Autism and Representation

Routledge Research in Cultural and Media Studies

1. Video, War and the Diasporic
Imagination
Dona Kolar-Panov

2. Reporting the Israeli-Arab Conflict
How Hegemony Works
Tamar Liebes

3. Karaoke Around the World
Global Technology, Local Singing
Edited by Toru Mitsui and Shuhei
Hosokawa

4. News of the World
World Cultures Look at Television
News
Edited by Klaus Bruhn Jensen

5. From Satellite to Single Market
New Communication Technology and
European Public Service Television
Richard Collins

6. The Nationwide Television Studies
David Morley and Charlotte Bronsdon

7. The New Communications
Landscape
Demystifying Media Globalization
Edited by Georgette Wang

8. Media and Migration
Edited by Russel King and Nancy
Wood

9. Media Reform
Edited by Beata Rozumilowicz and
Monroe E. Price

10. Political Communication in a
New Era
Edited by Gadi Wolfsfeld and Philippe
Maarek

11. Writers' Houses and the Making
of Memory
Edited by Harald Hendrix

12. Autism and Representation
Edited by Mark Osteen

Autism and Representation

Edited by
Mark Osteen

Routledge
Taylor & Francis Group
New York   London

First published 2008
by Routledge
270 Madison Ave, New York, NY 10016

Simultaneously published in the UK
by Routledge
2 Park Square, Milton Park, Abingdon, Oxon OX14 4RN

Routledge is an imprint of the Taylor & Francis Group, an informa business

Transferred to Digital Printing 2009

© 2008 Taylor and Francis

Typeset in 10 point Sabon Roman by IBT Global.

Library of Congress Cataloging in Publication Data
Autism and representation / edited by Mark Osteen.
p. cm. — (Routledge research in cultural and media studies)
Includes bibliographical references and index.
ISBN 978-0-415-95644-4 (hardback : alk. paper)
1. Autism. 2. Autism in literature. I. Osteen, Mark.

RC553.A88A833 2007
362.196'85882—dc22   2007015997

ISBN10: 0-415-95644-7 (hbk)
ISBN10: 0-415-80627-5 (pbk)
ISBN10: 0-203-93508-X (ebk)

ISBN13: 978-0-415-95644-4 (hbk)
ISBN13: 978-0-415-80627-5 (pbk)
ISBN13: 978-0-203-93508-8 (ebk)

Contents

Acknowledgments   vii

Autism and Representation: A Comprehensive Introduction   1
MARK OSTEEN

PART I
Clinical Constructions   49

1   No Search, No Subject? Autism and the
    American Conversion Narrative   51
    JAMES T. FISHER

2   Bruno Bettelheim, Autism, and the Rhetoric
    of Scientific Authority   65
    KATHERINE DEMARIA SEVERSON, JAMES ARNT AUNE,
    AND DENISE JODLOWSKI

3   Constructing Autism: A Brief Genealogy   78
    MAJIA HOLMER NADESAN

PART II
Autistry   97

4   Autism and Modernism: A Genealogical Exploration   99
    PATRICK MCDONAGH

5   Autism and the Imagination   117
    BRUCE MILLS

6   Fractioned Idiom: Metonymy and the Language of Autism   133
    KRISTINA CHEW

7   Imagination and the Awareness of Self in Autistic Spectrum
    Poets   145
    ILONA ROTH

8   Human, but More So: What the Autistic Brain Tells Us
    about the Process of Narrative   166
    MATTHEW K. BELMONTE

PART III
Autist Biography   181

9   Crossing Over: Writing the Autistic Memoir   183
    DEBRA L. CUMBERLAND

10 (M)Othering and Autism: Maternal Rhetorics of Self-Revision 197
    SHERYL STEVENSON

11 Urinetown: A Chronicle of the Potty Wars   212
    MARK OSTEEN

PART IV
Popular Representations   227

12 Recognizing Jake: Contending with Formulaic and
    Spectacularized Representations of Autism in Film   229
    ANTHONY D. BAKER

13 Hollywood and the Fascination of Autism   244
    STUART MURRAY

14 Film as a Vehicle for Raising Consciousness
    among Autistic Peers   256
    PHIL SCHWARZ

15 Alterity and Autism: Mark Haddon's *Curious Incident*
    in the Neurological Spectrum   271
    JAMES BERGER

16 Mark Haddon's Popularity and Other Curious Incidents
    in My Life as an Autistic   289
    GYASI BURKS-ABBOTT

    Conclusion: Toward an Empathetic Scholarship   297
    MARK OSTEEN

Contributors   303
Index   307

Acknowledgments

The chapters gathered herein derive from an October 2005 conference entitled "Representing Autism: Writing, Cognition, Disability," held at Case Western Reserve University in Cleveland, Ohio, and sponsored by the Society for Critical Exchange. I gratefully acknowledge the support of the SCE's Executive Director, Martha Woodmansee, and Nicholas Petzlak, as well as the rest of the Case faculty and staff who worked at the conference, presided at sessions, and generally helped to assure its success. Special thanks goes to the SCE's Associate Director Kurt Koenigsberger for his diligence and support. I would also like to thank those conference participants whose work does not appear here, but whose valuable contributions furthered the conference's aims and fostered its atmosphere of congeniality: Lisa Janice Cohen, Barbara Crooker, Ann Jurecic, Kristen Loutensock, Erika Nanes, Irene Rose, Chloe Silverman, Michael Turnheim, and especially Ruth Burks, who assembled the panel of people on the autism spectrum.

I also wish to thank the Loyola College Committee on Research and Sabbaticals for providing a summer research grant that helped me complete this project; Loyola's Dean of the College of Arts and Sciences, James Buckley; and my colleagues in the Loyola English Department. I'm also grateful to the anonymous readers of the proposal for this book, who offered numerous suggestions that strengthened the volume, and to Max Novick, the Routledge Acquisitions Editor, for his encouragement.

Most of all I thank my wife and son: Leslie for her unflagging support and simply for being there, and Cam for being the prime motivator of this work.

Autism and Representation
A Comprehensive Introduction

Mark Osteen

AUTISM AND DISABILITY STUDIES

What Is Disability Studies?

Until recent years, research on disability was usually consigned to the clinical or practical fields, which employ a "deficit" or "medical" model that represents disability as an individual problem or impairment to be cured or at least mitigated (Linton, *Claiming* 85). These disciplines pay little attention to the social and political contexts—constructed discourses of normality, for example—through which disabilities are molded and measured. Not only was the "voice of the disabled subject" (Linton 87) usually missing from this scholarship, but often the disability itself existed only as a symptom or ghost, in that the object of research was to abolish or at least render insignificant the disability being portrayed. In contrast, disability studies, as defined by James Wilson and Cynthia Lewiecki-Wilson, "sets aside the . . . medical model of disability as an accidental disease, trauma, deficit, or defect, . . . extending the insights of feminist, postmodern, and postcolonial theory and social and rhetorical studies to . . . analyze disability as a sociopolitical construct" ("Disability" 10).

Disability scholars have adhered tenaciously to this social-constructionist model. To put it in Ian Hacking's terms, disability studies is "against inevitability," aiming to demonstrate that the medical concept of disability emerged at a specific time in history and can therefore be changed (19).[1] As Hacking observes, such approaches (which dominate cultural studies) employ a "species of nominalism" (33) that view disabilities as artifacts of the disciplines that measure them, and as possessing no physical reality apart from the discursive practices that assess them (see Allen 94). In this view, disability is imposed on bodies by governmental and professional authorities. According to Simi Linton, "disability studies is the sociopolitical-cultural model of disability incarnate" (*Claiming* 133). Should it be?

Disability studies has raised public and academic consciousness by investigating the historical and cultural contingencies amidst which "disability" has been conceptualized and constructed while also improving the lives of disabled people. The field has also provided a valuable and necessary alternative to clinical discourses' objectification of disabled people. But disability studies has concentrated so heavily on the sociocultural construction of disability that it has largely ignored the physical realities on which its discipline is founded. Although the field's hostility toward science is an understandable reaction to contemporary medicine's sometimes oppressive discursive and financial power, it has also limited its disciplinary range. And just as disability studies repudiates the medical model (despite many scholars' reliance on medical interventions), so the field of "medical humanities" pays little attention to disability studies, distrusting "its infinitely malleable social construction of the body" (Herndl 597). This mutual animosity has foreclosed opportunities for cross-disciplinary exchanges that could enhance our understanding of disabilities' somatic and psychic aspects. As Diane Price Herndl argues, both the medical humanities and disability studies err by representing disability and disease as things rather than as relations (593–4). These reifications have, in turn, engendered two discrete fields whose individual presuppositions have grown ossified, and scholars who seldom cite each other's work, while repeatedly preaching to the converted.

This division has also left some questions begging, among them the problem of what counts as a disability (Swan 285). Linton writes that a condition must "significantly" affect daily life in order to qualify (*Claiming* 13). But that gets us no further: What constitutes significance? Is disability a matter of degree or of essence? Does the rubric encompass mental "illnesses?" Neurological differences? Obesity? Disabilities are not *either* physical facts or discursive constructs, but both; as Jim Swan concludes, "terms like *disabled* and *nondisabled* are not binary opposites but ... variable positions on a multidimensional gradient" (293). Therefore, as Lennard Davis notes in his groundbreaking book, *Enforcing Normalcy*, the term *disability* inevitably "serves two masters"—both the disabled and those who seek to discipline or "cure" them (xv). Many disability scholars perforce acknowledge the nebulousness of the term, which, as Rosemarie Garland-Thomson points out, incorporates "ideological categories as varied as sick, deformed, ugly, old, crazy, maimed, afflicted, abnormal, or debilitated" (74). Tom Shakespeare and Nicholas Watson have even suggested that disability—so complex, variable, and contingent, so uneasily poised at the "intersection of biology and society and of agency and structure"—is "the quintessential postmodern concept" (19). "Disability," it seems, is an "extraordinarily unstable category" (Davis, *Enforcing* xv) with "indeterminate boundaries" (Brueggeman 319).

Yet many disability scholars have felt the need to police the discipline, barring anything faintly redolent of the medical model (see, e.g., Linton, *Claiming* 141,149), and bristling at anyone with the temerity to suggest that disabilities are also impairments. Such efforts fail to recognize that the term cannot adequately encompass the many different forms of disability under its umbrella. This disciplinary vigilance has also reinforced a tendency to overlook or minimize tensions in the field's guiding principles, not the least of them one that mirrors a problem within the medical model: although disability scholars and advocates seek to celebrate disabilities as differences and redress the social and cultural conditions that render disability disabling, in so doing they work to eliminate the terms under which these differences become worthy of discussion.

More broadly, disability studies' adherence to the social-constructionist model, with its heavy debt to Foucault, has helped to foster a set of biases and misrepresentations that, ironically, replicate those historically aimed at disabled people. First, disability studies has been unwilling or unable to theorize impairment, suffering and pain—somatic conditions that accompany or precede disability—or to theorize the body itself, perhaps because doing so would seem to yield the floor to medicine. Second, Foucaultian paradigms that view subjects as pure products of a competition for power minimize human agency. Third, the breadth of its disciplinary reach has swept together a wide array of different conditions and embodiments, many of which have little in common. Fourth, disability studies' focus on visible physical disabilities has blinded it to the existence of other, perhaps less obvious but equally significant (and widespread) disabilities. Last, and most important for the purposes of this volume, disability scholarship has ignored cognitive, intellectual, or neurological disabilities, thereby excluding the intellectually disabled just as mainstream society has done. These missing discursive pieces have, in short, disabled disability studies, preventing the field from achieving sturdier and more sophisticated theoretical foundations.

A Neo-Cartesian Duality?

The medical model represents disabilities as the result of physical impairments, whereas the social-constructionist model depicts impairments as, in effect, "implanted" in the body "by the discipline that measures deviation" (Allen 96). Impairments are bodily realities; disabilities are discursive constructions. Thus, although most disability scholars dutifully claim not to deny the reality of impairment, they generally focus on everything *but* impairment, thereby accepting the dichotomy that their work should seek to bridge. However, over the past several years, this binary has come under attack. According to Mairian Corker and Sally French, for example, disability scholars too often present impairment as a "fixed surface onto which disability is 'projected' by culture" (3), abandoning impairment to the clinical fields. Ironically enough, this separation produces a "disembodied notion of disability," a neo-Cartesian mind/body dualism that merely replaces "biological essentialism with discursive essentialism" (Hughes and Paterson 330, 329, 333; cf. Jeffreys 39), and that dissolves the body into an aftereffect, or symptom, of discourse (Hughes, "What" 85). Yet if impairment is a prerequisite for disability (a necessary, if not sufficient, cause), then, as Shelley Tremain rightly observes, the distinction is ultimately a "chimera" (10). Mark Jeffreys aptly notes that it is "well enough to talk about making our culture accommodate physical difference; but only in acknowledging that there is some physical reality beyond culture can that accommodation be reached" (35).

Nor can this discursive essentialism explain embodied knowledge: What place does the social model allow for, say, the blend of bodily and intellectual knowledge that enables one to play a musical instrument (not just read notes), dance, or use a needle well (Allen 104)? The socially constructed subject is, indeed, a docile subject with a docile body—and, thus, an empty or unapproachable subject with little ability to alter its circumstances. Yet the history of disability refutes this idea: if power-driven discourses *determine* the conditions under which subjects are formed and bodies assessed, as the Foucaultian model implies, then how do people ever create new conditions? How, Bill Hughes asks, do we explain disability advocacy movements ("What" 90)? Where, in short, is agency? Again the irony: these scholars' discourses end up wedded to the same notion of passive subjectivity as the discursive powers they excoriate. Disability studies has yet to craft a coherent alternative to this disabling binary.[2]

Blind Spots

Most major scholarship on disability—aside, perhaps, from research on deafness and Deaf culture—has also concentrated almost exclusively on visible physical disabilities (see Murray, "Contemporary" 25). Conditions the naked eye cannot detect have been, in disability studies, truly invisible. Disability studies, one might say, possesses its own visual impairment. Some of this neglect might be chalked up to disability studies' close ties with disability advocacy, which has been led by physically disabled and Deaf persons, and whose results—access ramps, captions, ASL interpretations, and so on—are obvious to all. Accommodations for invisible disabilities are more difficult to produce or detect. In addition, much early work in disability studies employed psychoanalytic theories of the gaze and ideas about the spectacularization (or "enfreakment") of the disabled, using what Bill Hughes calls a "correspondence theory of perception in which vision provides immediate access to the external world" ("Constitution" 160). Thus, Hughes argues, "the impaired body is rendered disorderly . . . by the 'positive' observational practices that produce it" (158). Staring objectifies the person being stared at. But what of the body whose impairment cannot be readily seen? How is it rendered disorderly? Hughes's analysis actually reproduces the visual bias he critiques. But he is scarcely the only offender: this bias is evident throughout the recently published MLA volume on disability studies, and even in books such as Davis's, whose very subtitle implies a visually defined concept of disability.

In this way, the field's neo-Cartesian duality—its separation of body from mind, impairment from disability—has given birth to a curious paradox: although disability studies has, as I've suggested, failed to produce a systematic theory of the body, it has nonetheless focused intensely on the visible body and ignored what can't be seen—for example, the brain. In other words, disability studies has almost entirely neglected cognitive and intellectual disabilities. For example, a recent issue of *PMLA* containing the proceedings of a major 2004 conference on disability in the university presents about 30 essays on disability and the humanities. Of these, only three even mention cognitive or intellectual disabilities, and only two—articles by Michael Bérubé and Christopher Krentz—discuss cognitive or neurological differences in any significant way. Krentz explains why: intellectual disabilities lie "at the bottom of the disability hierarchy, largely contemned or ignored" (555).

John Radford likewise declares that "our culture has not only marginalized people with an intellectual disability; it has also marginalized the study of intellectual disability" (22). Again the situation in disability studies mirrors the situation in the broader culture: although physically disabled people are increasingly involved in all aspects of labor and social life, the intellectually disabled are shoved to the side. Our society's ideology of bourgeois individualism and personal productivity does not know what to do with those who cannot "compete" or "produce." Indeed, as Lewiecki-Wilson notes, "even within disability communities, stigma against severely disabled people who cannot communicate remains high" ("Rethinking" 159). Unusual bodies are one thing; unusual minds, it seems, are quite something else.[3] Why? One reason may be that, as Davis notes, academics are "high-functioning people without . . . serious cognitive disabilities" ("Disability" 530): we are hardly immune from competitiveness, and may even be more prone to value intellectual capabilities and achievements than other people. Does this mean that because intellectual disabilities are not *our* disabilities, we don't care as much about them? Are academics—even disabled academics—unaware of our cognitive privilege? Is disability studies guilty of cognitive ableism—a prejudice against those who cannot compose articles and books, compete for advocacy space, and contribute to disability scholarship?

One hopes not. One hopes, rather, that this oversight is due to the nature of such disabilities. That is, most cognitive disabilities derive from an impaired brain or neurology. Though the brain is, of course, an organ, the effects of neurological disabilities are both systemic and subtle. In many cases (aside from conditions such as Down syndrome or fragile X syndrome) there are no obvious physical abnormalities. Thus, theories that address visual enfreakment, pictorial representation, and so forth, don't fit well. And the lines between normality and neurological difference are often difficult to discern: a person with ADHD looks just like a person without ADHD. Are such people, then, "really" disabled? More to the point: Are people with Asperger's syndrome disabled or merely different? As Lewiecki-Wilson points out, "mental impairments are the hardest test cases in thinking through the relation between nature . . . and social construction" (157). At once a part of the body and the primary source of consciousness, the brain breaks down the lines of dualistic paradigms. Yet for that very reason cognitive and neurological disabilities may *best* represent that "seam where body joins culture" (Jeffreys 33), which disability scholars identify as the essence of the field. Moreover, if, as Krentz remarks, cognitive disabilities represent a "disruptive force, challenging our conceptions of intelligence, agency, and what it means to be human" (553), they perfectly epitomize the aims of disability studies. Cognitive and neurological disabilities, in sum, both exemplify disability as defined in disability studies *and* challenge the discipline's dominant models. The present volume, which examines the construction and (mis)representation of autism and offers innovative alternatives, is thus uniquely placed to question the orthodoxies of both disability studies and the medical model, to open spaces within both fields for new paradigms, and to provide opportunities for multidisciplinary exchange.

Who Speaks?

People with serious cognitive or neurological difficulties often cannot communicate well enough to advocate for themselves. This circumstance presents another reason for disability studies' relative neglect of cognitive disabilities, and may also help to explain why autism and other cognitive disabilities have been so misrepresented: cognitively disabled people are often deemed incompetent to manage their own therapy, or even their own daily lives, let alone write about those lives. Thus, autism has been represented over the years mostly by non-autistic people. Hence, as the first two chapters in this volume demonstrate, early clinical approaches to autism that drew from clinical psychology or Freudian ideas about childhood trauma ended up building what Ann Jurecic describes as a "fortress of words" around their subjects (8)—thereby demonstrating a "mind-blindness" that mirrored the weak "theory of mind" often cited as one of autism's core deficits.

This state of affairs has begun to change, thanks to publishers such as Jessica Kingsley, and to a flourishing online community devoted to disseminating information about autistic people and their lives.[4] Certain high-functioning autists and those diagnosed with Asperger's syndrome (self-described "Aspies") have seized the reins of representation, some of them volubly proclaiming that they are not sick and don't need to be "cured." Such declarations echo those of an earlier generation of disability activists and rely upon the same discursive models.[5] It is essential and right for autistic people to challenge misrepresentations; that is why this volume includes two chapters written by persons on the autism spectrum, Phil Schwarz and Gyasi Burks-Abbott.

However, this generally heartening trend has also exposed and possibly deepened a significant rift in autism culture, which runs from educational institutions and clinical theories and praxis, all the way through the publishing industry and online communities: the gap between so-called "high-functioning" and "low-functioning" people. In certain ways, these terms do perpetuate what Phil Schwarz, in his chapter in this volume, calls a "false dichotomy," for many autistic people function capably in some respects but are quite disabled in others. No doubt it's more accurate as well as more fruitful to recognize that autism is indeed a *spectrum*, and that any given autistic person's abilities will occupy different locations on it at different times. Moreover, the terms can create self-fulfilling prophecies: being labeled "low-functioning" may create low expectations that foster hopelessness or passivity. Yet, this admittedly rough distinction can be useful. Thus, for example, measures that may benefit more able people on the spectrum (such as attending mainstream schools) can harm the more severely disabled. Moreover, the distinction is crucial for the disability/difference conundrum. For although it is plausible to argue that the differences between Asperger's folks and neurotypical people are largely matters of style or adjustments, it is something else entirely to claim that a teenager who can't speak or write, smears his feces, and slaps himself repeatedly is not disabled but only different. Without denying that diagnostic and cultural discourses shape expectations and definitions for all autistic people, it's also true that the most severely disabled autistic people offer a prime example of that "physical reality beyond culture" to which Jeffreys alludes. And because autism self-advocacy is dominated by those who can communicate well, those who can't speak or write, or who are severely antisocial or intellectually impaired, are often left out in the cold. Who speaks for them?

This question is related to another issue often dodged or dismissed in disability studies: Who should participate in the field? Should it be restricted to those who identify themselves as disabled? What about people who don't consider themselves disabled, but who use assistive devices in their daily lives? Disabled people are understandably suspicious of being colonized by the nondisabled. After all, the historical oppression of the disabled was a consequence of others silencing their voices. But reserving disability studies for those who identify themselves as disabled makes it difficult for the nondisabled to "find a location from which to comment" (Linton, "What is" 520). And because people with significant cognitive impairments cannot self-advocate or write articles, "saving" disability studies for the disabled in effect permits only certain disabled people—the most cognitively privileged—to enter. Once again, the more severely disabled—who constitute a significant portion of autistic people—are doubly disenfranchised: first, by their disorder, and second, by the very community that should welcome them.[6]

Empathy or Compassion?

To escape this bind, we need new ways to engage and include those with significant cognitive impairments yet avoid presumptuousness or colonization. That is, we must strive to speak not *for* but *with* those unable or unwilling to communicate through orthodox modes. For this enterprise,

Cynthia Lewiecki-Wilson offers the concept of "mediated rhetoricity," defined as "language used for the benefit of the disabled person that is (co) constructed by parents, advocates and/or committed caregivers" ("Rethinking" 161). Such mediation requires "thoughtful attention" to the disabled person's "embodied nonverbal performances and gestures," so that their interlocutors and advocates can "carefully and ethically co-construct narratives and arguments from the perspective of the disabled person" (161–2). This "negotiated knowledge" is thus built, as Jurecic puts it, in "dialogue" with the subject (16).

How do we carry on these mediated dialogues and still respect the agency of those with whom and for whom we speak? Clearly we need empathy, which legal philosopher Martha Nussbaum defines as the "imaginative reconstruction of another's experience, without any particular evaluation of that experience" (302). Nussbaum distinguishes empathy from compassion, which she defines as "painful emotion occasioned by the awareness of another person's undeserved misfortune" (301) and which, she argues, presumes "responsibility or blame"—a belief that the person with whom we compassionate does not deserve to suffer (314). The distinction is significant for our project, because compassion may go hand in hand with a feeling of superiority ("you poor thing") that even severely disabled people rightly resent as patronizing. Compassion, that is, can easily lead to colonization.

But empathy and compassion are not easily separated. Although empathy, as a more neutral term, is less burdened with the baggage of pity, true empathy, I would argue, requires what Nussbaum terms a "eudaimonistic quality": the recognition that we are not aliens to one another but alike (317).[7] Still, her definition of "empathy" helps us preserve a "twofold attention" in which one "both imagines what it is like to be in" another's place yet retains "securely the awareness that one is not" (328). Hence, I propose instead of "mediated rhetoricity" a broader term, *empathetic scholarship*, which not only captures the aim of speaking *with* those unable to communicate entirely on their own, but also describes this volume's larger project: to combine rigorous scholarship with the experiential knowledge our non-autistic contributors have gained as family members and friends of autistic persons. Indeed, "empathetic scholarship" also encompasses the broader goals of disability studies: to produce and disseminate work that combines scholars' personal and professional lives in mutually beneficial ways and also makes a difference in the non-academic world.

The best scholarship in disability studies always has been empathetic, and many previous essay collections have included both standard scholarly essays and personal or autobiographical reflections.[8] But empathetic scholarship is a particularly valuable model for non-autists who hope to represent authentically and accurately what it means and how it feels to be autistic. For despite the proliferation of writing by and about autistic people, much of it is not truly *representative*: it too often misleadingly implies that most autistic people are savants while also suggesting that autistic people are worthy only if they overcome their disorder. Such representations may be compassionate, but in failing to respect difference, they are not truly empathetic. Most popular representations of autism indeed either make spectacles of autists or impose neurotypical formulae or conventions on them, thereby eliding difference in order to validate neurotypical experiences. More challenging or complex literary or cinematic portrayals are deemed uncommercial, consigned to small presses or independent production companies, or, perhaps more likely, not made or published at all. Once again, people with the most significant cognitive, sensory or communicative difficulties are silenced or erased.

This volume's empathetic scholarship aims to rectify these patterns. Our authors seek to produce "negotiated knowledge" in a variety of ways: by analyzing autism's clinical construction and cultural contexts (Fisher, Severson et al., Nadesan, McDonagh); through aesthetic or neurological research balanced by encounters with autistic people and their creative artifacts (Mills, Roth, Chew, Belmonte); by recounting and investigating their own and others' experiences of living with and learning from autistic people (Cumberland, Stevenson, my own chapter); or by scrutinizing how autism has been represented in popular culture (Baker, Murray, Schwarz, Berger, Burks-Abbott). This book is thus designed to place autism and other cognitive disorders within the ambit of disability studies, to explore how autistic representations may expand and enrich the field, and to demonstrate again that autistic people occupy a unique and valuable place on the human spectrum.

CLINICAL CONSTRUCTIONS

What Is Autism?

The prevailing diagnostic classification of autism lists a triad of impairments: in social interaction, language acquisition and use, "imaginative" interests and behaviors. A consensus has begun to emerge that autism (or some percentage of autism spectrum disorders) is caused by a not-yet-understood confluence of genetic predisposition and environmental influence.[9] Beyond these orthodoxies, however, the disorder remains nebulous. One reason is that the diagnostic categories themselves are constantly evolving. Ian Hacking's analysis of "indifferent kinds" and "interactive kinds" is instructive here. Indifferent kinds are entities or conditions with no awareness of being measured; they are not affected by their classifications. Thus "calling a quark a quark makes no difference to the quark" (105). Interactive kinds, in contrast, are involved in a "looping effect" whereby the very fact of their classification alters their behavior; that alteration in turn influences the classification. As Majia Nadesan explains in her book, in such cases "classificatory systems engender practices and institutions having the effect of producing what was classified" (24). Autism, argues Hacking, is both indifferent and interactive: its neurological or physiological aspects are indifferent, but individual autistic people and their families may be changed by being labeled, and the collective behavior of people responding to their labels in turn alters the classification. For instance, families of autistic children were "severely influenced . . . by the [obsolete] doctrine of the refrigerator mother" (Hacking 115), and some of the original symptoms identified by Leo Kanner and Hans Asperger, the psychiatrists who independently originated the autism diagnosis, are seldom used or seen today. Hacking thus concludes that autism is not "a linear continuum at all, but an extremely dense manifold of problems" (121).

Indeed, the shifting and at times vague diagnostic categories—autism, Asperger's syndrome, PDD-NOS, and others—suggest that autism is not one but several disorders, each with a different etiology, prognosis, and suitable treatments. Nor are the widely different levels of (dis)ability truly explained (they may even be elided) by the term "autism spectrum." As Nadesan writes in her important study of autism's construction, "the determination of which symptoms constitute difference and which constitute impairment remains vague" (208). Autism spectrum disorders (ASDs) reveal how complex are the interactions between somatic states and mental states, bodies and minds. At once indifferent and interactive, a physical condition with profound effects on consciousness and social life manifested at markedly different levels of severity, "autism" is an extraordinarily unstable category. In this instance, Foucault's description of a discursive formation as "a space of multiple dissensions; a set of different oppositions whose levels and roles must be described" (155) seems particularly apt. "Autism" indeed epitomizes the ambiguities of "disability" itself.

Conversion and Restitution

Given such complexities, it is hardly surprising that autism has been diagnosed, explained, and treated in widely disparate ways in its relatively brief history. Nor is it surprising that most of these explanations have sought to erect a monolithic concept of autism in order to promote a particular therapy and buttress a clinician's authority. In this way, writes Mitzi Waltz, early autism "experts" Melanie Klein and Bruno Bettelheim employed clinical narratives to assure "practitioners and students that taking on the mantle of the child analyst [would] provide them with a high degree of personal competence and power"; their documents promised to "reveal secret techniques that, once mastered, [would] convey special status" (427).

The first three chapters in this volume offer detailed analyses of these and other early clinical constructions of autism. First, James T. Fisher examines Virginia Axline's once-famous but now nearly forgotten text, *Dibs: In Search of Self*, which asserts that "disordered selfhood" (a result of unfeeling parents) rather than neurological wiring is responsible for autism. But, as Fisher shows, *Dibs* does not merely exemplify an obsolete and dubious clinical model; serves as a paradigm for much current writing on autism. Even today, Fisher suggests, many autism narratives adhere to the conventions of the "conversion narrative"—a quest for a "transformed or redeemed self"—inherited largely from the Augustinian sensibility of American Protestantism.

In the medical register, the theological idea of "conversion" is generally transposed into "recovery." Hence, the prevailing autism story is a version of what Arthur Frank terms the "restitution narrative"—institutional medicine's "preferred narrative" (79)—in which a patient is cured through a doctor's expertise. In such accounts, the cure comes not through the patient's actions but through the healer, drug or therapeutic regimen (Frank 115). Whether the force is God (as in the conversion story), or a drug or doctor (as in the restitution narrative), the agent of change in these stories is not the patient but some external power, while the patient accepts a place in a "moral order that subordinates him [or her] as an individual" (Frank 93).

In their chapter, Katherine Severson, James Arnt Aune, and Denise Jodlowski adduce a specific example of such subordination in the work of Bruno Bettelheim, who acquired fame through books such as *The Empty Fortress*, where he claimed to have cured autistic children by removing them from their parents and psychoanalyzing them. Our authors show how Bettelheim generated moral authority from his experiences a Holocaust survivor, and deployed ingenious rhetorical strategies to prevent the clinical establishment from questioning his claims. Bettelheim's primary goal, they argue, was not really to help children, but to reinforce his own image as a benevolent but overpowering presence: The Good Doctor. Bettelheim's theory that autism is caused by cold or neglectful parents (the seeds of which were sown in Leo Kanner's original writings) has been thoroughly discredited. Nevertheless, as I further suggest in the following section and in my conclusion to this volume, covert parent-blaming endures throughout contemporary autism literature (as well as in autistic people's actual families). Like that of Virginia Axline, the ghost of Bruno Bettelheim still haunts the house of autism.

Yet Bettelheim was scarcely the sole clinician who wove a version of autism from the strands of prevailing discourses, as Majia Nadesan's book comprehensively details. Her chapter in this volume summarizes the book's genealogy—the probable existence of, but failure to recognize, autism until the 1940s; its representation in various clinical discourses; the emergence of Asperger's syndrome as a diagnostic category in the 1990s—then explores how institutional relationships, expert authorities, and bodies of knowledge have thereafter represented, classified, and acted on autism, which she describes as a "biologically based, but socially shaped and expressed, behavioral and cognitive difference." Whereas earlier generations pointed the finger at parents, today's autism culture fixates on symbolic sites of contamination such as vaccinations, and represents autism through postmodern tropes such as the cyborg or computer. And while earlier generations appropriated models from Freudian or developmental psychiatry, today's popular imagination seeks the magic bullet in genetics. Yet current scientific understandings of autism, Nadesan shows, still reductionistically seek a single agent to explain this multivalent condition.[10] In other words, conversion and restitution narratives have not disappeared; instead, like popular culture's ubiquitous cyborgs and mutants, they have merely changed form.

AUTISTRY

Savants and Geniuses

Although autism was not recognized as a condition until the mid-twentieth century, its biological components would suggest that autistic people have existed throughout history. A few writers have therefore applied clinical criteria to diagnose historical figures with autism.[11] Other clinicians have taken a cue from Hans Asperger, who recognized that his young patients possessed undeniable gifts along with their impairments, to speculate about autistic creativity. Foremost in many of these efforts to celebrate rather than pathologize autistic traits is the sense that the unique qualities of perception, concentration, and selfhood among autistic people may also give rise to extraordinary creative abilities.

Combining these historical and diagnostic approaches, psychiatrist Michael Fitzgerald argues in his recent book *Autism and Creativity* that a number of noted nineteenth- and twentieth-century artists, scientists, and political figures displayed signs of high-functioning autism or Asperger's syndrome (Fitzgerald sees no significant difference between the two categories: 29–30), and that their contributions occurred *because*, not in spite of, their autism. Though Fitzgerald's attempt to champion autistic creativity is laudable, his project ultimately fails. One problem is that his psychobiographies range from the plausible (Ludwig Wittgenstein) to the frankly absurd (W. B. Yeats and, most alarmingly, Adolf Hitler); the less believable ones cast doubt on his entire enterprise. Further, though he warns against bending individuals' works and acts to "fit the paradigm imposed by the psychiatrist" (15), he repeatedly does just that, reshaping reported traits into straitjacketing diagnoses. Nowhere does he question if diagnosing the dead is permissible or even possible, nor whether the disparate forms of creativity he discusses are truly comparable. Fitzgerald's stated view that genius is inborn (138) also ignores the effects of education, culture, and plain old hard work.[12] Thus, though Fitzgerald invokes the familiar machine metaphor to refer to Wittgenstein (123), what is truly mechanical is his own method, in which *every* slight eccentricity becomes a symptom of autism. Indeed, there's something "autistic" (in Fitzgerald's own terms) about his approach, which recalls a musician who announces different titles but plays the same melody again and again.

Efforts to address autistic creativity fall short when the author arrives at the scene carrying too much clinical baggage. The medical doctor does not merely sit uneasily beside the aesthetic philosopher; he constantly interferes and guides her toward preconceived conclusions. In this regard, the writings of neurologist Oliver Sacks provide a fascinating case in point. Though Sacks has been maligned in disability studies as a "colonialist" who aggrandizes himself at the expense of his patients (see Shakespeare, Review 139), Leonard Cassuto has argued that Sacks refreshingly eschews restitution narratives in favor of tales in which his own progress toward understanding is an essential part of the drama (127–8). If Cassuto is correct, Sacks's insertion of his own eccentricities into his essays reveals that eudaimonistic quality that Nussbaum recognizes as essential for empathy. According to Jurecic, indeed, Sacks's best work exemplifies that "negotiated knowledge" created in "dialogue" with the subject that I have called empathetic scholarship (16).

Like Fitzgerald, Sacks asks whether there is a "distinctive 'autistic' form of perception and art" (Sacks 196); unlike Fitzgerald, Sacks acknowledges a "most intricate (and potentially creative) interaction between the autistic traits and the other qualities of the individual" (250). But although Sacks's thoughtful and well-written essays display a clear respect for his subjects, his tone sometimes veers into the wondrous, and his choice to write primarily on exceptionally gifted people like animal scientist and author Temple Grandin and artist Stephen Wiltshire may encourage a freak-show response. Why not write about what Anthony Baker, in his chapter in this volume, calls the "normally autistic?" Sacks also remains somewhat hemmed in by his medical training, as when he remarks that Grandin has succeeded in spite of her autism (244), when she herself asserts that her autism, as manifested in her acute visual/spatial mind and in her powers of concentration, is what has made her success possible (*Thinking in Pictures* 188).

More troublingly, Sacks speculates that Wiltshire—who creates meticulous architectural drawings and expertly echoes others' voices and words—is a "perceptual missile . . . a sort of transmitter of all that rushe[s] past," yet remains "unchanged, unfed, by the experience" (218). Wiltshire, he speculates, abides in a "multiverse" of "vivid, isolated" moments "unconnected with each other or with him, and . . . devoid of any deeper continuity" (242, 201); hence, he suggests, Wiltshire cannot truly be an artist. But Sacks's Romantic concept of imagination, with its emphasis on originality and synthesis, obstructs his vision. He assumes that Wiltshire's quasi-photographic art indicates a merely reproductive, mirror-like mind. But putting aside Sacks's other questionable suppositions—that absolute "reproduction" is possible, that it is a lesser form of art, and that any art is entirely original— closer attention reveals that Wiltshire's drawings are not, as Sacks claims, "unconceptualized" (243). Rather, like all artists, Wiltshire emphasizes certain details and omits others: his work shows an artist sifting, selecting, and revising his raw perceptions. Sacks also asserts that Wiltshire's echolalia "carries no emotion, no intentionality" and remains "purely automatic" (233); but this claim is refuted not only by numerous other researchers, but also by many autistic authors and their families.[13] There is something marvelously witty and self-aware about Wiltshire's delight in echoing scenes from the movie *Rain Man*: here is an autistic savant impersonating a fictional portrayal of an autistic savant (234)! Sacks cannot decide whether there is a "distinctively autistic imagination" (242), but if Wiltshire's performance of *Rain Man* isn't just that, then what would be?

If Sacks remains somewhat handicapped by his medical skepticism and need to enfreak his subjects, his speculation that autist artists display a unique "genius" for mimesis (241) takes an important step toward apprehending autistic imaginations. Further, as I suggest later, Sacks's intuition about Wiltshire's need to "borrow" an identity (240) is borne out by a number of autistics' autobiographies. Still, doing justice to the aesthetics of autism and the nature of the autistic imagination requires approaches less steeped in the medical and better versed in the history of aesthetics.

Local Coherence

Patrick McDonagh, in his contribution to this volume, offers one such approach, investigating parallels between autism's appearance as a diagnostic category and the emergence of literary modernism. McDonagh suggests that the capacity to perceive autism in the 1940s is connected to the dissemination of modernist notions of the self as illustrated in the era's literature. Tracing similarities between high modernist literature and Kanner's and Asperger's clinical observations, McDonagh elucidates how modernism's articulation of modern identity may have enabled clinicians to perceive that new form of being, the autistic person, defined by extreme aloneness, apparent egoism, and an idiosyncratic use of language—also hallmarks of the work of modernists such as Virginia Woolf, James Joyce, and Albert Camus. In his book *Send in the Idiots*, Kamran Nazeer offers a term that helps us further expand on McDonagh's explorations. In tracking the young adult lives of four former classmates, Nazeer—himself once diagnosed as autistic—interprets a myriad of different behaviors, from one man's need to speak through puppets to his own compulsive fidgeting with alligator clips, as manifestations of autistics' quest for local coherence (see 37–39, 122). Autistic people, he asserts, need rules above all things; if they can't find any, they will invent some. This term sheds further light on the modernist art that McDonagh describes, for each feature he discerns—idiosyncratic language, aloneness, egoism—bespeaks a desire for local, even private, rather than global coherence.

In a 1997 article, Marion Glastonbury likewise finds autistic traits in the work of twentieth-century writers Samuel Beckett and Georges Perec, and defends works she describes as "monologic, devoid of intersubjective richness; works which may be said to be *about* barrenness, reflecting and projecting a single stance, an unremitting mood: the minimalist sigh of an attenuated self" (39). Her observations about an "autistic dynamic of certain works of art"—those that seem to discourage human relatedness—may broaden our understanding of autistic creativity; but her belief that the autistic self is "attenuated" and "barren" mirrors Sacks's limiting presumptions. For "attenuated," let us substitute "locally coherent"; for "devoid of richness" substitute "richly attentive to minute detail"; for "minimalist" substitute "metonymic"; for "monologic," insert "introverted." The latter terms, invoked by the contributors to the aesthetics section of this volume, more accurately apprehend autistic creativity.

In his chapter, Bruce Mills further illuminates the idea of local coherence. After explicating Emerson's and Coleridge's analyses of the unifying ("esemplastic") power of the imagination, he shows how these ideas continue to inform contemporary clinical accounts of autistic deficits in theory of mind and central coherence. But rather than viewing these traits as impairments, Mills asks, what if we see them as features along a spectrum of possibilities? Mills finds in the work of Jessy Park and Temple Grandin an art of local coherence that displays a brand of imagination "defined by close attention to mechanical or physical patterns not psychological or social rules," motivated by private rather than public symbols and fed by individual rather than typical sensory preferences. Attention to the art of local coherence, he concludes, will help us expand our definition of imagination and foster a richer idea of human possibility.

The following two chapters, by Kristina Chew and Ilona Roth, respectively, add local coherence to Mills's and McDonagh's more theoretical essays by examining specific instances of autistic poetry. Drawing on linguistic theory, Chew adduces examples from the language of both autistic (Jessy Park, Larry Bissonette, Tito Mukhopadhyay) and neurotypical artists (Anne Carson, G. M. Hopkins) to illustrate a significant tendency in autistic thinking: the preference for metonymy over metaphor. In this "fractioned idiom" Chew finds a key to the workings of autistic creativity and consciousness. This clue to autistic thinking, she suggests, may help dispel misconceptions and encourage better communication between autistic and neurotypical fellow-travelers.

Chew's chapter reveals how an empathetic poetics can shed light on autistic creativity; Ilona Roth's chapter demonstrates how a clinical approach that respects autistic agency can challenge conventional wisdom about autistic thinking. Her investigation of autistic poetry undermines the belief that autistic creativity is "attenuated" and lacks self-awareness, that autists live solely in "isolated moments," and are therefore less than fully human. As she points out, to minimize the achievement of autist artists because their work involves "mere" accurate representation depends on a criterion not universally applied to neurotypical artists' work. Roth concludes that, contrary to what clinical orthodoxy would lead us to expect, autistic poetry is neither formulaic, devoid of figurative language, nor lacking in self-reflexivity. Indeed, she suggests that because poetry lends itself more readily to local coherence than does prose, it may be an ideal vehicle for linguistic autistry.

Given this penchant for the local, one would expect that narrative, which demands links, linearity, and global coherence, would present a problem for autistic people. The relation between autistic consciousness and narrative organization is the subject of Matthew K. Belmonte's chapter. Marshaling recent neuroscientific research on autism to explain autists' lack of central coherence, Belmonte argues that the theory of mind and executive dysfunctions often named as core impairments in autism are more accurately viewed as disruptions of narrative organization: a propensity to perceive the world in parts rather than as a connected whole. Threatened by the chaos this perceptual style generates, autistic people must work harder to construct a theory of reality than do neurotypical people. Belmonte's literary examples, however, suggest that neurotypical humans have always also employed narrative as a defense against chaos. Viewed in this light, we can understand autistic people as prototypes for a universal human struggle to craft narrative meaning from the menacing surround: autists are human, but more so.

AUTIST BIOGRAPHY

Autism and Narrative

Narrative is indeed a primary way that humans organize experience. Hence it's not surprising that autistic people and their loved ones have told fictional and factual stories of their lives. These authors face many of the same obstacles that other authors of disability narratives confront. One problem, as G. Thomas Couser points out, is that disabled people are less likely to believe their lives worthy of being narrated, and hence may not write about them at all ("Empire" 307). Second, as Davis notes, in "narrativizing an impairment, one tends to sentimentalize it and link it to the bourgeois sensibility of individualism" (*Enforcing* 4). That is, although autobiography has long been the "threshold genre" for marginalized groups (Couser, "Conflicting" 78), it tends to present disability as an individual issue, and hence downplays the effects of culture and society. Further, as Couser observes, because publishers generally consider disability to be "'downbeat' or 'depressing,' its representation may be allowed only on the condition that the narrative take the form of a story of 'triumph.'" Not only does this "tyranny of the comic plot" minimize the challenges disabled people encounter; it also implies that those who do not "triumph" over their disability lack determination or character ("Empire" 308). Such conventions perpetuate autism's versions of disability's stereotypes of the Supercrip and the Heroic Overcomer—the Savant and the Recovered Autistic—while also making life more difficult for the large majority who don't fit them.

Autism stories also present a particular set of problems. Most autistic people crave sameness, and family members sometimes testify to the feeling that they live in the movie *Groundhog Day*, where every day is like the previous one. How does one craft a tale about events that never seem to change?

Autism would therefore seem to inspire what Frank calls "chaos narratives," which imagine "life never getting better" (97) and which scarcely fit publishers' idea of what sells. In other cases, autism strikes family members as an inexplicable eruption, a manifestation of pure chaos. What Frank reads in illness narratives seems especially true here: autism equals "living with perpetual interruption" (56). But how do you tell a cohesive narrative about continual interruption? As soon as chaos or interruption becomes a narrative, it is no longer chaos or interruption. For these reasons, as well as because of the neurological disconnections that Belmonte discusses, autism seems peculiarly resistant to narrative. As I suggest further below, a tension between narrative order and narrative disruption—whether figured as relentless repetition or as outbreaks of chaos—runs through virtually all family autism stories.

Lastly, family members of autistic people are constantly buffeted by competing or contradictory messages from the larger culture: that they should just work harder to remedy the disorder and if they can't they are failures; that this or that therapy offers a miracle cure, and if they don't try it, they are guilty of abuse or neglect; that autistic people are hopelessly "locked in" and should be put "somewhere." Yet they also hear from the Asperger's community that autism is merely a different "style" of being human and that they should accept the person and not try to change him or her—indeed, that doing so is a form of abuse. Parent and sibling authors' own local coherence thus becomes fractured by what Dona Avery calls "*dissoi logoi*, a scrambled collection of competing . . . 'truth claims' that frame our culture's disability story" (Avery 119). Parent and sibling memoirs thus represent efforts to negotiate among these competing claims and disorienting conflicts.

Parents and Children

Nevertheless, there is no shortage of memoirs by the family members of autistic people. Parents and siblings who tell of their lives with autism generally speak from an empathetic position. Often, however, the praiseworthy need to show respect for their loved ones and celebrate their achievements ends up confirming stereotypes and conventions. Hence, Waltz documents that the vast majority of parent accounts are either pathographies (i.e., illness narratives) or accounts of using a specific therapy (428). In the first instance, the memoir may become the story of the family member's struggle with his or her own stigmatization rather than an account of the autist's life; in the second case, the biography metamorphoses into yet another restitution or conversion narrative.

Perhaps because autism was then less familiar and its stereotypes less prevalent, the earliest parent memoirs are still among the best. Clara Claiborne Park's eloquent and thoughtful *The Siege* (1967), about her daughter Jessy's early years and the family's struggle to treat and understand her, was "a watershed event in the history of autism" (Waltz 429) not only because

Park dared to challenge the psychiatric establishment's refrigerator-parent model, but also because she and her family comprehended that Jessy (called "Elly" in the book) was not just an impairment but a complex and talented human being. Clara Park's scrupulous recording of Jessy's rage for order—of the ways she satisfied her need for local coherence—remains one of the best accounts of an autistic "system." Park's sequel, *Exiting Nirvana*, which tells of Jessy's early adulthood and the refinement of her artistic talent, makes hers perhaps the most thoroughly documented autistic life in history (see Sacks's Foreword, x). Few parent writers have matched Clara Park's meticulousness and grace.

The other notable early parent memoir is Josh Greenfeld's 1970 *A Child Called Noah*, which uses a journal format to recount his family's struggles to diagnose and help his autistic son Noah. Much rawer and more driven by emotional torrents than Park's coolly elegant book, Greenfeld's is the first memoir featuring a "low-functioning"child, as it portrays the family's early life with Noah as a constant struggle against chaos, fear and the ignorance of the medical profession. No other autism parent memoirs appeared until the early 1990s, when Jane Taylor McDonnell's *News from the Border* (with an afterword by her son Paul), Judy and Sean Barron's *There's a Boy In Here* and therapy-centered books by Catherine Maurice and Annabel Stehli inaugurated the current surge of parent-written autism memoirs.

The first two chapters in this volume's "Autist Biography" section analyze these early memoirs. Blending literary analysis with reminiscences of life with her autistic brother, Debra Cumberland addresses the challenges facing parents of autistic children. In *A Child Called Noah*, she detects not a "male" quest tale but a chaos narrative of the sort delineated above. Conversely, she discovers in Park's and McDonnell's books vestiges of the "male" quest and war narratives, arguing that *The Siege* depicts Clara Park's use of domestic space as a fortress from which to battle both psychiatry and contemporary ideologies of motherhood. In contrast, McDonnell struggles to escape domesticity and fulfill herself professionally. Cumberland hears in each story echoes of her own mother's battle to define herself in relation to her son and his autism. Though none of these mothers ultimately defeated the prevailing belief that moms are responsible for their children's success or failure, Cumberland uses their stories to suggest why the proliferation of parent-authored memoirs constitutes an important positive development: by reading of others' experiences with autism, parents may find reassurance, or at least confirmation, of their own experiences and emotions.

In her chapter, Sheryl Stevenson also extracts from Park's and McDonnell's texts crucial insights about women's struggles to cope not just with autism but with irreconcilable conceptions of motherhood. She suggests that to ward off mother-blaming, each memoirist incorporates examples of her child's self-representations (Jessy's paintings, Paul's writing); yet these efforts also expose the gulf between the parent's and child's cognitive abilities. Stevenson further demonstrates how each author struggles with the questions of empathy—of speaking for her child—that I've just outlined, pointing out that each mother seeks to balance moments of "wondrous" discourse with quotidian details designed to claim "the ordinary world" for the autistic person. Ultimately, Stevenson argues, Clara Park manages to represent her daughter as at once strange and ordinary, both able and disabled. And in Clara Park's self-revisions—particularly her abandonment in *Exiting Nirvana* of *The Siege*'s controlling tropes—Stevenson locates an empathetic standpoint from which parent authors may learn to recognize our own developmental delays in understanding our autistic children, and thus finds a model for future parent memoirs.

The proliferation of parent-written accounts over the past 15 years seems to mirror the "epidemic" of autism diagnoses. There are far too many to discuss them all here. A few trends, however, are obvious. First, the gap between "high-" and "low-functioning" autistic people is painfully evident in this swelling library: even the smartest and best written of these books either adhere to the conventions of the recovery or restitution narrative, or depict children on the highest end of the autism spectrum. Well-intended though most of them are, the fact that they so far outnumber other representations fuels the misconception of ASDs as a set of temporary, even quaint eccentricities that can be remedied by undaunted parents. Some of these cure stories seem designed mostly to absolve the parent from guilt by singling out some other scapegoat (such as vaccines or diet) and portraying the parent's heroism. Indeed, *How I Saved My Child from Autism and Became a Better Person* could be the title of too many parent memoirs. A handful of recent memoirs have dared to buck this trend, and within this group some patterns have emerged that allow us to delineate the contours of an emerging genre.[14]

First, each memoir copes with the conflict between autism as lived and autism as it can be narrated by seeking a strategy with which to depict stasis or constant disruption. Second, each parent negotiates the "looping" effects of the diagnosis: is being labeled "autistic" liberating or imprisoning? Third, each finds a method—whether in denial, indignation, or stoic acceptance—of dealing with the shock, grief, rage and guilt that usually arise after the diagnosis and sometimes become parents' constant companions. Fourth, each author seeks a path through those *dissoi logoi*—between the feeling that autism is a terrible demon, an unconquerable, debilitating force, and the (sometimes elusive) sense that it may also be a gift. Lastly, although the nature of autobiography seems to demand a celebration or at least acknowledgment of the autistic child's individuality, parent authors often use their children as opportunities to generalize about education, medicine, drugs, and so on. This pattern is partly a function of audience: because autism is still not well understood by the public, these books often try both to tell a story and to educate the public about the disorder. But these competing aims often strain the books, prompting the authors to reach for a universality that their examples may contradict.

One recent memoir that wrestles with these issues is Paul Collins's *Not Even Wrong*, which couples the story of his son Morgan's autism diagnosis and their therapeutic interventions with forays into the lives of historical figures—Peter the Wild Boy, "outsider" artist Henry Darger, Alan Turing—who may have been autistic. Though Collins is a much nimbler writer than Michael Fitzgerald and refrains from Fitzgerald's one-size-fits-all methodology, his thesis is similar: that these "autistic" people's creative accomplishments would have been impossible had they been "normal." Though these anecdotes are fascinating, they interrupt the more compelling and immediate narrative of Collins's son and family. When Collins focuses his acute writerly eye on Morgan—when, for instance, he compares the boy's penchant for collecting broken bits of language to a "magpie gathering stray threads . . . into a nest" (81)—the book sings. But nearly every time Collins touches on a painful issue (Morgan's loneliness; the challenges he'll face in the future), he recoils; hence, the historical excursions seem like pretexts to avoid confronting the implications of his son's diagnosis. Collins's explicit comments reinforce the sense that he hasn't really grasped what this means. For example, he writes that Morgan is "happy when he is left alone, doing what he wants. It's the outside world that is the problem" (77). No doubt: but does he really believe that Morgan should just be left alone? Collins's search for the silver lining ultimately leads him to argue that autism is "*an ability and a disability*: it is as much about what is abundant as what is missing, an overexpression of the very traits that make our species human" (161). In this regard he concurs with Belmonte. Collins also concludes that this story isn't a tragedy but simply a factual account of "my family" (229). But because Morgan is still a pre-schooler at the close of the book, both statements seem premature. Collins lacks the experience that would lend authority to his conclusions; it's hard not to feel that he has written the book too soon.

In contrast to Collins's evasive tactics, Robert Hughes's *Running with Walker* gives it to us straight, albeit sprinkled with plenty of sardonic humor, as he candidly recounts his son Walker's chronic insomnia, seizures, maddening behaviors and regression, as well as his own depression, rage, feelings of imprisonment and inadequacy. Many scenes—Walker's obsession with Disney videos, the ongoing medication trials, the moments of insane danger and panic, and those astonishing (and frustrating) moments of apparent typicality—will strike a chord with many parents of autistic children. Nor is Hughes is afraid to stare unblinkingly at Walker's pain. For example, following a horrible episode in the aftermath of Walker's first seizure, this usually nonverbal boy touchingly proclaims, "No doctors today!" (64). Out of such moments of despair, Hughes conjures hope: after another sleepless night in which Walker's dangerous leaps from staircase to floor drive Hughes to spank him, the father eventually arrives at an epiphany—"Nothing is written" (132). In other words, he is free to adopt any attitude he chooses about his son. And he insists that Walker is "much, much more than a victim" of autism (20), railing with ferocious indignation at the physicians and specialists who misdiagnosed his son and dismissed all hope (see 135, 211). Understandably, these experiences cause Hughes to overgeneralize about educators and specialists.

Hughes also resists the "autism" label, arguing that it "vaporize[s] the mystery," and turns his son "into something simple, comprehensible, and finally boring" (81). But although in one section Hughes describes Walker as "low-functioning" (15), he also emphasizes the gifts—the intelligence and sheer *joie de vivre*—that render Walker a fascinating character and loveable son and brother. The book thus strikes a somewhat uneasy balance between the highlights and lowlights of life with autism. But Hughes does not fully succeed in turning this compelling material into a compact story: because Walker's improvements are not dramatic enough to call him "cured," the book remains a series of episodes leading to an anticlimactic conclusion.

Kate Rankin's amusing and frequently astonishing *Growing Up Severely Autistic: They Call Me Gabriel* displays a similar tension. Although Rankin records her agony at the diagnosis, there's no suggestion that the label imprisons her son, who may be the most seriously impaired child depicted in any parent memoir: at age seventeen, he is not toilet-trained, doesn't speak at all, has almost no ordinary play, social or academic skills, climbs compulsively, runs away, destroys furniture. Rankin recounts her experiences in an understated (though at times cliché-ridden) style—appropriately enough, for Gabriel's eccentricities (e.g., his rubber-glove fetish, his penchant for opening padlocked windows and climbing onto the roof, his relentless energy) require no rhetorical flourishes. In contrast to Hughes's volatility, Rankin narrates with an unsentimental (and very English) stoicism that lets us see Gabriel clearly. Near the end, she even acknowledges that her son has provided her and her family with opportunities to grow and understand themselves better (163). Though Rankin registers the nearly intolerable frustration and chaos of life with this child (in one scene she bites him in frustration: 75), her love and acceptance of Gabriel are apparent most in the honesty she displays, an honesty made possible by empathy. Gabriel is an unforgettable character, but the book's narrative never gains momentum. Perhaps such severely autistic children, with their intractable rigidity and destructive habits, resist treatment narratively just as they do therapeutically.

Though a more skilled writer than Rankin, Charlotte Moore shares her no-time-for-moaning attitude as she portrays the challenges of living with *two* autistic sons in *George and Sam* (her testimony that she never railed against fate or cast about for explanations is thus a remarkable tribute, but whether to optimism or to denial isn't clear: see 13). Moore resists the temptation to extol a specific therapy, noting that the audio integration therapy that benefited her older son George had no effect on Sam, and that dietary interventions that did nothing for George helped Sam immensely. Sensible, humorous and down-to-earth, Moore's text—as much a self-help book as a memoir—comprises brief essays on particular issues such as education, food, imagination, and diagnostics. But the desire to educate her audience often prompts Moore to over-generalize from her tiny sample (autists do this or that), to explain research on, for example, theory of mind, without a hint of skepticism (see 73–4), and to dismiss all autism drugs as useless (102). Moore seems compelled to reach a general audience, and this aim both interferes with the story and leads to the troubling conclusion that because autistic people retain a child-like innocence, their most valuable quality is to "provide a yardstick for neurotypical moral behavior" (222). This assertion perpetuates the "how autism made me a better person" convention, which represents autists not as ends in themselves but as means to neurotypical moral improvement.[15]

If none of these memoirs entirely succeeds in balancing narrative with truth, or in squaring specificity with generality, their existence nonetheless proves that the previously invisible segment of autistic persons—more severely impaired children who do not "recover" and whose stories don't make neurotypical readers feel uplifted—are at last emerging into view. My own chapter in this volume, which tells of our family's struggle to toilet train my autistic son, attempts to contribute to this emergence. If, as Frank argues, restitution narratives portray how medicine produces disciplined bodies (41), our story dramatizes how one autistic person resisted such disciplining. The chapter also exemplifies the tensions between narrative and authenticity I've outlined: it is at once a chaos narrative that records our fear that life would never improve and a tale of near constant disruption—a mixture of repetition and upheaval. In representing my son's behavior not as recalcitrance but as an effort to communicate his desires and assert his identity, I aim to demonstrate the kind of empathetic attention I've just outlined, as well as to dramatize how a "low-functioning" autistic child tries, against overwhelming odds, to generate local coherence and preserve agency.

Brothers and Sisters

Autistic children demand inordinate amounts of attention; they often disrupt families' social lives, wreck their houses, and create second-hand stigmas for their siblings. Their brothers and sisters—even the majority who testify to feeling protective and proud of their autistic siblings—may also feel neglected, envious, and resentful. Hence, though the shelf of sibling memoirs is less packed than the parent portion, these books provide an essential perspective on life with autism. They prove that living with an autistic sibling means adjusting expectations and definitions of normality, and requires learning to accept themselves, as well as their brothers or sisters, as both similar to and different from others. One powerful tool siblings employ to handle their anger and jealousy is humor, which is even more prominent in sibling memoirs than in the parent-authored books I've discussed. Indeed, by treating their brothers or sisters as amusing or annoying but fully aware, these authors honor their loved ones' humanity by refusing to condescend.

Two recent sibling memoirs offer abundant humor as they recount life with autistic siblings in the days when little was known about the condition. Mary-Ann Tirone Smith's *Girls of Tender Age* combines a charming and often hilarious story of growing up in the1950s with her (undiagnosed but clearly) autistic brother Tyler, and a true-crime tale about the murder of a classmate by a sociopathic ex-sailor named Bob Malm. Life with Tyler was often a trial: his hearing was so sensitive that the family couldn't play the piano, listen to records, or even cry in the house (Tyler testifies that hearing someone cry is like having "a cloud of needles [fly] into my face": 33). Whenever he hears a loud noise or sees the color red, Tyler becomes so anxious that he must complete a long series of "rounds" through the house, striding up and down the stairs and through each room over and over, while repeating the syllable "kish" (53). His uncontrollable anxiety also drives him to bite his wrist so habitually that it becomes callused and chronically infected. Though called "retarded," Tyler is far from it: he obsessively reads and quotes books about World War II, and the scenes in which Tyler orders his family members around like a military commander (50) are among the book's funniest episodes. Tirone Smith narrates these scenes with a bemused affection.

But Tyler's eccentricities were no doubt less amusing at the time and far from the only problems in this household. Tirone Smith inadvertently invokes the shade of Bruno Bettelheim in her description of her parents. Although her saintly father, Yutch, comes home every day from his job at a ball-bearing plant to cook and care for Tyler, her mother, Florence—a brittle, selfish woman always "on the verge of a breakdown" who once fractures Mary-Ann's arm while punishing her—seems more interested in perfecting her golf game than in dealing with her son. Though the author doesn't say so explicitly, she implies that Yutch's refusal to get help and Florence's chilly neglect added to Tyler's—and Mary-Ann's (Mickey's)—problems. Mickey's inability to cry also becomes part of the book's theme of denial—"my family's religion, my brother Tyler our god, and the Reverend Dr. Peale our pastor" (143)—as Tyler becomes a household Hitler who bends the family to his whims, knowing "exactly what he's doing" (86) all the while. On retirement, Yutch makes himself "a living tool . . . to fix the world so that Tyler can be kept in an agitation-free state" (171). But only after a college psychology professor reads Mickey's autobiography and tells her she lived in a "rigid, narrow grid constructed by your brother, who forced you and your parents to run yourselves ragged catering to his every obsession and compulsion" does she begin to understand how she has been affected (158).

In the second half of the book, Tirone Smith endeavors to connect Malm's crime and the sexism that contributed to her classmate's death with her family's suppression of her own voice. Just as Irene was strangled, we understand, Mickey was metaphorically strangled by Catholicism, the working-class mentality of toughing it out, and her brother's autistic manipulations. Malm, who denied responsibility for his actions throughout his life, instead blamed a monster inside him for his homicidal impulses. Tirone Smith comments: "Neither Bob nor the monster has any idea what remorse is. Neither did my brother. . . . Tyler did, in fact, have a monster that lived inside him. The monster's name was autism. So maybe sociopathic behavior is within the ever-widening spectrum of autism" (237). One not need have an autistic loved one to find this statement offensive. But Tirone Smith redeems the book with a touching story of Tyler's final illness, concluding that "autistics demonstrate love oddly . . . but their love is mighty just the same" (257).

Girls of Tender Age is really two books: a memoir of living in an autistic family, and a crime tale carrying a feminist thesis about male oppression. Despite lapses such as the one cited above, she manages to turn her rage and jealousy into a poignant tale that transcends its awkward parallels. Indeed, the book's unmatched parts well illustrate the author's ambivalence about her autistic family. A similar duality is displayed in another recent sibling memoir, Paul and Judy Karasik's *The Ride Together*, which juxtaposes Paul's comic strip vignettes with Judy's more conventional account to create a moving portrait of life with their autistic older brother David. Paul's comic strips are particularly trenchant in illustrating the world according to David, who recites and enacts dozens of television shows he has memorized, most notably *Superman*. David, whose echolalia exemplifies that extraordinary mimetic ability that Oliver Sacks describes, forges his identity out of scraps salvaged from mediated images: the voices, behavior, and characters of politicians, reporters and superheroes. Paul's own work reflects a similar talent.

The main story here, however, is about acceptance and love, and both siblings furnish anecdotes about how their jealousy and resentment turned into acceptance. In one set of panels, Paul fights with David and is sent to his room, then imagines himself living in *Superman* comics' Bizarro World where all conventions are inverted. He envisions a fictional, but perfectly rendered, 1960s public service ad about his brother's "Invisible Handicap"; after tearing up the comic book, bizarro Paul falls asleep, mumbling words from one of David's *Superman* scripts. Paul, we understand, has learned to enter David's world: indeed, he has become him. Which of the brothers is normal and which is bizarro? Another effective sequence depicts Paul taking David to a Three Stooges' film festival where he is initially mortified by David's shouts of "Moe, Larry, cheese!" But then the panels show the Stooges' world spilling into the theater, causing a pie fight and general mayhem (127–9). Back in "reality," David walks out, but his departure provides a pretext for Paul to chat up a pretty theater worker. The vignette ends with the brothers gleefully shouting in unison "Moe, Larry, Cheese!!" Paul has learned to accept his brother as a kind of Lord of Misrule, a "hole blown through ordinary . . . behavior," as Judy puts it (139). Rarely has the chaos of life with autism been better rendered.

Judy's quieter story also dramatizes her efforts to understand David (for whom she employs a series of metaphors, such as that of the "wild card" in the family deck [58]) and to transpose him in her mind from a nuisance to someone needing protection. After David's adulthood devolves into a perpetual round of unsuccessful residential placements, one of which ends when years of physical and sexual abuse come to light, Judy is agonizingly forced to reassess her complacency about David's supposedly self-inflicted injuries: "I had shaken the hand that had pulled back my brother's finger until the bone cracked. And I had smiled at the man . . . and left my brother with him. I left David to be hit again and to be told, 'This is because you are bad.' . . . I left my brother alone" (181). As in Tirone Smith's final pages, the inability to protect one's autistic sibling reminds the author that she has never truly understood him (185).

Yet Judy belatedly learns that David also protects her: after a ride together from one of his placement facilities, he questions her about the upcoming holidays and then gives her a kiss. Only later does she realize that although she thought she was reassuring David, he was actually reassuring her, telling her not to feel guilty about leaving him (152). Like the Stooges crashing through frames, David breaks out of the box into which others place him. Judy further illustrates this complexity in a scene in which she watches the movie *Rain Man* (about autistic savant Raymond Babbitt and his brother) while David sleeps beside her. The film, which once moved her, now leaves her cold, and she realizes that she doesn't want David to see it, not because he couldn't handle it, but because *she* can't. "I couldn't be with the movie . . . that I had used to make a neat package out of David, and be with David at the same time" (151). Autistic fact—that wild card—trumps autistic fiction. Through these vivid episodes, the Karasiks demonstrate that their brother is not just a disorder, but a complex, creative and loving human being who can't be fully captured by the label of "autism."

Tirone Smith and the Karasiks are able to create compelling narratives partly because they tell their stories in retrospect, when the shape of their brothers' lives is more complete. Even so, they never lapse into conversion or recovery stereotypes, and present their autistic brothers as agents, not patients. Perhaps most important, these memoirs suggest that autism is not just an individual disorder but also a family condition that responds to and generates interpersonal dynamics not so different from those in ordinary families. Each story, indeed, illustrates how other family members "become autistic," and are forced to learn empathy—that "eudaimonistic quality" of perceiving the world as another sees it—in order to inhabit the worlds their brothers create. These siblings come to appreciate what their brothers have given them, not as "yardsticks" for neurotypical morality, but as mixes of abilities and disabilities, of impairments and gifts, like those of other human beings. These siblings stories prove, in short, that an autistic person is one of us.

Doors and Mirrors

Even so, the library of memoirs by autistic people remains small. But this fact is not remarkable, given that autism often involves linguistic difficulties and cognitive impairments. Indeed, in some respects an autist autobiography seems a "contradiction in terms" (Sacks 253), and autism a form of embodiment that, as Michael Bérubé observes, cannot "narrate itself but can only be narrated" (572). Until 1986, when Temple Grandin's *Emergence: Labeled Autistic* appeared, there were no published autobiographies of autistic people. Grandin's book, co-authored by Margaret Scariano, also exemplifies other significant obstacles for autist autobiographies. For example, because of the communication problems associated with autism, these authors confront questions about "agency, authority, voice, and authenticity" that do not arise for most other disabled authors (Couser, "Conflicting" 79). For example, if, as is commonly believed, autistic people lack intelligence and a cohesive identity, then it's easy to assume that their works are really ghostwritten. On the other hand, if a person is capable of writing a book, can she really be autistic (see S. Smith, "Limit" 243)? And if the author is indeed "recovered," as Bernard Rimland's foreword to *Emergence* declares of Grandin (7), are the book's perspectives authentically autistic, or merely reconstructed through neurotypical perspectives?

Autistic authors thus encounter the same dilemma as parent authors: how to represent their lives as both uniquely autistic and akin to those of other humans. Perhaps that is why these early autist autobiographers present their accounts as recovery stories—why, for example, Bernard Rimland's and William Carlock's prefatory materials emphasize Temple Grandin's "rescue" from autism. Her own perspective, however, is more ambiguous. For one thing, her obsessive reiteration of the same tropes—particularly doors and entryways—indicates a mind that, though capable of both metonymic and metaphoric thinking, remains an *autistic* mind focused tightly on a narrow set of images. *Emergence* thus typifies Nazeer's and Mills's descriptions of local coherence. And though Grandin recognizes that her autism has caused great difficulties in her social and academic life, she also demonstrates that her autistic obsession with cattle chutes helped her construct a psychic or developmental tunnel through which she could exit her autistic world. That is, though moving through her symbolic door may have freed Grandin (80), her autism enabled her to generate the image that permitted her "emergence." Her autism, then, cannot be separated from her creativity and identity; she thus concludes that it would *not* be a good thing if all autistic people were "cured" (140). In other words, Grandin didn't emerge from autism so much as *merge with* it, crafting a self from within autism that enabled her to keep one foot on each side of the threshold.

Grandin also emerges by learning to merge with others. For example, a comparison of the occasionally florid writing in *Emergence* with the matter-of-fact style of her later autobiography *Thinking In Pictures* suggests that many passages in the book come from the hand of Margaret Scariano (see, for example, 15, 25, 32). Further, *Emergence* is remarkable for the frequency with which Grandin yields the page to other voices. The book is full of interpolated texts—letters from Temple's mother to professionals and to Temple

(47–53, 55–58; 100–102; 120–21), letters from clinicians (61–2, 143) and her Aunt Ann (92–4), writings by the youthful Temple (31, 112–14, 131, 133). This tactic may partly reflect Grandin's authorial insecurity, but it also instances a tendency dramatized repeatedly in autistic representations: that autistic selfhood and creativity are best shaped and expressed by appropriating others' identities and voices. The text's interpolations indeed imply that Grandin has cobbled together her identity from the remnants of others' and the residue of her own alter egos, including Alfred Costello (36, 77), an imaginary self who mocked her but whose voice she assumed, and Bisban, a mischievous character she borrowed from the Little Rascals films (35).

This pattern is even more apparent in the second autist autobiography to be published, Donna Williams's 1992 *Nobody Nowhere*. Williams's text is also framed by two prefatory or paratextual introductions written by experts who praise her "transition from autism to near-normalcy" (Rimland, Foreword to *Nobody* ix). Nevertheless, Williams's voice and viewpoint—blunt, headlong, self-obsessed but curiously unreflective—bespeaks an *autistic* consciousness that rarely generalizes or condenses, shows little comprehension of or interest in how others think, and possesses a weak grasp of narrative connection. Whereas Grandin defines her emergence via the trope of doors, Williams portrays her evolution through repeated scenes involving mirrors (see 56, 209) and shadows (95). Like Grandin's, however, her self-formation occurs through self-effacement, as young Donna repeatedly attaches herself to particular friends, imitating their actions and echoing their voices (31, 33), and invents personae with histories distinct from her actual one (80, 82). Most significantly, she conjures up and hides behind two long-time internal companions—soft-hearted, vulnerable, sunny Carol; assertive, prickly, controlling Willie—each of whom embodies selected shards of her "fractured" or "shattered" identity (102).

The other shadow in the book is her mother, and Williams suggests that she created those imaginary selves partly in response to her mother's abuse (thus again invoking the shade of Bettelheim). But none of these alter egos heals her fractures, and hers remains a "world under glass" (66) where Donna is walled off from her own consciousness by the mirror images she has crafted. Thus in one epiphanic scene, she gazes into a mirror and sees not Willie but herself look back (131); yet Willie eventually returns. Williams finally emerges only when she learns not to banish but to incorporate her alternate selves—to make them her minions rather than her dictators (see 192). A culminating game of shadow-dancing with a final alter-ego, a young autistic girl named Anne, illustrates that Donna has finally stepped from behind glass (196).

In contrast to Temple Grandin, whose adult identity is shaped by her negotiation with the "autism" label, Donna Williams doesn't receive a diagnosis until adulthood. Critic Sidonie Smith thus suggests that whereas Grandin constitutes herself "out of polarization" with the experts who have defined her (241), Williams uses her diagnosis as a "shape-shifting opportunity" through which to combine her many identities into a single cohesive self (237). But these subjects' negotiations with autism are not so clear-cut: the word "autism" barely figures at all in Grandin's own narrative, and both books reflect an autistic cognitive and narrative style. And despite *Nobody Nowhere*'s episodic structure, Williams sustains one theme throughout: her quest to bring her world—the intensely private world of Carol and Willie—into closer contact with the world of others. Like *Emergence*, then, *Nobody Nowhere* is a narrative of normalization.

In some respects, Grandin's and Williams's stories resemble those of the classic Bildungsroman protagonist, who battles oppressive authorities (Grandin's teachers, Williams's abusive or distant parents) and endures degrading love affairs (Williams's early adulthood is rendered as a repeated round of failed romances), but borrows from positive role models to synthesize a coherent identity and discover a vocation—which is embodied by the book we are reading.[16] Yet crafting an identity is far more difficult for these autist autobiographers, because their perceptions and alter egos arrive in bits and pieces. Thus they resort to strategies of bricolage—echolalia, imitation, fixations—that enable them to build identity from ramshackle assemblages of spare parts.[17] As Belmonte suggests, these autist authors seek to anchor themselves in the chaotic sea of sensation by battening upon stray flotsam. One thinks again of David Karasik's elaborate echolalia, of Stephen Wiltshire's impersonations of Rain Man, of Tyler Tirone's habitation in the house of World War II. These portrayals indicate that autistic creativity and identity are paradoxically synthesized through an arduous process of self-effacement, an emergence that occurs simultaneously with submergence.

Given the piecemeal strategies by which autistic authors construct themselves, one wonders whether autobiography, with its inherited chronological form and linear momentum, is a suitable genre. How can one authentically render an autistic consciousness when the demands of narrative order seem to violate its essence? Nazeer's *Send in the Idiots* offers an alternative: not a single story, but four vignettes, in each of which the author figures as both reporter and subject. Nazeer also inserts lengthy digressions about topics such as the art of conversation, autistic socialization, and the nature of autistic consciousness. This blend of narrative and interpretation, of empathetic involvement and authorial distance, allows Nazeer (himself a "former" autistic) to bypass the conventions of the recovery narrative and attain a compelling authority. His authorial position therefore fits the masking pattern we've detected in other autist autobiographies: by investigating and inhabiting the lives of other autistic adults, Nazeer not only learns that his original aims for the book were autistically rigid (88), but also solidifies a hybrid adult identity that is at times autistic, at other times neurotypical. Thus Nazeer resists reifying autism, instead offering complex examples that demonstrate again that autism is not one thing but many different things.

Grandin's and Williams's texts may send mixed signals to autistic readers: We are autistic and have written books, so you can too—but only if you present them as a "recovery" or emergence from it. The more complex inner narrative of merger and consolidation may be lost within the formulaic framework. Nazeer's subjects are also successful, but each of them (aside perhaps, from himself) remains significantly disabled. Yet the fact that these authors have written at all is of paramount importance, not just because they can serve as models for other aspiring autist authors, but also because the process of writing their lives has enabled them to *compose* those lives: their authorial selves are both doors and mirrors. Their texts challenge neurotypical readers to reconsider conventional notions of selfhood, authorship and agency, and encourage us to become their empathetic collaborators. Even if, as autistic author Jasmine O'Neill asserts, non-autistic people will never truly comprehend "what a life with Autism is like" (12), these texts serve as entryways into the room of autistic consciousness, and as mirrors in which to see ourselves *as* them.

POPULAR REPRESENTATIONS

Barely There

In Matthew David Hoge's 2004 film *The United States of Leland*, a confused teenager named Leland stabs to death an autistic boy named Ryan Pollard.[18] The day after his murder, Ryan's mother (Ann Magnuson) wonders aloud how anyone could hate Ryan enough to want him dead. After all, she concludes, "He was barely there." Though it's difficult to imagine any mother of a disabled child actually saying such a thing, the phrase sums up Ryan's role in this film, which devotes most of its attention to Leland (Ryan Gosling), whose prison teacher, Pearl (Don Cheadle), prods him into writing his story inside his U.S. history textbook. We eventually learn that Leland, who had developed a close relationship with Ryan, killed the boy because Ryan seemed to Leland a symbol of world's engulfing sadness. Subject to prejudice and taunting (which we never see), Ryan was, according to Leland, "trapped" inside his body. Judging by Leland's sensitive narration, his gentle chides about Pearl's infidelity, and his relationships with Ryan and his troubled sister Becky, we are supposed to view him as a misguided but moral young man whose murder was, paradoxically, aimed at "protecting" Ryan. "Even when you try to do something good," Leland laments near the end of the film, "it turns out bad."

This morality is confused, and so is the film, which constantly diverts our attention from Ryan—the autistic boy who was stabbed by his "friend"— and generally indicates that he scarcely matters. Ryan's family may care that he's dead, but the greater loss, we're led to believe, is Leland (who is ultimately stabbed in revenge by a young man who lives with the Pollards): after all, Ryan was "barely there" in the first place. The film's earnest manner and careful delineation of its other characters makes its cavalier treatment of Ryan all the more troubling. Despite *Leland*'s relatively accurate rendering of Ryan's disability, it depicts him as a mere symbol, as what David Mitchell and Sharon Snyder call a "narrative prosthesis": an artificial means to mobilize the plot, a "crutch on which . . . narratives lean for their representational power, disruptive potential, and social critique" (17). Ryan, that is, exists only to reflect the values of the *other*, non-autistic characters (47); as himself, he's barely there.

This phrase also sums up autism's place in both popular film and cinematic scholarship. As Stuart Murray points out in his chapter in this volume, even Martin Norden's expansive survey of disability in film, *The Cinema of Isolation*, has barely a word to say about intellectual disabilities in general or autism in particular. Of course, numerous autistic characters appear in recent cinema but, as in *Leland*, they function primarily as archetypes, symbols, ideas, or props, seldom as fully human beings. These autistic stereotypes resemble those Norden outlines for physically disabled characters. One common figure, for example, is an autistic version of Norden's "Sweet Innocent"—a childlike or passive character, like *Leland's* Ryan, who embodies the "mainstream belief that disabled people must depend on others for their every need" (33). Another is a variation on Norden's "Civilian Superstar": a resourceful, courageous person who happens to have a disability, usually enacted by a well-known performer, such as Dustin Hoffman, who played autistic savant Raymond Babbitt in *Rain Man* (51). The recent film *Mozart and the Whale*, about a love affair between two Asperger's adults played by Josh Hartnett and Radha Mitchell, offers a recent instance of this type. Also ubiquitous are examples of Norden's "High-tech Guru"— characters who seem "part machine" (299)—autists with computer or math skills, such as *Cube's* Kazan, or *Mercury Rising's* autistic boy Simon. These "gurus" are themselves subtypes of the most common cliché, autism's variation on the Supercrip (the overachieving disabled person who triumphs over tragedy): the Savant.

Tom Shakespeare argues that we should not be too rigid in our expectations for cinematic portrayals of disability, and that "it is dangerous to develop hard and fast rules of representation" that may further harden into dogmas ("Art" 170). But is it too much to expect simple accuracy? As it stands today, misleading stereotypes have shoved out virtually all other representations of autism from mainstream cinema. Rather than providing a stage on which to celebrate or at least explore autistic identity and agency, movies have placed a screen between their audience and any authentic sense of life with autism.

Screening Autism

Even those who know little about autism know about *Rain Man*, Barry Levinson's well-crafted buddy/road movie about Raymond and his callous brother Charlie (Tom Cruise), which first thrust autism into popular awareness. *Rain Man* also initiated the Savant and Yardstick stereotypes that, as Murray's and Anthony Baker's chapters demonstrate, still dominate cinematic depictions of autism. Such films select one or two characteristics (usually savant memory or math skills and echolalia) and erect them into one-dimensional portraits of the autist. The worst abuses of this phenomenon are on display in the 1994 film *Silent Fall*, in which autistic youngster Timmy Warden is the sole witness to his parents' murder. Ruining this intriguing premise, Akiva Goldsman's screenplay ludicrously exaggerates Timmy's echolalic skills and the healing powers of psychiatrist Jake Rainer (Richard Dreyfuss), who opines that Timmy is "trapped behind a wall" where it's "safer to be others." But Rainer could surely save Timmy if only given a chance: in one scene, Timmy magically stops stimming as soon as Rainer claps his hands. Eventually Rainer induces Timmy to use his super-human powers of mimicry to replay the sounds of the murder; Timmy later impersonates the sheriff to trick his sister into giving herself away as the murderer. Yet we also learn that Timmy can speak in his own voice when he has a compelling reason to do so. Autism, in short, is represented as a performance, a brand of ventriloquism that can be exploited or exploded by an ingenious shrink. Rainer's therapies are literally no more sophisticated than card tricks, as the film reduces doctor and autistic boy to a magician and his freak-show dummy.

Though most autism films are not quite this atrocious, *Silent Fall* is far from an anomaly in its use of autism as a handy plot gimmick. Indeed, in his chapter in the present volume, Anthony Baker analyzes the formulas popular films employ to represent autism. He notes that the character is usually a child possessed of some savant skill that generates a spectacle for audiences; the child is endangered and then rescued by a neurotypical hero, reassuring audiences that the neurotypical are truly able, truly valuable. The autistic characters are, in contrast, worthwhile *only* as savants; otherwise they possess neither agency nor real selfhood. Autism becomes a set of reified skills and quirks. Although the ghosts of Bettelheim and Kanner loom over these films' frequent missing or neglectful parents, Baker suggests that parents of autistic children may nonetheless find within them brief redeeming moments—a glance at neurotypical children playing, a close up of a child's PECS booklet—that validate their and their child's experiences. In its blend of experiential knowledge and rigorous taxonomy, Baker's essay exemplifies the goals of a truly empathetic scholarship.

Oliver Sacks notes that autism has long "attracted in the popular mind an amazed, fearful or bewildered attention" that evokes "mythical or archetypal figures—the alien, the changeling, the child bewitched" (190). In a recent essay on autism in contemporary fiction, Stuart Murray similarly demonstrates how some recent novels with autistic characters treat them as personifications "of difference and otherness" who symbolize "the alien within the human, the mystical within the rational, the ultimate enigma" (25–6). In his chapter in this collection, Murray argues that mainstream cinema also depicts autistic characters as emblems of the enigmatic or inexplicable. These representations frequently couple autistic with non-autistic characters (the autistic character serving as Yardstick), and require the autistic characters to "perform" autism by acting out some savant skill or stereotypical autistic behavior. Although these films invite audiences to gaze at the autist and speculate on the human condition, they almost always end up resorting to generic conventions that render them formless, formulaic or sentimental. Autism, Murray argues, generally becomes an excuse to reinforce conventional ideas about family love; rather than exploring autistic agency or presence, such films serve the needs and pacify the expectations of the majority audience.

Even films that aim to flout these patterns eventually fall victim to them. For example, *Mozart and the Whale* (written by Ron Bass, who also scripted *Rain Man*), based on the actual experiences of two Asperger's adults, at first seems to transcend these trite approaches. Donald Morton (Josh Hartnett) and Isabelle Sorenson (Radha Mitchell) meet at a support group for autistic adults. Some of the other members—including Janice, who shouts at everyone and never makes eye contact; Gracie, who laughs inappropriately and spouts obscure trivia about presidents; and a man who stims with an egg-beater—are believably autistic. The filmmakers also comment on them cinematically: throughout this group scene—filmed on steps leading to a pond—director Peter Naess consistently places his camera well above or below the speaking character, and positions the speaker somewhere left or right of center frame. These unbalanced compositions and extreme angles illustrate a neurotypical viewpoint: autistic people are either greater or less than the rest of us, and live at the margins of human life. The scene's ultimate effect is that of a zoo exhibit, or what Isabelle calls a "fish tank."

The sense that Isabelle and Donald are specimens on display is reinforced by their constant association with animals (Donald's disheveled apartment is full of birds; Isabelle owns an eclectic menagerie) and by their first date, which occurs on Halloween. After donning a whale costume, Donald can't bring himself to go out; Isabelle, clad in eighteenth-century male garb, eventually tires of waiting and fetches Donald, who explains that the whale costume reveals his desire to be "in the parade" rather than watching it from the sidelines. He's definitely in the parade on this night, as he and "Mozart" attract curious gazes from passersby. But for much of this sequence Donald is again placed off-center in the frame: he's in the parade, but mostly as a sideshow, right next to the bearded lady. In the next sequence Isabelle is seen standing, a bird perched on her left hand, simultaneously painting a picture and composing music. Ah yes, she is a savant (though we never see her actually do anything valuable with her powers), and so is Donald, who possesses extraordinary mathematical ability. The filmmakers do contrive an imaginative way to illustrate Donald's math skills: as he explains his fascination to Isabelle, numbers float above his head, responding to his manipulations. But these clever moments don't dispel the overriding sense that autistic people can be either geniuses or freaks; what they are *not* is regular people.

Josh Hartnett's Donald is authentically awkward and appealing, but Radha Mitchell's performance, complete with barking laugh and zany humor, renders Isabelle less as an Asperger's woman than as a conventionally ditsy romantic comedy protagonist. Just so we know that she's not merely a flake, the filmmakers give her a public meltdown scene when Donald tries to interest her in a carnival game of ring-toss. As the sound of metal clanking sends her into screaming agony, the camera rises to the kind of overhead shot usually reserved for murder or horror sequences; Isabelle hunkers in the center of the frame, surrounded by gawking spectators. The carnival-goers no longer need the booths, for they now have a more fascinating exhibit to behold: an autistic person freaking out.

The couple's difficulties in finding common ground, which culminates in a bitter argument in which Isabelle accuses Donald of trying to be normal and pandering to his neurotypical boss, highlights a genuine issue in the autism community. But aside from its quirky characters, the film is a standard romantic comedy, complete with a meet-cute sequence (the costume scene), commitment problems, miscommunication about expectations, and a breakup followed by a climactic reunion. That Donald and Isabelle can sustain a relationship may suggest that autistic people have the same needs and desires as others, but the film mostly affirms conventional ideas about marriage and mainstream views of normality. It thus exemplifies Murray's thesis: autism films invariably lapse into formula or sentimentality and certify neurotypical values.

In addressing a neurotypical audience, these films are, of course, seeking commercial success. But can autistic viewers find themselves in them? They may see glimmers in *Mozart*'s minor variation on the romantic comedy, but they probably do not relate to savant children rescued by shrinks, and will likely be offended by *Leland*'s insulting treatment of Ryan Pollard. Phil Schwarz, in his chapter in the present volume, offers some more positive alternatives. In documenting how a group of autistic adults responded to four films—none with a character identified as autistic—Schwarz (himself an adult on the autism spectrum) demonstrates how each film represents one stage of a possible journey toward autistic self-advocacy, moving from finding role models and coping with negative stereotypes, to asserting autistic identity and finally to conveying positive self-awareness to friends and family. The biographical films about pianist Glenn Gould and cryptographer Alan Turing provided historical perspectives and possible heroes. Turing's alienation and reluctant disclosure of his homosexuality also raised the question of whether to reveal one's autism. *Smoke Signals*, a film about Native American youth, exposed parallels between its protagonists' internalization of negative stereotypes and those to which autists are exposed. Finally, from John Sayles's fable *The Secret of Roan Inish* the audience drew a compelling metaphor for autistic people's role in neurotypical families. All four films, Schwarz persuasively argues, present important ideas about the positive construction of autistic identity and self-awareness without sensationalizing, romanticizing, or demonizing autism. One can only hope that filmmakers intent on explicitly representing autistic people will someday do the same.

Props and Puzzles

In the past ten years, several authors—some of them parents of autistic children—have published novels with autistic characters. As in the parent- or sibling-authored memoirs, the autistic characters generally appear as an eruption of chaos, an impenetrable enigma, a catalyst for another character's development, or as a force that must be transformed or erased.[19] As Murray notes, autism serves in some of them as a "prosthetic device" to enable "the discussion of a range of other issues," such as masculine identity, family cohesion, and adult responsibility ("Contemporary" 40). I would add that it also functions as a pretext for romances of female empowerment, as an emblem of social and familial dysfunction, and as a means to explore sibling jealousy. These authors' apparent need to harness their autistic characters to some conventional genre tale—romance, recovery narrative, coming-of-age story, or murder mystery—indicates not only a bow to popular tastes, but a fear that autism resists or defeats narrative, and is thus unsuitable novelistic material. Yet in each of these novels, the scenes in which the autistic child appears are the most thoughtful, realistic and evocatively written.

Two recent autism novels, both written by mothers of autistic children, exemplify these patterns, albeit in slightly different ways. Marti Leimbach's *Daniel Isn't Talking* centers on Melanie, whose three-year-old autistic son Daniel eventually makes (rather implausibly) rapid progress via an adapted ABA therapy/play program. Early on, Leimbach affectingly portrays Daniel's behaviors (toe-walking, a fixation on Thomas the Tank, and so on) and Melanie's fears about him. Unfortunately, she tethers this compelling material to a trite female empowerment romance filled with cardboard characters. For example, virtually every professional Melanie consults is a narrow-minded fool who functions only as an obstacle to Daniel's progress. Even less believable are the major male figures: Melanie's husband Stephen does little but patronize her, shout into his cell phone, and carry on an affair with another woman, whereas Andy, the Irish therapist who enters Melanie's life and rescues Daniel, is simply a female fantasy figure—not only is he full of brilliant therapeutic ideas, loaded with patience and armed with every right answer, but he's a great lover too! Striving to link Melanie's and Daniel's emergences, Leimbach marries two formulas—the autism restitution narrative and the romance novel—but fails to improve upon either one.

Yet when she concentrates on Melanie's relationship with Daniel, Leimbach often effectively captures the emotions many parents of autistic children feel. Her pangs of loss (49) and guilt over her perceived inadequacies

("I feel . . . that I've ruined him": 53); her devout wish that Daniel become simply "an average child" (70); her alienation (184) and embarrassment when parents of typical children brush her off because she and Daniel are "living proof that there are no guarantees with our children, that bad things happen" (107); her fear of what may happen to Daniel after she dies (73)—these insights carry an authority born of lived experience. Leimbach also trenchantly addresses the low-functioning/high-functioning gulf in Melanie's resentment of parents who proclaim that their child's autism is not a disability but merely a "difference": "What you know about such people," she writes, "is that they have a child who functions very well . . . that they have probably not scrubbed feces from their carpet, or watched their child cry and rock in what looks like agony because he cannot speak" (250). Such glimmers hint at another, better novel that Leimbach might have written. As is, however, Daniel's autism is translated into a metaphor for his mother's escape from an oppressive marriage and discovery of her identity—a crutch with which Melanie can limp to a better life.

Cammie McGovern's *Eye Contact* also weds an autism novel to a genre story—in this case, a murder mystery. Protagonist Cara is the mother of autistic nine-year-old Adam, who (revisiting the premise so poorly served by *Silent Fall*) witnesses the murder of his only friend, a girl named Amelia. Adam's relationships with his mother and with an otherwise friendless older boy named Morgan (who himself seems to be an undiagnosed Asperger's child) give the novel a strong emotional center and help to explain its title: eye contact is what enables humans to establish intimate relationships, yet each person sees the world with a different set of eyes. Cara's observation that Adam may be friendless because she can't give him an example of a healthy relationship (198) thus helps to explain the odd isolation of all the novel's adults: the eye contact through which humans form relationships is both a missing piece in Adam and necessary equipment for functional adulthood. Adam's condition, then, serves as a synecdoche for the "autistic" society in which he abides.

Unfortunately, Cara's self-absorbed friends (disabled and disturbed Kevin, agoraphobic Suzette) fail to engage the reader. *Eye Contact* also suffers from McGovern's attempt to do too many things: scatter the rather contrived mystery plot with red herrings and track Cara's efforts to find the murderer and a partner, while also tracing Adam's social development and recovery from trauma. As with *Daniel Isn't Talking*, *Eye Contact*'s strongest scenes revolve around the autistic boy and especially his relationship with his mother. For example, one brief scene when an intrusive litany of "r" words interferes with Adam's intended words (149–50) reveals an author actually trying to explore autistic consciousness. We also witness Cara become a domestic detective who must learn to decrypt Adam's words and pictures. For example, she recalls insisting that Adam learn to *ride* his bicycle rather than compulsively tilting the training wheels. After she finally removed the training wheels, Adam, frustrated at his mother's obtuseness, poured glue into the bike's gears (45): he simply saw the bike differently than she did. If Cara's realization that Adam will always remain to some degree a mystery to her (188) seems to make him more a puzzle than a person, nonetheless this is a feeling shared by the loved ones of many autistic people. Her growing capacity to see through Adam's eyes—to achieve empathy—offers a useful guideline for understanding real-life autistic people while respecting autistic agency and humanity.

In contrast, the novel's other neurotypical people often fail to see what's right in front of them: Morgan's mother's blindness to his needs prompts him to commit an act of vandalism, and the police constantly interrogate the wrong people, though Adam possesses the key clues to solve the murder. The implication is that if regular people like Cara and the cops would only make better eye contact with autists—as Morgan does with Adam, thereby discovering important truths about his own motives and obsessions—perhaps we would understand both them and ourselves more clearly. Indeed, the novel implies that all human beings are somewhat mysterious, which furnishes another good reason to make better eye contact.

Little Men

If Cammie McGovern sometimes uses autism as a metaphor for neurotypical problems, at least she gives her autistic character his own thoughts and wishes. Most other recent novels with autistic characters do much worse. For example, Simon Armitage's *Little Green Man* exploits its autistic character merely to expose (already obvious) flaws in its neurotypical protagonist. The main plot follows Barney, the novel's immature and rather unpleasant narrator, as he engineers an elaborate game of dares with his equally repellent boyhood friends, all of them vying for the titular (allegedly valuable) sculpture. Barney is also the father of Travis, an autistic seven year old who displays many now-standard autistic traits: an obsession with videos, odd postures, lining up toys, etc. As Murray notes, Travis seems to be trotted onstage to "perform autism" and thus lend some humanity to his father ("Contemporary Sentimental" 36). Even so, Travis's scenes are far more engaging than the rest of the novel. In the book's most lyrical passage, Barney recollects Travis's conception at Lighthouse Farm, and as Barney projects a film of the place onto a wall, Travis's shadow fills the screen, creating an "empty likeness with his arms outstretched" as he reaches out "to touch that impossible, invisible thing only he could see" (124–5). Though this scene indicates that Barney sustains a fascinated affection for his son, it also illustrates that Travis functions mostly as an embodiment of his father's longing for lost innocence: like his father, Travis is a lighthouse shining with no purpose. Though Barney does change, eventually tossing his childish things from a cliff, Travis cannot, for he isn't a character but a symbol—a shadow or statue, a little man standing for his father's arrested development.

Recent sibling novels with autistic characters do little better in representing autistic humanity. Eli Gottlieb's *The Boy Who Went Away*, for example, tracks thirteen-year-old narrator Denny Graubart's final summer at home with his "disturbed" (probably autistic) older brother James, known as Fad.[20] In this often-sharp coming-of-age tale, Gottlieb humorously conveys Denny's confusion and resentment at being the brother of what he calls an "authentic genetic fuckup" (142). Denny also envies Fad for the attention he receives from their mother, who is obsessed with her older son and determined to keep him out of an institution, a goal that Denny feels is destroying the family (18). What Denny most despises about his brother, however, is that "this person was almost me" (12): Fad embodies Denny's own feelings of inadequacy and alienation. At the novel's end, after their mother's efforts fail and Fad must depart, Denny achieves a modicum of sympathy for his brother, even giving him a reluctant hug. Yet he remains ambivalent: asked later if he misses his brother, he describes his feelings as "padded with . . . thick, smothering clouds of numbness." He despises those who ridicule Fad, but his love has been "scoured clean by all those years of superheated steam" (206). Although Fad is the boy who goes away, in a sense he was never really there, for he exists mostly as an objective correlative for *Denny's* self-hatred and growth.

The brother in Martha Witt's *Broken as Things Are* occupies a similar position. In this Southern gothic/family melodrama, narrator Morgan-Lee, an adolescent North Carolina girl, develops a quasi-incestuous relationship with her probably autistic older brother, Ginx.[21] The two have created a private language and world of stories that only they share. But as he ages, Ginx becomes pathologically jealous and possessive of his sister, digging a fallout shelter where he hopes the two will live when the atomic bombs strike, and later beating her when he discovers she has slept with another boy. But again Ginx—always seen through Morgan-Lee's eyes—is less a character than a symbol: of his mother's repressed Oedipal desires, his father's chronic denial, his sister's sexual confusion and alienation, and most of all of familial dysfunction. Ginx thus functions as a kind of reverse prosthesis—an obstacle that Morgan-Lee must leap, a disability she must overcome. As in Armitage's and Gottlieb's novels, Witt's autistic character exists primarily as a foil—a shadow self or little man whom the protagonist must discard to achieve selfhood.

From the Inside

Each of these novels is in some way stymied by the narrative problem of autism. Though Leimbach and McGovern represent their autistic children empathetically, they eventually turn their novels into less problematic genre tales; Armitage's, Gottlieb's and Witt's autistic characters are bundles of quirks, fun-house mirrors for their dysfunctional protagonists' self-assessments. Perhaps someday an autistic person will write a novel dramatizing autistic consciousness and self-formation from the other side of the mirror. In the meantime, there are two recent novels, one an international best-seller, that portray autistic narrators. Both are, of course, "high-functioning," because an entirely nonverbal or intellectually impaired narrator would present seemingly insurmountable challenges to storytelling. Both protagonists also encounter many obstacles and conflicts typical of the coming-of-age story: recalcitrant or hostile authority figures; influential peers; a society inhospitable to those with peculiar needs; a climactic discovery of identity and/or vocation. Yet the two are quite different in their execution and ideas about autistic selfhood.

Elizabeth Moon's science fiction novel *The Speed of Dark* tells of Lou Arrendale, a young man whose company employs a number of Asperger's and autistic people. In this near-future world, Lou's employer accommodates its autistic employees by, for example, setting aside rooms equipped with trampolines. Lou's autist cohorts frequently engage in spirited discussion, and the novel offers the possibility of a genuine autistic community—an imagined nation—like those many present-day autism advocates have called for. And though Moon empathetically portrays Lou's problems in establishing relationships, his need for routine and sensory calming, she also depicts his phenomenal gifts at pattern recognition, which he uses to become a successful "bioinformatics" specialist as well as an accomplished fencer. Though not a savant, Lou is a reasonably successful man. So it is difficult to accept when, given the chance to undergo an operation that will cure him of autism, Lou agrees to be normalized (not all of his autistic friends make the same decision). The ethical questions involved in his decision brush the essence of the disability versus difference controversy: should autistic people try to be like others, or should they preserve and celebrate their differences as intrinsic elements of their identities? Lou maintains that he is not ashamed of his autistic self; rather, he decides to have the operation in order to "learn what I want to learn and do what I want to do" (300)—to gain better opportunities for personal, professional, and social development.

Moon must be applauded for reaching inside of Lou's mind to show him wrestling with a difficult decision, whether or not we agree with it. Yet Lou's predicament is less involving than it should be because it does not grow naturally from the novel's action but seems imposed on it. Is Lou behaving as his character would, or following a prescripted authorial program designed to provoke an argument or provide another recovery narrative? Because Moon is a neurotypical writer (and the mother of an autistic son), readers may suspect that her protagonist's decision is more a neurotypical wish-fulfilment than a free choice. As in the classic Bildungsroman, Lou discovers his vocation; yet this vocation seems to unravel the self-formation he has undergone up to that point. How ironic that autistic agency is ultimately employed here to choose *not* to be autistic! Can one be "normally autistic?" That is, can individual autists fashion personal norms and use them to achieve self-fulfillment? Certainly. But those norms would ideally emerge *from within* autism and eventually be integrated with it.

Though we root for Lou, he's difficult to love because he doesn't seem to love himself. In contrast, fifteen-year-old Christopher Boone, the autistic narrator of Mark Haddon's best-selling novel *The Curious Incident of the Dog in the Night-Time*, is quite pleased with himself just as he is. And unlike Lou's narration—whose monotonously similar sentences become wearying over the course of the novel—Christopher's voice represents autistic thinking as pictorially imaginative, self-aware, even witty. Although the predominance of sentences beginning with "and" illustrates Christopher's difficulty in sorting out hierarchies, his astute observations of his world make him an engaging narrator as well as a fairly competent detective. And he needs to be, for the novel's plot traces Christopher's quest to discover who has killed Wellington, a neighbor's poodle, with a garden fork.

Curious Incident appeals to neurotypical readers with its often uproarious humor, which emerges from Christopher's deadpan descriptions of others' quirks and his own preferences and fixations: his hatred of yellow and brown, his love of dogs and math, his myriad adjustments to and compensations for the neurotypical world. Christopher's inability to comprehend others' emotions also enables Haddon to filter the bathos from potentially overwrought scenes. For example, when Christopher finally arrives at his estranged mother Judy's apartment following a harrowing train journey to London, he informs her that his father, Ed, had told him she was dead. Christopher—a big fan of TV nature shows—blandly tells us, "And then she made a loud wailing noise like an animal on a nature program on television" (193). Christopher's neutral narration makes the scene more powerful. But perhaps the novel's greatest triumph is Haddon's graphic rendering of Christopher's inner world via a variety of quasi-postmodernist tactics: drawings, math problems, maps, lists and, in one very effective scene, a chaotic barrage of signs that illustrates his disorientation in a noisy train station (170). As Murray notes, Christopher is not a symbol of someone else's dysfunction, but always and only himself ("Contemporary Sentimental" 37): his autism is an essential part of his nature, and his decisions and development emerge through, not in spite of, his condition. Although Christopher does not imitate others, aside from that, his Bildung follows a fairly typical path: he defies his parents, discovers previously unknown abilities, defeats his own fears, and develops a vocation as he passes his math A-level exams. He triumphs, but remains autistic. In short, Christopher is both disabled and gifted, both unusual and typical, definitively himself yet capable of growth.

Haddon does not entirely sidestep the pitfalls that doom other popular representations of autism. For example, although Christopher astutely recognizes that "normal" people also have "special needs"—of which Ed's rage (he's the one who kills Wellington), drinking problem and lying, as well as Judy's weakness and instability, provide ample evidence—this idea comes dangerously close to the banal axiom that "everybody is disabled." And though Haddon poignantly dramatizes the trials involved in rearing even an extremely talented autist such as Christopher, he also invokes the shade of Bettelheim in Judy's decision to abandon her son and husband. Christopher, then, does serve partly as a yardstick for his parents' behavior and as a catalyst for their emotional problems. In addition, Christopher's mathematical gifts fit popular notions of the autistic savant, and his eccentricities conform to what Murray calls a "media conception of autism" (38–9). Nevertheless, *Curious Incident* is by far the best novel with an autistic character yet published, and though it promulgates certain stereotypes, it presents autism as just another way of being human. When I've taught the novel in undergraduate literature classes, an initial caution not to interpret Christopher's traits as typical of all autistic people helps to counteract the perils of stereotyping. My students—most of whom start the novel with little or no knowledge of autism—end up learning something about the disorder and, just as important, about their own cognitive and sensory (dis)abilities. Aren't those primary goals of disability studies?

Given *Curious Incident*'s popular appeal, it seems fitting to end this collection with two essays discussing the novel. First, James A. Berger examines the novel's treatment of language and social relations. Drawing from evolutionary theory, Berger hypothesizes that Christopher, like many real-life autistic people, is more comfortable with indexical than symbolic thinking. He then suggests that although Christopher is adept at mapping space, he sometimes feels lost in time and hence would prefer to live in a world of routine and habit, of problems or puzzles to solve, but devoid of life-altering decisions. In other words, Berger implies that Christopher embodies (and overcomes, to some degree) one of autism's principal challenges to narrative—stasis. Although Berger also discovers a theme of social dysfunction in the isolation of Christopher's neighbors and their inability to communicate with each other, ultimately he reads this quasi-autistic social condition as a function of autistic tendencies wired into all human neural systems. He concludes that we should read *Curious Incident* as a kind of neurological *psychomacheia*, a drama of the struggle within every soul between the need for community and the desire for solitude. In this regard, Berger echoes Belmonte: to be autistic is to be human, but more so.

In his chapter, Gyasi Burks-Abbott reads *Curious Incident* in the light of his own experiences as an autistic, finding flaws in its portrayal of autistic consciousness. Though acknowledging its appeal, Burks-Abbott argues that the novel perpetuates stereotypes and generates a monolithic view of autism. He also points out inconsistencies in its treatment of Christopher's theory of mind: although Haddon has stated in an interview that Christopher cannot put himself in another's shoes, in the novel he offers sophisticated hypotheses about his father's mental states.[22] Burks-Abbott also questions Haddon's depiction of Christopher's literal mind, arguing that his distinction between metaphor and simile is specious, and implies that autistic people need a prosthesis to grasp figurative language (Burks-Abbott thus joins Ilona Roth in arguing that many autistic people handle figurative language quite well). *Curious Incident*, he concludes, is "the new *Rain Man*," and though it has evoked widespread interest in autism that could inspire more genuine autistic perspectives, it actually works against autistic self-representation.

These chapters offer a multitude of perspectives on autism: historical and rhetorical investigations of its clinical construction; inquiries into autistic art and creativity; analyses and examples of autobiographical writing; critical examinations of how autism has been—or could be—represented in cinema and fiction. What links them? A desire to give voice to a segment of the population that has heretofore been silent and invisible even in the disability community; a willingness to sweep away stereotypes and misconceptions about autism; a commitment to see and hear autistic people's abilities and disabilities with fresh eyes and ears; a wish to create a community of empathetic readers and viewers who respect autistic agency and humanity; a recognition that there are many ways to be autistic—as many ways as there are to be human.

In the conclusion to the volume, I summarize other major issues, statements and questions these essays raise, and offer directions for the future. But now I yield the floor to our contributors.

NOTES

1. Hacking charts six grades of constructionism, ranging from the "historical" (the most neutral approach) through the "reformist" and "revolutionary"; Hacking's analysis of social constructionism is itself social constructionist in what he would call an "unmasking" or "reformist" mode (19–20).
2. Susan Gabel and Susan Peters propose "resistance theory" as a better way to frame "the complex relationships and negotiations between divergent ideas like discourse, the material body, sociopolitical systems and processes, power relations, cultural contexts of disability, impairments, and the like" (586). Resistance theory, they claim, recognizes agency, in that "individual resistance to disciplining power exists at both the individual and collective levels" (594). Resistance theory can also encompass medical interventions such as hearing aids, which are said to "resist" the body's impairment (597). But are hearing aids modes of resistance, or rather means of accommodating and mitigating disabilities? As Gabel and Peters present it, "resistance" comes to mean so many different things in different contexts that its explanatory power fades; in trying to expand its reach, they turn it into a one-size-all muumuu hiding the very contours that distinguish terms and conditions and render them worth studying.
3. David Mitchell and Sharon Snyder likewise note that "[w]hile most of the work in the humanities to date has centered upon physical disability . . . one of the major new areas of research in disability studies will need to be that of cognitive disabilities" (39). Yet their own definition of cognitive disability focuses almost entirely on mental illnesses such as schizophrenia, not on retardation or autism.
4. Valuable Web sites about autism include neurodiversity.com and autistics.org, among others; sarnet.org provides a weekly digest of news about autism. I also

recommend Kristina Chew's "Autismland" and "Autismvox" pages, accessible through www.kristinachew.com.

5. In *Send in the Idiots*, Kamran Nazeer (who is, or was, himself autistic) rebuts these claims by arguing that the instances in which autism is an advantage—even for "high-functioning" people—are far outweighed by its disadvantages (215). According to Nazeer, the view that autistic people are not disabled but merely different derives from a belief (mistaken, in his view) that they cannot change and should not be expected to measure up to social norms (227).

6. An example in the autism community comes from the Web site autistics.org, which carries the header "The Real Voice of Autism," because the site is managed and operated by people with autism spectrum disorders. This declaration accompanies a contention that non-autistic people, such as those who head the Autism Society of America, are presumptuous in claiming to speak for autistics or for autism research. But the belief that autistic people's ideas and opinions should trump all other views of autism would, if carried to its logical extreme, prevent the most severely disabled autistic people from having *any* voice. Such defensive positions also perpetrate a form of reverse elitism and may reinforce the belief that autistic people are irremediably alien.

7. Nussbaum also eventually concludes that it is difficult to feel compassion without empathy or empathy without compassion.

8. For example, Corker and French's collection begins with a set of personal narratives by disabled scholars, and includes Judy Singer's remembrance of her possibly autistic mother and her Asperger's daughter; Snyder, Brueggemann and Garland-Thomson's volume incorporates hybrid essays, such as those by Mark Jeffreys and Nancy Mairs, along with more standard scholarly pieces.

9. For a summary and analysis of recent work in these areas see Nadesan 160–73. See also "Environmental Health and Autism" for a set of brief articles outlining these approaches.

10. A quick survey of the literature bears out this contention: most clinical books and many parent accounts are still designed to tout a specific therapy or approach, be it theory of mind (Baron-Cohen), executive functioning (Russell), "floortime" play therapy (Greenspan and Wieder, Stacey), Audio Integration Therapy (Stehli), Facilitated Communication (Martin, Savarese), or Applied Behavioral Analysis (Lovaas, Maurice).

11. For example, Rab Houston and Uta Frith examine the life of Hugh Blair, an eighteenth-century Scottish laird, concluding that he indeed had (unrecognized) autism (149). Frith also speculates more briefly about other historical cases of autism in *Autism: Explaining the Enigma* (17–35), and Paul Collins discusses some of the same figures in his *Not Even Wrong*.

12. As Nazeer notes, such an individualistic understanding of genius amounts to an "autistic view of intellectual and social progress, one focused on the role of the *autos*" (85).

13. Autistic authors Jasmine O'Neill (48) and Donna Williams (209), for instance, attest to the volitional and social properties of their echolalia. Wiltshire's drawings of Sacks's own house also refute the contention that he simply "reproduces" what he sees (Sacks 212). For further discussion of Wiltshire's drawings, see Ilona Roth's chapter in this volume.

14. Among the best of these are Beth Kephart's *A Slant of Sun* and Valerie Paradiž's *Elijah's Cup*. Three notable father-authored memoirs, Michael Blastland's *The Only Boy in the World*, Ralph Savarese's *Reasonable People*, his account of his son's adoption and emergence via Facilitated Communication, and Roy Richard Grinker's *Unstrange Minds*, an anthropology of contemporary autism written by the father of an autistic daughter, were published too recently to

be included in my remarks. For a fairly comprehensive list of autism-related books, see neurodiversity.org. In addition, www.kristinachew.com offers capsule reviews and summaries of many recent autism titles.

15. The term *yardstick* provides the title for Patricia Puccinelli's brief study of retarded characters in literature (see also 11, 28). Puccinelli's book lacks a firm theoretical basis (for example, she uses IQ as her measurement 5–6), and her classifications blend into each other; yet this "yardstick" concept does provide its own helpful way of measuring how autistic characters are represented in terms of neurotypical needs and definitions. Bérubé likewise notes that intellectually disabled characters often serve as "indexes of *everyone else's* moral standing" (569–70).

16. These conventions were codified more than thirty years ago by critic Jerome Buckley in *Season of Youth* (17).

17. Nazeer offers another example. One of his adult autistic subjects, man named Andre, becomes so anxious when conversations grow too personal that he will speak *only* through one of his hand-crafted puppets. Nazeer speculates that the puppets allow Andre to "stop[ ] being himself" (24) and hide behind an inanimate persona. Andre's employment of the puppets is, however, autistically rigid: if anyone interrupts one of his puppet monologues, he becomes incensed. Thus, when Nazeer inserts a brief sentence during one monologue, Andre locks the author in a bathroom for several hours (24–35).

18. Although Ryan is never labeled "autistic" (a newscaster calls him "retarded"), the few scenes in which Ryan appears—which depict him avoiding eye contact, repeatedly requesting to "sing a song," and refusing to ride his bike around a fallen tree limb—suggest a moderately impaired autistic child.

19. The Catalyst is another of Puccinelli's terms for the roles of intellectually disabled fictional characters: see 45.

20. Like Ryan Pollard, Fad is never specifically called "autistic," but he too displays many autistic traits, including obsessive rocking, severe anxiety (which he calls "volts"), withdrawal (197), rigidity, aggression and self-injurious behaviors. Because the novel is set in the 1960s, the specialists who examine Fad fail to arrive at a suitable diagnosis, though "childhood autism" is listed as one possibility (11).

21. Witt never names Ginx's disorder, though many of his habits—rocking, tactile defensiveness, hatred of eye contact, savant-like factual memory—are autistic stereotypes. The Library of Congress cataloging data inside the novel, however, lists "Autistic youths—fiction," and Ginx is called autistic on the back cover of the paperback edition.

22. Stuart Murray makes a similar point in "Contemporary Sentimental" 38–9.

WORKS CITED

Allen, Barry. "Foucault's Nominalism." Tremain 93–107.

Armitage, Simon. *Little Green Man*. London: Viking, 2001.

Avery, Dona. "Talking 'tragedy': Identity Issues in the Parental Story of Disability." Corker and French 117–26.

Baron-Cohen, Simon. *Mindblindness: An Essay on Autism and Theory of Mind*. Cambridge, MA: MIT P, 1997.

Barron, Judy and Sean Barron. *There's a Boy in Here*. New York: Simon & Schuster, 1992.

Bérubé, Michael. "Disability and Narrative." *PMLA* 120 (2005): 568–76.

Blastland, Michael. *The Only Boy in the World: A Father Explores the Mysteries of Autism*. New York: Marlowe and Company, 2006.

Brueggemann, Brenda Jo. "An Enabling Pedagogy." Snyder, Brueggemann, and Garland-Thomson 317–36.

Buckley, Jerome. *Season of Youth: The Bildungsroman from Dickens to Golding.* Cambridge, MA: Harvard UP, 1974.

Cassuto, Leonard. "Oliver Sacks and the Medical Case Narrative." Snyder, Brueggemann, and Garland-Thomson 118–30.

Collins, Paul. *Not Even Wrong: Adventures in Autism.* New York and London: Bloomsbury, 2004.

Corker, Mairian, and Sally French, eds. *Disability Discourse.* Buckingham and Philadelphia: Open UP, 1999.

———. "Reclaiming Discourse in Disability Studies." Corker and French 1–11.

Couser, G. Thomas. "Conflicting Paradigms: The Rhetorics of Disability Memoir." Wilson and Lewiecki-Wilson 78–91.

———. "The Empire of the 'Normal': A Forum on Disability and Self-Representation: Introduction." *American Quarterly* 52 (2000): 305–10.

———. "Signifying Bodies: Life Writing and Disability Studies." Snyder, Brueggemann, and Garland-Thomson 109–17.

Davis, Lennard J. *Enforcing Normalcy: Disability, Deafness and the Body.* London and New York: Verso, 1995.

———. "Disability: The Next Wave or Twilight of the Gods?" *PMLA* 120 (2005): 527–32.

"Environmental Health and Autism." Special Issue of *Autism Advocate.* 45.5 (Fall 2006).

Fitzgerald, Michael. *Autism and Creativity: Is there a link between autism in men and exceptional creativity?* Hove and New York: Brunner-Routledge, 2004.

Foucault, Michel. *The Archaeology of Knowledge.* Trans. A. M. Sheridan Smith. New York: Routledge, 1972.

Frank, Arthur W. *The Wounded Storyteller: Body Illness, and Ethics.* Chicago: U of Chicago P, 1995.

Frith, Uta. *Autism: Explaining the Enigma.* Oxford: Blackwell, 1989.

Gabel, Susan, and Susan Peters. "Presage of a paradigm shift? Beyond the social model of disability toward resistance theories of disability." *Disability & Society* 19.6 (October 2004): 585–600.

Garland-Thomson, Rosemarie. "Disability and Representation." *PMLA* 120 (2005): 522–27.

Glastonbury, Marion. "The Cultural Presence of Autistic Lives." *Raritan* 17.1 (Summer 1997): 24–44.

Gottlieb, Eli. *The Boy Who Went Away.* New York: St. Martin's, 1997.

Grandin, Temple. *Thinking in Pictures and Other Reports from My Life with Autism.* Foreword by Oliver Sacks. New York: Doubleday, 1995.

———., and Margaret M. Scariano. *Emergence: Labeled Autistic.* Novato, CA: Arena, 1986.

Greenfeld, Josh. *A Child Called Noah: A Family Journey.* New York: Holt, Rinehart and Winston, 1970.

Greenspan, Stanley, I. and Serena Wieder. *Engaging Autism: Helping Children Relate, Communicate, and Think with the DIR Floortime Approach.* New York: Da Capo, 2006.

Grinker, Roy Richard. *Unstrange Minds: Remapping the World of Autism.* New York: Basic Books, 2007.

Hacking, Ian. *The Social Construction of What?* Cambridge, MA: Harvard UP, 1999.

Haddon, Mark. *The Curious Incident of the Dog in the Night-Time.* New York: Doubleday, 2003.

Herndl, Diana Price. "Disease Versus Disability: The Medical Humanities and Disability Studies." *PMLA* 120 (2005): 593–97.

Houston, Rab, and Uta Frith. *Autism in History: The Case of Hugh Blair of Borgue.* Oxford: Blackwell, 2000.

Hughes, Bill. "The Constitution of Impairment: modernity and the aesthetic of oppression." *Disability & Society* 14.2 (1999): 155–72.

———. "What Can a Foucauldian Analysis Contribute to Disability Theory?" *Tremain* 78–92.

———., and Kevin Paterson. "The Social Model of Disability and the Disappearing Body: towards a sociology of impairment." *Disability & Society* 12.2 (1997): 325–40.

Hughes, Robert. *Running with Walker: A Memoir.* London and Philadelphia: Jessica Kingsley, 2003.

Jeffreys, Mark. "The Visible Cripple (Scars and Other Disfiguring Displays Included)." Snyder, Brueggemann, and Garland-Thomson 31–39.

Jurecic, Ann. "Mindblindness: Autism, Writing, and the Problem of Empathy." *Literature and Medicine* 25.1 (Spring 2006): 1–23.

Karasik, Paul and Judy Karasik. *The Ride Together: A Brother and Sister's Memoir of Autism in the Family.* New York: Washington Square, 2003.

Kephart, Beth. *A Slant of Son: One Child's Courage.* New York: Norton, 1998.

Krentz, Christopher. "A 'Vacant Receptacle'? Blind Tom, Cognitive Difference, and Pedagogy." *PMLA* 120 (2005): 552–57.

Leimbach, Marti. *Daniel Isn't Talking.* New York: Nan A. Talese/Doubleday, 2006.

Lewiecki-Wilson, Cynthia. "Rethinking Rhetoric through Mental Disabilities." *Rhetoric Review* 22.2 (2003): 156–67.

Linton, Simi. *Claiming Disability: Knowledge and Identity.* New York: New York UP, 1998.

———. "What Is Disability Studies?" *PMLA* 120 (2005): 518–22.

Lovaas, O. Ivar. *The Autistic Child: Language Development through Behavior Modification.* New York: Irvington, 1977.

Martin, Russell. *Out of Silence: A Journey into Language.* New York: Holt, 1994.

Maurice, Catherine. *Let Me Hear Your Voice: A Family's Triumph over Autism.* New York: Knopf, 1993.

McDonnell, Jane Taylor. *News from the Border: A Mother's Memoir of her Autistic Son.* Afterword by Paul McDonnell. New York: Ticknor & Fields, 1993.

McGovern, Cammie. *Eye Contact.* New York: Viking, 2006.

Mitchell, David T., and Sharon L. Snyder. *Narrative Prosthesis: Disability and the Dependencies of Discourse.* Ann Arbor: U of Michigan P, 2001.

Moon, Elizabeth. *The Speed of Dark.* New York: Ballantine, 2003.

Moore, Charlotte. *George and Sam.* Introduction by Nick Hornby. London: Viking, 2004.

Mozart and the Whale. Dir: Peter Naess. Scr: Ron Bass. Perf. Josh Hartnett, Radha Mitchell. Millennium Films, 2006.

Murray, Stuart. "Autism and the Contemporary Sentimental: Fiction and the Narrative Fascination of the Present." *Literature and Medicine* 25.1 (Spring 2006): 24–45.

Nadesan, Majia Holmer. *Constructing Autism: Unravelling the 'Truth' and Understanding the Social.* London and New York: Routledge, 2005.

Nazeer, Kamran. *Send in the Idiots: Stories from the Other Side of Autism.* New York and London: Bloomsbury, 2006.

Norden, Martin F. *The Cinema of Isolation: A History of Physical Disability in the Movies.* New Brunswick, NJ: Rutgers UP, 1994.

Nussbaum, Martha C. *Upheavals of Thought: The Intelligence of Emotions.* Cambridge: Cambridge UP, 2001.

Paradiž, Valerie. *Elijah's Cup: A Family's Journey into the Community and Culture of High-Functioning Autism and Asperger's Syndrome.* New York: Free Press, 2002.

Park, Clara Claiborne. *Exiting Nirvana: A Daughter's Life with Autism*. Foreword by Oliver Sacks. Boston: Little, Brown, 2001.

———. *The Siege: The First Eight Years of an Autistic Child*. 1967. Rev ed. Boston: Little, Brown, 1982.

Puccinelli, Patricia M. *Yardsticks: Retarded Characters and Their Roles in Fiction*. New York: Peter Lang, 1995.

Rain Man. Dir. Barry Levinson. Perf. Dustin Hoffman, Tom Cruise. Scr. Ron Bass. United Artists, 1988.

Rankin, Kate. *Growing Up Severely Autistic: They Call Me Gabriel*. London and Philadelphia: Jessica Kingsley, 2000.

Rimland, Bernard. Foreword. *Emergence: Labeled Autistic*. By Temple Grandin and Margaret M. Scariano. Novato, CA: Arena, 1986. 5–8.

———. Foreword. *Nobody Nowhere: The Extraordinary Autobiography of an Autistic*. By Donna Williams. New York: Times Books, 1992. ix–xii.

Russell, James, ed. *Autism as an Executive Disorder*. Oxford: Oxford UP, 1997.

Sacks, Oliver. *An Anthropologist on Mars: Seven Paradoxical Tales*. New York: Knopf, 1995.

———. Foreword. *Exiting Nirvana*. By Clara Claiborne Park. Boston: Little, Brown, 2001. ix–xiv.

Savarese, Ralph James. *Reasonable People: A Memoir of Autism and Adoption. On the Meaning of Family and the Politics of Neurological Difference*. New York: Other P, 2007.

Shakespeare, Tom. "Art and Lies? Representations of Disability on Film." Corker and French 164–72.

———. Review of *An Anthropologist on Mars* by Oliver Sacks. *Disability & Society* 11.1 (1996): 137–42.

———. and Nicholas Watson. "The Social model of disability: An outdated ideology?" *Exploring Theories and Expanding Methodologies: where we are and where we need to go*. Ed. Sharon N. Barnartt and Barbara M. Altman. Amsterdam and New York: JAI, 2001. 9–28.

Silent Fall. Dir: Bruce Beresford. Scr: Akiva Goldsman. Perf: Richard Dreyfuss, Liv Tyler, Ben Faulkner. Kouf/Bigelow Productions/Morgan Creek Productions/Warner Bros., 1994.

Smith, Mary-Ann Tirone. *Girls of Tender Age*. New York: Free P, 2006.

Smith, Sidonie. "Taking It to a Limit One More Time: Autobiography and Autism." *Getting a Life: Everyday Uses of Autobiography*. Ed. Sidonie Smith and Julia Watson. Minneapolis: U of Minnesota P, 1996. 226–46.

Snyder, Sharon L., Brenda Jo Brueggemann, and Rosemarie Garland-Thomson, eds. *Disability Studies: Enabling the Humanities*. New York: MLA, 2002.

Stehli, Annabel. *The Sound of a Miracle*. New York: Avon, 1991.

Swan, Jim. "Disabilities, Bodies, Voices." Snyder, Brueggemann, and Garland-Thomson 283–95.

Stacey, Patricia. *The Boy Who Loved Windows: Opening the Heart and Mind of a Child Threatened with Autism*. Cambridge, MA: Da Capo, 2003.

Tremain, Shelley, ed. *Foucault and the Government of Disability*. Ann Arbor: U of Michigan P, 2005.

The United States of Leland. Dir. Matthew Ryan Hoge. Perf. Ryan Gosling, Don Cheadle. MDP Worldwide/Media8Entertainment/Thousand Words/Trigger Street Productions, 2003.

Waltz, Mitzi. "Reading case studies of people with autistic spectrum disorders: a cultural studies approach to issues of disability representation." *Disability & Society* 20.4 (2005): 421–35.

Williams, Donna. *Nobody Nowhere: The Extraordinary Autobiography of an Autistic*. New York: Times Books, 1992.

Wilson, James C. and Cynthia Lewiecki-Wilson, eds. *Embodied Rhetorics: Disability in Language and Culture*. Carbondale: Southern Illinois UP, 2001.

———. "Disability, Rhetoric, and the Body." Wilson and Lewiecki-Wilson 1–24.

Witt, Martha. *Broken as Things Are*. New York: Holt, 2004.

Part I

Clinical Constructions

1   No Search, No Subject?
Autism and the American Conversion Narrative

James T. Fisher

Autism is widely understood as a disorder of selfhood in which persons fail by virtue of their condition to fulfill the birthright of developing, disclosing, and searching for an individual identity. The presence of autistic persons thus constitutes a kind of scandal in a culture where the subject in search of self is virtually equated with what makes us human. The best-known literary works treating autism in America are conversion narratives: these texts resuscitate the imperiled humanity of their subjects while confirming the efficacy of therapeutic interventions, which, in the twentieth century, rivaled traditional religious practices as chosen vehicles for personal transformation. As heirs to a tradition—with deep roots in the Augustinian sensibility of Puritanism—packing as much normative power as American culture permits, these narratives tend to immunize themselves from interrogation.

The conversion narrative—a record of the quest for a transformed or redeemed self—is such a pervasive motif in the American idiom that contemporary versions are rarely identified as such or contextualized against the genre's evolving history, from colonial-era Protestant narratives of spiritual conversion to its many subsequent permutations in classic and vernacular American literature. In seventeenth-century New England, "potential church members had to deliver conversion narratives—oral testimonies—to prove themselves worthy to the minister and church elders before they were allowed to become full members and participate in the Lord's Supper and vote in church meetings" (Reis 22). This ritual was designed to ensure "that all members were among the saved" (22). In the eighteenth and nineteenth centuries African-American slaves and free persons of color, westward-expanding White Protestants, and many others adapted the conversion narrative to their own forms of evangelical piety, the public expression of which often conferred cultural and spiritual authority on the bearer. Even immigrant Catholics developed a communal variant of the conversion narrative through the intercession of the parish mission, which exposed urban congregations to the heart-rending sermons of itinerant revival preachers (Dolan). In the twentieth century, the conversion narrative served widely diverse purposes, from the southern "racial conversion narratives" charted by literature scholar Fred Hobson (in which white authors "confess racial wrongdoings and are 'converted,' in varying degrees, from racism to something approaching racial enlightenment": 2) to ubiquitous popular chronicles of recovery from addiction.

Though the contemporary literature of self-help/recovery has been lampooned by scolding critics as symptomatic of a post-Christian "triumph of the therapeutic" (Rieff) or a "culture of narcissism" (Lasch), the distinction between religion and psychology was often creatively blurred in twentieth-century conversion narratives. The broader tradition was grounded, as historian John O. King explained in *The Iron of Melancholy*, in "a certain literary genre and style of self-examination—the idea that to be of the saints is to be mentally beset" (331). King argues that the conversion narrative evolved across a trajectory marked by the shift from "Puritan conscience to Victorian neurosis" (his subtitle) where it stalled out amid the struggles of secularizing late-nineteenth-century Protestant intellectuals to work through obsessive ideations that rendered them "mentally beset" but spiritually stranded without access to the consolations of saintliness. William James's monumental *Varieties of Religious Experience* (1902) was conceived in large part as a response to this dilemma; a series of lectures informed by classic conversion narratives, *Varieties* also charted the stages of James's own personal "transformation, refashioning the landscape of the pilgrim's journey in the terms of the new psychology" (King 192), a modern psychology of unfolding selfhood that James himself helped construct. James and the cohort of psychologists, psychoanalysts and social critics who came after him grafted new layers of meaning onto the traditional conversion narrative, yet the practice of psychotherapy in the twentieth century found its cash nexus primarily in the treatment of "neuroses" that rarely yielded dramatic cures to rival the transformative personal narratives animating the older tradition that James found so compelling.

By the time "infantile autism" was isolated as a distinct disorder by Johns Hopkins psychiatrist Leo Kanner in 1943, the psychoanalytic interpretive categories that enjoyed hegemony among American cultural elites tended to highlight the grinding labor of adjusting instinct to the civilizing process. Autism was dramatically different: a condition whose alternative label—childhood schizophrenia—evoked a terrifying blend of innocence and madness. The temptation for some psychoanalytic theorists and psychotherapists to manipulate this new disorder so as to showcase their prowess at treating the most challenging mental pathologies (in this case by transforming mute subjects into authentic selves) proved irresistible. The threat of competing counternarratives authored by parents or other nonprofessionals (or autistic persons themselves) was quickly subdued by Kanner in his published accounts of "refrigerator mothers," a motif ritually invoked in virtually all authoritative autism narratives published over the next two decades and beyond.

Kanner was a gifted clinician who came to understand the damage wrought by that one most infelicitous turn of phrase. He deigned finally to "acquit you people as parents" (Park, *Exiting* 11) at a meeting of the fledgling National Society for Autistic Children in 1968, but not before a small but profoundly influential subgenre of autism conversion narratives had emerged, exalting visionary therapists who rescued children from toxic parents and the hostile culture threatening sensitive young people in postwar America. Although the psychoanalyst-manqué Bruno Bettelheim would achieve great celebrity for his 1967 work, *The Empty Fortress: Infantile Autism and the Birth of the Self*, with its claims of "cure" for numerous autistic children, the most enduring work in the genre is surely Virginia Mae Axline's 1964 best-seller, *Dibs: In Search of Self*. This remarkably durable, perpetually reprinted work—originally subtitled *Personality Development in Play Therapy*—is structured after the classic American conversion narrative: a youthful (extraordinarily youthful, in this case) subject, an estranged or "divided self" (the category first devised by William James in 1902), achieves wholeness and authentic selfhood following an arduous journey of self-discovery:

> This is the story of a child in search of self through the process of psychotherapy. It was created out of the experience of a living person—a little boy named Dibs. As this child came forth to meet the abrupt forces of life, there grew within him a new awareness of selfhood, and a breathless discovery that he had within himself a stature and a wisdom that expanded and contracted even as do the shadows that are influence by the sun and the clouds. (Axline xi)

"Dibs" was a semi-mute, withdrawn and tormented child attending a fancy Manhattan private school when his desperate parents reached out to Axline, who worked in a Child Guidance Center at an undisclosed nearby location. Over the course of a handful of weekly play therapy sessions Dibs undergoes a miraculous transformation from an echolalic (echolalia is the repetition of words or phrases one has heard), obsessively pronoun-reversing, miserable young soul to perhaps the most adult-sounding, self-aware six-year-old in the annals of American literature. Axline used dollhouse figures to "unlock" Dibs from the source of his antisocial rage, his cold and unfeeling parents, especially Dibs's mother, a former surgeon who reportedly confessed to Axline: "It was bad enough to have a child, but to have a mentally retarded child was really more than we could bear" (65). At a crucial stage of his recovery, Axline encourages Dibs to fantasize about his parents trapped in their burning home. "They scream and cry and beat on the door," intones Dibs. "They want to get out. But the house is burning and they are locked in and they can't get out. They scream and cry for help." Axline writes: "Dibs clasped his hands together and tears streamed down his face. 'I weep! I weep!' he cried to me. 'Because of this I weep.' Do you weep because the mother and father are locked in the house and can't get out and the house is burning?" Axline asks. " 'Oh no!' Dibs replied. A sob caught his voice and broke it. He stumbled across the room to me and flung his arms around my neck while he wept bitter tears. 'I weep because I feel again the hurt of doors closed and locked against me,' he sobbed. I put my arm around him" (125–126). His parents could put out their own damn fire.

Although it is sorely tempting to dismiss this work as a hoax, or one very bad novel, *Dibs* is in fact a landmark autism conversion narrative, in which "autism" as such is revealingly invoked but twice in the book and never by Axline (Dibs's nameless mother and teachers separately confess their fear of the diagnosis before Axline saves him), though "there can be no doubt," as Catherine Maurice writes in *Let Me Hear Your Voice*, "that Dibs is indeed autistic" (279). Axline eschewed applying a formal diagnosis to Dibs, a strategically potent move at a time when autism was still viewed as extremely rare. She linked Dibs's condition to an emotional injury susceptible to cure by a gifted, empathetic healer such as herself. Because autism itself continued to be viewed as an emotional disorder caused by bad parenting, Axline could draw on the Kanner/Bettelheim mother-bashing tradition (though *The Empty Fortress* would not appear until 1967, Bettelheim's theories were familiar via his earlier writings) while reaching out to a much wider general audience than those writers had found. Her relative humility was a key to the book's everlasting popularity: while Dibs's symptoms clearly indicate autism, the treatment is grounded in a simple approach accessible to readers and practitioners alike. Inadvertently, perhaps, Axline shifted the public perception of autism from its location in a bizarre precinct of abnormal psychology into a metaphor for the human condition itself, a literary coup that was astonishingly successful.

Dibs, as best-seller and conversation piece, surely exposed millions of Americans to autism for the first time, albeit to an egregiously inaccurate if clinically validated version of emotional malaise rather than to a neurological condition. Though not widely reviewed or aggressively marketed at the time of its initial publication (and Axline totally evaded the glare of celebrity in the decades prior to her death in 1988), the *New York Times* reported in 1969 that *Dibs* ("the most unlikely-sounding best-seller ever") was still "selling madly"; by 1979 more than one and one-half million copies were in print. Dozens of printings later, *Dibs* soldiers on in a life wholly independent of the autism wars: school children honor its compassionate spirit in book reports; online customer reviews tout it as a miracle text holding the key to recovery from autism and less daunting ailments alike.

The popular reception of *Dibs* is testament to the enduring centrality of conversion narratives in American culture, especially those blending an inclusive postdenominational spirituality with a highly accessible therapeutic ethos. Axline's skill in this genre was first evidenced in *Play Therapy: The Inner Dynamics of Childhood* (1947), a casebook grounded in the application of "Eight Basic Principles" she devised to guide therapists in this relatively new psychotherapeutic technique (75–76). These principles—designed for therapists but structured in a spiritually progressive manner akin to the 12 Steps of Alcoholics Anonymous—urge a radical acceptance of each child's unique selfhood and a "non-intrusive" technique adapted from the work of Axline's mentor Carl Rogers (1902–1987), an erstwhile Protestant seminarian turned therapist/guru of untapped human potential. Axline studied under Rogers at Ohio State University and followed him to the University of Chicago in 1945, where he established a Counseling Center that included a play therapy room. "Next to Rogers," writes his biographer, Virginia Axline "became the best-known figure in the Center" (Kirschenbaum 155) and a leading practitioner of the "nondirective, client-centered" (later known as "person-centered") therapy associated with her mentor. In1948, Axline moved to New York City, where she studied and taught at Columbia Teachers College while continuing her clinical work in child guidance.

Axline was regarded as the most gifted "Rogerian" of her generation. Rogers himself was awed by his protégé's "complete acceptance of the client" as he or she is. "I learned courage from her," he later testified (Kirschenbaum 163). Rogers had rejected both his fundamentalist Protestant childhood religion and the liberal theology he imbibed at Union Theological Seminary; yet it is hard not to view Rogerian therapy as a form of spiritual encounter shorn of all doctrine beyond a belief in the inherent ability of every human being to achieve "self-actualization." Or as Axline writes in *Play Therapy*: "the client is the source of the living power that directs the growth within himself" (24).

Dibs: In Search of Self is the case study par excellence of nondirective therapy. Axline roots Dibs's recovery in his own resources, particularly his willingness to partake of a risky spiritual journey: "He had gone in search of a self that he could claim with proud identity" (167). Axline claims only to foster "confidence in the inner resources of this child" and surround him with a "relaxed, optimistic, sensitive" therapeutic environment. "Now he was beginning to build a concept of self that was more in harmony with the capacities within him. He was achieving personal integration" (168). Nondirective therapy, she explains in *Play Therapy*, "is really more than a technique. It is a basic philosophy of human capacities which stresses the ability within the individual to be self-directive." The therapeutic process "involves two persons" and "gives unity of purpose to the one who is seeking help—that of realizing as completely as possible his self-concept and of becoming the kind of person that satisfies the self" (27). The therapist's role in this conversion experience is crucial: as theologian Terry Cooper elucidates, "healing is relational, not individual" (31) in the Rogerian scheme.

This dualistic component of the conversion process signaled a shift in the genre to accommodate the therapist's role. The classic American conversion narrative was marked by its unmediated character: human being before God and nature, striving for redemption in a distinctly Protestant idiom. The subject was expected to speak in his or her own true voice. But Dibs speaks solely through Axline's healing intercession, in words she selects: his salvation is achieved via the mediation of the omnipotent therapist turned omniscient author, who first saves Dibs's soul, then imprints her priestly authority on the pages of the conversion/recovery narrative, merging her persona with her practice. The play therapist was protected from hubris by the demands of the discipline; as Axline explains in introducing her "eight basic principles," "they are great in their possibilities when followed sincerely, consistently and intelligently by the therapist" (75). There was also great risk of misapplication and misinterpretation, errors less likely to be committed by a therapist who had undergone her own conversion into methods of genuine discernment and nonjudgmental listening. Ironically, the "non-intrusive" character of Rogerian play therapy prompted the therapist to feed back the words of the client virtually unmodified by interpretation; the idea was to generate self-discovery but the effect often simulated a kind of therapeutic echolalia.

Although the "nondirective" method appeared to honor the classic Protestant-American tradition privileging personal experience over the claims of doctrine or hierarchy, one of the most revealing passages in *Dibs* suggests that the therapeutic subject could never fully "self-actualize" until he recognized the unique prowess of his therapist. Nearing the end of his work with Axline, Dibs confesses: "I can't figure this all out." "What can't you figure out?" she asks. "All this. And you. You're not a mother. You're not a teacher. You're not a member of mother's bridge club. What are you?" "You can't quite figure out just what kind of a person I am, h'm? I said." " 'No, I can't,' Dibs said. He shrugged his shoulders. 'But it really doesn't matter,' he said, slowly gazing into my eyes. 'You are the lady of the wonderful playroom' " (171–172). This is the moment at which the conversion narrative triumphs over the grueling demands of traditional psychoanalytic authority. Dibs suddenly throws the "nursing bottle" with which he had taken comfort against a radiator, smashing it to bits: "six-year-old Dibs does not need you now. Goodbye, baby bottle, goodbye" (172). In detailing Dibs's conversion to self-actualized child Axline emerges as *both* Dibs's "heroic" therapist (Waltz 3) and his liberator from dependence on therapy itself.

This young subject's recovery is astonishingly rapid—even miraculous—by the standards of any therapeutic precedent: as the *New York Times* noted admiringly in 1965, Axline "guided a virtually mute boy of 5 to release his dammed-up intelligence through an hour a week of play therapy" ("Books—Authors"). During his second session with Axline at the Child Guidance Center Dibs began to overcome his echolalia; articulated strongly negative feelings about his home life; and for the first time identified himself by the personal pronoun (accompanied by "a brief, fleeting smile," another first). In attempting to "lock up" a doll house in the therapy room, Dibs also demonstrated in this session that "he could observe and define problems. He could solve these problems" (33–34). There is no evidence that any of these reported rapid gains were viewed skeptically by readers or clinicians for several decades after the book first appeared. Axline enshrined an extraordinarily high standard for play therapy in *Dibs*, yet her "eight basic principles" enjoyed normative status for decades. Writing in 1983, another play therapist somewhat sheepishly confessed: "I found it difficult to consistently maintain the degree of saintliness which Axline seemed to advocate" (qtd. in Peoples 77).

"If Dibs was an emotionally deprived child—and indications were that he was—to attempt to develop an emotional attachment at this point might seem to be satisfying a deep need of the child, but it would create a problem that must of necessity ultimately be resolved by him" (17), Axline writes in explaining how she instantly discerned the ideal balance between supporting Dibs and encouraging his independence. Such assertions inspired so much confidence in her readers that precious few ever registered uneasiness with her jarringly equivocal warranty of the narrative's authenticity. The text, Axline briefly explained, is drawn from "recorded material" documenting her sessions with Dibs, but "the records have been edited to disguise all identifying information, to remove false starts . . . to facilitate a smoother report. The dialogue between Dibs and his therapist is essentially verbatim in sessions held at the Child Guidance Center. . . . [N]o words were used that were not originally those of Dibs" (185–186). Axline flouted the conventions of empirical social scientific reportage from a posture not of defiance but serenity, as though Dibs's rebirth rendered all things anew, the classic posture of the born-again subject. Axline never even bothered to acknowledge in the 1964 text that "Dibs" had made a cameo appearance seventeen years earlier in *Play Therapy*. In that earlier text "Dibs" is quoted as musing on the "big, big church" at which he gazes through a window during a play therapy session (25). In his 1964 incarnation "Dibs" speculates that God "must be awfully, awfully big to need such a big, big house" (173).

In both books Axline also made bold claims for her use of technology; these begged for scrutiny that never materialized. She suggested in *Play Therapy* that the ideal therapy room "can be wired for phonographic recordings" to be used strictly "for the furtherance of research and as a teaching aid for student therapists" (55–56) at places like the University of Chicago Counseling Center where she worked. Yet in 1947 the state of recording technology (including at professional studios) made it extremely unlikely that play therapy sessions with highly active children ranging across a room could have been electronically recorded with any degree of fidelity. In *Play Therapy* she reproduces transcripts of group therapy sessions in their entirety, involving as many as six "behavior-problem" (211) boys at a time, with each young voice clearly differentiated; the transcriptions come complete with parenthetical renderings of facial expressions and the children's unfolding emotional responses to the proceedings. Few works for the theater are as elaborately drawn as these transcriptions. By 1964 the same six-year-old "Dibs" as reinvented from *Play Therapy* had been transported from the phonographic age to the era of reel-to-reel recording technology, his adept handling of which is described in several passages from *Dibs*.

Given Axline's admission that the identity of her subject in search of self is camouflaged in the narrative, none of this textual history disproves the existence of a "historical" Dibs. It does however support the most generous conclusion, that "Dibs" was at best a composite figure drawn from Axline's lengthy clinical experience. The author was blithely unconcerned to cover her tracks: she never indicated just when the Dibs sessions had taken place (though she revealed in the 1964 text that Dibs had turned fifteen sometime prior to the publication of *Dibs: In Search of Self*; in 1969 she told a *New York Times* reporter that Dibs was currently in graduate school: Stock 26). Dibs's existence both in and outside of time only enhances the work's power as a kind of miracle/conversion narrative that also somehow maintains its credibility as a case study in play therapy—a remarkable feat given the work's transparently novelistic features.

The cultural context in which *Dibs* was validated as an *autism* conversion narrative featured a deeply ingrained hostility to parents of children with "mental" disorders, an ongoing need to treat autism as a product of emotional deprivation, and a highly charged investment in childhood and adolescent sensitivity as a barometer of the culture's humanness. Virginia Mae Axline did not invent these themes from postwar American culture so much as she absorbed them. Carl Rogers seemed to regard her as a guileless, simple soul: "a schoolteacher who always remained a schoolteacher" (Rogers and Russell 271). Axline's very rare public statements reveal the extent of her own susceptibility to the culture-shaping psychoanalytic orthodoxy of the era. She took a compassionate interest in multiply handicapped children also suffering with emotional disorders, especially blind children. When asked during testimony before a Congressional subcommittee on special education in 1959 why so many blind children were also "emotionally disturbed" she explained: "they are born lightweight and not physically attractive. . . . [W]hen they do get home, people are afraid to pick them up" ("Blind Children"). Every kind of disability could be linked in this way to a heightened risk of developing autism or something like it at a time when both early childhood and adolescence were viewed as highly perilous states fraught with social-psychological and even political implications. By the time *Dibs* was published in 1964, American readers were well versed in this emerging tradition of grave concern, represented across an array of genres from Dr. Benjamin Spock's *Baby and Child Care* (expert child-rearing advice) to J.D. Salinger's *Catcher in the Rye* (fiction of teenage alienation) to Paul Goodman's *Growing Up Absurd* (nonfiction social criticism).

Dibs's withdrawal in early childhood from the cold brutal world marks him as one of the archetypal sensitive literary heroes of the era, a kind of Holden Caulfield *in extremis*: at the conclusion of *Dibs* Axline even includes a letter purportedly written by the now-fifteen-year-old subject, nearly a decade removed from her care (183–184). The letter protests the expulsion of one of Dibs's friends from their private school. Though clearly intended by Axline to demonstrate his superior sensitivity and leadership, the quoted missive evokes the smug tone of every insufferable adolescent immortalized in postwar boarding-school fiction. But beyond the text's derivative character, Axline carves a space in *Dibs* for contemplating autism as a metaphor for the human personality facing extreme danger from an increasingly dehumanized mass culture. Bruno Bettelheim's similar diagnosis of autism as a response to the "extreme" threat posed by mothers who wished their children did not exist was always linked with an analysis of totalitarianism grounded in his experience as a refugee from Nazism. Prominent social critics like Erich Fromm concurred with Bettelheim: as Mitzi Waltz puts it, Fromm and many others claimed "that an alienating culture actually causes the condition autism" (8). Axline's account of Dibs's suffering is drawn directly from this tradition. What sane person, asks the author, would not retreat from the onslaught of monstrously uncaring parents who in turn, by her magnanimous account, are merely victims themselves of the malnourished environment that produced them?

There was no "autism crisis" in the 1960s; there *was* a perceived crisis of humanity in which young people who suffered for their sensitivity and adults gifted with the ability to heal autistic persons were conjoined as saviors for the whole culture. In lauding the "holy work" of Bruno Bettelheim in the pages of *Commonweal*, a magazine of the liberal Catholic laity, a mental health professional concluded in a review of *The Empty Fortress*: "Bettelheim's lessons are useful for anyone concerned with humanity; they are absolutely essential for all concerned about the present crisis of poverty and inequality in America" (qtd. in Pollak 270). In this sense it did not matter whether Axline diagnosed Dibs with autism or not: his early childhood emotional malaise marked him as a subject on whose search for self the fate of a humane cultural order rested. Autism was reconfigured in the 1960s as the quintessential disorder of un-actualized selfhood: its purported healers—or the healers of any condition that required such a dramatic conversion into authentic selfhood—achieved a priestly purchase on enduring cultural authority.

This was the cultural context in which the autism conversion narrative achieved unchallenged canonical status. Dibs became the world's first recovered autistic person to be offered up by his healer as an antidote to a dehumanized mass culture. At the conclusion of *Dibs* he charges educators to do for others what Axline has done for him: save the children. As Dibs reportedly lectured the faculty at his prep school, "You *must* unlock the door of ignorance and prejudice and meanness." The friend who brought this letter to Axline's attention asks: "Do you want to keep it for your collection of brave new words for justice and equality for all?" Axline responds by admiringly repeating Dibs's bold assertion (or threat) of his "intent to act" against school authorities, invoking a Rogerian mantra that links the self-actualizing theory of play therapy with the spirit of the 1960s counterculture, looking beyond Marx or Jesus or even Freud toward the liberationist ideology of the human potential movement (184). Axline now enters the pantheon of postwar authors whose works served as existential guides to highly sensitive subjects in search of self. A correspondent lamented in a 1969 letter to Axline: "I wish your book had been written fifteen years ago so I wouldn't have to lock the door to my room because my parents don't understand" (qtd. in Stock), as though the text possessed the cautionary power to preemptively spare *parents* from inflicting psychic damage on their offspring.

Carl Rogers once recalled that Axline "vowed she could never ever work with a rejecting parent, and before she was through she was working with all kinds of parents" (Rogers and Russell 271). Yet she wrote about only one kind. "From page one of both her books," writes Catherine Maurice, "her message is pure and simple. Parents are the enemy, coldly selfish, abusive of their children" (Maurice 279). Axline's avowed wish to keep her distance from "rejecting" parents is mirrored in her books by the distance she maintains between accounts of her work and any acknowledgment of play therapy's roots in post-Freudian child psychiatry and in hostility to parenting. Melanie Klein was an Austrian-born British therapist who formulated her own principles of play therapy prior to Axline and who—according to her disciple Frances Tustin (a leading proponent of the "psychogenic" theory of autism's causation)—believed that children starved of affection by their parents "could be cured" of autism (Grosskurth 187). Virginia Axline clearly shared the view of Klein and her followers that play therapy could liberate children from their "autistic trap"; as the text of *Dibs* amply confirms, she also more than shared their vitriolic attitude toward the parents of children with special needs. When the receptionist at Axline's Child Guidance Center expresses her disdain for Dibs's father ("Why doesn't he go jump in the East River"), Axline readily concurs: "Yes . . . why doesn't he?" (59).

Entire chapters of *Dibs* are devoted to exposing the extravagant deficiencies of Dibs's mother, an archetypal "refrigerator mother" who—despite her sophisticated vocabulary—was emotionally more mute than Dibs himself. "What must this woman really think and feel about Dibs," Axline pondered, "and the part she played in his young life to be so terrorized at the prospect of being interviewed and questioned about the situation?" But Dibs's mother was lucky: she proved capable of being "changed in understanding and appreciation of his growth" (140). Axline's representation of Dibs's mother shows that mother-blaming was a cultural reflex far too pervasive to ascribe to the baleful influence of Bruno Bettelheim, who is routinely singled out for well-deserved denunciation. In fact, as discrepancies in Bettelheim's life story—and reports of his abusive treatment of children—gradually began to emerge in the decades following the publication of *The Empty Fortress*, his stature as visionary healer of autistic children was undermined, but the ideas he had championed remained very much in circulation in the work of Virginia Mae Axline, a Bettelheim without the baggage.

A specter is haunting the contemporary autism wars and its name is *Dibs*: an inextinguishable text sustaining a faith that disordered selfhood not wiring is at the heart of the autism phenomenon. The popular-canonical status of Axline's work, coupled with her nearly unchallenged reputation as a virtuoso play therapist, helped preserve well beyond its deserved shelf life a formulation that undermines the human dignity of persons with autism: a subject is "made human" in its search for "self." The corollary of this formula has virtually never been acknowledged by its champions: that the subject indifferent or immune to the expectations of selfhood fails the test of authentic humanity.

When the "existential" approach to autism was finally challenged by a neurological model in the 1980s and 1990s, the trajectory of Axline's narrative continued to echo even in works that explicitly rejected her premises, most notably in Catherine Maurice's *Let Me Hear Your Voice*, which redefined the conversion narrative from a mother's perspective and substituted Applied Behavioral Analysis for play therapy. Maurice vociferously denounced Axline's hostility to parents, yet it can be argued—the merits of ABA notwithstanding—that *Let Me Hear Your Voice* extends the literary tradition of "no search, no subject"; or to put it in commercial terms, "no recovery, no story." *Let Me Hear Your Voice* shares features with *Dibs* that, far from incidental, are markers of contemporary narratives of conversion/ recovery. Like Dibs, Maurice's children are ultimately declared "normal" (cured, recovered) and even gifted (Maurice 299–300) by competent authorities (Dibs tests to an IQ of 168). Like Dibs, these children are protected from the glare of publicity, their names changed (along with that of the author), just as "all identifying information" was "disguised so completely" by Axline that "no one will ever be able to know or be able to guess the true identity of Dibs" (20). No conversion, of course, is consummated without a leap of faith, a leap that readers with a will to believe are invited to make by the authors of these autism conversion narratives.

The American literary marketplace clearly privileges if it does not demand narratives of heroic triumph over seemingly insuperable obstacles. In recent years in autism literature, those obstacles have come to include the Kanner/Bettelheim/Axline legacy itself; nonbelievers in the efficacy of Facilitated Communication (Russell Martin's *Out of Silence*); pharmaceutical makers (see the women whose transformed lives are chronicled in David Kirby's best-selling *Evidence of Harm*); and the pediatrics establishment. The latter two interest groups were tackled head-on by Karyn Seroussi in *Unraveling the Mystery of Autism*. Seroussi and others have generated a subgenre of autism recovery narratives that—in their focus on dietary purity, alternative medicine and the purging of toxins through such practices as chelation—evoke a venerable American tradition of conversion/recovery through avoidance of contaminants both physical and spiritual. The most successful of these works obscure their own literary/therapeutic sources and smooth away autism's rougher edges. Sometimes they occlude the autistic subject altogether, leaving in its place a born-again self shorn of memory or history.

A counternarrative challenging the compulsory equation of the autistic subject with a search for autonomous selfhood first emerged in 1967 with the publication of Clara Claiborne Park's *The Siege*. The "phenomenological" approach—introduced by Park and embraced by a growing cohort of contemporary writers—is grounded in an ethic of hard-earned acceptance and a way of seeing that replaces abstractions (e.g., "recovery") with faithful chronicling of lives in progress. The conversions experienced in this small but growing cohort of works (Kephart; Pearson-Vasey and Vasey) more often center on the non-autistic author's transformed perceptions of normalcy than on the "recovery" of the autistic subject. As Cammie McGovern—the author of *Eye Contact* (2006), a novel that extends this tradition—writes in an op-ed piece for the *New York Times*, "I've never met a recovered child outside the pages of those old books" ("Autism's").

In recent years an autism literature has finally emerged in which subject and author are one and the same (e.g., Prince-Hughes; Nazeer). These works do not adhere strictly to the conventions of the conversion narrative (not even those of the best-selling author Temple Grandin, who has occasionally identified herself as a "recovered autistic"). At the same time, the novelty of these works—when coupled with evidence of the author's persistent "difference" as manifested in social communication practices—has revived notions of a submerged, articulate (articulate, that is, in the idiom identified as normative by audiences invested in neurotypical modes of self-expression) autistic self struggling to escape the disabled subject. These responses are more reflective of book-industry promotional practices and cultural expectations than of the author's intentions, in the same way that Virginia Mae Axline might have argued that *Dibs* was never meant to signify more than the potential of play therapy to treat children with strictly emotional disorders.

Most recently, an autistic culture has emerged to vociferously challenge remnants of the autism conversion narrative as fundamentally inimical to human rights. Centered primarily in blogs and Web sites (neurodiversity. org; autistics.org) the voices of this movement reject the contention "that I was 'broken' and needed to be 'fixed,' " a theme that resonates across the spectrum of conversion narratives from early Christianity to the autism wars of the present. The struggle to clear a safe space for authentic autistic personhood reveals the ways in which a venerable if often overlooked literary genre continues to organize discourses on recovery and resistance alike. As it was for the great historian Oscar Handlin ("once I thought to write a history of the immigrants in America. Then I discovered that the immigrants *were* American history": 3) so it shall be for the historians of this most highly contested form of developmental difference/disability: the history of the autism conversion narrative *is* the history of autism in America.

WORKS CITED

Axline, Virginia. *Play Therapy: The Inner Dynamics of Childhood*. Boston: Houghton Mifflin, 1947.

———. *Dibs: In Search of Self; Personality Development in Play Therapy*. Boston: Houghton Mifflin, 1964.

Bettelheim, Bruno. *The Empty Fortress: Infantile Autism and the Birth of the Self*. New York: Free P, 1967.

"Blind Children Said to Need Aid." *The New York Times* 17 March 1959: 36.

"Books—Authors." *The New York Times* 11 March 1965: 30.

Cooper, Terry D. *Sin, Pride & Self-Acceptance: The Problem of Identity in Theology and Psychology*. Downers Grove, IL: InterVarsity P, 2003.

Dolan, Jay P. *Catholic Revivalism: The American Experience, 1830–1900*. Notre Dame, IN: U of Notre Dame P, 1978.

Goodman, Paul. *Growing Up Absurd: Problems of Youth in the Organized Society*. New York: Vintage, 1960.

Grosskurth, Phyllis. *Melanie Klein: Her World and Her Work*. New York: Knopf, 1986.

Handlin, Oscar. *The Uprooted: The Epic Story of the Great Migrations that Made the American People*. Boston: Little, Brown, 1973.

Hobson, Fred. *But Now I See: The White Southern Racial Conversion Narrative*. Baton Rouge: Louisiana State UP, 1999.

James, William. *The Varieties of Religious Experience: A Study in Human Nature*. 1902. New York: Penguin, 1982.

Kanner, Leo. "Autistic Disturbances of Affective Contact." *The Nervous Child* 2 (1943): 217–250.

Kephart, Beth. *A Slant of Sun: One Child's Courage*. New York: Norton, 1998.

King, John Owen. *The Iron of Melancholy: Structures of Spiritual Conversion in America from the Puritan Conscience to Victorian Neurosis*. Middletown, CT: Wesleyan UP, 1983.

Kirby, David. *Evidence of Harm: Mercury in Vaccines and the Autism Epidemic: A Medical Controversy*. New York: St. Martin's, 2005.

Kirschenbaum, Howard. *On Becoming Carl Rogers*. New York: Delacorte, 1979.

Lasch, Christopher. *The Culture of Narcissism: American Life in an Age of Diminishing Expectations*. New York: Norton, 1979.

McGovern, Cammie. "Autism's Parent Trap." *The New York Times*, 5 June, 2006. http://www.nytimes.com/2006/06/05/opinion/05mcgovern.html?ex=1163912400&en=4c72e5652a7cdb72&ei=5070.

———. *Eye Contact*. New York: Viking, 2006.

Martin, Russell. *Out of Silence: An Autistic Boy's Journey Into Language and Communication*. New York: Penguin, 1994.

Maurice, Catherine. *Let Me Hear Your Voice: A Family's Triumph Over Autism*. New York: Fawcett Columbine, 1993.

Nazeer, Kamran. *Send in the Idiots: Stories from the Other Side of Autism*. New York: Bloomsbury, 2006.

Park, Clara Claiborne. *Exiting Nirvana: A Daughter's Life with Autism*. Boston: Little Brown, 2001.

———. *The Siege: The First Eight Years of an Autistic Child*. Boston: Little, Brown, 1967.

Pearson-Vasey, Gloria and Kevin J. Vasey. *The Road Trip: Life with Autism*. Ottawa: Novalis, 2005.

Peoples, Crocker. "Fair Play Therapy." *Handbook of Play Therapy*. Eds. Charles E. Schaefer and Kevin J. O'Connor. New York: John Wiley, 1983. 76–88.

Pollak, Richard. *The Creation of Dr. B: A Biography of Bruno Bettelheim.* New York: Simon & Schuster, 1997.

Prince-Hughes, Dawn. *Songs of the Gorilla Nation: My Journey Through Autism.* New York: Harmony, 2004.

Rieff, Philip. *The Triumph of the Therapeutic: Uses of Faith After Freud.*1966. Chicago: U of Chicago P, 1987.

Reis, Elizabeth. "Seventeenth-Century Puritan Conversion Narratives." *Religions of the United States in Practice.* Ed. Colleen McDannell. Volume 1. Princeton: Princeton UP, 1999. 22–31.

Rogers, Carl R., and David E. Russell. *Carl Rogers: The Quiet Revolutionary: An Oral History.* Roseville, CA: Penmarin, 2002.

Salinger, J.D. *The Catcher in the Rye.* Boston: Little, Brown, 1951.

Seroussi, Karyn. *Unraveling the Mystery of Autism and Pervasive Developmental Disorder: A Mother's Story of Research and Recovery.* New York: Simon & Schuster, 2000.

Spock, Benjamin. *Dr. Spock's Baby and Child Care.* Rev Ed. New York: Pocket, 1998.

Stock, Robert W. "Underground in Oshkosh." *The New York Times* 16 February 1969: BRA26.

Waltz, Mitzi. "Metaphors of Autism, and Autism as Metaphor: An Exploration of Representation." 2003. http://www.interdisciplinary.net/mso/hid/hid2/hid03pap/waltz%20paper.pdf

2 Bruno Bettelheim, Autism, and the Rhetoric of Scientific Authority

Katherine DeMaria Severson
James Arnt Aune
Denise Jodlowski

In 1967 Bruno Bettelheim published *The Empty Fortress: Infantile Autism and the Birth of the Self*, forever affecting the world's view of autism. Hailed by the popular press, the book showed how Bettelheim effectively treated three children with severe autism at the University of Chicago's Orthogenic School by applying psychoanalytic theory and milieu therapy. Children who had once exhibited bizarre antisocial behavior were, in some cases, completely cured. No one had ever achieved such success with this enigmatic disorder. Although Bettelheim's book did have its critics, the overflow of praise from Bettelheim's advocates drowned out the voices of the few detractors. As a result, Bettelheim's thesis, that the infant's relationship with her "refrigerator mother" caused autism, soon became the accepted explanation in popular and in some professional circles.[1]

For the next twenty-three years, the writings of researchers, parents of autistic children, and adults with autism served to discredit Bettelheim's claim of maternal causation. However, shortly after Bettelheim, a Holocaust survivor, committed suicide in 1990 at the age of 89, the world suddenly had reason to question more than his hypothesis. Letters poured in to newspapers from former students of the Orthogenic School. Bettelheim, the staunch advocate of safe and comforting environments for children with emotional disabilities, allegedly had physically and emotionally abused the children in his care. Some of the adults that Bettelheim claimed to have "cured" of severe developmental disabilities, including autism, charged that they had entered the school with nothing more than behavioral problems. The shocking revelation that Bruno Bettelheim had neither a degree in psychology nor therapeutic training also emerged during this time. We have learned that in fact he wrote his dissertation on aesthetics, and while in Vienna was a lumber merchant.

These and many other posthumous revelations about Bettelheim prompt serious questions for academics and lay people alike. How did he acquire a directorship at a school for children with psychological disorders, at a major American university, without a degree in psychology? Moreover, how did he escape the supervision of an administrative governing board during his entire twenty-nine-year tenure as director of the School? How did he convince so many to give so much to fund the School and his research? Why did none of the several individuals in the psychoanalytic field who knew of Bettelheim's false credentials bring this fact to light?

Despite the overwhelming evidence against both Bettelheim's character and his account of the etiology of autism, true believers still exist. Peter Hobson, a prominent English psychologist, affirms the "refrigerator mother" hypothesis in his 2002 book *The Cradle of Thought*. Alfred A. Knopf, one of the most prestigious publishers in the United States, published in 2002 a biography of Bettelheim by his longtime literary agent, Theron Raines. The book accepts Bettelheim's account of his career at face value. Some 70% of French psychiatrists continue to treat autism and Tourette's disorder, as well as depression, with psychoanalytic methods. Lacanian psychoanalysis remains a significant force in literary and cultural studies, despite the consistent failure of its scientific claims. Parents of autistic children, including the senior author of this paper, can attest to the widespread belief among social workers and other ostensibly educated professionals that autism results from a failure in maternal bonding.[2]

This chapter investigates a little-studied phenomenon in the rhetoric of science: the persistence of false beliefs in an ostensibly scientific community. We proceed by analyzing generally how Bettelheim constructed his ethos during his lifetime and then focus more narrowly on the specific rhetorical strategies he used throughout *The Empty Fortress*.

CONTEXT, ETHOS, AUDIENCE

The success of Bettelheim in American academic circles and of *The Empty Fortress* must be understood within their respective historical contexts. Bettelheim's authority derived from his fabricated credentials and from the state of the American university in the 1940s, when academe still bowed to the prestige of European intellectuals. *The Empty Fortress* benefits from Bettelheim's expert authority as well from as the American fascination with the Holocaust and with psychoanalysis.

Bettelheim received his first academic position teaching art history at Rockford College in Illinois and participated in the Eight-Year Study, which examined art education in American schools. These two positions served as his springboards into the Orthogenic School. At this time, Bettelheim first began to embellish his credentials, calling himself a psychologist and claiming to have treated a child with autism while living in Vienna. Consequently, when the University of Chicago sought a qualified person to take over the failing Orthogenic School, one of Bettelheim's colleagues from the Eight-Year Study suggested his name.

The social context and intellectual fads of the era led to the effectiveness of *The Empty Fortress*, published in 1967. Indeed, the historical situation answers many of the preliminary questions about how Bettelheim became an influential voice in the public sphere and managed to elude censure from the psychoanalytic community. As Pollak has noted, Bettelheim arrived on the academic scene at a time when " 'the cause'[i.e., Freudian psychoanalysis] so transfixed the populace that in 1941 a singing analysand and her dreams starred on Broadway in *Lady in the Dark*"(127). Freud had become so famous that his theories had reached into American popular culture. However, America's captivation with psychoanalysis and the Holocaust is not enough to explain Bettelheim's ascendancy.

Bettelheim actively created his own myth. His first academic essay, "Individual and Mass Behavior in Extreme Situations," published in 1943, gave him his authority in psychology and his mystique in the public arena. "Extreme Situations" was the first widely read essay in the United States on the Nazi concentration camps.[3] In this essay, Bettelheim offers a psychoanalytic account of the mental deterioration of the camp prisoners at the hands of the SS guards. While rendering Bettelheim an "expert" on the camps, this essay also made his name in psychoanalysis. Additionally, in writing "Extreme Situations" Bettelheim first used "science" to lend credence to his assertions. Although he continued to write for academic journals for the next decade, he mostly co-authored them with the Orthogenic School's original psychologist, Emmy Sylvester. His solo academic career was far less notable.

On finding that legitimate scholarly journals did not accept his "science" merely on his word (his last essay for a scientific journal was in 1950), Bettelheim turned his attention almost entirely to writing for a mass audience. He wrote a column for *Ladies Home Journal* from 1965–1975, and his audience grew from the early 1960s onward, devouring his articles in *Redbook*, *Parents*, *Harper's*, the *Saturday Evening Post*, *Scientific American*, and *Playboy*. He had something to say about everything from "Why Working Mothers Feel Guilty" to "Speaking Out: Stop Pampering Gifted Children." Bettelheim recycled a great deal of his material. For example, an abbreviated version of "Joey the Mechanical Boy," one of the case studies in *The Empty Fortress*, was originally published in *Scientific American* (116–127). These and other essays made him a household authority in psychology in the 1960s. Although he criticized others for using their patients to make them famous, this practice became his hallmark (Pollak 328). Bettelheim further augmented his celebrity by publishing several books about parenting and the children at the Orthogenic School before the publication of *The Empty Fortress*.

The accessibility of Bettelheim's vivid, clear prose further added to his popularity. He employed *Encyclopedia Britannica* editor Ruth Marquis to make his texts more readable and used pictures, films, and the students' illustrations in many of his public presentations: he hired professional photographers and filmmakers to capture the students in action, then conveniently interpreted the images for his audience to highlight the students' progress. These films, illustrations, and pictures became mainstays of his fundraising campaigns, and their success is evident from the fact that Bettelheim led donation solicitation for the University of Chicago during his tenure there.

The psychoanalytic community probably gave Bettelheim quite a bit of leeway initially for his shabby scholarship because of the subject matter of "Extreme Situations": a large portion of the early psychoanalytic community in America consisted of exiled Viennese and German Jews. Additionally, Bettelheim's public success helped to disseminate psychoanalysis to a wide audience. However, by 1963, the height of Bettelheim's popularity, when his lack of theoretical framing and questionable methodology could do the most harm, it was too late: many of his colleagues felt that he was so "well known and respected by the lay public that any challengers risked being accused of sour grapes" (Pollak 224–225). Yet the psychoanalytic community never allowed Bettelheim into the fold, excluding him almost entirely from all associations, a fact that troubled him to his dying day. It was the same fear that kept Bettelheim's ex-wife, Gina Weinmann, from telling anyone that she, not Bettelheim, had treated the young "autistic" girl, Patsy.

Bettelheim's expert ethos, then, stems from a conjunction of factors: postwar fascination with Freud and the Holocaust; his careful management of his public image; his careful attention to writing for a popular audience; and a generalized anxiety about the family in 1950s and 1960s America. We turn now to focus on the rhetorical strategies Bettelheim adopted to construct his comprehensive treatise on autism, *The Empty Fortress*.

ANALYZING BETTELHEIM'S RHETORICAL STRATEGIES

Many have called Bruno Bettelheim's *The Empty Fortress* "the empty book"; he himself has been called much worse. However, if *The Empty Fortress* is indeed so devoid of value and Bettelheim such a monster, how did his arguments gain credence? In *The Empty Fortress*, Bettelheim had two goals. First, he wanted to prove that autism paralleled the condition—caused by "extreme situations"—experienced by concentration camp "moslems" (i.e., those who withdrew or shut down their emotions). In autism, he asserted, the child's parents (more specifically, the mother) created similarly extreme situations, forcing the child to turn inward or withdraw altogether. Second, Bettelheim attempted to create a stage theory of infant development that paralleled Erikson's adolescent developmental theory.

It is no real surprise that Bettelheim's theory of development didn't gain acceptance. First, he spends little effort in pursuing this argumentative avenue. Second, developmental theory belongs primarily to the domain of child psychology. Although Anna Freud had for some time used psychoanalysis to explain child behavior, the more "rigorous" divisions of psychology did not accept this practice. Classical psychology dismissed Bettelheim for his lack of scientific rigor, his ties to psychoanalysis, and his intentionally sensationalistic prose. When they chose to speak out against him they did so in academic journals and out of sight from the popular media. Yet although he still violated scientific standards, Bettelheim aimed for acceptance with the community by using scientific terminology, form, and "statistics."

Though Bettelheim's science was shoddy, his rhetorical strategies were clever. As Alan Gross explains in the *Rhetoric of Science*, even "objective" scientific fields use traditional rhetorical strategies to persuade readers. As Gross argues, these rhetorical strategies necessitate viewing rhetoric as epistemic. That is, rhetorical methods not only help to communicate knowledge; they also help us acquire knowledge in the first place. Robert L. Scott elucidates the theory of a rhetorical epistemology, arguing that to view rhetoric as epistemic requires that one relinquish the possibility of definitively knowing the "truth." Nonetheless, understanding can be and is achieved within traditions and communities, which act as check and balance systems for those arguing within their tradition. Hence, if an understanding achieved within a specific tradition is consistent with their standards and knowledge, it is "true" for that community. Scientific communities must police their own.[4] The specialization of knowledge and language has created a gap in the laity's ability to criticize most scientific writing. It is precisely this chasm of expectation and knowledge that Bettelheim exploits in *The Empty Fortress*. Thus, an analysis of Bettelheim's *The Empty Fortress* writes a new chapter in the evolving field of the rhetoric of science.

In further examining success of *The Empty Fortress* with a general audience, we first turn to the more recent rhetorical theory of Chaim Perelman, who discusses the difference between the universal and the particular audience. Bettelheim's community consists of the lay audience and those on the border of science: social workers, school counselors, and administrators. He geared his message to them, but always with an eye towards achieving the ever-elusive scientific legitimacy. So although Bettelheim sought to persuade two particular audiences, the psychological and psychoanalytical communities, he also wrote for what Perelman calls the "universal audience"—the ideal reasonable audience.

Common beliefs unite a particular audience, and the rhetor's burden is to maintain the integrity of his arguments while still shaping them to the belief system of the particular audience in order to maximize persuasion. However, as Perelman notes, the rhetor cannot ignore the larger universal audience, the ideal reasonable audience. In this configuration, the particular audience offers the rhetor the less difficult playing field: perspective is *de facto* limited, rules are apparent, and beliefs are shared.

The universal audience presents a very different rhetorical challenge. The universal audience is a construct of the rhetor's mind. As Perelman states: "Everyone constitutes the universal audience from what he knows of his fellow men, in such a way as to transcend the few oppositions he is aware of. Each individual, each culture, has thus its own conception of the universal audience" (33). The rhetor's idea of the universal audience affects the nature of his/her arguments to the extent that they "must convince the reader that the reasons adduced are of a compelling character, that they are self-evident, and possess an absolute and timeless validity, independent of local or historical contingencies" (32). The rhetor's construction of the universal audience is telling, since through arguments appealing strictly to the reason of this imaginary audience he or she reveals what it is he/she believes to be self-evident.

Oddly, in this case, Bettelheim succeeds in persuading his imagined universal audience but fails with the particular audiences. His primary argument is that autism, in both its source and symptoms, parallels the condition of the "moslems" in the Nazi concentration camps. Yet it is not enough for Bettelheim simply to argue the parallel case; his study must also appear scientific to shield him against accusations that he is merely projecting his major frame of reference onto his theory of autism.

Hallmarks of good science include elevating inductive over deductive reasoning, following a standardized report format, and using case studies as illustration. Science's purposeful preference for inductive over deductive reasoning is a check for objectivity in invention.[5] Traditionally, invention is where one looks for arguments. To reason inductively is to look toward the observed phenomenon to make the arguments; to reason deductively is to seek in the phenomenon rationalization for existing arguments. Although never certain of its outcome, induction best serves the goal of objectivity. Bettelheim's deductive approach to autism thus proves the most damaging of his violations of the scientific method.

The overarching arrangement of *The Empty Fortress* demonstrates Bettelheim's reliance on deductive reasoning. The persuasive value of arrangement, first taught by Cicero, was modified by the sciences to mimic the process of induction so that the experiment (discovery process) comes first, followed by a results/discussion section (what was proved). The standard scientific article reviews the topic literature, indicates a contradiction or space for further research, shows how the particular study will contribute, and then fills the intellectual space created (including a description of the theory, rationale, and methodology to be used).[6] On its face, *The Empty Fortress* appears to maintain the scientific format. There is an introduction in which Bettelheim describes his theory, methodology, and rationale. He then situates himself and his theory within the literature and uses case studies. He provides a conclusion and discusses the implications of his study. But that is where the similarities end. In both arrangement and content, Bettelheim's format is inconsistent with scientific norms.

First, his own introspection, or his personal experience in observing the extreme conditions in Nazi concentration camps, serves as the rationale for both his theory and his methodology. This is a particularly suitable approach since, according to Bettelheim, the constraints of science make it impossible to examine the human mind in all its complexity. This rationale is an appeal both to the psychoanalytic audience and to the humanity of the universal audience. Anticipating accusations that he operates out of personal bias, Bettelheim invokes the "scientific" claim that his conclusions were verified by his team of researchers. As Bettelheim states, "the uses of introspection for understanding others would be a projection of one's own experience, with little scientific merit" (8). However, as his biographies have exposed, Bettelheim trained each of his otherwise unqualified therapists, thereby calling into question the objectivity and capability of these women either to vouch for or invalidate his hypothesis. On the basis of this balancing act, Bettelheim claims that his conclusions are informed, yet scientific, experiential, yet objective.

Bettelheim's theoretical rationale is no less suspect. He describes his "milieu therapy" essentially as a journey without a map:

> [O]ur task as we see it is to create for him a world that is totally different from the one he abandoned in despair, and moreover a world he can enter right now, as he is. . . . Each of us is implying in his way that one cannot help another in his ascent from hell unless one has first joined him there, to whatever degree. There is no "direct confrontation" available to the sick child, unless somebody offers himself for the confrontation. This will always, to some degree, mean a descent to one's own hell. . . . At the same time there is no purpose to such a venture if all that happens is our offering to accept the child in his desolation. What we also have to demonstrate is that together we can make a go of it, even down there—something that he alone at this point cannot do. . . . Hence at the heart of our work is not any particular knowledge or any procedure as such, but an inner attitude to life and to those caught up in its struggle, even as we are. (10–11)

Although appealing in its sympathetic and moving sense of how to approach a child with a severe mental disorder, Bettelheim's "milieu therapy" lacks precision and even the most general of guidelines. But the lack of rigor in "milieu therapy" would likely be ignored in the psychoanalytic community where the analysand/patient guides the treatment and "knowing the other" is contingent on "knowing the self" (3).[7]

Thus, if the introduction to the scientific article is the point at which the researcher situates himself within a community of knowledge, it still remains unclear precisely in which community Bettelheim chooses to locate himself. Here the construction of his universal audience takes form. If knowledge depends on communal agreement, it is in the diversity of appeals—to the communities of science, psychoanalysis, and those transfixed by the horrors of Nazi Germany—that Bettelheim creates his universal audience and hence his grounds for understanding.

Bettelheim continues to develop his theory of causation in the following two chapters. He situates himself within the literature, but not within autism case studies, of which there were many. He reserves his discussion of studies on autism to the end of the book, where they occupy the argumentative space of rebuttal. Instead he manipulates animal behavior studies and research findings on both typical children and children with a variety of psychological disturbances to suit his needs. This tactic serves several functions. First, Bettelheim retains the guise of science by backing up his claims with scientific research findings. Second, he develops his hypothesis about the cause of autism without having to deal with any counterexplanations. Finally, the alternative literature that Bettelheim selects as foundational to his theory implicitly persuades his audience to view autism as a disorder of nurture, since each of his subjects at least began life as "normal." Bettelheim fully immerses his readers in his theory, which he then reinforces with case studies; he does all of this long before he concerns himself with the major works on autism. To anyone unfamiliar with child development or autism, Bettelheim's theory sounds impressive, even groundbreaking.

The case studies exemplify Bettelheim's penchant for deduction rather than induction. As indicated by his grant application and comments to friends, Bettelheim sought the cause of autism in the parents. Before he admitted a single student with autism, that is, he had already determined the source of the disorder. Committing himself to treating autism as a psychological disorder rising out of environmental causes, he precluded any other explanation. Within each case study, his deliberate inclusion of the environmental background serves as a crucial means to foreground his own theory within his observations. To advance his notion of the "refrigerator mother," he outlined Marcia's, Laurie's, and Joey's tragic lives pre- and post-birth, before any discussion about their symptoms. Of course, to make his case more cogent, Bettelheim appears to select the most "hopeless," most infantile, of his students for his case studies.

The opening sentence to Laurie's "Background and History" discussion reads: "Laurie's mother, by her own account, had known little happiness in her life" (95). Bettelheim quickly moves to discuss her mother's first troubled marriage, her marriage to Laurie's father, and his unwillingness to talk with Bettelheim (he writes: "the father was not interested in giving us a history; he was 'too busy'" [96]). Thus he implicitly diagnoses Laurie's condition by pointing to the actions of Laurie's mother and her nursemaid (Bettelheim is sure to note that the nursemaid played a prominent role in Laurie's infancy because her mother had to go back to work immediately). In one of his more direct accusations, Bettelheim writes: "A comparison with the history of other autistic children we have known makes it possible to speculate further: namely, that the maid herself may have never behaved as a total person toward Laurie" (119). From here, Bettelheim begins his discussion of Laurie's autism.

Bettelheim reveals in "Marcia's History" that her family's disturbances began even before she was born. Marcia's mother and father had difficult childhoods, and both were "indifferent" about marrying each other but did so because previous loving relationships were tragically terminated. Bettelheim also describes Marcia's father's mental health problems: he had difficulty providing for his wife because of extreme fear and anxiety. After Marcia was born, Bettelheim further notes, both parents realized that they no longer wanted their child. Her father thought "Marcia was simply 'an ugly little baby.' She was 'really no interest to me. I felt she was my wife's child'" (158). Additionally, Bettelheim remarks that the father wanted Marcia gone "so that he could have more of the mother" (159). Meanwhile, Marcia's mother felt trapped in her marriage and considered leaving both her husband and her child. Therefore, Marcia spent most of her time with babysitters, "some of whom seemed to inspire Marcia with great fear" (158). Such problems, Bettelheim surmises, led Marcia to seek nonexistence, yet remain alive to gain revenge on her parents. At age two, for example, Marcia no longer had regular bowel movements, which Bettelheim interprets as a symbolic protest against her mother. He reaches a similar conclusion in his third case, Joey, in his observation of Joey's problems with language, including his gradual loss of concrete language and his inability to use personal pronouns, attributing these problems to personal choice or protest rather than to disability.

In effect, the deductions in these case studies open a Freudian back door for Bettelheim into the science of child development. If autism has an environmental rather than a physiological cause, Bettelheim might find clues to normal infant development through the recovery process of children with autism. In addition to creating the appearance of a parental or maternal cause of autism in his case studies, his arrangement is necessary to give scientific credibility to his Freudian interpretations of the children's behavior. For instance, under this arrangement, Laurie's alleged looking upward toward the elusive "good breast" seems far more reasonable, since Bettelheim has already shown that nursing is "the nuclear experience out of which develop all later feelings about oneself and other persons" (19). Not merely another Freudian obsessed with breasts, Bettelheim indicates that in feeding the infant begins to develop a sense of self, and that this frustrated yearning for the breast shows the autistic child acting out his/her blocked sense of self.

Circularly, the theory section helps validate Bettelheim's interpretations, and his interpretations help validate his theory. Perelman's concept of "presence" best explains the interplay between his theory and interpretations. Perelman writes that "one of the preoccupations of a speaker is to make present, by verbal magic alone, what is actually absent but what he considers important to his argument or, by making them more present, to enhance the value of some of the elements of which one has actually made conscious" (29). The case studies of Laurie, Marcia, and Joey recreate actual instances of his theory, thereby "enhanc[ing] the value" of his theory. After the strategically placed "history" in his case studies, Bettelheim does not simply describe the children's behavior; he interprets it through the framework of his theory. As a result, he makes present what was actually absent in these children's behavior. Because of the bizarre behaviors exhibited by the children in the case studies, his interpretations begin to seem the only means of explaining these deviancies. Yet the fact that none of these behaviors goes unexplained is rather suspect.

When Bettelheim finally turns his attention to the arguments of Kanner and Rimland he intends to refute their claims that autism is an innate disorder. He takes these theories to task on two points: (1) they cannot explain the autistic child's inability to differentiate the "I" and the "you" in language use, and (2) they cannot explain why autistic children shy away from stimuli if it is a disorder of the part of the brain dealing with arousal.

Kanner notes that children with autism avoid using the pronoun "I" in favor of the pronoun "you," and concludes that this reversal, like the autistic child's tendency to memorize long lists of information, is symptomatic of the fact that language holds little meaning for them.[8] Kanner and Rimland both agree that the child with autism can repeat words without understanding them. Bettelheim states that "Rimland, a psychologist, seems uninterested in the psyche of autistic children, since he did not study them as persons but inquired only into the neurological structure of their brains" (433; this is a particularly biting comment because Rimland's own son is autistic). If Rimland and Kanner were more astute, according to Bettelheim, they would have realized that the child with autism does not use the pronoun "I" for several reasons, none of which is a lack of understanding of language. The autistic child may avoid using "I" so that he/she can hide his/her innermost thoughts. In some cases, it could be "either a denial of selfhood or denote[] an absence of awareness of selfhood, while the substitution of 'you' shows some awareness of the selfhood of others" (Bettelheim 427). But primarily for Bettelheim, the child who avoids "I" "is complying with what he considers a parental wish that he should not exist" (429). Finally, the autistic child performs the aforementioned feats of memory not as exercises in repetition but as indications to the world that he does not have a feeble mind. Because these children fear speaking "freely," they must covertly prove to the world their intelligence (430).

Like Kanner's, Rimland's neurological theory of autism presents autism as an innate disorder. Rimland holds that a dysfunction in the reticular formation of the brain stem, the portion of the brain responsible for arousal, causes autism. In response, Bettelheim argues that even if someone discovers a definitive neurological source of autism, that does not preclude the psychological explanation. There might be periods during which certain neurological systems must receive stimulation in order to maintain normal development. If, as Bettelheim argues, the child has a poor emotional environment, this may explain why the central nervous system becomes dysfunctional. Moreover, Bettelheim holds that Rimland's argument that autism is caused by a dysfunction of the area of the brain responsible for arousal contradicts the behaviors these children exhibit. If Rimland were correct, Bettelheim posits, it would make no sense for many children with autism to plug their ears, close their eyes, or scream in the attempt to shut out stimuli. Bettelheim writes: "It is exactly because they can be aroused, but do not wish to be, that they try to block out stimuli through motor behavior like twiddling, or to drown them out through music which they hear as 'white' noise without content" (402). He believes that "[t]hrough their shutting out of sensation they [avoid being] confronted by a frustrating reality" (402). Bettelheim may be partly correct about autistic people's capacity for arousal, but he is clearly wrong about the cause.

Bettelheim does agree with Rimland that blaming parents gains clinicians no ground. Instilling a sense of guilt in the parents of these children is useless since whatever they may have done to cause their child's disorder, Bettelheim writes, we can be certain that "they did [it] because they could not help themselves to do otherwise" and "[t]hey suffer more than enough in having such a child" (404). Keeping this in mind, we still should not cease searching in the parent/child relationship for anything that may aid our understanding. In Bettelheim's view, both Kanner and Rimland see autism as a problem to be solved while ignoring the human element (for example, he rebuts Kanner's argument that children with autism cannot relate to others. Bettelheim responds that they do relate, but in their own fashion).[9] Kanner's and Rimland's studies can never definitively refute Bettelheim's causal claims until someone constructs a test that can detect the biological existence of autism at birth; thus Bettelheim's claim is proven because it cannot be disproved.

But Bettelheim does not believe that his theory should be accepted by default; rather, he decides to meet the scientists on their own ground: characteristically, whenever he sees the potential for doubt in his findings, he invokes "science." Thus he argues that we should select the theory that best explains autism's cause according to the effectiveness of the treatment driven by that theory. As a result, he engages in a statistical comparison with the only long-term study taken from Kanner's and Rimland's research. According to Bettelheim, the statistical improvement in his patients is significantly better than that resulting from the other approaches. Because the methods based on his theory create better results, his theory must be right.

However, Bettelheim's statistics are problematic. In his grant application he states that he planned to admit 12 children with autism for his study. Yet the school records show that he admitted ten, only two of whom had entered with the diagnosis of autism. And Bettelheim gives a base number of 46, 40 of whom he will use for comparison. Where are these children? Bettelheim can safely make his success rate claims since the children's records are sealed. Hence, no one will ever know the true success of Bettelheim's "milieu therapy."

In summary, Bettelheim's career benefitted from his ability to construct an ethos that appealed to an audience beyond the scientific community. His status as a European intellectual propelled him to fame with an American mass audience. Furthermore, his desire to produce readable texts secured his position as an expert on child behavior. *The Empty Fortress* reveals additional reasons for Bettelheim's success: it seeks to capture the ideal universal audience rather than attempting to gain the acceptance of the scientific community. On the surface, *The Empty Fortress* appears scientific, though we have noted that Bettelheim violated several principles of good research. His willingness to take on counterarguments further solidified the persuasive appeal of the text.

Most importantly, according to Bettelheim, he is the only researcher who has treated autistic children as people. For those unfamiliar with his history, Bettelheim reviews in the introduction that he has written extensively on child psychology. As a Holocaust survivor, he presents himself as the only person capable of truly understanding the cause of autism, having first-hand experience of such extreme situations. His insights into the children's behavior, his "milieu therapy," his expressed sympathy for the children ravaged by autism, all further his image of the Good Doctor. It is perhaps the fundamental need to believe in the figure of the Good Doctor that underlies the mythic rhetorical structure of the persistent belief in the maternal-cause theory of autism. Viewed in hindsight, it appears that Bettelheim's work, like that of Freud himself, was less a modernist effort to replace religion with science than an effort to preserve a space for traditional, allegedly humanist values. It was an attempt, finally, to affirm that we have minds and souls rather than simply brains. That a more humane treatment for autistic persons eventually came from focusing on their neurology rather than on the "meaning" of their lives is but one of the many ironies of the career of Dr. Bettelheim.

NOTES

1. This hypothesis was originally hinted at by Leo Kanner. See, for example, Kanner's article in *American Journal of Orthopsychiatry* (425).
2. A social worker in Rice County, Minnesota, in the 1990s was notorious for pulling autistic children from their homes on the ground of child abuse.
3. In England Bettelheim published two other essays on the camps that received little attention in the United States (Pollak 116).
4. Gross (129–143) elaborates on this in his analysis of the peer review process, framing peer review as a conjunction of speech act theory and Habermas's ideal speech situation so that editing and revising becomes an ideal interaction. He does, however, omit that the peer review process also encompasses the more specific audience issues referred to here.
5. To say that science privileges inductive over deductive reasoning does not mean that a researcher engages in a study without a theory or a methodology. Often, as research proceeds, theory and method are revised according to the particulars of the specific phenomenon. This revision typically does not

compromise the integrity of the study, but is rather built into the scientific method to allow for the best possible understanding.

6. For a discussion of the reenactment of the inductive process see Medawar. For a commentary on the introductions of scientific article see Swales.

7. As the statements of former students have attested, Bettelheim's confrontation was often physically and mentally abusive. This contradiction between Bettelheim's statements and actions makes his therapeutic methodology even more suspect (Pollak 191–211).

8. Researchers still differ on why pronoun reversal occurs in some autistic children. Those who support a theory-of-mind explanation, for example, view pronoun reversal as a problem related to malfunctions within interconnected brain functions that make it difficult for the child to differentiate between the self, the other, and their respective motives.

9. Bettelheim is also right about this. Most researchers at the time, including Kanner, believed that people with autism did not relate to others.

WORKS CITED

Bettelheim, Bruno. *The Empty Fortress: Infantile Autism and the Birth of the Self.* New York: Free P, 1967.

———. "Individual and Mass Behavior in Extreme Situations." *Journal of Abnormal and Social Psychology* 38 (Oct. 1943): 417–452.

———. "Joey: A 'Mechanical Boy.'" *Scientific American* 200 (1959): 116–127.

———. "Speaking Out: Stop Pampering Gifted Children." *Saturday Evening Post* 11 April 1964: 8–10

———. "Why Working Mothers Feel Guilty." *Redbook* March 1966: 55, 131–33, 144–47.

———, and Leo Kanner. "Early Infantile Autism, 1943–1955." *American Journal of Orthopsychiatry* 26 (1956): 556–566.

Gross, Alan. *The Rhetoric of Science.* Cambridge, MA: Harvard UP, 1990.

Hobson, Peter. *The Cradle of Thought.* London: Macmillan, 2002.

Kanner, Leo. "Problems of Nosology and Psychodynamics of Early Infantile Autism." *American Journal of Orthopsychiatry* 19 (July 1949): 425.

Medawar, Peter. "Is the Scientific Report Fraudulent? Yes; It Misrepresents Scientific Thought." *Saturday Review* 1 August 1964: 42–43.

Perelman, Chaim, and Lucy Olbrechts-Tyteca. *The New Rhetoric: A Treatise on Argumentation.* Trans. J. Wilkinson and P. Weaver. London: U of Notre Dame P, 1969.

Pollak, Richard. *The Creation of Dr. B: A Biography of Bruno Bettelheim.* New York: Simon & Schuster, 1997.

Raines, Theron. *Rising to the Light: A Portrait of Bruno Bettelheim.* New York: Knopf, 2002.

Scott, Robert L. "On Viewing Rhetoric as Epistemic." *Central States Speech Journal* 28.1 (1967): 9–17.

———. "On Viewing Rhetoric as Epistemic: Ten Years Later." *Central States Speech Journal* 27 (1976): 258–266.

Sutton, Nina. *Bettelheim: A Life and Legacy.* New York: Basic Books, 1996.

Swales, Gene. *Analysis: English and American Research Settings.* Cambridge: Cambridge UP, 1990

3   Constructing Autism
A Brief Genealogy

Majia Holmer Nadesan

Autism, a neurological disorder, is now regarded as reaching epidemic pro-
portions ("Evidence mounts") and considered a major public health problem. The dramatic increase in autistic diagnoses parallels a huge increase
in scientific research on autism and related disorders such as Pervasive
Developmental Disorder (PDD), Asperger's syndrome, and nonverbal communication disorders. For example, acting in response to the dramatic rates
of increase in its autism diagnoses—up to 1000%—the state of California
recently allocated $34 million to autism research ("California"). A range
of media information directed toward popular audiences complements the
scientific research. Information about autism can be found in an array of
popular periodicals, including such varied titles as *Time* (Nash and Bonesteel), *Newsweek* (Cowley), *The Economist* ("Science and Technology"),
and *Scientific American* (Rodier), and on a seemingly infinite supply of Web
sites (e.g., www.autism.com; www.autismcenter.org; www.nichd.nih.gov/
autism/). Articles about the relationship between autism and vaccinations
can be found in almost every daily newspaper within the United States (e.g.,
Bandler; "Drug Lawsuits") and representations of autism find wide expression within the popular media, as illustrated by the well-known film *Rain
Man* and others. More recently, the popular media have speculated on a
causal relationship between autism and computer "geekiness" (Chapman;
Nash and Bonesteel).

Across many of these representations of autism—both scientific and popular—is an unwritten but foundational premise that autism is a *disease* (or
sometimes *condition*) that will, ultimately, be rendered transparent through
the ceaseless efforts of scientific authorities. Typically, this quest for trans-
parency entails a reductionistic search for origins, although speculations
regarding the nature of these origins have changed across time, reflecting
historically specific preoccupations and research paradigms. Currently, a
positivistic preoccupation with genetic mutations and/or faulty biochem-
istry has replaced the 1950s "refrigerator mother"(commonly attributed to
Bettelheim) thesis for the ontogenesis of autism (Gardner).[1] Today, efforts
to localize epidemiological centers for the disorder hint at the promise of its
remediation through gene therapy or medication. Thus, although estimates

of the autistic population grow, the underlying articulation of the "condition" as pathological remains relatively intact. The few voices that argue for the disorder's functionality in the information age do not question its location outside the norm.

This chapter contributes to current efforts to redress the positivistic biases in the vast corpus of literature on autism by exploring the social-historical conditions and practices that enabled autism to be identified, labeled, and therapied in the early twentieth century as well as the conditions today that permit childhood autism, particularly high-functioning childhood autism, to be labeled an "epidemic" ("Evidence mounts" 1). As the idea of an autism epidemic has captured the public imagination, the disorder has been regarded as both threatening and fascinating. Therefore, exploration of the social conditions involved in the production, interpretation, and remediation of autism is important not only for people intimately involved with autism but also for those interested in how social institutions such as medicine, psychology and psychiatry, and the popular media shape our ideas about normality and difference in shifting economic and political environments. Thus, the stakes in this exploration extend beyond autism to include the ideas and practices whereby we constitute everyday life and social institutions and the processes that will, ultimately, produce the concepts of and opportunities for personhood in the twenty-first century.

Accordingly, this chapter provides a brief genealogy of autism to contextualize the conditions of possibility for contemporary understandings of autism. This genealogy questions whether autism is a homogeneous, pathological condition that can be exhaustively known—or transparently represented—by scientists and their representational technologies (e.g., MRIs). Although I deconstruct the idea of autism as a uniform, biological essence shared by all people labeled as "autistic," I do *not* reject the idea that biological phenomena contribute to the expression of "autistic" symptoms. I believe we need to explore how various institutional relationships, expert authorities, and bodies of knowledge have sought to represent, divide, understand, and act on *biologically based, but socially shaped and expressed*, behavioral and cognitive differences such as autism. What follows constitutes a preliminary and partial response to this need.

CONSTRUCTING AUTISM IN THE MEDICAL LITERATURE

Autism, as a meaningful diagnostic category, emerged in the early 1940s. This timing is not accidental but rather reflects an emergent matrix of practices and interpretive vocabularies that marked the transition into the twentieth century (see Nadesan, *Constructing* 9–28). We must understand the emergence of autism as a diagnostic category in the 1940s in relation to a matrix of professional and parental practices that marked the cultural and economic transition to the twentieth century, just as we must understand the emergence of high-functioning forms of autism in terms of practices that mark late-twentieth-century and early twenty-first century life. The conditions of possibility for diagnosing children as autistic or high-functioning autistic are ultimately less rooted in the biology of their conditions than in the cultural practices and economy of their times. For example, in the 1800s, the standards for classifying individuals as disordered were much less nuanced, the standards of normality much broader, and the mechanisms for social and individual surveillance that we take for granted today simply did not exist. Prior to the late 1800s, children would not have been subject to any form of "developmental" or psychological examination unless their conditions were particularly severe and their parents particularly economically privileged. Indeed, it was not until the 1930s that guidelines were created and used in tracking children's "developmental" progress.[2] The historical contingencies of autism diagnoses call into question artificial distinctions between biology and culture, and disease and social representation.

In our everyday thinking and communication, most of us visualize disease as either caused by a scientifically discernable agent such as a virus or bacterium (e.g., AIDS or meningitis) or as emanating from a detectable, localized bodily dysfunction (e.g., heart disease or diabetes). The disease-causing agent or diseased bodily system is seen as objective, available to visual representation (through a microscope, electromagnetic scan, or scientific diagram), and ultimately treatable (even if a "cure" eludes current medical understanding). In effect, disease is represented in our everyday understanding as available to empirical identification, interpretation, and intervention. This everyday understanding of disease derives from nineteenth-century positivism, which held that the laws of nature could be identified and understood univocally through detached, empirical inquiry. Positivist conceptions of medicine presume a mind/body dichotomy in which diseases are primarily if not exclusively located in the biological body, and presume that each disease is caused by a specific and (ultimately) identifiable element.[3]

Although medical theory has long rejected many positivist assumptions about the nature and origin of disease, our popular understandings and much medical practice continue to invoke them in diagnosing and treating various diseases. The formulation also lingers in the popular imagination and in expert efforts to identify "agents" responsible for causing autism or capable of curing autism. But autism is probably a heterogeneous condition that is more properly called a syndrome than a disease. Moreover, the causal pathways engendering autistic symptoms are most likely multiple and contingent on level upon level of loosely coupled, synergistic, biological and social systems. Most medical experts would agree that all, or even most, people with autism do not share the same underlying biological condition. Moreover, people with autism, like everyone else, grow and change in relation to their familial and social environments. Built environments and social practices elicit and constrain, enable and shape the developing person, whether that person bears a label or not. And yet autism is often represented in popular discourse—in the media, in parental accounts of autistic children, and in some medical research—as caused by discernable, distinct, and mechanistic agents whose operations will inevitably be revealed to an anxious public. Such accounts erase or minimize the complex and irreducible biological and social synergies that operate across genetic, molecular, psychological, social, and cultural environments in favor of reductionistic, linear, biogenetic formulations.

Efforts to reject positivist models confront age-old Western (i.e., Platonic and Cartesian) dualisms between body and mind/soul, corporeality and symbolic representation, materialism and idealism. Ridding theory of ancient but false dichotomies is not an easy task, as illustrated when scholars argue that diseases or disabilities are socially constituted. Too often efforts to view disease as socially constructed oscillate between the binaries of materialism and idealism because of the difficulties in synthesizing them. On the one hand, the built environment contributes to disease (e.g., through diet and pollution); yet the causes cannot be reduced to built environments. On the other hand, although disease may appear as brute facticity (e.g., through pain or dehabilitation), bodily symptoms are always/already interpreted within symbolic systems of meanings, social practices, and historically and culturally variable expert authorities. Prevailing socially constituted ideas about disease shape and constrain medical researchers' observations, interpretations, and interventions, whereas bodily symptoms and processes can at times offer material refutation of prevailing ideas about causation and cure. In short, disease, disability, and bodily difference are at once material and symbolic, both socially constructed and materially inscribed.

Recently, scholars in the sociology of medicine and disability studies have offered more synthetic accounts of the relationship between body and mind, disease and representation, materialism and idealism. Nicholas Fox, for example, suggests that rather than becoming locked within the dualism of nature/biology and culture, we should eschew the search for the "truth" of how the body (or brain) "really is" (or should be), and reject the search for the body's facticity. Instead, he contends, research should focus on the *becoming* of the body/mind as it is constituted by and relates to cultural processes (9). Fox's approach need not necessitate rejecting a biological component of autism. Rather, it entails viewing the biological and the cultural as mutually constitutive, inseparable in their constitution of personhood. An approach such as Fox's would not emphasize the mechanistic and reductionistic search for definitive origins but would instead focus on the *becoming* of autism as it is bioculturally constituted, interpreted, experienced, and resisted.

In seeking to unravel the becoming of autism, the work of Ian Hacking provides useful models and heuristics. In *The Social Construction of*

What? Hacking demonstrates the interaction of biology and culture, materiality and ideas, through a variety of examples including schizophrenia, child abuse, and childhood autism. Hacking uses the idea of "interactive kinds" to explain the mediation of socially constructed ideas and material existence: "'Interactive' is a new concept that applies not to people but to classifications, to kinds . . . that can influence what is classified. And because kinds can interact with what is classified, the classification itself may be modified or replaced" (103). Unlike "indifferent kinds," which are entities not affected by their classifications as such, "interactive kinds" are fundamentally affected—produced in relation to—the categories and labels used to describe them. Interactive kinds are affected by the process of classification to such a degree that the classification may itself require eventual modification or replacement. The construct of child television viewers, Hacking observes, illustrates the kind of classificatory "looping" specific to interactive kinds: the behavior of child television viewers is, no doubt, irrevocably changed by the classification and research of children as child viewers. Interactive kinds are classificatory systems that emerge within matrices of institutions and practices and that, once articulated, engender practices and institutions that produce and shape what was classified. However, human beings are subject to unintended effects because of the reflexive nature of consciousness (among other factors). That is, the awareness of one's classification as a particular kind of being, a particular kind of subject, can engender resistance and/or behavioral variation.

Hacking goes on to distinguish the kind of classificatory looping illustrated by child viewers from another form of looping he describes as "biolooping" (109), which he illustrates in relation to the brain chemical, serotonin. Serotonin levels, Hacking observes, are correlated with depression. Yet behavioral treatments directed toward reducing depressive states can be as effective as chemical therapy in raising serotonin levels. Biolooping thus refers to the process whereby mental states, individual comportment, and cultural practices can affect biological outcomes such as serotonin levels. Hacking argues that biolooping and classificatory looping could both be at work simultaneously in some forms of psychopathologies, particularly schizophrenia and childhood autism.

Autism, like schizophrenia according to Hacking, is an interactive kind that may be subject to the looping effect as a consequence of the interpretations of parents, caregivers, autistic patients and even experts' very understandings of the diseases at issue. Accordingly, Hacking suggests that understandings of the nature and manifestations of distinct diseases and pathologies may change significantly over time, leading to different therapeutic approaches and, consequently, disease progressions. For example, Hacking notes that many of the symptoms identified by Kanner and Asperger are no longer regarded as primary symptoms of autism: for example, "flat affect," which both original researchers observed and remarked on, is no longer regarded as a determinate diagnostic criterion. Moreover, many severely affected children who today bear the label of classical autism would probably have been diagnosed by Kanner or Asperger as psychotic or mentally retarded.

Consequently, autism is a particularly compelling example of the intersection of biology and culture, because although it is arguably an interactive kind, it also evidences the characteristics of an indifferent kind in that its symptoms are in some way rooted in genetics, epigenetics, or molecular chemistry. These biogenetic factors, however, do not "motivate" fixed, uniform symptoms such as "flat affect." Moreover, the underlying biogenetic factors are not themselves fixed or uniform. The effects of parental expectations and reinforcements, therapy programs, and individual experiences loop back to affect or even constitute the expression of biogenetic factors. Further, drugs such as Prozac do not merely reduce symptoms but may actually alter the brain chemistry and neural topography of autistic patients, illustrating Hacking's idea of bio-looping.

Prozac and other drugs that target neural chemistry are themselves cultural artifacts and thereby show how cultural models of the mind/brain undergird scientific authorities' efforts toward bioengineering. Although the current biogenetic/chemical model of the brain–mind relationship is not exhaustive (or even necessarily valid), biomedical interventions generated using this model tend to alter subtly the expression of that which they presuppose. Moreover, patient and caregiver expectations, based on the perceived validity of the biogenetic model of the brain, no doubt alter the experience and expression of the effects of biomedical interventions.

Hacking's work points to many compelling avenues of research for those investigating the symbolic aspects of autism. I am most interested in the emergence of autism in the early twentieth century and the emergence of more high-functioning forms of the disorder in the late twentieth century as "niche" disorders. In Hacking's 1998 text, *Mad Travelers*, he investigates "transient" mental illness:

> By a "transient mental illness" I mean an illness that appears at a time, in a place, and later fades away. It may spread from place to place and reappear from time to time. It may be selective for social class or gender, preferring poor women or rich women. I do not mean that it comes and goes in this or that patient, but that this type of madness exists only at certain times and places. The most famous candidate for a transient mental illness is hysteria. (1)

Hacking questions whether a variety of neuroses such as PMS, ADHD, and multiple personality disorder are real or culturally produced. In that regard, so-called "shadow syndromes" such as subclinical autism and depression seem particularly suspect.

Although there is some discontinuity in Hacking's formulations of subclinical autism as a transient mental illness in *Mad Travelers* and his later formulation of it as both an interactive and indifferent kind in *The Social Construction of What?*, I feel that the disorder exemplifies this niche effect, even though it undoubtedly has a biological component. In the section that follows, I briefly introduce the thesis—argued at much greater length in my book—that autism is a disorder that emerged and was created in relation to cultural practices and discourses specific to particular points in time: the transition from the nineteenth to the twentieth century and, more recently, the transition from the twentieth to the twenty-first century.

CONSTRUCTING AUTISM: A BRIEF GENEALOGY OF THE TWENTIETH CENTURY

Following Hacking's idea of a niche effect, I suggest that autism is a disorder of the early twentieth century, whereas high-functioning variants such as Asperger's syndrome (AS), and Pervasive Development Disorder (PDD) are disorders of the late twentieth- and early twenty-first centuries. This is to say that as a distinct psychological disorder or psychiatric disease, autism could not have emerged in the nineteenth century, though I concede that there have no doubt been people throughout history who have displayed the symptoms we now define as autism.

Autism could not have emerged as a distinct disorder because within the diagnostic categories of nineteenth-century (and earlier) thought, it was unthinkable. Childhood psychosis was not widely recognized professionally until the closing decades of the nineteenth century, and the idea of the developmental disorder was a twentieth-century psychiatric innovation. Moreover, the institution of child psychiatry as a profession awaited the twentieth century.

If autism was unthinkable within the scientific taxonomies, medical nosologies, and medical practices of nineteenth-century thought, so high-functioning variants of autism were largely unthinkable diagnostic categories until the mid- to late twentieth century.[4] In the first half of the twentieth century, the eccentricities we now associate with AS would have most likely resulted in the diagnosis of a personality disorder such as a schizoid personality, if anything. Childhood eccentricities would have gone unremarked or undiagnosed unless particularly troubling. Psychiatric diagnoses involving moral pathology, preschizophrenia, or developmental neuroses would have been called on to explain more overt expressions of childhood "deviance." The relatively mild characteristics delimiting the outer edges of autistic spectrum disorders such as semantic-pragmatic disorder and ADHD would have typically escaped parental concern and expert observation. Identification of individuals with "mild" autism spectrum conditions awaited a host of conditions: the invention of intensive mothering, the standardization of (narrowly delineated) benchmarks of developmental normality, and widespread pediatric surveillance of very young children.

And so we must contextualize the history of autism in all of its forms within the evolution and transformation of medical practices and the development of professions such as psychiatry, psychology, social work, and special education, all of which either emerged or were professionalized in the early twentieth century. We must further understand the history of AS and PDD in the context of new standards for parenting that emerged in the mid-twentieth century and of new economic conditions surrounding the purported "information revolution" that began in the 1960s. I argue that the public's fascination with autism stems in large part from the notion that autistic people are technologically gifted and particularly adept with computer technology.[5] We must also comprehend the scientific search for understanding autism in the late twentieth century within a new matrix of practices seeking to explain social behaviors in terms of genes, which are commonly seen as entities that will ultimately deterministically explain a whole repertoire of human behaviors.

Finally, we must view the "cures" for autism—the various remediations and therapies promoted by professional practitioners and parents alike—in the context of late twentieth-century social fears about environmental contamination and pollution, fears engendered by environmental catastrophes but also, I argue, motivated by latent cultural taboos and anxieties. In modern times, social fears and anxieties have been transferred from dragons and demons to our own creations, particularly our technological creations (Mulgan 1). Industrial toxins constitute a potent locus of anxiety and create ambivalence about the fruits of technological innovations designed to maximize our health and wealth. Medical technologies created to minimize "risks" to the populace, such as vaccinations, have also generated anxiety, ironically, because of their risks to susceptible populations. Anxieties about the unintended effects of our technological creations merge with ancient distinctions between the pure and the impure, the untouched and the contaminated (Turner 207).

The empirically real and symbolically imagined threats posed by technological pollution collide with the notion of the pure, innocent infant, untouched by culture and technology. In addition, the infant has become an imagined site for class mobility in a time of increased economic competitiveness. Disabled children, who fail to conform to regimented standards of (hyper)normality, may therefore be viewed as damaged or contaminated, rather than merely different. Nonfamily members may also view such children as dangerous or contaminated. Indeed, the late nineteenth-century sentiment that society needs to be protected from its disabled (Braddock and Parish 34) persists in the contemporary popular imagination, which may explain some of the resistance to mainstreaming disabled children. Aspiring parents are always vigilant to real and imagined threats to their children's purity.

Although the threats posed by industrial toxins are indisputably real, their environmental ubiquity prevents easy remediation. Parental angst is therefore displaced to symbolic sites of contamination. Vaccinations are one of them. However, despite their demonstrable potential harms, the fear of vaccinations may obscure and deflect attention from more diffuse and perhaps more potent threats such as industrial effluences, pesticides, air pollution or viral agents. The public fear of autistic contamination and, conversely, our fascination with "autistic intelligence," together point to the symbolic complexity of autism, and to the contradictions associated with its interpretations and remediations. The range and complexity of autistic symbolism preclude singular or definitive understandings. This chapter pursues but a few avenues of investigation.

For the sake of simplicity, I represent the various strands involved in the constitution, interpretation, and remediation of autism as "social discourses," while acknowledging that discourses cannot be severed from the institutional relations that engender, reproduce and transform them. The various discourses that I briefly introduce here include those of twentieth-century pediatric psychiatry, childhood, cognition, genetics, the environment, and disability advocacy.

The first set of discursive practices concerns the psychiatric articulation of boundaries between normality and pathology. Genealogies of mental illness provided by Berrios, Berrios and Porter, Foucault, and Porter, among others, reveal the historical contingencies and institutional practices that provided the conditions of possibility for increasingly refined ideas about the nature of, and divisions between, psychological normality and pathology in the early twentieth century. The modern state in the nineteenth century extended governmental practices over more domains of social life, resulting in new bodies of knowledge, social institutions, and authorities who aimed to divide populations according to finer wrought distinctions of health and pathology, sanity and insanity, intellectual acuity and mental retardation (see Foucault, "Governmentality"). Accordingly, by the beginning of the twentieth century, new divisions, institutions, and authorities enabled the identification and articulation of autistic spectrum disorders that formerly would have either gone undiagnosed or, contrastingly, would have been pathologized as personal dangerousness, moral degeneracy, or "idiocy."[6]

Nineteenth-century governmental practices included expansion of compulsory education, which resulted in more social and expert surveillance of children. Moreover, the articulation and popularization of Freudian and Darwinian theories in the second half of the nineteenth century resulted in new cultural anxieties about childhood in general and the childhood of potential social "degenerates" in particular (see Morss 24, 4, 154). Changing ideas about childhood also enabled identification and articulation of autism within the early twentieth century. Although much early research and social work focused on adjusting lower-class immigrant children in the United States, the increasing psychiatric interest in preventing social maladjustment brought middle-class children into focus by the early twentieth century. New educational and psychological authorities developed to meet the new imperatives of social adjustment (see Rose, *Governing* 123–81), challenging the boundaries between normality and pathology, and eventually replacing binary distinctions with a continuum of pathologized and pre-pathological states associated with (Freudian) neuroses, preschizophrenic or schizophrenic-like conditions, and finally with personality disorders (as articulated by Kurt Schneider). Educational psychologists, community psychiatrists, and pediatricians—all newly instituted experts—found apparent manifestations of a vast range of disorders among the children they surveyed (also see Jones).

These historical circumstances—the convergence of new ideas about childhood, new systems of surveillance, new expert authorities, and new institutional arrangements—provided the conditions of possibility for autism to be identified, named and interpreted. We must place Hans Asperger's pediatric practice and Leo Kanner's child psychiatry within these historical contexts. Similarly, we must contextualize efforts to understand what autism *meant* for each of these individuals within a genealogy of Bleuler's schizophrenia, Freudian psychoanalysis, German phenomenology, and Kurt Schneider's personality theory—conceptual frameworks for the explanation of mind, perception, and pathology that shaped Asperger's and Kanner's ideas about autism. For example, both Kanner and Asperger appropriated Bleuler's description of the schizophrenic's "autistic" style of thinking, which Bleuler had appropriated from Freud. This intellectual heritage engendered the assumption that autism was characterized by aloneness, solipsism, and a turning away from the social world, resulting in a failure to develop a "normal" ego. However, whereas Kanner viewed autistic thinking in relation to psychosis, as an underdeveloped or disintegrating ego ("Autistic Disturbances" 48, 50), Asperger was more inclined to regard the children under his care as afflicted with a particular type of (nonpsychotic but disordered) ego that afforded unique insight into the natural world even while it created social discord ("Autistic Psychopathy" 67, 70–74). Both Kanner and Asperger felt that autistic thinking resulted from inborn, biological forces; however, Kanner also noted behavioral and personality similarities in the parents of his autistic children ("Autistic Disturbances" 50), thereby implying the possibility for some level of social influence in creating autistic symptoms.

Psychodynamic forces that allegedly produced autism captured the public imagination in the United States and Western Europe after World War II. Popular accounts of child development promulgated by such diverse figures as D. W. Winnicott and Bruno Bettelheim emphasized the mother's role in fostering stable ego development. They helped create the sense that normal, healthy child development was fraught with peril and thus required the mother's ever-present guidance. Autism and other developmental disorders were thus sometimes inadvertently and other times directly attributed to maternal negligence or transgression. In the postwar period, earlier psychoanalytic accounts that emphasized infant *perceptions* (such as those proposed by

Melanie Klein) gave way to object-relations accounts that attributed developmental problems to mothers' actual (or purported) behaviors. In popular psychology, mother-blaming continued to be used to explain many forms of child psychopathology until the late 1970s and early 1980s.

Toward the close of the twentieth century new institutional conditions, expert authorities, and systems of knowledge shaped ideas about normality and pathology in the context of new "niche" conditions. Cognitive psychology, in particular, replaced the psychoanalytic framework for understanding "developmental disorders." And so autism was reconceptualized in the popular imagination from an ego shipwrecked on the shores of object relations to a computer with modular dysfunctions. Accordingly, "high-functioning" autism (e.g., Asperger's syndrome and semantic pragmatic disorder) and Pervasive Developmental Disorders (PDD) were carved out as distinct disorders by several important social/cultural discourses, including the metaphors of cognitive psychology (which view minds in terms of isolated modules), and by parent-centered bourgeois discourses that present childhood as the locus of class mobility, particularly in the information age (see Ehrenreich; Nadesan, "Engineering"411).

The coupling of cognitive psychology with cognitive neuroscience, and the popularization of this coupling in late twentieth-century discourses of early childhood brain science (see Bruer) lent urgency to the public and academic interest in "developmental disorders," further expanding the continuum of possible autistic symptoms and diagnostic assessments. In relation to these discourses, childhood autism has acquired multiple valences in late twentieth- and early twenty-first century life. Autism signifies pathology and difference in an epoch that increasingly emphasizes physical and psychological health, yet also signifies technological aptitude, as illustrated in this Los Angeles *Times* article on the prototypical computer "geek": "There is some fascinating speculation going on these days that the well-known stereotype of the computer geek or nerd may actually be a description of mild autism, especially a form of autism known as Asperger's syndrome" (Chapman 1). The simultaneous elevation and denigration of "high-functioning" autistic traits may speak more to cultural preoccupations and anxieties with technology and masculinity than to any "essential" autistic personality (see Nadesan, *Constructing* 128–132). But most troubling are the representations of autistic intelligence as at once alien and machine-like: the common idea that autistic intelligence is typified by a computer's computational processes strips autistic people of their consciousness, their emotions, their humanity. Autistic intelligence has become a site of condensation for the cultural fascination with, and fear of, self-regulating, cybernetic machines devoid of human emotion and sociality.

Childhood autism has also been caught up and dissected in the various cultural discourses of medical, environmental, and genetic risk. Across the twentieth century, risk assessment and prevention became primary operating logics of biopolitical authorities ranging from public health officials to environmentalists, from family doctors to school authorities (see Castel; Petersen and Lupton 18–22). Today, the risk factors for adult mental and physical illnesses have proliferated (e.g., diet, poverty, working mothers, pesticides), perhaps matched only by proliferating disease categories (ADHD, fibromyalgia, etc). Environmental contaminants, diet, and susceptibility genes are among the expanded categories for identifying and calculating risk. As the range of risk factors grows, more and more people are subject to surveillance, contributing further to the proliferation of risk categories.

The sociological literature on medical risk suggests two main categories of risk interpretation and assessment: (1) external risks posed by an ever-expanding array of real and imagined environental threats ranging from lifestyle to environmental pollutants; and (2) internal risks posed by the dynamics of the corporeal body, including the immune system and genetic forces (see Armstrong; Martin; Petersen and Bunton; Petersen and Lupton). Within these two general categories of risk, autism has been understood as an environmental illness, a genetic impairment, and a form of immune deficiency.

Accordingly, discourses of environmental risk management, environmental degradation and, more generally, ideas of a modern "malaise" offer a range of interpretive frameworks for understanding autism as an environmentally induced and mediated condition. Figuring prominently in discourses of alternative medicine and health, autism is interpreted as embodying the human cost of ruthless capitalism, government mandated health protocols, and poor environmental stewardship. For example, Seroussi's popular *Unraveling the Mystery of Autism and Pervasive Developmental Disorder* blames the MMR vaccination, whereas Alecson's *Alternative Treatments for Children within the Autistic Spectrum* views autism in relation to a wide range of environmental insults. Framed from this perspective, "autism" sometimes signifies a disease of modernization whose remediation depends largely on practicing alternative medicine and pure living. Autism has become the outermost pole of a whole range of contemporary environmentally mediated diseases including ADHD, chronic fatigue syndrome, and fibromyalgia that, following the argument of David B. Morris, "possess the power to define or represent an entire era" (56).

And yet, so far cultural anxieties about autism and environmental risk have resulted less in organized, expert efforts to confront sources and forms of environmental dangers than in research and resource allocations dedicated to identifying susceptibility genes. Facilitating the shift in focus from (external) environmental risk to (internal) genetic risk are genetically linked immune system "deficiencies," which are viewed in the popular imagination as rendering individuals susceptible to environmental contaminants. In *Flexible Bodies*, Emily Martin traces the evolution of popular understandings of the immune system's role in creating and maintaining healthy bodies. Martin suggests that such beliefs imply that some people possess inherently superior or more "fit" systems (231, 235) because of their genetic makeup

(237). Martin worries that this emphasis on genetic fitness could lead to new forms of stigmatization (239) or even a veiled form of social Darwinism (229).

Hence, the current discourse of genetically linked susceptibilities for autism has the potential to stigmatize autistic people and their families as genetically unfit. Although the susceptibility formulation also implies environmental catalysts, genes are what capture public attention, along with private and public funding. For example, the state of Arizona recently appropriated $7.1 million for research on autism susceptibility genes with the goals of developing diagnostic tests and pharmaceutical interventions (Snyder B1). When financial funding is at issue, discourses of the active gene promulgated by pharmacological and bioengineering interests take precedence over efforts to curb potential environmental catalysts and mediations.

Therefore, we must explore the social construction of autism in the context of an emerging hegemonic discourse that critics have labeled the "geneticization thesis" (Lippman 175; Ten Have 295), which posits risk as residing within the individual. Critics of this discourse argue that it reifies the gene as a unified biological agent and reductive causal principle to explain ever more aspects of social life.[7] Some even fear that the geneticization thesis will lead to the resurrection of old eugenics politics and policies. These fears may be well founded, given that the identification of susceptibility genes will inevitably lead to development of techniques for prenatal screening. However, unlike the old eugenics, which entailed state intervention, the new eugenics will be characterized by individualized decisions made in the context of marketized health care (see Petersen and Bunton 45–57).

Critics of these genetic technologies also point to their predictive limitations. For example, causal and mechanistic models of gene action are unlikely to explain or predict the range of autistic conditions or the severity of autistic symptoms. Part of the problem with such models is that they presuppose that complex disease and psychiatric phenotypes can be reduced to, or mapped on, clearly definable genotypes. This reductionist model of the gene ignores the complexity of synergistic bodily systems whose operations are always/already mediated by molecular contingencies and environmental influences.

The growing field of epigenetics demonstrates how changes in gene expression can occur in the absence of any alteration of DNA sequencing. Epigenetic changes can be caused by forces internal or external to the body. Reiner Veitia contends that very idea of a clone needs to be rethought because of the phenotypic variations that can be expressed in an organism that are not encoded in its genome (21). By decoupling the direct Mendelian relationship between genotype and phenotype, epigenetic findings raise questions about the (seemingly) singular quest for autism susceptibility genes.

However, although the discourse of genetic determinism is fraught with limitations, it has emerged as an important social discourse in that, as Lemke writes, it produces "truth" by organizing "an epistemo-political field of the visible and the expressible, which controls the diverse forms of signification, and defines the conditions for truth and falsehood" (553). In other words, the new genetics discourse constructs individuals as particular kinds of subjects at risk due to their genetic susceptibility.

Thus, Lemke suggests that the "social power" of genetic information "lies less in the resurrection of genetic determinism and more in the construction of genetic risks" (551). That is, the power of genetics discourses lies less in their capacity to predict determinate outcomes than in their capacity to calculate risks in relation to "deviations" from statistically generated profiles of normality. Hence, Novas and Rose suggest that genetic risk has been afforded a "new calculability" that may lead to new strategies and technologies designed to assess and ameliorate risky personhood (486), defined in relation to a new and normatively constituted "consensus genome" (Lemke 553), which may lead to a new "discourse of deficiency" that constructs individuals in according to the disposition of their genetic variation (Lemke 553).

The desire to represent and control the human genome illustrates in the extreme Foucault's description of biopower—a form of power that seeks to govern populations through technologies of life (*History of Sexuality* 139). As a disease of modernization, autism speaks to new practices of biopower as well as to new technologies for the surveillance and governance of populations but also opens up new strategies of resistance by individuals seeking respect and social justice on the basis of their biogenetic differences (see Rose, "Politics"). Certain autism advocates illustrate this strategy of affirming difference and demanding accommodation rather than seeking a cure or remediation (see http://ani.autistics.org).

Novas and Rose suggest that "somatic" individuals who relate to themselves on the basis of some underlying genetic identity do so in a context of inalienable legal rights granting them entitlements as well as obligations (501). This somatic subject is also embedded within a humanistic psychological discourse of self-actualization that demands certain ethical accountabilities from those providing services or caring for them. Therefore, biogenetic medical discourses that construct individuals as "somatic" selves also intersect with other legal and humanistic discourses stressing "autonomy, self-actualization, prudence, responsibility and choice" (502). Disability and patients' rights advocates use these legal and humanistic discourses in their efforts to optimize care, social respect, and accommodation.

A wide and diverse range of autism advocates have seized genetic discourses and used them advantageously, whereas other advocates have rejected such discourses for pathologizing social difference. Understanding the social construction of autism thus requires exploring the ambiguities, contradictions, and ambivalences posed by efforts to appropriate and resist genetic discourses.

Perhaps autism will always remain enigmatic, as does so much of the human condition. Thus, I have not attempted to locate the "truth" of autism because I suggest that there is no singular, fixed, universal biological truth to be located. Autism is articulated discursively through the nosological clustering of symptoms and through clinical practices of remediation. It is produced through the practices that materially implement the various social discourses I have briefly described. I do not deny that there are biological differences: I do not deny that genetics, ontogenetic socialization factors, and environmental chemicals shape the emergence and expression of our embodiment. Ràther, following Hacking's vocabulary, I argue that autism is an interactive kind and that individuals labeled autistic are fundamentally transformed by that labeling and the subsequent interventions that follow, thereby creating what Hacking describes as a looping effect. Thus, I argue that the processes of identifying, interpreting, remediating, and performing embodied differences are cultural and historically specific. Autism is not outside of the symbolic awaiting discovery, but inscribed and produced through the symbolic. Investigating these processes of inscription and production reveals current desires, anxieties, and opportunities for personhood in the twenty-first century.

NOTES

1. Although Bettelheim is typically held responsible for the idea that mothers cause their children's autism, the idea that mothers' behaviors lead to mental illness predates Bettelheim's work. Lauretta Bender suggests that Frieda Fromm-Reichmann's 1948 concept of the "schizophrenogenic mother" may have helped catalyze mother blaming (109–24). Popular renditions of objects relations theory promulgated by figures such as D. W. Winnicott held mothers responsible for their infants' successes or failures in achieving stable egos (see Nadesan, *Constructing* 95–102). However, the force and simplicity of Bettelheim's writing in *The Empty Fortress* led credence to his claims within a Zeitgeist willing to blame mothers for all manner of developmental irregularities.
2. See Rose and Armstrong for discussions of the emergence of developmental norms.
3. See Freund and McGuire's discussion of the Western medical model, 6–7.
4. Many people who today are diagnosed with high-functioning autism would likely have escaped diagnosis entirely in the early part of the twentieth century. In the mid-twentieth century, such high-functioning individuals might have been diagnosed with a personality disorder or regarded as sociopathic or psychopathic.
5. For example, *Wired* magazine's article, "The Geek Syndrome," written by Steve Silberman, speculates that some technologically "gifted" individuals may have Asperger's syndrome and that autism and Asperger's syndrome diagnoses are surging among the children of Silicon Valley (174–183). Silberman speculates that "math and tech genes" may be to blame (see also Nash and Bonesteel).
6. For an excellent discussion of the history of "dangerous" personalities see McCallum. For histories of mental illness see Trent, and Wright and Digby.
7. For discussion and evaluation of genetic discourses see works by Keller (both citations), Hedgecoe, Petersen and Bunton, Rabinow, and Ten Have. Bunton and Petersen's recent collection *Genetic Governance* is also an excellent resource.

WORKS CITED

Alecson, Deborah. *Alternative Treatments for Children within the Autistic Spectrum.* New York: McGraw-Hill, 1999.

Armstrong, David. *A New History of Identity.* Houndmills: Palgrave, 2002.

Asperger, Hans. "'Autistic Psychopathy' in Childhood." Trans. Uta Frith. *Autism and Asperger Syndrome.* Ed. Frith. Cambridge: Cambridge UP, 1991. 37–91.

———. "Problems of Infantile Autism." *Communication* 13 (1979): 45–52.

Bandler, James. "Children's Vaccines Raise Seizure Risk, Don't Cause Autism." *Wall Street Journal* 30 August 2001: B2.

Bender, Lauretta. "The Historical Background of the Concept of Childhood Schizophrenia." *The Concept of Schizophrenia: Historical Perspectives.* Ed. J. G. Howells. Washington, DC: American Psychiatric P, 1991.109–124.

Berrios, Germane E. *The History of Mental Symptoms: Descriptive Psychopathology Since the Nineteenth Century.* Cambridge: Cambridge UP, 1996.

Berrios, Germane E., and Roy Porter, eds. *A History of Clinical Psychiatry: The Origin and History of Psychiatric Disorders.* London: Athlone, 1995.

Bettelheim, Bruno. *The Empty Fortress: Infantile Autism and the Birth of the Self.* New York: Free P, 1967.

Bleuler, Eugen. "Dementia Praecox Oder Gruppe der Schizophrenien." *Handbuch der Psychiatrie. Spezieller Teil. 4 Abteilung. 1. Halfte.* Ed. G. Aschaffenburg. Leipzig: Franz Deuticke, 1911. 1–420.

———. "Die Prognose der Dementia Praecox (Schizophreniegruppe)." *Allgemeine Zeitschrift fur Psychiatrie und Psychisch-Gerichtliche Medizin* 65 (1908): 436–464.

Braddock, David, and Susan Parish. "An Institutional History of Disability." *Handbook of Disability Studies.* Ed. Gary L. Albrecht, Katherine D. Seelman, and Michael Bury. Thousands Oaks, CA: Sage, 2001. 11–68.

Bruer, John T. "Brain Science, Brain Fiction." *Educational Leadership* 56. 3 (1998): 14–18.

———. "In Search of Brain-Based Education." *Phi-Delta Kappan* 80. 9 (1999): 649–657.

Bunton, Robin, and Alan A. Petersen. *Genetic Governance: Health, Risk and Ethics in the Biotech Era.* New York: Routledge, 2005.

"California: $34 Million Allocated for Autism Spectrum Disorders Research." *Autism Research Review* 14.2 (2000): 1.

Chapman, Gary. "The Cutting Edge: Focus on Technology; Digital Nation: Even If 'Geekiness' is a Disorder, There's No Rush to Find a Cure." *Los Angeles Times* 27 September 1999: 1.

Cowley, Geoffrey. "Understanding Autism." *Newsweek* 31 July 2000: 46–54.

Darwin, Charles. "A Biographical Sketch of an Infant." *Mind* 2 (1877): 285–294.

"Drug Lawsuits Pursue Mercury Link to Autism." *The Arizona Republic* 3 October 2001: A4.

Ehrenreich, Barbara. *Fear of Falling: The Inner Life of the Middle Class.* New York: Pantheon, 1989.

"Evidence Mounts for Epidemic of Autism." *Autism Research Review* 14.2 (2000): 1.

Foucault, Michel. "Governmentality." *The Foucault Effect.* Ed. Graham Burchell, Colin Gordon, and Peter Miller. London: Harvester Wheatsheaf, 1991. 97–104.

———. *The History of Sexuality: An Introduction.* Vol 1. Trans. Robert Hurley. New York: Vintage, 1990.

———. *Madness and Civilization: A History of Insanity in the Age of Reason.* Trans. Richard Howard. New York: Vintage, 1988.

————. *Mental Illness and Psychology*. Trans. Alan Sheridan. Berkeley: U of California P, 1987.

Fox, Nicholas. *Beyond Health: Postmodernism and Embodiment*. London: Free Association, 1999.

Freud, Sigmund. *The Standard Edition: Five Lectures on Psychoanalysis, Leonardo da Vinci and Other Works* Vol. 11. 1910. London: Hogarth, 1957.

Freund, Peter E. S., and Meredith B. McGuire. *Health, Illness, and the Social Body: A Critical Sociology*. Englewood Cliffs, NJ: Prentice Hall, 1991.

Gardner, Martin. "The Brutality of Dr. Bettelheim." *Skeptical-Inquirer* 24.6 (2000): 12–14.

Hacking, Ian. *Mad Travelers*. Charlottesville: UP of Virginia, 1998.

————. *The Social Construction of What?* Cambridge, MA: Harvard UP, 1999.

Hedgecoe, Adam. "Schizophrenia and the Narrative of Enlightened Geneticization." *Social Studies of Science* 31.6 (2001): 875–911.

Houston, Rab and Uta Frith. *Autism in History: The Case of Hugh Blair of Borgue*. Padstow, Cornwall: Blackwell, 2000.

Jones, Kathleen W. *Taming the Troublesome Child: American Families, Child Guidance, and the Limits of Psychiatric Authority*. Cambridge, MA: Harvard UP, 1999.

Kanner, Leo. "Autistic Disturbances of Affective Contact."1943. *Classic Readings in Autism*. Ed. Anne M. Donnellan. New York: Columbia UP, 1985. 11–49.

————. and Leon Eisenberg. "Early Infantile Autism 1943–1955." *American Journal of Orthopsychiatry* 26 (1956): 55–65.

Keller, Evelyn F. *Refiguring Life: Metaphors of Twentieth-Century Biology*. New York: Columbia UP, 1995.

————. *The Century of the Gene*. Cambridge, MA: Harvard UP, 2000.

Klein, Melanie. "A Contribution to the Theory of Intellectual Inhibition." *Contributions to Psycho-Analysis 1921–1945 Melanie Klein*. Ed. Ernst Jones. 1931. London: Hogarth, 1950. 254–66.

————. "Notes on Some Schizoid Mechanisms." 1946. *Identity: A Reader*. Ed. Paul DuGay, Jessica Evans, and Peter Redman. London: Sage, 2000. 130–143.

Lippman, Abby. "Prenatal Genetic Testing and Screening." *American Journal of Law and Medicine* 1 (1991): 15–50.

Lemke, Thomas. "Disposition and Determinism—Genetic Diagnostics in Risk Society." *Sociological Review* 22.4 (2004): 550–566.

Martin, Emily. *Flexible Bodies: Tracking Immunity in American Culture—From the Days of Polio to the Age of Aids*. Boston: Beacon, 1994

————. "Flexible Bodies: Health and Work in an Age of Systems." *The Ecologist* 25.6 (1995): 221–226.

McCallum, David. *Personality and Dangerousness: Genealogies of Antisocial Personality Disorder*. Cambridge: Cambridge UP, 2001.

Morris, David B. *Illness and Culture in the Postmodern Age*. Berkeley: U of California P, 1998.

Morss, John R. *The Biologising of Childhood: Developmental Psychology and the Darwinian Myth*. Hove, UK: Lawrence Erlbaum Associates, 1990.

Mulgan, Geoff. "High Tech and High Angst." *The Age of Anxiety*. Ed. Sarah Dunant and Roy Porter. London: Virago, 1996. 1–20.

Nadesan, Majia Holmer. *Constructing Autism: Unraveling the "Truth" and Understanding the Social*. London: Routledge, 2005.

————. "Engineering the Entrepreneurial Infant: Brain Science, Infant Development Toys, and Governmentality." *Cultural Studies* 16 (2002): 401–432.

Nash, Madeleine J., and Amy Bonesteel. "The Geek Syndrome." *Time* 6 May 2002: 90–94.

Novas, Carlos, and Nikolas Rose. "Genetic Risk and the Birth of the Somatic Individual." *Economy and Society* 29.4 (2000): 485–513.

Petersen, Alan, and Robin Bunton. *The New Genetics and the Public's Health*. London: Routledge, 2002.

Petersen, Alan, and Deborah Lupton. *The New Public Health: Health and Self in the Age of Risk*. London: Sage, 1996.

Porter, Roy. *Madness: A Brief History*. Oxford: Oxford UP, 2002.

Rabinow, Paul. *French DNA: Trouble in Purgatory*. Chicago: U of Chicago P, 1999.

Rodier, Patricia M. "The Early Origins of Autism." *Scientific American* 282.2 (2000): 56–63.

Rose, Nikolas. *Governing the Soul: The Shaping of the Private Self*. 2nd ed. London: Routledge, 1999.

———. "The Politics of Life Itself." *Theory, Culture and Society* 18 (2001): 1–30.

Schneider, Kurt. *Die Psychopathischen Persoenlichkeiten* [The Psychopathic Personalities]. Leipzig: Thieme, 1923.

———. "Ueber die Grenzen der Psychologisierung. [The Limits of Psychologization]." *Ner venarzt* 24 (1953): 89–90.

"Science and Technology: Pointing the Finger." *Economist* 93. 24 March 2001. http://web.lexis-nexis.com.ezproxy1.lib.asu.edu/universaldocument?m=068758857ffb6d0.

Seroussi, Karyn. *Unraveling the Mystery of Autism and Pervasive Developmental Disorder: A Mother's Story of Research & Recovery*. New York: Broadway, 2002.

Silberman, Steve. "The Geek Syndrome." *Wired Magazine* 9.12 (2001): 174–183. http://www.wired.com/wired/archive/9.12/aspergers_pr.html.

Snyder, Jodie. "State Dollars Jump-Start Autism Research." *The Arizona Republic*. 25 July 2006: B1.

Ten Have, H. A.M.J. "Genetics and Culture: The Geneticization Thesis." *Medicine Health Care and Philosophy* 4 (2001): 295–304.

Trent, James W. *Inventing the Feeble Mind: A History of Mental Retardation in the United States*. Berkeley: U of California P, 1994.

Turner, Victor. *Dramas, Fields, and Metaphors: Symbolic Action in Human Society*. Ithaca: Cornell UP, 1974.

Veitia, Reiner A. "Stochasticity or the Fatal 'Imperfection' of Cloning." *Journal of Bioscience* 30.1 (2005): 21–30.

Wing, Lorna. "Asperger's Syndrome: A Clinical Account." *Psychological Medicine* 11 (1981):115–130.

Winnicott, D. W. "Mirror-Role of Mother and Family in Child Development."1967. *Identity: A Reader*. Ed. Paul DuGay, Jessica Evans, and Peter Redman. London: Sage, 2000. 144–149.

Wright, David and Anne Digby, eds. *From Idiocy to Mental Deficiency: Historical Perspectives on People with Learning Disabilities*. London: Routledge, 1996.

Part II
Autistry

4 Autism and Modernism
A Genealogical Exploration

Patrick McDonagh

In 1943 Leo Kanner published "Autistic Disturbances of Affective Contact," his groundbreaking article defining a new condition that he called autism. In 1944, unaware of Kanner's work, Hans Asperger published "Autistic Psychopathy in Childhood" ("Die 'Autistichen Psychopathen' im Kindesalter"), describing a very similar condition and also giving it the name autism. Uta Frith notes the "remarkable coincidence" that Kanner, working at the Johns Hopkins University in Baltimore, and Asperger, at the University Paediatric Clinic, Vienna, "independently described exactly the same type of disturbed child to whom nobody had paid much attention before and both used the label autistic" (*Autism and Asperger* 6). Although the conditions they describe are at some points distinct, Kanner and Asperger are generally accepted as having traveled the same road: Asperger's syndrome is now a subcategory of autism, afforded a place at the "higher functioning" end of what Lorna Wing designates the "autistic continuum" (111). Asperger himself, writing in 1979, commented on the "astonishing similarities within these two groups which accounted for the same choice of name" (qtd. in Wing 98).

It is striking that independent researchers should simultaneously identify a hitherto unrecognized psychopathology and assign it a diagnostic category with the same name. If people with autism, or at least common autistic characteristics, had existed previously, as presumably they had, why had it taken so long to recognize them as sharing a particular condition? What confluence of events and ideas created the circumstances that allowed Kanner (1894–1981) and Asperger (1906–1980) to see certain children as belonging to a particular type, when those before them had not?

Autism, Frith claims, did indeed exist before the 1940s. In *Autism in History*, cowritten with social historian Rab Houston, she describes the case of Hugh Blair, "cognosced" as a "natural fool" in 1747. Using extensive statements by witnesses from the case of Blair vs Blair (as Hugh's capacity was called into question by his younger brother), she builds a case that Hugh was in fact autistic. She also argues that Jean Itard's famous subject, Victor, the "wild boy of Aveyron," displays features of an autistic child and concludes, with some confidence, that "the evidence . . . allows us to assume that Victor was autistic" (*Autism* 26). And she cites reports of an individual with autistic-like qualities admitted to London's Bethlehem Hospital in 1799, noting that "the boy never engaged in play with other children or became attached to them, but played in an absorbed, isolated way with toy soldiers," and that this case has "often been quoted and never contested, as early evidence of Autism" (*Autism* 16). Recently, Michael Fitzgerald has retroactively diagnosed a number of historical figures—among them Mozart, Beethoven, Melville and Yeats—as having had Asperger's syndrome. In the literary realm, Thelma Grove has argued that Charles Dickens's character Barnaby Rudge, from the 1841 novel of the same name, is the first autistic hero in English literature (evidence of Dickens's fine skills of observation), and Frith has offered the fictional detective Sherlock Holmes as a possible case study in autism (*Autism* 43). However, we must take such historical and literary assessments with hefty servings of salt; as Richard Ellmann has observed, "posthumous diagnosis by biographers [is] as hazardous as diagnosis by doctors when the patient is alive" (11). Early autism sightings, alluring as they may be, should prompt us to ask why these apparently autistic individuals were not identified in their own time as having a specific condition distinct from "idiocy," at one end of the autistic spectrum, or mere "eccentricity" at the other.

My resistance to reading historical figures or literary characters as autistic or aspergian is based on one of the fundamental precepts of this paper: that autism, even should it turn out to be a single pathology with an organic cause and thus "real," is also perceived within a social dynamic, and our recognition and understanding of autism takes form within this dynamic. If the social circumstances allowing us to perceive autism did not exist before some point relatively early in the twentieth century, and if the perception and articulation of autism is an important part of its being, then to what extent can we say the condition existed previously? Certainly the organic foundation of autism is most likely continuous (although some argue for organic causes linked to recent environmental conditions), but without the social dynamic, can this organic component alone actually represent autism as we understand the term? In *The Social Construction of What?*, Ian Hacking suggests that autism as a condition may be both "indifferent"—that is, existing as a real thing, whether or not we recognize it—and "interactive," engaged in a dynamic relation with the social world, and understood and altered through this interaction (117–22). The biological component of autism, the "indifferent" element, may have a long history upon which biomedical and neurological research might one day shed some light, but autism as a diagnostic category has also, since its creation, been engaged in a dynamic social exchange that is as crucial as its indifferent element. Thus, although a pre-twentieth-century autism is possible in terms of simple pathology, it seems to be something of a conceptual anachronism.

Autism makes most sense if we consider it as something other than a diagnostic category, a mere act of nosology. Majia Holmer Nadesan has offered an extensive account of issues at play in what she defines as the social construction of autism; in the concept's earlier articulations, these include the growth of psychiatry and psychological discourses and the development of the idea of childhood. Priscilla Alderson and Christopher Goodey, in an article on autism and inclusion, note in passing the possible role played by sociopolitical factors, including the Second World War, in creating a theme of exclusion in the lives of both Kanner and Asperger, and suggest that this sensitivity to exclusion may have influenced their perception of autistic aloneness, although they do not explore this notion in detail (notably, Bruno Bettelheim, in his introduction to *The Empty Fortress*, is explicit about how he translated his experience as a prisoner in a German concentration camp into his theory that autism is an extreme withdrawal from an intolerably hostile environment).

I would like to propose another overlooked factor: the growth of modernism and modernist ideas of the self. A link between modernism and autism has been hinted at previously by Marion Glastonbury, who explores what she calls the "autistic dynamic of certain works of art" (39), noting especially the works of Ludwig Wittgenstein, Franz Kafka, Samuel Beckett and Georges Perec. In her analysis, these authors—whom she diagnoses as autistic—are responsible for artistic, intellectual and significantly autistic contributions to our understanding of identity. "[T]he house of Art has many mansions; as many, one might suppose, as there are energetic recesses in the human brain," she writes. "It follows that there is scope, within the multiplicity of twentieth-century culture, for forms of art that are monologic, devoid of intersubjective richness; works that may be said to be *about* barrenness, reflecting and projecting a single stance, an unremitting mood: the minimalist sigh of an attenuated self" (39; italics in the original). Though I am wary of diagnosing the dead, her notion of an "autistic dynamic" is compelling—as is her observation that this art flourishes in the "multiplicity of twentieth-century culture." Was Beckett writing as a modernist or an autist? My inclination is toward the former, given the impossibility of actual diagnosis. But as I argue, modernity and modernism made possible the recognition of autism, and would have also created a space for Glastonbury's "autistic dynamic" in artistic expression.

Aesthetic modernism grew in parallel with psychology, psychiatry and psychoanalysis, writes Mark Micale, who observes that "on the eve of the emergence of modern dynamic psychiatry, physicians were as influenced by cultural representations and popular stereotypes as novelists were knowledgeable about the findings of medical science" (4). And as Judith Ryan has shown, empiricist psychology and literature experienced an "extraordinary symbiosis" in the first decades of the twentieth century, especially in the cultural hothouses of Vienna and Prague (22). There are strong parallels between these modernist notions of identity and those emerging in Kanner's and Asperger's descriptions of autism, suggesting that the capacity to perceive autism in the 1940s may be connected to the proliferation of modern, and modernist, notions of the self, which were given shape in the literary works of the era. To support this hypothesis, I look first at the history of autism, and then at the relation between autism and aesthetic modernism, with a glance over some literary case studies.

THE CREATION OF AUTISM

Eugen Bleuler coined the term *autism* in his 1911 work *Dementia Praecox*, using it to describe "the most severe schizophrenics . . . [who] live in a world of their own" (63). In a monograph published the following year, *The Theory of Schizophrenic Negativism*, he writes that "autistic schizophrenics" have "turned away from reality; they have retired into a dream life, or at least the essential part of their dissociated ego lives in a world of subjective ideas and wishes, so that to them reality can bring only interruptions" (20). However, Bleuler clearly represents autism as characteristic of certain types of schizophrenia (another of his coinages), and, although there are similarities to the Kannerian and Aspergian applications of the term, his diagnostic criteria do not match what they defined as autism. The concept continued to circulate throughout the 1920s and 1930s, although without affixing itself strongly to any distinct condition but rather remaining a subspecies of schizophrenia.

"As the meanings of autism proliferated it became increasingly possible to discuss the presence of autistic thinking in individuals who did not evidence the delusions and hallucinations of psychoses," writes Nadesan. "Autism was a phrase with wide currency and applicability, particularly in the German psychiatry with which both Kanner and Asperger were familiar" (40). In his 1943 "Co-editor's Introduction" to *Nervous Child 2*, the journal in which his article appears, Kanner cites the German/Austrian psychotherapeutic heritage of Sigmund Freud, Carl Jung, Alfred Adler, Ernst Kretschmer, Adolf Meyer, and others—although not Bleuler. Asperger's conclusion also includes a reference to a professional lineage, including Kretschmer, Jung and Erich Jaensch. And as Hacking has noted, both were educated in the ideas of August Homburger, a specialist in childhood schizophrenia and developmental disorders ("What is Tom" 3, 6). Both writers, then, shared roots in the vibrant world of Austrian and German psychology of the early twentieth century. Certainly the influence of psychodynamic theories of the mind, identity and relationships are evident throughout the writing of Kanner and Asperger, as close readings of their articles demonstrate.

Kanner and Asperger share biographical as well as professional similarities. Both were Austrian, with Kanner coming from a Galician Jewish background. Kanner moved with his family to Berlin in 1906, when he was twelve, served in the Austro-Hungarian army in the First World War, and later returned to Berlin for his training as a physician and specialist in the new field of electrocardiography. While a student in Berlin, he also reveled in the city's cultural vitality, writing poetry and actively participating in its artistic community (Neumärker 215). He left in 1924, driven by the poor economic situation to the United States, eventually settling at Johns Hopkins University. Of Asperger's biography, less information is readily available. He was born and died in Vienna and traveled little in between, working at that city's University Paediatric Clinic beginning in 1932, a year after receiving his doctorate. We also know he was an introverted child—and later considered himself an "introverted" adult (in the Jungian sense)—who showed early precocity in language and would quote the nineteenth-century Austrian poet Franz Grillparzer to his elementary school classmates.

Given their shared roots in German and Austrian psychodynamic research, then, it is not quite so astonishing that Kanner and Asperger would both appropriate the term "autism" for their own uses (although it remains unusual that their uses would be so similar). Perhaps the term was current enough that Kanner did not even feel the need to refer to Bleuler at all when he adopted it, although Asperger did, admiring Bleuler's contribution in writing that "The name 'autism' . . . is undoubtedly one of the great linguistic and conceptual creations in medical nomenclature" (38).

Despite its linguistic brilliance, for years Bleuler's coinage remained without a clear referent, a vague signifier condemned to a free-floating existence. All of this changed, though, in 1943, when Leo Kanner applied the term to the case subjects—eight boys and three girls—with whom he had been working since 1938. "The outstanding, 'pathognomic,' fundamental disorder is the children's *inability to relate themselves* in the ordinary way to people and situations from the beginning of life," he writes (242; italics in the original). An "*extreme autistic aloneness*" (242; italics his) defines their lives from the start; a "profound aloneness dominates all their behavior," he notes, going on to observe that the children also bear "strikingly intelligent physiognomies" and, when alone, may even assume "an expression of beatitude" (247). Kanner writes that his subjects could often speak at an apparently advanced level, usually being "capable of clear articulation and phonation"; however, language was not used for the purposes of communication but "was deflected in a considerable measure to a self-sufficient, semantically or conversationally valueless or grossly distorted memory exercise" (243). For instance, Kanner's first case history describes a boy, Donald, as taking

> much pleasure in ejaculating words or phrases, such as "Chrysanthemum"; "Dahlia, dahlia, dahlia"; "Business"; "Trumpet vine"; "The right one is on, the left one is off"; "Through the dark clouds shining." Irrelevant utterances such as these were his ordinary mode of speech. He often seemed to be parroting what he had heard said to him at one time or another. (219)

Later in the same case history, Kanner describes Donald's father trying to teach his son the meanings of "yes" and "no," asking the boy, "Do you want me to put you on my shoulder?"

> Don expressed his agreement by repeating the question literally, echo-lalia-like. His father said, "If you want me to, say 'Yes'; but if you don't want me to, say 'No.'"

> Don said "yes" when asked. But thereafter "yes" came to mean that he desired to be put up on his father's shoulder. (220)

In the case of Paul G., Kanner recounts how the boy

> cut a sheet of paper into small bits, singing the phrase "cutting pa-per," many times. He helped himself to a toy engine, ran around the room holding it up high and singing over and over again, "The engine is flying." While these utterances, made always with the same inflec-tion, were clearly connected with his actions, he ejaculated others that could not be linked up with immediate situations. These are a few ex-amples: "The people in the hotel"; "Did you hurt your leg?"; "Candy is all gone, candy is empty"; "You'll fall off the bicycle and bump your head." However, some of those exclamations could be definitely traced to previous experiences. He was in the habit of saying almost every day, "Don't throw the dog off the balcony." His mother recalled that she had said those words to him about a toy dog while they were still in England. (227)

Kanner concludes that "None of these remarks was meant to have commu-nicative value" (227).

All the children in his survey come from "highly intelligent parents," he writes, noting that "All but three of the families are represented either in *Who's Who in America* or in *American Men of Science*" (249). Perhaps more significantly, he notes, out of this group "there are very few really warm-hearted fathers and mothers" (250). The parents, like their children, are also "strongly preoccupied with abstractions" and "limited in genuine interest in people" (250). Kanner concludes that "these children have come into the world with innate inability to form the usual, biologically provided affective contact with people, just as other children come into the world with innate physical or intellectual handicaps. . . . [H]ere we seem to have pure-culture examples of *inborn autistic disturbances of affective contact*" (250; italics in the original).

In this first description of autism we hit several themes that will rever-berate in writings over the years. Kanner identifies autism as "inborn," an assertion that remains dominant, although the exact nature of this inborn quality remains unknown. He also notes the intelligent but emotionally cold parents—which can be seen as grist for the geneticist argument, but also was developed by Bettelheim into his environmentalist "refrigerator mothers" theory of autism (the term, of course, was Kanner's originally). He stresses the noncommunicative, idiosyncratic, almost experimental uses of language. And, most of all, he foregrounds the children's "profound aloneness."

In Asperger's notion of autism, the autistic person is, again, characterized by isolation. "The autist is only himself," he writes, "and not an active member of a greater organism which he is influenced by and which he influences constantly" (38); people with autism are, rather, "intelligent automata" (58). This intelligence has restrictions, however. "Autistic children *are* able to produce original ideas. Indeed, they can *only* be original, and mechanical learning is hard for them. They are simply not set to assimilate and learn an adult's knowledge" (70; italics in the original). Asperger then identifies autistic language as being especially representative of autistic intelligence. "[Autistic children], and especially the intellectually gifted among them, undoubtedly have a special creative attitude towards language. They are able to express their own original experience in a linguistically original form. This is seen in the choice of unusual words which one would suppose to be totally outside the sphere of these children" (70–71). Asperger cites an eleven-year-old boy whose language was especially rich and idiosyncratic as uttering such phrases as "I can't do this orally, only headily," "My sleep today was long but thin," "To an art-eye, these pictures might be nice, but I don't like them," and "I don't like the blinding sun, nor the dark, but best I like the mottled shadow" (71).

Asperger concludes that "Behind the originality of language formations stands the originality of experience. Autistic children have the ability to see things and events around them from a new point of view, which often shows surprising maturity. The problems that these children think about are usually far beyond the interests of other children of the same age" (71). Autism here is shaped as a radical interpretation of personal experience, a form of hyperindividuality that cannot be shared.

Another of Asperger's striking observations is his description of autistic children as "egocentric in the extreme. They follow only their own wishes, interests and spontaneous impulses, without considering restrictions or prescriptions imposed from outside" (81). He also writes, anticipating later work by Simon Baron-Cohen, that

> The autistic personality is an extreme variant of male intelligence. . . . Boys . . . tend to have a gift for logical ability, abstraction, precise thinking and formulating, and for independent scientific observation. . . . In the autistic individual abstraction is so highly developed that the relationship to the concrete, to objects and to people, has largely been lost, and as a result the instinctual aspects of adaptation are heavily reduced. (84–5)

Kanner and Asperger describe conditions that appear markedly similar, and I have stressed these similarities in recounting them here. Both agree that the children in their respective studies are characterized by "striking," perhaps even "inevitable," affinities. Asperger writes that "those who know such children never cease to be surprised at the striking coincidences of detail" (67), and Kanner writes that "even a quick review of the [case] material makes the emergence of a number of essential common characteristics appear inevitable. These characteristics form a unique 'syndrome,' not heretofore reported" (242).

But—to return to my original question—if the coincidences of detail are so striking, if the common characteristics are essential and inevitable, where were these children before 1943? As Kanner hypothesizes, "It is quite possible that some such children have been viewed as feebleminded or schizophrenic. In fact, several children of our group were introduced to us as idiots or imbeciles, one still resides in a state school for the feebleminded, and two had been previously considered as schizophrenic" (242); he repeats later that "most of these children were one time or another looked upon as feebleminded" (247). Asperger draws the same conclusion. Observing a wild variance on the intelligence test scores of individual children depending on who was doing the testing, he notes that "Clearly, it is possible to consider such individuals as both child prodigies and as imbeciles with ample justification" (46). Asperger writes also that "autism occurs at different levels of ability," noting that "there is a smooth transition further along the range to those mentally retarded people who show highly stereotyped automaton-like behavior" (75).

But, this gradient notwithstanding, why, if these individuals shared striking characteristics, had they not been previously identified as common to a particular condition? After all, it is not as if the superintendents of institutions for "idiots" and the "feeble-minded" were oblivious to the physiological and psychological taxonomies that could be created out of the asylum's residents. As early as 1861, P. Martin Duncan had identified six forms of idiocy, along with accessory cases—a typology he expanded further in collaboration with William Millard. In 1866 John Langdon Down discerned five "ethnic types of idiots" (the Caucasian, the Ethiopian, the Malay, the North American Indian and the Mongolian), conditions he hypothesized were caused by phylogenetic recapitulation, among the population of the National Institute for Idiots in the United Kingdom. In 1872 William Ireland came up with ten different categories of "idiocy," among them hydrocephalic idiocy, epileptic idiocy, traumatic idiocy, congenital idiocy, and idiocy by deprivation. And these physicians were hardly alone in their endeavors: asylum supervisors were constantly on the lookout for new ways of conceptualizing their charges, and new divisions and categories were continually being proposed, based on criteria ranging from physical appearances to apparent causes of mental deficiency to an individual's level of educability. Clearly, there was no lack of professional interest in the different ways of seeing mental deviance; yet the closest we come to anything resembling autism is in the rogue category of the "idiot savant," referring to someone who has apparently diminished skills, yet certain areas of unusual capacity, and even these individuals are understood in a manner clearly very different from those children described in Kanner's and Asperger's papers. For some reason, autism was invisible in the nineteenth century, despite the existence of physical resources—the asylums that gathered together the necessary sample population—that would have made further classification possible. So what had changed between 1900 and 1940?

MODERN IDENTITIES AND AUTISTIC IDENTITIES

"[I]n or about December, 1910, human character changed. I'm not saying that one went out, as one might into a garden, and there saw that a rose had flowered, or a hen had laid an egg. The change was not sudden and definite like that. But a change there was, nevertheless; and since one must be arbitrary, let us date it about the year 1910," writes Virginia Woolf in the essay "Mr. Bennett and Mrs. Brown" (320). The evidence is everywhere, she observes: in religion, conduct, politics, and literature; indeed, in all human relations. Whether or not Woolf's date holds up to historical analysis (and she does concede its arbitrariness), there is plenty to suggest that the concept of identity and relations between people were indeed in flux, thanks both to dramatic changes in social structure and to historical events. Tim Armstrong, writing about modernism in the United Kingdom, notes that any Englishman falling asleep in 1900 and, Rip Van Winkle-like, not rising for twenty or thirty years would confront an unrecognizable landscape:

> he would have missed the war; the Liberal reforms culminating in the National Insurance Act of 1911; the rise of the Labour Party; the enfranchisement of women; the Russian Revolution; the re-arrangement of Europe and the establishment of the League of Nations. And more: Einstein's demolition of the Newtonian world-view; the aeroplane, cinema, television; the *Titanic*. (*Modernism, a Cultural History* 1)

Revolutions were occurring: in science and technology, in demographics and politics, in art and philosophy.

These revolutions characterize modernity, especially in the twentieth century. Modernity, argues Anthony Giddens, is best understood as a juggernaut, a "runaway engine of enormous power which, collectively as human beings, we can drive to some extent but which also threatens to rush out of our control and which could rend itself asunder" (139). Thanks to the inherent dangers of riding this juggernaut, "we shall never be able to feel entirely secure. . . . Feelings of ontological security and existential anxiety will coexist in ambivalence" (139). Singling out the "late modernity" of the twentieth century (growing from a process lasting four centuries), Giddens stresses the "discontinuities which separate modern social institutions from traditional social orders" (6), such as the pace and scope of change. He develops a psycho-philosophical explanation of what he calls "ontological security," referring to "the confidence that most humans beings have in the continuity of their self-identity and in the constancy of the surrounding social and material environments of action" (92). However, the discontinuities of the modern world threaten this security, displacing it with a sense of existential anxiety, which is characterized in part by a sense of isolation from other people (Giddens uses the phrase "polite estrangement" [81] to describe modern relations). Thus, similar processes occur at the communal and the individual levels: the breakdown of routines and traditions creates broad social and cultural insecurity that forms a societal analogue to personal angst. Increasingly, alienation and displacement become the norm.

These processes of late modernity create new possibilities (and indeed impose new demands) on the construction of identity. Armstrong argues that modernism embraces the scientific and technological revolutions of the nineteenth and early twentieth centuries, using knowledge and craft to reform and restructure identity, especially as the self becomes more open to analysis and alteration. "Modernism," he writes, "is characterized by the desire to intervene in the body; to render it part of modernity by techniques which may be biological, mechanical, or behavioral" (*Modernism, Technology* 6)—a desire manifested in psychological and psychiatric techniques, as well as in the diagnosis and treatment of new psychological conditions. Significantly, this process places a profound emphasis on the individual subject.

Although science and technology are central to modernity, aesthetic modernism has also been critical in articulating cultural perceptions of the modern identity. In his landmark study of aesthetic modernism, Michael Levenson foregrounds the importance of the intense subjectivism central to identity in much literature, tracking its literary roots to Max Stirner's 1844 work *Der Einzige und sein Eigentum* (translated as *The Ego and His Own*). Stirner writes: "I am unique. Hence my wants too are unique, and my deeds; in short, everything about me is unique. And it is only as this unique I that I take everything for my own, as I set myself to work, and develop myself, only as this. I do not develop man, nor as man, but, as I, I develop—myself" (qtd. in Levenson 64). This "early and extreme statement of philosophic egoism" (Levenson 64) enjoyed a brief success, lapsed into obscurity—possibly, Levenson suggests, because of the distracting political storms of 1848—and was reborn into a more welcoming climate at the turn of the century; between 1900 and 1929 the work appeared in 49 editions, and this "Stirner revival" also inspired the biweekly journal the *New Freewoman*, a vanguard of English modernism launched by Dora Marsden in June 1913 (Levenson 66). By January 1914, the *New Freewoman* had been rechristened *The Egoist*, and it became one of the most important vehicles for getting out the modernist word, publishing works by James Joyce, H.D., Ezra Pound, and T. S. Eliot, among others.

These writers also share an interest in the idiosyncratic use of language that is often reminiscent of the language structures identified by Kanner and Asperger as characteristic of autistic children. In Joyce's *A Portrait of the Artist as a Young Man*, for instance, the author signals his interest in the capacities of modern language in the opening lines: "Once upon a time and a very good time it was there was a moocow coming down along the road and this moocow that was coming down along the road met a nicens little boy named baby tuckoo" (7). The repetition and the use of baby talk immediately introduce the notion of language as both individual and communal—the tone is immediately recognizable as that of an adult talking to a child, but at the same time the actual words are unique in the literary corpus. Joyce was arguably the most influential of modernist novelists, and one can dip into his works at random to find examples of linguistic experimentation that many readers might have found distinctly noncommunicative, such as the analysis of Leopold Bloom's "meditations" with which he "accompan[ied] his demonstration to his companion of various constellations":

> Meditations of evolution increasingly vaster: of the moon invisible in incipient lunation, approaching perigree: of the infinite lattiginous scintillating uncondensed milky way, discernible by daylight by an observer placed at the lower end of a cylindrical vertical shaft 5000 ft deep sunk from the surface towards the centre of the earth: of Sirius (alpha in Canis Major)10 lightyears (57,000,000,000,000 miles) distant and in volume 900 times the dimension of our planet: of Arcturus: of the procession of equinoxes: of Orion with belt and sextuple sun theta and nebula in which 100 of our solar systems could be contained: of moribund and of nascent new stars such as Nova in 1901. . . . (*Ulysses* 819)

And so forth. The language is both florid and precise, but passes dramatically beyond simple communication.

Of course, Joyce is hardly alone in his experimentation. Consider, for instance, this passage from Gertrude Stein's *The Making of Americans* (1930), in which the narrator ponders the nature of anxiety:

> As I was saying there are many ways of having anxious feeling in them in men and women. Anxious feeling in some is almost the whole living that they have in them, some have the anxious feeling every minute of their living every minute is a whole to them with an anxious feeling which each minute ends them. Some have very much anxious feeling in them but not every minute in their living, with some of such of them anxious feeling never makes an end to them, it goes on repeating in them but it does not ever to them make an end of them. (193)

Stein's narrator continues to write anxiously about anxiety, repeating or developing slight variants of sentence structures, and obscuring the referent of the pronoun "them." The result is a highly individualized description, a passage that defines its own idiosyncratic logic while enacting its obsession with anxiety. Intriguingly, as a researcher in the late 1890s at the Harvard Psychological Laboratory, Stein had written at least two important articles on automatic writing, and although, as Armstrong argues, her writing itself is not "automatic," the "conceptual framework" provided by this research may "validate Stein's textual production" (*Modernism, Technology* 200).

The modernist text thus articulated a highly subjective response to the surrounding world. Such a position also implied that reality was provisional at best, that the meaning one could perceive in the external world was little more than a wishful fabrication. The modern individual was thus divided: a being capable of expressing particular articulations of identity, and engaging with the world as an independent actor; and at the same time an isolated being compelled to abandon the notion of a shared reality. Hypotheses on the nature of reality have since been explored in countless phenomenological and existential writings.

Thus the stage was being set. The opening decades of the twentieth century saw the growth of a sociocultural environment in which a condition like autism could seem possible. Aesthetic modernism articulated the complexities of the modern identity, and in so doing enabled physicians to perceive that new form of being, the autistic person, defined by an extreme aloneness, apparent egoism, and an idiosyncratic use of language.

THE MODERN PROTAGONIST

Asperger's description of autistic subjects being "egocentric in the extreme" and "follow[ing] only their own wishes, interests and spontaneous impulses, without considering restrictions or prescriptions imposed from outside" (81) could apply to the protagonist of many a novel from the first decades of the century—so let us consider a few literary case histories. By the 1920s, egoism was becoming a common character trait in literature, as writers experimented with variations on the themes of identity and isolation. In a Stirneresque paean to the individual subject, D.H. Lawrence observed that "Insofar as I am I, and only I am I, and I am only I, insofar as I am inevitably and eternally alone, it is my last blessedness to know it, and to accept it, and to live with this as the core of my self-knowledge" (qtd. in Howe 34–35). This subjectivism inevitably demands an understanding of the subject as occupying an isolated and even defensive position. When James Joyce's Stephen Dedalus, in *A Portrait of the Artist as a Young Man*, plans his future, he imagines securing his integrity as an individual and an artist by "using for my defence the only arms I allow myself to use—silence, exile, and cunning" (247). And in Jean-Paul Sartre's 1944 play *Huis clos*, dramatizing themes treated by the author in earlier literary and philosophical writings, the character Garcin observes famously that "l'enfer, c'est les Autres" (92)—that is, "hell is other people." Indeed, as the familiarity of the Joyce and Sartre quotations suggests, one does not have to search very hard to find egoist assertions. They were almost clichés among modernist writers, entering the cultural consciousness so effectively because they spoke to pervasive concerns over social and individual identity.

Modernist writers also explored the loss of faith in the value of social convention and the uncertain relation of the individual to external reality. The Austrian writer Robert Musil's three-volume *Man Without Qualities* features as its protagonist Ulrich, a mathematician struggling to understand his life. When we first meet him in Volume One (1930), Ulrich is standing before his window, trying to calculate the energy and forces involved in observing the activity on the street outside. "'It doesn't matter what one does,' the Man Without Qualities said to himself, shrugging his shoulders. 'In a tangle of forces like this, it doesn't make a scrap of difference.' He turned away like a man who had learned renunciation, almost indeed like a sick man who shrinks from any intensity of contact" (8). The narrator then poses the question, "since the possession of qualities presupposes that one must take a certain pleasure in their reality, all this gives us a glimpse of how it may all of a sudden happen to someone who cannot summon up any sense of reality—even in relation to himself—that one day he appears to himself as a man without qualities" (14). Musil's Ulrich, like the young patients of Kanner and Asperger, shrinks from contact with the external world and, retreating into himself, risks disappearing.

Modernist novels almost inevitably wrestled with questions of who we are and how we manage to communicate with others. Daniel Albright, writing on the novels of Virginia Woolf, refers to their pervasive "agony of identity" (96) as Woolf attempts, in *Mrs. Dalloway*, to develop a theory of personality that is distinct from the "repulsive" (101), "remorseless" (107) Human Nature, "[the] brute with the red nostrils . . . snuffing into every secret place" (161), that characterizes the established and oppressive expectations of the human as represented by the rational physicians Holmes and Bradshaw.

Mrs. Dalloway spans one day in which Clarissa Dalloway prepares for her evening party and Septimus Warren Smith rushes toward his death. Party preparations also include the process of composing oneself—that is, creating a public version of one's self. Woolf describes Clarissa Dalloway unselfconsciously preparing her public identity before the mirror.

> How many million times she had seen her face, and always with the same imperceptible contraction! She pursed her lips when she looked in the glass. It was to give her face point. That was her self—pointed; dart-like; definite. That was her self when some effort, some call on her to be her self, drew the parts together, she alone knew how different, how

> incompatible and composed so for the world only into one centre, one
> diamond, one woman who sat in her drawing room. . . . (40)

And if oneself is unknowable, others are even more so. Peter Walsh recalls
Clarissa's youthful speculations on communication and identity: "Clarissa
had a theory . . . to explain the feeling they had of dissatisfaction; not knowing people; not being known. For how could they know each other?" (167).
Such isolation is part of the state of being human in *Mrs. Dalloway*, but it
reaches its extreme expression in the subplot of Septimus Warren Smith, a
veteran of the Great War. When his beloved friend Evans is killed in battle,
Smith, "far from showing any emotion or recognising that here was the end
of a friendship, congratulated himself on feeling very little and very reasonably. The War had taught him" (94–95); he then becomes engaged to marry,
"when the panic was on him—that he could not feel" (95). But Smith's withdrawal is present to a lesser degree in other characters: Richard Dalloway,
who wants to tell his wife he loves her but can only articulate it by giving
flowers (130); Peter Walsh, who confesses that he does not know what he
feels, and thus cannot state it (210).

At the end of the novel, on hearing from Sir William Bradshaw of Smith's
suicide, Clarissa experiences a sensation of profound empathy unusual in
the world of this novel. "Death was defiance," she thinks. "Death was an
attempt to communicate; people feeling the impossibility of reaching the
centre which, mystically, evaded them; closeness drew apart; rapture faded,
one was alone. There was an embrace in death" (202). Suicide, a willed end
rather than a passive acceptance of mortality, becomes a form of communication, of self-expression. It is a profoundly solitary, internal expression, of
course: not an extended dialogue, but certainly a statement. In Woolf's ren-
dition, the modern individual, though longing for closeness and communication, becomes resigned to acknowledging the inadequacy of any attempts
to fulfill these desires.

Let us consider one last case history. In a 1943 article, Jean-Paul Sartre
provides an interesting interpretation of early reader responses to Meursault,
the protagonist of Albert Camus's 1942 novel *L'Etranger* (translated as both
The Outsider, and, in United States, *The Stranger*): "'He's a poor fool, an
idiot,' some people said; others, with greater insight, said, 'He's innocent.'
The meaning of this innocence remains to be understood" ("Camus" 26).
Sartre then explains this innocence as an expression of the logical absurdity of existence, noting that "[t]he 'absurd' man is the man who does not
hesitate to draw the inevitable conclusions from a fundamental absurdity"
(27). The novel itself takes what Camus calls the "benign indifference of the
universe" (154) and incorporates it in Meursault. On trial for shooting an
Arab, Meursault tells his lawyer, "I'd rather lost the habit of noting my feelings" (80), and, thinking over allegations that he experienced no regret for
his actions, concludes, "I have never been able to really regret anything in

all my life. I've always been far too much absorbed in the present moment, or the immediate future, to think back" (127). As Sartre writes, "the absurd . . . resides neither in man nor in the world, if you consider each separately. But since man's dominant characteristic is 'being-in-the-world,' the absurd is, in the end, an inseparable part of the human condition" ("Camus" 28). Sartre's commentary stresses what is ostensibly universal in Camus's character. If one were to indulge in a piece of reductive literary criticism, Meursault could be said to "lack harmony between affect and intellect"—but the diagnosis here is not from one of Camus's readers, but rather from Hans Asperger describing his patients (79).

AUTISM IMAGERY

As Glastonbury has noted, the twentieth century found room for an "autistic dynamic" in art, and I suggest that this opening of aesthetic space also contributed to the recognition of the condition. Modernism created a new perceptual framework, one in which it would be possible for Kanner and Asperger to understand their patients—and the idea of autistic alienation, a "profound aloneness"—in a manner unimagined by their predecessors. The children who would have seemed to be part of a largely homogenous group of "idiot" children fifty years earlier assumed new features for Kanner and Asperger, features their predecessors could not have recognized. Autism appeared as a diagnostic category when its primary qualities—isolation and alienation, the need to establish personal rituals to impose order on the world, the removal of referential and conventionally communicative functions from language—also appeared as critical components of the modern (and modernist) identity.

The stars presiding over autism's birth play an important role in how it continues to be represented in popular culture. Freud, writing of the "uncanny effect of epilepsy and of madness," suggests that "the layman sees in them the working of forces hitherto unsuspected in his fellow-men, but at the same time he is dimly aware of them in remote corners of his own being" (366). Similarly, Leslie Fiedler argues that "freaks" are expressions of a "secret self," evoking an "aboriginal shudder" in onlookers (17). Fiedler's ideal freak "challenges the conventional boundaries between . . . self and other" (24). If Freud and Fiedler are correct, could not autism be, in part at any rate, an expression of our secret (and very modern) fear of and fascination with isolation, alienation and disintegration? Cultural representations, especially the profoundly influential film *Rain Man* and, more recently, Mark Haddon's *The Curious Incident of the Dog in the Night-Time*, but also a host of other texts, have been critical in planting autism in the public mind. There is also a ready market for the growing body of autobiographies by autistic writers, who have taken a prominent role in defining the condition.

Donna Williams, whose memoir *Nobody Nowhere* placed her among the first of the now-swelling ranks of autistic autobiographers, describes autism as an "emotional disability," hypothesizing that autism involves an

> inability to comprehend closeness [which] constrains the formation of attachments and inhibits attempts to make sense of one's environment in infancy. Without this, perhaps the child creates within itself what it perceives as missing and in effect becomes a world within itself to which all else is simply irrelevant, external and redundant. The child . . . does not perceive the absence of emotional attachment until he or she begins to be imposed upon by a world that expects it, along with the desire to learn and to be part of things, which usually springs from emotional attachment and belonging. (203)

Williams's assessment of autism is reminiscent of contemporary concerns about alienation and the inability to communicate needs and desires that has bequeathed to contemporary western culture a burgeoning self-help industry; as she describes it, autism is an extreme expression of themes that permeate contemporary society and culture. And at the start of the twenty-first century, many people seem very interested in autism and what it means to be autistic: Simon Baron-Cohen's *The Essential Difference* even includes a series of quizzes at the end of the book, so that readers can test how aspergian/autistic they are. And though Baron-Cohen offers a disclaimer that these tests do not prove or disprove one's aspergian/autistic status, he provides them all the same, undoubtedly because of the popular interest and anxiety excited by autism.

In contemporary fictional narratives, autism imagery usually appears in relation to characters negotiating the problems of identity and language, and to the dysfunctional relationship of the individual to his or her family or community (McDonagh). That this should be one of autism's dominant metaphorical uses in popular culture is hardly surprising, and indeed seems inevitable, given that autism may well have emerged when it did because we, as a culture, require a repository for our anxieties concerning the subjective, isolated self bequeathed by modernism, as well as more recent—postmodern, perhaps—expressions of subjectivity as destabilized, fragmented and hypermediated by the pervasive images generated by popular culture. I suggest that this "autism anxiety" lies at the root not only of popular representations of autism, but of the diagnostic category "autism" itself. Autism has become a useful metaphor for some aspect of what we think of as human. The intensity of cultural interest in autism is reflected in the ever-increasing ranks of autism-related books and films, with an emphasis on fiction, documentary and autobiography. But in a very important sense, this symbolic or metaphorical function has always been a part of autism—at least in how it has been formed as a concept, a syndrome, and a diagnostic category. Autism in film and literature is used as a metaphor because, as a metaphor, it makes sense to us: it appeals to our own secret fears. And it has worked so well as a pathology, a diagnostic category, for the same reason: because we understand it as a metaphor for something we carry within ourselves.

ACKNOWLEDGMENTS

I would like to thank Mark Osteen and Tim Stainton for their comments on earlier drafts, as well as the participants at the Autism and Representation conferences in Cleveland and Liverpool, especially Chris Goodey, Irene Rose and Kristen Loutensock.

WORKS CITED

Albright, Daniel. *Personality and Impersonality: Lawrence, Woolf and Mann*. Chicago: U of Chicago P, 1978.

Alderson, Priscilla, and Christopher Goodey. "Autism in Special and Inclusive Schools: 'There has to be a point to their being there.'" *Disability & Society* 14 (1999): 249–61.

Armstrong, Tim. *Modernism: A Cultural History*. Cambridge, UK: Polity, 2005.

———. *Modernism, Technology and the Body: A Cultural Study*. Cambridge: Cambridge UP, 1998.

Asperger, Hans "'Autistic Psychopathy' in Childhood." 1944. Trans. Uta Frith. *Autism and Asperger Syndrome*. Ed. Uta Frith. Cambridge: Cambridge UP, 1991. 37–92.

Baron-Cohen, Simon. *The Essential Difference: Male and Female Brains and the Truth About Autism*. New York: Basic, 2003.

Bleuler, Eugen. *Dementia Praecox or the Group of Schizophrenias*. 1911.Trans. Joseph Zinkin. New York: International Universities P, 1950.

———. *The Theory of Schizophrenic Negativism*. Trans. William A. White. New York: Journal of Nervous and Mental Disease, 1912.

Camus, Albert. *The Stranger*. Trans. Stuart Gilbert. New York: Knopf, 1981.

Down, John Langdon. "Observations on the Ethnic Classification of Idiots." *Clinical Lecture Reports of the London Hospital* 3 (1866): 259–62.

Duncan, P. Martin. "Notes on Idiocy." *Journal of Mental Science* 7 (1861): 232–52.

Ellmann, Richard. *Golden Codgers: Biographical Speculations*. Oxford: Oxford UP, 1973.

Fiedler, Leslie. *Freaks: Myths and Images of the Secret Self*. New York: Touchstone, 1978.

Fitzgerald, Michael. *The Genesis of Artistic Creativity: Asperger's Syndrome and the Arts*. London: Jessica Kingsley, 2005.

Frith, Uta. *Autism: Explaining the Enigma*. Cambridge, UK: Blackwell, 1989.

———., ed. *Autism and Asperger Syndrome*. Cambridge: Cambridge UP, 1991.

Freud, Sigmund. "The 'Uncanny.'" Trans James Strachey. *The Penguin Freud Library*, Vol 14: Art and Literature. Harmondsworth: Penguin, 1985. 335–376.

Giddens, Anthony. *The Consequences of Modernity*. Stanford, CA: Stanford UP, 1990.

Glastonbury, Marion. "The Cultural Presence of Autistic Lives." *Raritan* 17 (Summer 1997): 24–44.

Grove, Thelma. "Barnaby Rudge: A Case Study in Autism." *Dickensian* 83 (1987): 139–48.

Hacking, Ian. *The Social Construction of What?* Cambridge, MA: Harvard UP, 1999.

———. "What is Tom saying to Maureen?" *London Review of Books* 28.9 (11 May 2006): 3, 6–7.

Houston, Rab, and Uta Frith. *Autism in History: the Case of Hugh Blair of Borgue.* Padstow, Cornwall: Blackwell, 2000.

Howe, Irving. "The Idea of the Modern." *Literary Modernism.* Ed Irving Howe. Greenwich, CT: Fawcett, 1967. 11–40.

Ireland, William W. "The Classification and Prognosis of Idiocy." *Journal of Mental Science* 18 (1872): 333–354.

Joyce, James. *A Portrait of the Artist as a Young Man.* 1916. Harmondsworth: Penguin, 1976.

———. *Ulysses.* 1922. Harmondsworth: Penguin, 2000.

Kanner, Leo. "Autistic Disturbances of Affective Contact." *Nervous Child* 2 (1943): 217–250.

Levenson, Michael. *A Genealogy of Modernism: A Study of English Literary Doctrine 1908–1922.* Cambridge: Cambridge UP, 1984.

McDonagh, Patrick. "Autism and the Modern Identity: Autism Anxiety in Popular Discourse." *Disability Studies Quarterly* 19 (1999): 184–191.

Micale, Mark S. "The Modernist Mind: A Map." *The Mind of Modernism: Medicine, Psychology and the Cultural Arts in Europe and America, 1880–1940.* Ed Mark S. Micale. Stanford CA: Stanford UP, 2004. 1–19.

Musil, Robert. *The Man Without Qualities.* Vol. 1. 1930. Trans. Eithne Wilkins and Ernst Kaiser. London: Picador, 1979.

Neumärker, K.-J. "Leo Kanner: His Years in Berlin, 1906–1924. The roots of autistic disorder." *History of Psychiatry* 14 (2003): 205–18.

Ryan, Judith. *The Vanishing Subject: Early Psychology and Literary Modernism.* Chicago: U of Chicago P, 1991.

Sartre, Jean-Paul. "Camus' *The Outsider*." 1943. Trans Annette Michelson. *Literary and Philosophical Essays.* New York: Collier, 1962. 26–44.

———. *Huis clos* (suivi de *Les mouches*). Paris: Gallimard, 1947.

Stein, Gertrude. *The Making of Americans.* 1925. New York: Something Else, 1966.

Williams, Donna. *Nobody Nowhere: The Extraordinary Autobiography of an Autistic.* New York: Times Books, 1992.

Wing, Lorna. "The Relationship between Asperger's syndrome and Kanner's autism." *Autism and Asperger Syndrome.* Ed. Uta Frith. Cambridge: Cambridge UP, 1991. 93–121.

Woolf, Virginia. "Mr. Bennett and Mrs. Brown." *Collected Essays.* London: Hogarth, 1966.

———. *Mrs. Dalloway.* 1925. London: Penguin, 1992.

5   Autism and the Imagination

Bruce Mills

We associate much with the imagination: the power to evoke images of absent objects and people, to generate inner pictures of past events or memories, and to create artistic representations of important experiences and desires. We attribute the highest order of moral, intellectual, and emotional growth to the ability to engage the imagination; we see "imaginative play" as necessary for the development of empathy and thus healthy familial and social bonds. In art, such associations and attributions arise from a history of understanding the imagination as more than the passive ability to recollect images and instead as an active and transformative faculty of the mind. Ralph Waldo Emerson, Samuel Taylor Coleridge, and others argued that, through the productive or constructive power of the imagination, we literally create the world by giving order or larger meaning to seemingly disparate and discrete elements. In light of these notions, an impaired imagination might manifest itself in a lack of empathy, literal-mindedness, or a tendency to get caught up in the individual and distinct impression. Within a continuum of definitions that elevate the liberating (and humanizing) nature of the imagination, such qualities suggest profound limitations—and a vision of the world that closes off the possibility of great art and wisdom.

Given current definitions and descriptions of autism spectrum disorders (ASD), it is reasonable to conclude that those with the impairment lack the possibility of experiencing the full, imaginative life of "neurotypical" individuals. In the *Diagnostic and Statistical Manual of Mental Disorders, 4th Edition* or *DSM–IV*, clinicians address this deficit in the last of the triad of impairments. Noting the "restricted repetitive and stereotyped patterns of behavior, interests, and activities" of those on the spectrum, the manual defines the nature of this impairment by underscoring how it presents itself through "delays or abnormal functioning" in the area of "symbolic or imaginative play." Though it grounds such diagnostic criteria in empirical studies, this representation of autism still reveals underlying assumptions concerning the nature of the imagination and an "ideal" or "natural" creative process; it positions certain cognitive processes in relation to the imagination as "normal." In its implied emphasis on the synthesizing power of the imagination, for instance, the *DSM–IV* invites readers to devalue the heightened ability of those with autism to discern the sometimes subtle and distinct features of a discrete image, activity, or experience. Instead it favors the capacity to move quickly to a more generalized or symbolic understanding. Moreover, if autism is theorized as an impaired ability (or inability) to develop what Uta Frith terms the "drive for central coherence," then those on the spectrum seem to lack definitive features of the imagination. That is, Frith asserts that "[i]n the normal cognitive system there is a built-in propensity to form coherence over as wide a range of stimuli as possible, and to generalize over as wide a range of contexts as possible" (*Autism*, 2nd ed. 159–60); such a view resonates with the belief that the highest manifestations of the imaginative faculty embody the capacity to unify seemingly distinct images and memories.

Motivated by observations of my own son's autistic filtering of the world and guided by professional interest in the nature of the imagination, in this chapter I explore the implications of these resonating conceptual legacies. In recent Western thought, poet-philosophers consistently linked notions regarding the imagination to the anatomy of the mind. In the even more immediate study of the biology of mind, psychologists and scientists hypothesize a peculiar mentalizing ability (or theory of mind) within the particular neurological wiring of the brain. With the increased incidence of autism and the insights arising from biographical and autobiographical narratives, however, we might begin to rethink past paradigms that oppose typical/normal with atypical/abnormal imaginative processes. In the continuum that marks the different cognitive processes that produce art, we might begin to refine an understanding of the imagination in relation to autism.

A UNIFYING INSTINCT: ROMANTIC NOTIONS OF THE IMAGINATION

Considering the law of the human mind and equating the process of creation with the act of thought itself, Emerson voices an influential notion of the creative self in a language that recalls current models of intellectual development:

> To the young mind every thing is individual, stands by itself. By and by, it finds how to join two things and sees in them one nature; then three, then three thousand; and so, tyrannized over by its own unifying instinct, it goes on tying things together, diminishing anomalies, discovering roots running under ground whereby contrary and remote things cohere and flower out from one stem. It presently learns that since the dawn of history there has been a constant accumulation and classifying of facts. But what is classification but the perceiving that these objects are not chaotic, and are not foreign, but have a law which is also a law of the human mind? (65–66)

Delivered to students at Harvard College in 1837, Emerson's assertions offer his era an image of the evolving intellect and thus an antebellum rendering of what William G. Perry, Jr. and others might term a form of "intellectual and ethical development in the college years." Interestingly, Emerson envisions such growth as the unfolding of an internal and eternal law; it is a transcendental vision rooted in biological fact. The "duty" of the individual, then, is to attend to and foster the insights arising from this "unifying instinct" or "law of the human mind." For Emerson, this imaginative life involved more than rigidly applying the thoughts of other times and writers; it demanded that the past be used to construct a response to the present, to develop new generalizations that harmonized the seemingly unrelated aspects of changing conditions. Given his reflections in "The American Scholar," one could argue that, by its very nature, the ideal mind promised flexibility and fluidity of thought.

Emerson's ideas represent just one example of the tendency to link the nature of thought and cognitive processes to the physiology of the brain itself. Starting in the late eighteenth century, the discussion of the imagination often formed the site of this speculation. By the second and third decades of the nineteenth century, prominent encyclopedia definitions of the imagination offer some of the clearest merging of the literary, metaphysical, and physiological. According to Abraham Rees's entry in *The Cyclopaedia* (1824), the imagination "is a power or faculty of the soul, whereby it conceives and forms ideas of things, by means of impressions made on the fibers of the brain, by sensation." In fact, the definition of this faculty or power arises more from new findings in relation to the anatomy of the brain and the neurology of perception than from past philosophical or literary models. Thus, after distinguishing between the passive imagination (i.e., the "simple impression of objects") and active imagination (i.e., the capacity to arrange and combine received images in a "thousand ways"), Rees devotes the rest of the initial paragraph to how the brain processes sensations associated with present and absent objects. This is to say that modern notions of the imagination arise from the era's conceptions of cognitive processes, from its ideas about the nature of the mind itself.

Such notions resemble Coleridge's influential distinctions among the primary imagination, secondary imagination, and fancy articulated in *Biographia Literaria*. In a sense, his distinctions present features of the imagination along a continuum. At the most advanced place on this continuum, Coleridge posits the primary imagination or "the living Power and prime Agent of all human perception" and "repetition in the finite mind of the eternal act of creation in the infinite *I am*." The secondary imagination differs differs from the primary only in "degree" and "mode of its operation": "It dissolves, diffuses, dissipates, in order to re-create; or where this process is rendered impossible, yet still at all events it struggles to idealize and to unify." Finally, Coleridge argues that the "Fancy, on the contrary, has no other counters to play with, but fixities and definites"; it is "no other than a mode of Memory emancipated from the order of time and space; and blended with, and modified by that empirical phenomenon of the will, which we express by the word *choice*" (304–5). Along this spectrum, then, we move from the more limited capacity to attend to ("play with") objects provided by memory to the ability to create anew, that is, to transform ("dissolve, diffuse, and dissipate") in order to give new order to the seemingly fixed elements of sensation and memory. And though this idea is not clearly articulated in these excerpts, Coleridge viewed those who display fancy to be lesser thinkers and artists.

In defining the "sensual man" as one who "conforms thoughts to things" and the "poet" as conforming "things to thoughts," Emerson integrates aspects of Coleridge's distinctions. "The Imagination," Emerson adds, "may be defined to be the use which the Reason [i.e., intuition or unifying instinct] makes of the material world" (44). In a sense, Fancy can be understood as a conventional mind that strains to move beyond the simple mirroring of rigid forms and laws; the Primary Imagination is the power to construct novel approaches and narratives and to grasp larger symbols or underlying structures in the prelude to and/or process of creation. In the Romantic period, the power of the primary imagination offered the potential for divinity within the limitations of a finite and material existence. Not surprisingly, the poet-artist was described in terms that captured the capacity to unify aspects of the world. If not everyone had the ability to achieve such heights of the imagination, each person (created in God's image) contained the wiring for such a possibility.

By directly and indirectly connecting imagination to the mechanism of the mind itself (and how this mechanism or structure renders in material form the infinite dimensions of divine creation), Coleridge, Emerson, and others mark a definitive aspect of a modern turn in Western thought. In tracing an "archaeology of the human sciences," Michel Foucault describes this epistemological transition or new episteme:

> For the threshold of our modernity is situated not by the attempt to apply objective methods to the study of man, but rather by the constitution of an empirico-transcendental doublet which was called *man*. . . . There are those that operate within the space of the body, and—by studying perception, sensorial mechanisms, neuro-motor diagrams, and the articulation common to things and to the organism—function as a sort of transcendental aesthetic; these led to the discovery that knowledge has anatomo-physiological conditions, that it is formed gradually within the structures of the body, that it may have a privileged place within it, but that its forms cannot be dissociated from its peculiar functioning; in short, that there is a *nature* of human knowledge that determines its forms and that can at the same time be made manifest to it in its own empirical contents. (319)

From the time of the Enlightenment, Foucault underscores, such human faculties as reason and imagination took into account the physical or material nature of the human body. Although the ability to transcend the constraints of time and place through our imagination points toward a kind of metaphysical power, the ultimate check to such abilities, by definition, rests in the evolution and normal development of mind as much as in the formal education of the self. In the anatomy of mind, in the very wiring of the brain, we might discover—or, certainly, people came to believe in the possibility of discovering—peculiar capacities for knowing. In a sense, the imagination is a hardwired faculty that has its own rules. Descriptions of the imagination, then, can be traced back to the cognitive processes evolving from the brain.

Given this pattern of thought arising in the eighteenth century and gaining wider prominence in the nineteenth century, it is possible to argue that notions of the imagination were progressively connected to the laws of cognition. In other words, the metaphysical was merging with the physical, the philosophical with the biological. Artistic genius simply manifested the highest order of these inherent laws; moreover, the artistic productions inevitably embodied the laws of this unifying impulse, this drive toward greater visions of coherence and wholeness. Hence, with Coleridge and Emerson, we see the greatest praise directed toward those individuals who have done more than vividly record the discrete or individual sensation or memory. For the writers of the period, the imagination redeemed the seemingly unredeemable aspects of finite existence; it was the power that gave order and promised union where before had existed disharmony and disconnection.

CENTRAL COHERENCE, THEORY OF MIND, AND THE IMAGINATION

Our current understanding of autism draws from theories that echo in striking ways eighteenth- and nineteenth-century concepts of imagination that have become normalized over two centuries. And although such views of what constitutes the imagination might not directly inform studies of autism, they do form at least an underlying conceptual and cultural framework. We hear past efforts to define the peculiar faculty of the imagination in two ideas concerning information processing that have influenced how we comprehend autism: the notion of central coherence and mentalizing or theory of mind.

In her first edition of *Autism: Explaining the Enigma* published in 1989, Uta Frith explained differences between the drive for central coherence and local coherence in terms that cannot help but recall Coleridge's distinction between the primary imagination and fancy. In a particularly vivid illustration of her ideas, she depicts information processing as a force not unlike the main channel of a large river. For most individuals, this force "pulls together large amounts of information (many tributaries)." However, she also posits a drive toward what she terms "local coherence," arguing that even smaller pieces of information must be "pulled together . . . by some locally acting cohesive force" (97). Though Frith does not discount the importance of this drive toward local coherence, she does—at least in this first edition—see the more embracing pattern-making force as on a higher level. Similar to the way Coleridge (and Emerson) framed the higher mental faculty of the imagination, she sees the drive for central coherence as the capacity to give order and unify; more specifically, she reframes notions of the primary imagination (or Emerson's unifying instinct) in the terms of cognitive neuroscience. In this context, an intense focus on small pieces and thus an impaired capacity to give a unifying explanation to "local" information mirrors the shortcomings of the fancy.

With mentalizing or theory of mind, we have another framework within which to explain the particular set of impairments described in the *DSM–IV*, a framework that clearly resonates with or is related to powers attributed to the imagination. Frith prefers the term "mentalizing," defining this theory as "the ability to predict relationships between external states of affairs and internal states of mind" (2nd ed. 77). In *Mindblindness: An Essay on Autism and Theory of Mind*, Simon Baron-Cohen suggests that "the phrase 'theory of mind' . . . has come to be shorthand for the capacity to attribute mental states to oneself and to others and to interpret behavior in terms of mental states" (55). Significantly, Baron-Cohen postulates four important "mind-reading" mechanisms within the brain: Intentionality Detector (ID), or "a perceptual device that interprets motion stimuli in terms of the primitive volitional mental states of goal and desire" (32); Eye-Direction Detector (EDD), a mechanism that allows individuals to detect and make inferences from another's eyes (39); Shared-Attention Mechanism (SAM), or a mechanism that enables individuals to develop "triadic representations" or "relations among an Agent, the Self, and a (third) Object" (44); and, finally, Theory of Mind Mechanism (ToMM). Serving an especially important role in relation to these other mechanisms, ToMM "has the dual function of representing a set of epistemic mental states and turning all of this mentalistic knowledge into useful theory" (50). In effect, ToMM performs tasks often associated with the imagination.

Why is this drive toward central coherence and the presence of a theory of mind mechanism so important? In answering this question in evolutionary terms, Frith and Baron-Cohen speak of autistic cognitive tendencies as the sign of an abnormal mind, a mind marked by the absence of mechanisms fundamental to survival. (In this regard, the capacity to mentalize can be understood as a necessary presence and the inability to do so as a debilitating absence.) According to Frith, "without this type of high-level cohesion, pieces of information would just remain pieces, be they small pieces or large pieces" and "[a]s pieces they would be only of limited use in the organism's long-term program of intelligent adaptation to the environment" (*Autism*,

1st ed. 98). Baron-Cohen sees his work as a contribution to "evolutionary psychology," a field that "looks at the brain (and thus the mind) as an organ that, via natural selection, has evolved specific mechanisms to solve particular adaptive problems" (11). Drawing from an essay by L. Cosmides, et al., he writes that

> [the authors] use the metaphor of the brain as a Swiss Army knife to make this point. Each blade of the Swiss Army knife was, clearly, designed for a specific purpose: the corkscrew for pulling corks, the screwdriver for driving screws, the scissors for cutting thin materials, the saw for sawing thicker materials, and so on. It makes no sense to try to use the corkscrew to drive screws, or the screwdriver to pull corks, if the knife has a different "mechanism" for solving each of these problems. So it is with the brain, say Cosmides et al. We do not use our color-vision system to talk, or our language system to see color. We use specialized modules for the functions they evolved to solve. (11)

In light of such assumptions and beliefs, we can see ToMM as a critical mechanism, a specific evolutionary adaptation that enables individuals to go beyond superficial (e.g., mechanistic) interpretations of their environment to theorize and process interior causes for exterior actions. Through this mechanism we gain adaptive advantage, for we learn to anticipate behaviors, negotiate difficulties, and respond productively to change. In many respects, we can again understand ToMM as related to and/or depending on the functions associated with the imagination. That is, it is the mechanism that takes specific information, creates representations of mental (not real) states, and forms propositions. Moreover, it has a unifying function, that is, it takes these representations of possible mental states and constructs a "theory" of human behavior on which to base conclusions and potential choices.

In many respects, then, the theories that assert a drive for central coherence and describe inter-related mechanisms necessary for the capacity to hypothesize inner states represent a modern translation of Emerson's law of the human mind and Coleridge's speculation on the imagination. Again, according to Emerson, the mature mind embodies the ability to move beyond the local and discover how seemingly "contrary and remote things cohere and flower out from one stem." By inference, the mind would remain in perpetual adolescence if it attended solely to the individual thing, that is, to the object as it "stands by itself" (65). In effect, Emerson envisions what we might call the youth of "local coherence" and the maturity of "central coherence." In his notions of the creative mind, in fact, he conceptualizes an idealized individual ("Man Thinking") who allows the inherent capacity of mind to find fruition in any vocation or endeavor. The influence of Coleridge on this perception of the poet-unifier emerges clearly in the belief that the imagination is the faculty that constructs new forms and narratives from sensation and memory. To do so, of course, requires the ability to note particular objects and behaviors and then configure the discrete components of this "stuff" of memory into new scenarios and narratives. To understand present behaviors and anticipate future ones requires an "active imagination." In defining the dual function of ToMM as "representing a set of epistemic mental states and turning all of this mentalistic knowledge into useful theory" (50), Baron-Cohen asserts the fundamental place of "story" or narrative in human understanding. In other words, a story or narrative that explains the past and helps anticipate the future is a "useful theory." Representing and imagining name similar acts of mind.

Not surprisingly, psychologists and neuroscientists point to studies of children's play (or lack of it) as important evidence of an impaired imagination/theory of mind. If, as Baron-Cohen argues, normal development shows the ability to "pretend or recognize the pretending of others" (53), then a failure to show such play implies some dysfunction, impairment, or "absence." As stated in the *DSM–IV*, autism by definition manifests itself in play that fails to offer evidence of a normally developing theory of mind. Rather than pretending, children simply perform ritualistic actions, for example, the repetitive lining up of toys. They appear to lack a mechanism that builds representations founded in an understanding other minds and seem to have no drive to account for or give meaning to playmates' interior states. In short, individuals with ASD are "blind" to other minds, for their interactions show that they cannot build shared representations and pretend scenarios. It is not that they do not want to interact; it is that they lack the mechanisms of mind for developing mutual interests. In the terms of Emerson and Coleridge, such individuals seem stuck on the quality of things in and of themselves rather than formulating shared stories, so to speak, that might generate interactive not side-by-side play. The rigid lining up of toys, then, does not represent the mind in the act of recreating or reformulating observed behaviors for the purposes of modeling one's place in the world or communicating with another person. Rather, it is the act of a mind manifesting an isolating instinct rather than a unifying one.

That the *DSM–IV* links imaginative and symbolic play also underscores the affinity between cognitive and literary-philosophical perceptions of higher states of mind. (According to psychiatric manuals, an autism diagnosis can result if "delays or abnormal functioning" occur in one of the following: "(1) social interaction, (2) language as used in social communication, or (3) symbolic or imaginative play.") In other words, the goal or end should not be the thing itself. To revel in the spin of a wheel, in the scrolling credits at the end of videos, or in the repetition of arranging letters or plastic toy figures appear to be self-stimulatory not symbolic acts. Although such behaviors seem to demonstrate restrictive behaviors and may embody attempts to address an anxiety arising from a dysfunctional sensory processing system, however, they may not in all instances and with everyone on the spectrum represent the delays or dysfunction that notions of the imagination predispose us to see.

FROM DEFICITS TO STYLES OF KNOWING

If this admittedly brief history of the imagination and abridged summary of current cognitive theories of autism gesture toward one common denominator, it is the normalizing of styles of processing information that reflect less attention to the local and discrete. Or to frame this idea differently, these preceding reflections point toward the tendency to see the individual thing not as an end itself but as a means to an end. According to these influential views, to be human is to demonstrate a capacity for organizing broad pieces of information and giving special importance to inner or psychological states.

But what if we were to define the imagination with less attention to the "highest" manifestation of some unifying faculty and more attention to preferences for (or neurological predilection toward) different types of information processing? What if we read the drive for central coherence and theory of mind (at least the capacity and powerful inclination to account for psychological states in social interactions) not as signs of *normal* development but as features along a spectrum of possibilities? In other words, we might consider that some individuals thrive on the local and more private (or what Frith calls "self-limiting taxonomies"; *Autism* 2nd ed. 163) and others might orient themselves toward global arrangements and classifications. The expressive or artistic outcomes of such predispositions would inevitably vary. On this continuum of cognitive "styles," people at the extremes would be less able to build bridges toward other ways of knowing and thus would present peculiar challenges for the listener, viewer, and/or reader. It may be that, especially for those with the capacity to create expressive visual or verbal art, the play of the mind is not delayed or dysfunctional but manifestly unique. A different way of knowing would produce symbol structures (or taxonomies) not easily understood though not less inflected with the very human yearning to give shape to vast but uniquely experienced sensations and distinctively rendered memories.

In revising her chapter "A Fragmented World" for the second edition of *Autism: Explaining the Enigma*, Uta Frith suggestively directs readers toward these possibilities. Citing Francesca Happé's study of central coherence, she begins to reframe her earlier attempts to make sense of the fragmented perceptions of those with autism:

> Happé's work has been crucial in redirecting research interest away from the focus on deficits and toward the strengths in autism. She collected evidence for detail-focused processing in autism in three quite different domains: visual perception, auditory perception, and verbal semantics. She formulated the hypothesis that central coherence is a cognitive style that varies from weak to strong in the normal population and is reflected in a normal bell-shaped distribution of scores on relevant tests. The population of individuals with autism would also be

expected to show such a bell-shaped distribution, but with the mean shifted toward the weak extreme. (162)

Turning to work by Baron-Cohen and his team in Cambridge, she notes his identification of "an information-processing style" that he terms "systemizing" (163). Such a style, she summarizes, "is based on an intuitive understanding of how mechanical things work, and a preference for information about the physical as opposed to the psychological world." According to the study, "[s]tyle and content not only fit individuals with autism but also many normal people" (163). As researchers begin to assess and understand even more fully the meaning of "spectrum" in autism spectrum disorders, the limitations of past theories will give way to different configurations of what constitute cognitive strengths and weaknesses.

So how might we understand the nature of the imagination within this different way of processing the world? How would the art of local coherence manifest itself? In firsthand accounts of autism from observers and those on the spectrum, we discern the outlines of an imaginative faculty arising from different cognitive propensities. Within two classical texts in the literature of autism—Clara Claiborne Park's account of her daughter's life in *The Seige* and Temple Grandin's in *Emergence* and *Thinking in Pictures*—we witness how local coherence and the absence of theory of mind produce an imaginative faculty defined by close attention to mechanical or physical patterns not psychological or social rules, by a private not public symbol structure, and by an internal integrity or unity evolving in part from idiosyncratic sensory preferences.

To understand the different dimensions and terms of an "autistic" imagination, it is useful to focus on creative processes and products, for, although the imagination becomes critical to a broad range of human endeavors, its emblematic features might best be discerned in verbal and visual art. Moreover, in this context, it is also revealing to consider how a lack of interest in employing the imagination to connect with others shapes this type of imagination. We can think of verbal and visual compositions as representations of an internal vision—the imagination rendered in visible forms. In short, artistic acts convey efforts to communicate some internal state or understanding to others. However, what if the artist was not wired to care in fundamental ways about others' emotional or psychological states and the web of social relationships and rules that arise from or affect such states? And, in addition, what if an individual were cognitively predisposed to value or fear what the non-autistic would see as the odd or unusual sensory detail, for example, the touch of sand in the palm, the unexpected sound of a refrigerator or radiator kicking in or school alarm going off? With such an imagination, memory remains important, for, like anyone engaged in representing the world in play or art, the person with autism draws from the storehouse of memory and sensation. Still, he or she does so without the large and far-reaching desire to enter a broader human conversation.

What we know about the language impairment of those with autism can illuminate the nature of the locally coherent imagination. As shown in studies of language development, an impairment exists in pragmatics or the use of language to communicate, not in the ability to distinguish sound (phonetics), understand the mechanics of grammar (syntax), or use words and sentences to create meaning (semantics). Significantly, it is the delay or impairment in pragmatics that profoundly reconfigures the entire equation. So, too, it is with the imagination. If Emerson's description of the unifying instinct assumes a pragmatic consciousness and thus an imagination driven to understand the self within the complex web of social relationships, then we can only conclude that an autistic self must have a substantially different mode of receiving the world through the senses, recollecting experiences in memory, and producing this inner processing in expressive forms. Not unlike language, then, the supposed receiver of the communicative or expressive act—that is, the audience, listener, viewer—remains absent or distant from the equation for or definition of the imagination. In effect, the imaginative faculty is employed not to communicate but to develop a kind of internal order. An autist's art may evoke certainly intellectual and emotional responses from an audience, but, ultimately, is indifferent to them.

Near the end of *The Siege*, Clara Park speculates on the seeming absence of her daughter's imagination in ways that underscore this indifference and recall the absence of Emerson's unifying instinct. "All the autistic child's deficiencies," she writes,

> could be seen as converging in this one: the deficiency which renders it unable or unwilling to put together the primary building blocks of experience. . . . The autistic child does not move naturally from one sound to another, from one word to another, from one idea to another, from one experience to another. Yet reality, as human beings experience it, is a web of connections to be made. (267)

She goes on to suggest that this "lack of exploratory drive" embodies an absence of some "sense of purpose" and then concludes: "Purpose entails drive, and the capacity to sustain. But it entails another capacity as well, one which itself plays an obvious part in motivation—the capacity to *imagine*, to bring to mind and take seriously what is not, or not yet, present to immediate experience" (268). Working as she is within the template of past definitions and the common experience of the neurotypical, we can understand Park's conclusions. However, just as it is possible to have language without the desire to communicate, so too is it conceivable to have an imagination that lacks the motivation to represent or compose for the purposes of entering some broadly shared, meaning-making conversation. The discrete shape, the distinct color, and the individual pattern may speak sufficiently to the impulses of local coherence. In addition, such an imagination may be unable to see and thus include social knowledge within the artistic process.

In her epilogue to *The Siege* written fifteen years after the book's initial publication, Park returns with greater insight to this question of her daughter's imagination. She is able to do so, in part, because, in the intervening years, Jessy developed remarkable skills as an artist and because Park herself had come to understand the social dimensions that encompass motivation: "Motivation. I come back to the old mystery of Jessy's long passivity, and the related question of the role of cognitive and emotional factors in her disabilities" (314). Considering why any child might engage in the "myriad tasks of development" (and, thus, one could add, in acts of the imagination that motivate such engagement and further growth), she suggests more than biological forces: "But growth is social too. The baby has social reasons to pay attention to the sounds its mother makes, to make sounds in return, to notice what effects those sounds produce, to practice and refine them. It associates people with comfort and pleasure, it recognizes them, it wants to communicate with them" (315). To posit some inherent human instinct for finding such comfort and pleasure, Park implies, fails to account for her daughter's challenges as well as her unique potential to develop intellectually and emotionally. It is worth considering, then, that Jessy's symbolic and imaginative play is neither delayed nor abnormal but unmotivated, but rather, when self-initiated and without externally imposed structures, expresses an internal world with rules peculiar to her own private sensations and codes and with particular attention to local detail and desires.

In the fixation or perseveration on detail or private preferences, then, we might locate as much advantage as disadvantage. Though it confronts the "centrally coherent" imagination with questions of purpose or larger meaning, such focus can produce striking artistic works. Again, visual art offers some especially emblematic examples given the greater spatial abilities of those on the spectrum and the way such artistic media depend less on social intelligence. In her daughter's case, Clara Park describes what might be clearly classified as an art of the locally coherent:

> Jessy sits at her table, bent over a sheet of drawing paper, deftly outlining a rectangle with a sable brush. At hand are some thirty tubes of acrylics, but for today she has mixed only shades of green—five of them. Green is her favorite color. She is working from the pencil sketch she made at a friend's house some weeks ago, one of her quartz heater series, the successor to her series of radio dials and electric blanket controls. Her abstracting eye has reduced the heater to its essential design elements, 11 ranges of tiny rectangles, 72 to a range. For the painting she has enlarged them fourfold, but they still measure only a half-inch by a quarter. Today she will fill in only the greens, placing them unhesitatingly among the 792 rectangles according to a pattern we cannot see. But she can see it; she has already chosen the final color which will enclose the whole. (281–2)

Clara Park goes on to describe the completed painting with shades of color that "glow against the tan neutrality of the border with the surreal intensity of a heater in a dream" (282). This process and product are striking for a variety of reasons. First, the subject of the painting—it is one of many paintings in a quartz heater series—expresses a fascination that seems linked to sensations and memories associated with her peculiar response to heaters themselves. As a child, the unexpected sound of a heater kicking in was especially troublesome to Jessy. The subject matter is not a "normal" preference, however, for it fails to account for or attend more readily to viewers' inclinations and desires. Second, the process displays a rigid attention to some private logic, an order in shape and color that has an internal consistency if not a surreal quality to a pattern that her parents cannot see. Although the painting enacts central features of the imagination by giving order and form to sensation and memory, however, both process and product ensue from a different cognitive form and function.

With Temple Grandin's discussion of fixations in *Emergence* and *Thinking in Pictures*, we bear witness to similar displays of a locally coherent imagination. Her fixation on doors, for instance, embodied the need to find a concrete, visual translation of abstract ideas in order to negotiate complex emotions and social relationships. She writes that "[p]ersonal relationships made absolutely no sense to me until I developed visual symbols of doors and windows" (*Thinking in Pictures* 34), yet, as she originally describes in her autobiography *Emergence*, this discovery arose from a random association generated during a minister's sermon (*Emergence* 79–80). After developing this visual tool, Grandin then repeatedly employed it during especially difficult times of transition such as graduation from high school and college. Not surprisingly, in reflecting on this visual aid to her development, she cites the example of Jessy Park's seemingly idiosyncratic visual associations:

> A visual image or word becomes associated with an experience. Clara Park, Jessy's mother, described her daughter's fascination with objects such as electric blanket controls and heaters. She had no idea why the objects were so important to Jessy, though she did observe that Jessy was happiest, and her voice was no longer a monotone, when she was thinking about her special things. (*Thinking* 37)

Turning to another instance of an autistic man who demonstrated greater rigidity in behavior and difficulty in addressing transitions or unexpected occurrences, Grandin further offers a window into the nature of her imagination:

> I would speculate that such rigid behavior and lack of ability to generalize may be partly due to having little or no ability to change or modify visual memories. Even though my memories of things are stored as individual specific memories, I am able to modify my mental images. For

example, I can imagine a church painted in different colors or put the steeple of one church onto the roof of another; but when I hear somebody say the word "steeple," the first church that I see in my imagination is almost always a childhood memory and not a church image that I have manipulated. This ability to modify images in my imagination helped me to learn how to generalize. (*Thinking* 38)

Clearly, Grandin articulates the predilection to work from the discrete memory, and, though her abilities reflect a greater capacity to break out of the fixities presented in some of Jessy Park's behaviors, she shares a preference for the mechanistic not psychological, for associations connected with private not social or public meanings. Significantly, this associative process reflects a drive toward symbol-making as a means to understand the world. The "mechanistic" and concrete image, however, forms the vocabulary and shapes the private codes.

In our understanding of autism and in the terms that mold our definitions of this developmental disorder, then, we must not underestimate the degree to which a neurotypical sensibility or cognitive style has shaped the lens through which we view our concepts of the world. Notions of the imagination, central coherence, and theory of mind arise from interactions built on a social knowledge and impulse; more than this, they emerge from a neurological wiring that has seamlessly stitched in the fine but pervasive threads of social purposes. If there is another kind of mind, one where things not people condition ways of knowing and where the humanizing faculties of language and imagination function with more indifference to communication and human connection, then we must return to original assumptions and concepts—not because they are useless or inaccurate but because they remain incomplete or unaccommodating to the continuum of imaginative processes and acts.

Perhaps one outcome of such thinking is the need to conceive of creative processes and outcomes in terms of teams and networks that not only foster the arts of local coherence but also facilitate a communication and presentation of such artistic products and processes. It is important to emphasize that, although such a conclusion may not be profound, it demands a fundamental valuing of the local as well as the physical and mechanistic. Thus, the neurotypical drive toward central coherence, manifested in interventions, treatments, and educational curricula, might give less room for an attention to the local, for example, to an incessant focus toward multiple perspectives on a single object and how it looks or functions and to the necessity of certain fixations in the development of those on the spectrum. Preventing people from getting "stuck" (an important and necessary goal) must be balanced with an eye toward the developmental advantages of nurturing the narrow vision. As we have seen, evidence of the importance of finding this balance arises in the narratives about Jessy Park and by Temple Grandin. *Emergence* and *Thinking in Pictures* trace the positive outcome of identifying how certain fixations might open the door for meaningful insights, interactions, and careers. Without question, Grandin's obsession with doors as well as her squeeze machine (the device that enables her to apply calming pressure to her body and thus help address sensory needs) became one medium for an "emergence" from the more profoundly limiting aspects of her way of processing the world. In the life of her daughter, Clara Park's (and her family's) willingness to accept the need for behavioral motivations and wisdom to foster the odd subject matter of her finely detailed artwork provided the possibility of Jessy's own emergence.

In many respects, this chapter has simply endeavored to identify legacies that normalize certain styles of knowing and to suggest that such traditions of thought foster a view of autism that overlooks or tries to "correct" a drive toward local coherence. This is not to say that most people do not reflect an urge toward central coherence or a theory of mind or that ASD does not present itself in impairments that often have devastating effects on individuals and their families and communities. In other words, these reflections are not meant to dismiss the very real challenges of addressing limiting perseverative behaviors and harmful dimensions of an impaired sensory processing system. However, a conceptual shift is necessary before the special skills and potential contributions of those with autism can be fully realized and further intellectual, emotional, and spiritual development can take place. Moreover, in relation to the imagination, we need to rethink assumptions behind the *DSM–IV*'s perspective on imagination and autism. The nature of play—and its symbolic and imaginative dimensions—might vary in relation to the particular manner in which the player processes the world. The viewer also brings certain predilections to such observations. To begin to see the nature of the imagination through insights gleaned from autistic creation—its rendering of the particular in ways that enable the single thing, so to speak, to be seen in all its peculiarity—is an essential step. Becoming aware of a potential mindbindness in the drive toward central coherence is another.

WORKS CITED

Baron-Cohen, Simon. *Mindblindness: An Essay on Autism and Theory of Mind.* Cambridge: MIT P, 1997.

Coleridge, Samuel Taylor. *Biographia Literaria, or Biographical Sketches of My Literary Life and Opinions.* Vol. 7 of *The Collected Works of Samuel Taylor Coleridge.* Ed. James Engell and W. Jackson Bate. Princeton: Princeton UP, 1983.

Emerson, Ralph Waldo. "The American Scholar." *Selections from Ralph Waldo Emerson.* Ed. Stephen E. Whicher. Boston: Houghton Mifflin, 1957. 63–80.

Foucault, Michel. *The Order of Things: An Archeology of the Human Sciences.* New York: Vintage, 1970.

Frith, Uta. *Autism: Explaining the Enigma.* Oxford, UK: Blackwell, 1989.

———. *Autism: Explaining the Enigma.* 2nd ed. Oxford, UK: Blackwell, 2003.

Grandin, Temple. *Emergence: Labeled Autistic.* New York: Warner Books, 1986.

————. *Thinking in Pictures, and Other Reports from My Life with Autism*. New York: Vintage, 1995.

Park, Clara Claiborne. *The Siege: The First Eight Years of an Autistic Child*. Boston: Little, Brown, 1982.

————. *Exiting Nirvana: A Daughter's Life with Autism*. Boston: Little, Brown, 2001.

Perry, William G. *Forms of Intellectual and Ethical Development in the College Years*. New York: Holt, Rinehart & Winston, 1970.

Rees, Abraham. "Imagination." *The Cyclopedia*. Vol. 19. Philadelphia: S. F. Bradford, 1810–24. N. p.

6 Fractioned Idiom
Metonymy and the Language of Autism

Kristina Chew

Unfractioned idiom, immaculate sigh of stars

—from Hart Crane, "To Brooklyn Bridge"

Research on autistic children's language frequently notes that many children think concretely and have difficulty understanding abstract concepts.[1] Autistic children tend to take literally metaphoric language that draws on concrete images: parents relay stories of a child smashing his head into a screen door when told "Put your head in the door and call dad" or asking "Can I have an Oreo?" on hearing someone say "That's the way the cookie crumbles." Figurative language like metaphor or its less-well-known cousin, metonymy—which is the focus of this chapter—can be especially confusing for an autistic person because it seems to be about concrete things (cookies), but actually refers to an abstract concept (how some situation has turned out). Autistic language users, this chapter suggests, think metonymically, connecting and ordering concepts according to seemingly chance and arbitrary occurrences in an "autistic idiolect."

In *Exiting Nirvana: A Daughter's Life with Autism*, Clara Claiborne Park describes elaborate systems of "correlated" elements to reveal how her daughter Jessy thinks and talks. When Jessy makes herself a breakfast of eight pieces of bacon, she lives by "Analogies and Correlations": she makes eight pieces "[b]ecause of good" (Park 26). Silence (which is also good to Jessy, who was nonverbal until she was seven) is eight, "[a]nd between silence and sound is 7"; "[d]oing something fairly bad is only 3 and bad is 2 and very bad is 1" (26–7). Another system is based on clouds and doors, with the sun and four clouds and zero doors the "worst." She bases yet another system on "flavor tubes" and numbers: rice pudding is not good, and she associates numbers with each flavor ("0 light blueberry, 1 lime, 2 lemon, 3 orange, 4 strawberry . . . 8 grape, 9 or more, blueberry again": 81). Eating certain flavors or amounts of food in and of themselves means that a day is good, not so good, or just bad. Eight slices of bacon means that things are complete and need no supplementation (with eggs or toast): "If I have less than 5 and egg I have to cut that thin slices of toast" (27).[2]

We can understand Jessy Park's elaborate systems of correlations of tastes, sounds, and sights as being based on metonymical connections. Metonymy is classically defined as "trope in which one entity is used to stand for another associated entity" and, more specifically, as a "replacive relationship that is the basis for a number of conventional metonymic expressions occurring in ordinary language" such as "the pen is mightier than the sword" or "Nixon bombed Hanoi," in which "Nixon stands for the armed forces that Nixon controlled" (Loos et al., "Metonymy"). The basic definition of any literary trope is some entity used to stand for another entity; the twist of metonymy is the emphasis on *association*. Roman Jakobson elucidates this associative function of metonymy by comparing it to the more commonly used term metaphor, which is classically defined as "the expression of an understanding of one concept in terms of another concept, where there is some similarity or correlation between the two" (Loos et al., "Metaphor"). According to Jakobson in "Two aspects of language and two types of aphasic disturbances," metaphor and metonymy are the two fundamental modes to communicate meaning. In Jakobson's formulation, a metaphor—*Achilles is a lion*—links two disparate items on the basis of some similarity (strength and courage, the qualities conventionally attributed to a lion), whereas metonymy links two disparate items on the basis of contiguity or association (the equation by some now of Brad Pitt with Achilles, because the actor played the hero of the 2005 motion picture production of the *Iliad*: see Jakobson 76–82). In metonymy, one entity is related to another because those two items *happened* to occur in close succession to each other.

Here is an example of how, for my autistic son Charlie, two apparently unrelated terms came to be equated. The word "sushi" came to mean "bike ride" to Charlie because I had one day bought him sushi for lunch after he had been on a bike ride and not—metaphorically?—because of a resemblance between the wheels of his bike and the seaweed-edged rounds of sushi.[3] "Sushi" later became closely linked to "ShopRite" not so much because that was where we bought sushi but because a speech therapist, in teaching Charlie to talk about his everyday activities in longer sentences, taught Charlie the phrase "I get sushi at ShopRite" and the association stuck in his mind. This phrase then became a truth to Charlie, who insisted on always getting sushi when we went to a ShopRite grocery store or even when the word "ShopRite" or the similar-sounding "shopping cart" was spoken by us or by Charlie.[4] It is certainly true that, a store being where one buys sushi, it would be likely for anyone to connect said store to said food. The difference in an autistic idiolect is that *only* the sushi is associated with ShopRite—*only* sushi is mentioned when the child talks about ShopRite—and not the myriad of other things one can purchase there. ShopRite and sushi become one and the same.

"Idiolect" refers to a private language created by and understandable to one individual alone. The ancient Greek word *idiotes*, "private citizen," is the etymological root of the words "idiom" (which is "a manner of speaking that is natural to native speakers of a language" as well as "an expression whose meanings cannot be inferred from the meanings of the words that make it up") and "idiosyncratic" (denoting some eccentricity that is particular to an individual: *WordNet*). Due to an unusual use of words and syntax, we can classify the language of an autistic person as a language for a community of one—an idiolect. But rather than seeing this language as incomprehensible, we can better interpret it by seeking to understand the "system" that the user—my son Charlie, Jessy Park—has created, and, in particular, the metonymical basis of that system.

Clara Park presents Jessy's "marvelous yet sterile" systems with their equations of food and feeling without explaining their genesis.[5] Park describes these systems to suggest something about autistic thinking with its focus on concrete and controllable minutiae: "Her systems were designed to eliminate the unexpected, to capture uncertainties in a net of connections, to reduce them to rule" (83). As Jessy grows older, she loses the need for her cosmos of food, weather and number correlations. Indeed, her "emotions seemed independent of the weather," Park writes (82), only to discover twenty years later, when the neurologist Oliver Sacks speaks to Jessy, that the systems are still in her mind and even more elaborate than her mother had thought: now there are 55 new flavors (including three kinds of "espresso" and "dark rum").

The rationale behind Jessy Park's systems arises out of metonymic correlations between numbers and concrete phenomena that she uses to explain the world to herself and herself to the world. An excerpt from a journal kept by Fran, a "Jessy-friend"—someone who taught and took care of Jessy—suggests the origin of the system of clouds and the sky. "Pure blue sky. *While walking the long hill, a little cloud appeared and covered the sun briefly—oh, what sadness and anger—mumble, mumble, looking down at the ground, dragging the feet, stopping, answering no more questions about school. 'What is the matter, Jessy?'* 'The cloud over the sun'" (Park 77–78; italics in original). The clouds are said to be "full of numbers" ("multiples and powers of 37 and 73, with two bad 3's"); Jessy becomes happy when the cloud is gone. Another day, when there is a full moon and "low horrendous clouds"—"what a horrendous day," Fran writes—is full of crying, someone taking Jessy's "special" seat on the schoolbus, refusals to sing or answer questions, mumbling and telling Fran to go away (Fran herself walks home in tears: 78). Fran's journal suggests how differences, subtle and extreme, in the physical world seemed at times to coincide with bad days for Jessy, who then turns one day's happening into a general rule. She thus creates her system of clouds and doors, in which her greatest joy is represented by zero clouds and four doors: a bright, cloudless day, with plenty of protection (doors) to keep out unwanted stimuli? As a child, she also used this system to describe her reactions to music: hard rock, to which she listens "with an expression of the purest joy, rocking in her rocking chair, putting her hands over her ears" (Park and Youderian 315) is the music of no clouds and four doors, whereas a recording of the spoken word is the worst (four clouds and no doors).

All these systems draw on concrete stimuli—food, clouds—that often exert a strong effect on the senses. The correlation of clouds and rice pudding and bad days at first seems random and mysterious (though we often unconsciously equate objects, such as apple pie, with concepts such mom, on the basis of similarly arbitrary associations). But through them we can begin to understand the mind of an autistic person whose linguistic ability may be severely limited and whose neurological wiring fosters an unusual (I prefer not to say "abnormal") use of language. The language of autism might seem "bizarre" or "weird" (terms that I also use with reservation, due to the value judgments implicit in them) but it is no more so than the metonymical language we find in poetry.

Let us, then, consider some poetry by non-autistic poets that exhibits "autistic" language. The prose poem is the ideal form for the metonymic language of autism, as each sentence builds on the previous one through associations.[6] The sudden disruptions of topic and of meaning in prose poetry are similar to an autistic person's abrupt introduction of unrelated concepts and association of entities and ideas not based on logical connections. Canadian poet and classicist Anne Carson's "Short Talk on Autism," from *Short Talks* (1992),[7] presents a woman's experience of a doctor's language. "It is a large grey cheerful woman its language is boomings beckonings boulders boasts boomerangs bowler hats. Brother?" (Carson 25). The nameless "she" does not hear the content of the doctor's language. She is stuck on the sounds (especially the initial "b"): "*b*oomings *b*eckonings *b*oasts *b*oomerangs *b*owler hats. Brother? Tell me about your *b*rother?" The "booming" sound of the doctor's language leads to the woman's falling into a reverie of words starting with "b," so that the only word she hears of the doctor is a "b"-word, "brother." She hears (or believes she hears) "*what does it eat, light?*" from the doctor's pencil, and these words are repeated until, by the poem's end, their meaning is lost as they are repeated like a choral refrain: "*what does* wander yondering . . . *eat eat eat* who know what damage *eat light?*" (25). Carson's poem suggests that the woman's understanding of the doctor's language is not semantic but phonetic and rhythmic, so that "wander" generates "yondering." The woman experiences language and words as concrete objects, as groupings of "b" and "w" sounds. This concrete use of language is related to metonymy and links the language of autism to poetic language. In Carson's poem, the woman's understanding of her doctor-interlocutor is unknown and it is not clear what, if any, communication passes from patient to physician.

Similar wordplay and creation of meaning based on the sounds of words is evident when a person perceives an identity between two entities purely on the basis of their names having a similar sound: thus my son used to think "girl" and "squirrel" were the same purely on the basis of the consonant "ir" and "l" sounds. This finding meaning in the very sounds of language is at work in Carson's use of the "*and/ond*" equivalence in her "Short Talk on Autism" and even more prominent in the poetry of Gerard Manley Hopkins, which readers often experience as a mass of sound and images. Here are lines 6–9 of "That Nature is a Heraclitean Fire": "in pool and rutpeel parches / Squandering ooze to squeezed | dough, crúst, dust; stánches, stárches / Squadroned masks and manmarks | treadmire toil there / Foótfretted in it." The initial "sq" sounds in "squandering," "squeezed," and "squadroned" link those words sonically; the three words also develop an image of some concrete *thing* being molded and shaped from language, first semisolid "ooze," then clayey "dough" that first hardens into "crust" before crumbling into "dust." The sounds, words, and images linked with "squadroned" also refer to something manmade: soldiers in a "squadron," in military formation, stiffly "starched" and toiling and treading in the "mire," their marching feet making a fretwork-like pattern of "manmarks." In building the images of such manmade creations as bread or soldiers in military formation, Hopkins relies on the accumulated similarities and repetitions of sounds ("sq"; the long vowel sounds of "oo" and "ee" and "ough"; the staccato beats of "crust, dust; stanches, starches"). These lines represent an aspect of the experience of language for a child with autism who struggles just to distinguish among the phonemes and vowel sounds, who is most comfortable using concrete language, and has a very difficult time grasping abstract notions, such as "truth," or "faith." Hopkins heaps up *things*—the pool, the "ooze to squeezed dough, crust, dust," a splintering slice of bread (the Host?); his poem is packed with concrete images as he uses sounds concretely. Hopkins's poetry approaches an idiolect in its overwrought syntax and diction, as in this excerpt from "God's Grandeur":

> The world is charged with the grandeur of God.
> It will flame out, like shining from shook foil;
> It gathers to a greatness, like the ooze of oil
> Crushed. Why do men then now not reck his rod?

"Generations have trod, have trod, have trod": the thrice-repeated phrase with its monosyllabic words resembles how my son Charlie "plays" with language. He hears the repeated sound "*ear*" in "seared" and "bleared" and "smeared" but "*ear*" may be all he hears. If you try to listen only to the sounds of "God's Grandeur," you may experience an approximation of Charlie's language. Because they seem out of context, some of Charlie's verbal utterances seem as incomprehensible to most listeners as a line by Hopkins.

Lines like "sheer plod makes plough down sillion" from "God's Grandeur" have the kind of gnarling music reminiscent of a Baroque fugue, or of the commentary the autistic painter Larry Bissonnette writes for a painting entitled "Paints get really loused up by my signature so both art and letters learn to cohabitate": "Powered print treats painted images well as long as colors Larry selects match. Larry loves pink and purple because pressured painter gets to lighten stroke."[8] Like Hopkins's poetry, Bissonnette's writing engulfs us in language as sound and image, each syllable so overstuffed with sounds (the repeated initial "p") and potential meaning (the use of perfect participle-noun combinations, "powered print," "painted images," "pressured painter") that it can be unbearable to read. Bissonnette's painting, a rectangular canvas, is alike filled with paint, with swatches of brown on the top, red on the bottom, pale pink through the middle and on the right, and more.

What if such compact verbal utterances were the way we had to talk to each other—in such a fractioned idiom, in bits and pieces of words, in sounds knowable only to its speaker? Every word in Bissonnette's short commentary counts because there are so few, and because of the dense quality of his language with its many adjectives: the print is "powered"—it is empowered by the colors he uses; it is given force and movement by those colors—whereas the painter himself is "pressured" by the necessity of putting the paint into a contained space, by the world around him. The verbal utterances of Larry Bissonnette and Jessy Park—their fractioned idioms— suggest that an autistic person experiences language and the world as a continuous difficult poem steeped in metaphors, verbal echoes, word play. If we feel baffled by this mass of words, imagine a cognitively disabled child who has minimal speech trying to make sense of the nonsense-language of everyone else. Meanwhile, those everyone elses do not grasp the metonymical truths—that bike rides equal sushi, or four clouds make a bad day, that "booming" signifies "boomerang"—according to which he orders and understands the world.

Autistic language exemplifies Ferdinand du Saussure's notion of the "arbitrary" nature of the sign, of the relation between signifier and signified, in his *Cours de Linguistique Générale*. Figuring out language according to a Saussurean model of signifiers attached arbitrarily to a signified or meaning is in fact the lifelong language project of an autistic individual. The sounds of words all seem attached to a meaning for no particular reason; each example must be learned; nothing is natural. A child with autism can be described as living in a world of contingent relations. He/she does not grasp meaning automatically, inasmuch as this involves a symbolic register in which something can stand for something else because of a similarity. Thus do autistic individuals have "concrete" thinking and language. And therefore learning how to think using figurative language like metaphors must be part of his or her speech and cognitive education. What is the skill of generalization—understanding that "ball" means not just one flashcard of a beach ball but a soccer ball, a blue ball, a football, a koosh ball—but a lesson in thinking metaphorically?

Because metaphors and other types of figurative language are fundamentally woven into neurotypical cognitive processing and language, they are one aspect of language that is particularly difficult for autistic persons to understand. Words that say one thing and mean another can register as meaning more than one thing, as George Lakoff and Mark Turner write regarding metaphors in particular:

> [M]etaphor pervades our normal conceptual system. Because so many of the concepts that are important to us are either abstract or not clearly delineated in our experience (the emotions, ideas, time, etc.), we need to get a grasp on them by means of other concepts that we understand in clearer terms (spatial orientation, objects, etc.). *This need leads to metaphorical definition in our conceptual system* [my emphasis]. We have tried . . . to give some indication of just how extensive a role metaphor plays in the way we function, the way we conceptualize our experience, and the way we speak. (115)

As Lakoff and Turner note, we mistakenly relegate metaphors to the realm of "language only." But metaphors are intricately infused in our understanding: they are not "just words" but directly influence and create our thinking processes and understanding of the world. I would like to extend what Lakoff and Turner write regarding metaphor to figurative language more generally and to metonymy in particular. Both metonymy and metaphor refer to ways in which words are associated with the world, with concrete phenomena, with reality. The difference between the two terms lies in how the associations between the metonymy or metaphor—the signifier—and the concrete item in the world—the signified—are made. In metaphor, the signifier refers to its signified on the basis of a common-sense similarity agreed on by a community of speakers (for instance, neurotypical speakers) and generated by an ability to see sameness in difference—some similar quality in two different entities. Thus, bravery links Achilles to a lion. A lick of a fresh lemon leaves a sour taste in the mouth; finding out the used car you just bought is a "lemon" leaves the same sour feeling. In metaphor, connections rely on the ability to discern and select some similar feature of the lemon and the used car, or between a cookie crumbling and some situation not working out as desired. In metonymy, the reason for the linking of signifier to signified—of the referer to the referent—is not readily, logically discernible.[9] Richard Nixon alone could not bomb a city, Hanoi, yet we have read of "Nixon bombing Hanoi." A pen has come to mean a writer and still does metonymically, even though our culture has developed other implements for writing. (Because many writers might write using a keyboard, the saying could be revised to be "the keyboard is mightier than the sword" or, to update the entire phrase, "the keyboard is mightier than WMDs.") Yet different flavors of rice pudding have nothing to do with notions of goodness or badness.

Just as Lakoff claims that metaphors influence more than just our understanding of language, so metonymy embodies how the words of an autistic idiolect influence more than just an autistic person's understanding and use of language.[10] Our ability to see a similarity among entities is fundamental for our understanding of the world. This intrinsic functioning of metaphors in both our linguistic and general understanding further attests to how an autistic person's experience of language and of the world of senses and stimuli as a whole is fundamentally different from that of neurotypicals because theirs is a metonymic rather than a metaphorical cosmos. If it is the case that, as Lakoff and Johnson write, "concepts that occur in metaphorical definitions are those that correspond to *natural* kinds of experience" (118; emphasis mine), then we can further see the fundamental challenges to an autistic child's learning language. What is "natural" or essential to the majority of the population is not so for a child with autism's neurological and sensory impairments. What seems natural to the majority of the population—to those of us who are not autistic—seems so to an autistic person only by convention, habit, repeated occurrence. It may well be as conventional—as arbitrary, as accidental, as metonymical—to say that Achilles is a lion as it is to say that a bike ride is sushi. What is true to Charlie—that you go to ShopRite to buy sushi—is only one option within a range of possibilities to me: I go to ShopRite for vegetables, eggs, detergent, Advil, and coffee filters, to name a very few things. This difference would explain the often puzzling challenges that can arise in teaching language and communication to autistic children, because their use of language is different from that of neurotypical users. We must learn more about how an autistic understanding of language differs fundamentally from neurotypical usage as we seek to teach autistic persons to communicate more effectively and seek to understand and interpret autistic idiolect.

This difference is described by Tito Rajarshi Mukhopadhyay in his autobiographical *The Mind Tree*.[11] Mukhopadhyay's writing has been seen as exceptional due to the severity of his autism and his language disability, but what is particularly exceptional about it is his use of an autistic idiom. Mukhopadhyay's language provides clues to his way of thinking, just as do Jessy Park's more limited verbalizations and systems of correlations.

Although *The Mind Tree* is seemingly structured as a narrative—of the narrator's growth from self-absorbed autistic child to autistic author able to explain himself in language—Mukhopadhyay jumps from writing about himself as a child (of unclear age) to general observations about his difficulty in coordinating his mind and body, his thinking and his verbal output.[12] He intertwines a first-person and a third-person perspective, as in "The Window of my World," the first section of *The Mind Tree*: "I think about the little boy who had a way of expressing himself, not through speech but through a frustrated temper tantrum. The language was known but it did not relate to anything" (1). The third-person perspective gives Mukhopadhyay's writing an objective, distant quality, like that we associate with clinical reports. He writes about himself as a character in a story, "the little boy," the "little" indicating that he is looking back at a younger version of himself. He thus assumes the perspective on "the boy" of an omniscient narrator. An abstract noun ("the language") becomes the subject of a sentence: "the language" is a "known" and familiar entity that is not able to "relate to anything," just as a person might not be able to relate to another person. Mukhopadhyay describes "language" as not relating "to anything" (and whose language is it—his only? another person's? language in general?). It is as if it is not the autistic subject of the text who has difficulties relating but language itself. He writes about language as a thing foreign and external, separated and broken off from the subject, as it is in Carson's "Short Talk on Autism": "it is a large grey cheerful woman its language is boomings." In Mukhopadhyay's experience, language is an alien thing that he nonetheless must learn to use to express his needs and himself.

The Mind Tree's subject also describes himself as thoroughly disembodied, separate from his own body. Mukhopadhyay often seems almost surprised that a body part, such as his hand, is actually connected to his "self": "The hand had made a strange relationship with its shadow, and he fluttered it and spent his hours, contented with the long company of his shadow" (2). He writes about his hand as a foreign entity that he has accidentally discovered. "The hand" is like the disembodied, separate language referred to previously. The lack of connection between Mukhopadhyay's mind and body leads to him cut his fingers on a fan: "Once a table fan had attracted him and he went to touch it. He cut his fingers, of course, but could not caution himself, though he had full knowledge of current, electricity and the dangers involved with it. The two stayed in their own selves, isolated from each other" (77–78). He describes the fact that a table fan can cut his fingers as an accidental phenomenon that he comprehends almost incidentally. His writing suggests that, had he not had the experience of touching the fan, he would not have known not to (and he does not indicate whether he has since stopped touching fans, only that he knows he is not supposed to). As he writes in one of his poems about how others perceive his difference: "Men and women are puzzled by everything I do / Doctors use different terminologies to describe me / I just wonder. . . .? But it is a world full of improbabilities / Racing toward uncertainty" (201). Mukhopadhyay's understanding, like Jessy Park's of clouds in the sky, is metonymical in its reliance on the observation of chance occurrences that are elevated to truth. Investigating how poetic language works—through metonymy when metaphor is expected—can assist us in understanding Mukhopadhyay's thinking, and perhaps in understanding how an autistic person perceives the world with its many "improbabilities / Racing toward uncertainty."

What I have tried to describe in this chapter is the arbitrary way autistic people use language to communicate and to comprehend the world. To understand or interpret an autistic person's language, one must be not only a translator but also an interpreter who reads metonymically in order to uncover the relationship between two seemingly unrelated items like sushi and bike ride. The relationship between these two terms is temporally constructed when two events occur in succession (such as bike riding in a certain park and then eating sushi). The connection between the two events or terms is arbitrary, the result of historical-temporal accident or spatial proximity (in the phrase "daddy blue blanket," because the blanket happened to be on the bed once while the child's father was sleeping in it). Everyday words like "slide" or "beach house" can refer to a particular complex of meanings that are tightly enwrapped with a child's past experiences. These meanings are not immediately accessible to any listener. Neurotypical individuals recognize the coincidental and arbitrary nature of these associations, but for an autistic person the relationship is essential. It is part of the order of the universe, the person's own private cosmos. We can use the trope of metonymy to interpret what might seem arbitrary linguistic utterances of autistic individuals. Examining how metonymy works—how, in metonymy, language is linked to the world—can suggest how an autistic idiolect might arise through accidental associations that an autistic person might not see as such.

Autistic language is a fractioned idiom, its vocabulary created from contextual and seemingly arbitrary associations of word and thing, and peculiar to its sole speaker alone; this chapter has attempted to show why and how we can decode that idiolect, and to understand how its piecemeal utterances create meaning. Armed with tools drawn from poetry, we might try to listen harder and longer to the "random utterances" of those whose words may be few indeed. We can employ metaphor and metonymy, assonance and alliteration, meter and syntax, to interpret an autistic person's communicative attempts or even what seems to be unusual behavior, such as touching a moving fan or drawing rows of tubes and labeling them with strawberry, tangerine, lemon. The difference between metonymy and metaphor can also illustrate the divide in understanding between autistic and neurotypical persons. If we read autistic language with the presumption that the person saying a seemingly nonsensical phrase such as "bedtime orange" is communicating a message, if we assume the responsibility of translating flavor tubes and clouds, we might be able to understand some of what an autistic person is telling us. Reading autistic language as we read poetry, with attention to its tropes and the system behind seemingly unusual combinations of elements and images and to the music of language, can offer some clues for understanding and, most of all, for communication.

NOTES

1. Kanner noted the "literalness" of speech among autistic children in "Autistic Disturbances of Affective Contact"; "abnormalities associated with language and thought" are noted as a "major symptom of childhood autism" in Hermelin and Frith.
2. Jessy Park's flavor tubes and other systems of correlated elements are what Simon Baron-Cohen terms *a drive to systematize* that, paired with a tendency not to empathize, is characteristic of autistic individuals.

3. So, too, for Charlie, does "bedtime" stand for a whole complex of words and associations, including the feeling of "I love you" because Barney—with his signature song—was once Charlie's bedtime companion.

4. The metonymic thinking of autistic persons also helps explain why any augmentative communication system that uses a metaphoric/symbolic system, such as PECS, can be difficult for an autistic person to grasp. Generalization is easier said than done.

5. The systems are recorded in full detail in an article by David Park, Clara Park's husband, and Phil Youderian 315.

6. L=A=N=G=U=A=G=E poet Lyn Hejinian frequently writes prose poetry, as in *My Life*. Of the place of language in writing, she writes in her introduction to *The Language of Inquiry*, "language is nothing but meanings, and meanings are nothing but a flow of contexts. Such contexts rarely coalesce into images, rarely come to terms. They are transitions, transmutations, the endless radiating of denotation into relation" (1).

7. "Short Talk on Autism" appears in the first edition of *Short Talks* (1992) but is not included in the version of *Short Talks* incorporated in Carson's *Plainwater*.

8. The language of autistic persons is more and more accessible thanks to the growing number of books and other writings by autistic authors. Some of Bissonnette's paintings with his commentary are reproduced in his text, "Letters Ordered."

9. A teaching program based on the principles of Applied Behavior Analysis (ABA) can thus be highly effective in teaching language to a child with autism, because such a method teaches language as verbal behavior; see Lovaas et al., Koegel.

10. The need to understand autistic idiolect on its own terms and especially in regard to the function of metonymy is underscored by George Lakoff's observations about the prevalence of metaphor in our language, here in regard to President George W. Bush's Gulf War rhetoric: "One of the fundamental findings of cognitive science is that people think in terms of frames and metaphors—conceptual structures like those we have been describing. The frames are in the synapses of our brains—physically present in the form of neural circuitry. When the facts don't fit the frames, the frames are kept and the facts ignored" ("Metaphor and War"). An individual with autism has the frames but not the metaphors (which he or she might experience as metonymies).

11. Many sections of *The Mind Tree* appear in Mukhopadhyay's earlier book, *Beyond the Silence: My Life, the World, and Autism*.

12. The lack of temporal awareness—and the difficulty of constructing a chronological narrative—in *The Mind Tree* is also notable in autobiographical accounts by autistic writers such as Sue Rubin, Lucy Blackman, and Alberto Frugone.

WORKS CITED

Baron-Cohen, Simon. "The Male Condition." *New York Times on the Web* 8 August 2005. 9 January 2007 <http://www.nytimes.com/2005/08/08/opinion/08baron-cohen.html?ex=1168578000&en=31eb995dfbf17744&ei=5070

Biklen, Douglas. *Autism and the Metaphor of the Person Alone.* New York: New York UP, 2005.

Bissonnette, Larry. "Letters Ordered Through Typing Produce the Story of an Artist Stranded on the Island of Autism." Biklen 172–182.

Blackman, Lucy. "Reflections on Language (by Lucy Blackman)." Biklen 146–167.

Carson, Anne. *Plainwater: Essays and Poetry*. New York: Knopf, 1995.

———. *Short Talks*. London, Ontario: Brick Books, 1992.

Donnellan, Anne M., ed. *Classic Readings in Autism*. New York: Teachers College P, 1985.

Frugone, Alberto. "Salient Moments in the Life of Alberto, as a Child, a Youth, a Young Man." Biklen 185–197.

Hejinian, Lyn. *The Language of Inquiry*. Berkeley: U of California P, 2000.

———. *My Life*. Los Angeles: Sun & Moon, 1987.

Hermelin, Beate, and Uta Frith. "Psychological Studies of Childhood Autism: Can Autistic Children Make Sense of What They See and Hear?" Donnellan 210–235.

Hopkins, Gerard Manley. *The Poems of Gerard Manley Hopkins*. 4th edition. Ed. W.H. Gardner and N.H. MacKenzie. Oxford: Oxford UP, 1970.

Jakobson, Roman. "Two aspects of language and two types of aphasic disturbances." *Fundamentals of Language*. The Hague: Mouton, 1971. 55–82.

Kanner, Leo. "Autistic Disturbances of Affective Contact." Donnellan 11–52.

Koegel, Lynn Kern. "Communication and Language Intervention." *Teaching Children with Autism: Strategies for Initiating Positive Interactions and Improving Learning Opportunities*. Eds. Robert L. Koegel and Lynn Kern Koegel. Baltimore: Paul H. Brookes, 1995. 17–32.

Lakoff, George. "Metaphor and War, Again." 9 January 2005. http://www.alternet.org/story/15414>.

———. and Mark Johnson. *Metaphors We Live By*. Chicago: U of Chicago P, 2003.

———. and Mark Turner. *More than Cool Reason: A Field Guide to Poetic Metaphor*. Chicago: U of Chicago P, 1989.

Loos, Eugene E., Susan Anderson, Dwight H. Day, Jr., Paul C. Jordan and J. Douglas Wingate, eds. "What is a metaphor?" *Glossary of Linguistic Terms*. 29 January 2006.http://www.sil.org/linguistics/GlossaryOfLinguisticTerms/WhatIsAMetaphor.htm

———. "What is metonymy?" *Glossary of Linguistic Terms*. 29 January 2006. http://www.sil.org/linguistics/GlossaryOfLinguisticTerms/WhatIsMetonymy.htm

Lovaas, O. Ivar, John P. Berberich, Bernard F. Perloff, and Benson Schaeffer. "Acquisition of Imitative Speech by Schizophrenic Children." Donnellan 135–178.

Mukhopadyay, Tito Rajarshi. *Beyond the Silence: My Life, the World, and Autism*. London: National Autistic Society, 2000.

———. *The Mind Tree: A Miraculous Child Breaks the Silence of Autism*. New York: Arcade, 2003.

Park, Clara Claiborne. *Exiting Nirvana: A Daughter's Life with Autism*. Boston: Little, Brown, 2001.

Park, David and Philip Youderian. "Light and Number: Ordering Principles in the World of an Autistic Child." *Journal of Autism and Childhood Schizophrenia* 4.2 (1974): 315–8.

Rubin, Sue. "A Conversation with Leo Kanner (by Sue Rubin)." Biklen 82–109.

WordNet. Cognitive Science Laboratory, Princeton University. 2005. 7 January 2006. <http://wordnet.princeton.edu/>.

7   Imagination and the Awareness of Self in Autistic Spectrum Poets*

Ilona Roth

INTRODUCTION

> When I had been gifted this mind of mine
> I recall his voice very clearly
> To you I have given this mind
> And you shall be the only kind
> No one ever will like you be
> And I name you the mind tree
> I can't see or talk
> Yet I can imagine
> I can hope and I can expect
> I can feel pain but I cannot cry
> So I just be and wait for the pain to subside

> From "The Mind Tree," by Tito Mukhopadhyay
> (at age 11; from *Beyond the Silence* 104).

In this chapter I consider one of the most elusive but fundamental questions posed by autistic conditions: what is the mental world of the person with autism like? In particular, I focus on two faculties of mind—imagination and awareness of self—whose status in autistic spectrum individuals has been the subject of confusing and contradictory claims. The prevalent view—that imagination and self-awareness are impaired or even absent—might seem to imply that autistic persons do not really have an inner life: that they live entirely in the here and now, perceiving, recognizing and responding to the outer environment, but unable to reflect on experience, whether before, during or after its occurrence.

---

*In this chapter "autism" should be taken as generic shorthand for autism spectrum difficulties or disorders (ASD) and I use these terms more or less interchangeably. I favor the phrase "person with autism/ASD" over "autistic person." However, in the interests of economy of expression, I use both phrases. No disrespect is implied.

Imagination and self-awareness are beginning to gain recognition among cognitive scientists as key elements within the mental architecture that has played a central role in the exceptional evolutionary success of humans. Therefore, to suggest, as some in the research, clinical and lay communities do, that people with ASD lack these capacities is to deny their essential humanity. We need to understand the rationale for representing autism in this way, and highlight the evidence that challenges or qualifies this representation. An important resource is the significant volume of published literature by people on the autism spectrum, including poetry, stories and autobiographies.

PROSE AND POETRY AS A ROUTE TO THE AUTISTIC MIND

Prose and poetry written by people with ASD call for investigation because to write a poem without imagination, or to write about oneself without self-awareness, would seem an oxymoron. Though autistic individuals with literary talent are in a minority, we cannot simply dismiss this phenomenon as offering no wider insights into the autistic condition. Rather, it may provide a unique window into the mental world of autism, which, though unusual and hard to fathom, is by no means a void.

An isomorphic relationship between thought processes and use of language in ASD has been established in psychological research by Tager-Flusberg and others. She demonstrated that, just as people with ASD have impaired understanding of other people's thoughts and beliefs, so their spoken discourse tends to lack mental state terms such as "think," "know" and "believe." The rationale for exploring thought and its disorders through systematic analyses of *written* language also receives support from a recent study of the works of novelist Iris Murdoch. Garrard et al. carried out content analyses of Murdoch's late work, which showed that subtle changes in the scope and imaginative richness of the language were present well before she showed symptoms of Alzheimer's disease (see especially 254–60). Poetry, the focus of the present research, is an especially fruitful medium for a similar approach, being relatively unconstrained by the rules of written prose or spoken social discourse.

In this chapter I outline some of the conflicting claims about imagination and self-awareness that feature in representations of the autism spectrum. I then describe some of the insights that our research into autistic poetry is providing. First, however, I propose definitions of the two faculties of mind central to this discussion.

IMAGINATION AND AWARENESS OF SELF: DEFINITIONS

To define imagination and self-awareness is no easy matter, for they are among the most slippery phenomena that fall within the scope of psychology.

In previous eras scientifically minded psychologists have steered well clear of such complex, elusive faculties of mind, confining themselves instead to more methodologically tractable phenomena. As Fodor points out (107), traditional cognitive science has specialized in effective models of processes that are of marginal interest, presuming that the more interesting processes cannot be readily investigated. Fortunately, there is a growing realization that to avoid conformity to this First Law of the Nonexistence of Cognitive Science one must engage with the interesting phenomena, however difficult that might be. I offer the following working definitions of imagination and self-awareness in this spirit, and with the knowledge that they leave room for debate and improvement.

Imagination denotes a cluster of related phenomena including pretense and fantasy, metaphorical thinking (in "as if" mode), counterfactual thinking (in "what if?" mode), creative thinking and imagery. These are all mental processes in which the mind operates with concepts and ideas that may have no correspondence with past, current or future reality. With such wide scope, imagination might appear synonymous with thought in general: after all, what is human thought if it is not abstract, hypothetical, flexible and creative? I cannot give a full answer to this objection here. Suffice it to say that, despite some overlap with the broader concept of human thought, imagination denotes its most quintessential and special characteristics, and that these merit special and separate consideration.

Awareness of self refers to the capacity to be aware of one's own inner states, experiences and characteristic ways of engaging with the world. Such awareness comprises different levels, which include the following: awareness of one's own sensations and perceptions; awareness of one's own agency or effects on the environment; awareness of one's own mental states—thoughts, desires and emotions; awareness of one's enduring qualities, such as personality and identity; and awareness of one's relationship to others.

IMAGINATION AND AWARENESS OF SELF IN AUTISM: MEDICO-SCIENTIFIC PERSPECTIVES

Medical and scientific accounts of autistic spectrum conditions embrace some broad generalizations about mental processes such as imagination and self-awareness that, as we shall see, sit uncomfortably with the skills and achievements we encounter in some individuals on the spectrum.

Regarding imagination, the diagnostic criteria for ASD highlight as one cluster within the well-known diagnostic triad rigid, stereotyped behavior and a preference for sameness, all suggesting the antithesis of imaginative thought patterns. The absence of pretend play, which neurotypical children develop at 18 months, is considered a robust predictor of an incipient autistic condition (see Baird et al.). Both children and adults with ASD are said to have difficulty with metaphorical language (Happé) and with understanding or constructing narrative (Bruner and Feldman; Belmonte, this volume).

Their difficulties in imagining what other people are thinking and feeling—known as theory of mind or ToM—have been extensively documented over the last eighteen years (see Baron-Cohen, "Theory of Mind," for a review). Children with ASD also show difficulty in experimental tests of creativity, such as completing a fantasy story (Craig et al., "Story-telling"), drawing a fantastical creature (Craig et al., "Drawing"), or thinking of alternative uses for an object such as a brick (Craig and Baron-Cohen 321–23, 325).

The autistic capacity for mental imagery (roughly, the capacity for qua-siperceptual experiences in the absence of sensory stimulation) presents a mixed pattern. For instance, Temple Grandin, a prominent autistic academic, describes her own thinking style as heavily reliant on visual imagery (Grandin, *Thinking* 19–42). However, Craig's studies of children suggest that although their capacity to form veridical images of real objects and events is preserved, their ability to form images of unreal or fantastical things may be impaired.

Overall, then, people with autism appear to have difficulties with most if not all the forms of imagination outlined earlier. However, this simplifies a complex picture. Much of the evidence derives from experimental tasks that may not map well to real-life situations, and the character and severity of problems that autistic people experience differ substantially between sub-groups and individuals across the spectrum. For instance, many adults with high-functioning autism or Asperger's syndrome have some theory-of-mind skills, and children in these diagnostic subgroups have less difficulty with creativity and fantasy tasks than those with classic autism.

An apparently more fundamental challenge to the imaginative deficit model is the accomplishments that some people with ASD show in creative fields. From this group, sometimes known as savants, come the remarkable architectural drawings by Stephen Wiltshire and vibrant, lyrical paintings by Richard Wawro; Tony DeBlois's highly accomplished jazz improvisations and command of twenty instruments. In the domain of creative writing, we have poetry by writers such as Tito Mukhopadhyay, Craig Romkema, and Donna Williams. Yet, perhaps in the interests of parsimony, some experts have questioned the creativity suggested by such achievements. For instance, Treffert (194–5, 256–61) implies that because Stephen Wiltshire's drawings of buildings are highly accurate representations, his main talent derives from his remarkable memory—that he simply "reads out" images of the buildings from memory onto the page. Beate Hermelin, however, has demonstrated that this is mistaken: Wiltshire draws not what he sees, but what he knows the structures he depicts to be "really like," a transforma-tive process that is surely related to creativity (154–55). In any case, to dismiss autistic creativity because it involves accurate representation is to subject it to criteria not consistently applied to neurotypical people: we do not dismiss the work of Canaletto, for instance, because his paintings are precise and presumably accurate renditions of eighteenth-century Venetian scenes.

Further skepticism about autistic creativity appears in the claim that talented artists such as Wiltshire do not represent the spectrum. Yet we can also question this claim. If the assumption is that autistic artists are an exceptionally high-functioning group, this is incorrect: some of them (Wiltshire and Mukhopadhyay, for instance) have severe disabilities. Even if such creativity is uncharacteristic of the general autistic population, we find a similarly uneven distribution of creativity in the neurotypical population (Simonton 189, 196). If the claim is that *no* autistic individual other than these high-profile individuals has any creativity, this is also untrue. Most of us who work with autistic people know of many who can draw well, play music, or who have quirkily creative ideas, even if they cannot express them well on paper.

There has been comparatively little empirical work on autistic awareness of self, not least because of the difficulty of designing objective studies. At the level of sensory and perceptual experience, there is clinical and anecdotal evidence for both diminished and accentuated self-awareness (see, for instance Frith, "Asperger" 14–15). Autistic persons may not notice or report stimuli that would typically evoke pain, and may experience lights, colors and sounds as abnormally or even painfully strong. Claims about the autistic person's awareness of his or her own mental states mostly constitute extensions of the theory-of-mind approach. In this view, the process of reflecting on one's own thoughts, beliefs and feelings is considered essentially the same as reflecting on the thoughts, beliefs and feelings of others. In keeping with this approach, Frith and Happé propose that, to the extent that ToM capacity is impaired in people on the autistic spectrum, so too should be the capacity for self-reflection or self-awareness: people with ASD "may know as little about their own minds as about the minds of other people" (7).

Frith and Happé studied the introspections of three young autistic men who were asked to write down the contents of their thoughts at random intervals. In keeping with their model, the capacities for self- and other-awareness were correlated. The young man with the poorest ToM skills was completely unable to report mental experience. The young man with the best ToM skills produced the most sophisticated reflections, including some references to mental states. All three men found the task very difficult and unfamiliar, and their reports described visual images, invariably veridical rather than imaginary, which they experienced as "pictures in the mind" (14).

The notion that a person knows her own mind only to the extent, and in the way, that she knows other people's can be challenged both philosophically (see McGeer 243–46) and empirically. Neuropsychological evidence suggests that although the neural circuits involved in representing self and other are partly shared, they are also partly distinct (Decety and Sommerville 5–9). Correspondingly, there is evidence for selectively preserved self-awareness in some autistic children. For instance, Ziatas et al. found that the spontaneous speech of children with Asperger's syndrome made *more* assertions relating to their own internal states than that of typically developing controls (see especially 81–91). Klein et al. tested a young autistic adult on his knowledge of his own and other family members' personality characteristics. Although his ratings of the traits of other family members were indiscriminate and misjudged, his self-knowledge proved to be specific and accurate—it agreed well with others' ratings of him. Because this young man also had profound problems with episodic memory and semantic category acquisition, Klein and colleagues concluded that he had acquired his personality knowledge via a distinct mechanism dedicated to aspects of self-awareness (375–88).

To summarize, studies of self-awareness in people with ASD present a complex picture. The profile of self-awareness across the levels outlined earlier appears atypical, rather than uniformly diminished. This leaves open the question of how far and in what ways people with autism are self-aware. In the face of such contradictory views of both imagination and self-awareness in autism, I turn to what we can learn from autistic writings, especially poetry.

THE CONUNDRUM OF AUTISTIC POETRY

Autistic writers with enough talent to be published have begun to emerge during the last twenty years, with books such as Temple Grandin's *Emergence: Labeled Autistic* and Donna Williams's *Nobody Nowhere* being early examples. Williams's first and subsequent books are notable for including poetry as well as autobiographical reflections. Other more recent examples include Tito Mukhopadhyay's remarkable volume of autobiography and poetry, written when he was between the ages of eight and eleven, and Jennifer Fan's collection of poetry.

Two factors may have fostered the emergence of this genre. First, contemporary educational and therapeutic techniques place a premium on self-expressive and creative activities such as the writing of diaries and stories. Second, with growing interest in autistic writings, as evidenced by thriving specialist publishers such as Jessica Kingsley, autistic individuals may feel more encouraged to put pen to paper. However, autistic writing is not necessarily a new trend. In the past, the literary talents of diagnosed autistic individuals may have been known only within their own immediate circle of family and friends. Moreover, the possibility of latent autism among well-recognized writers and poets is receiving considerable attention. For instance, Marion Glastonbury argues that the eccentric life and bleak outlook of Samuel Beckett is consistent with an autistic condition ("Stain" and " 'I'll Teach' " 62–64), and Michael Fitzgerald has made similar claims for W. B. Yeats (171–93) and Lewis Carroll (194–205).

To write an autobiography without imagination or self-awareness would seem problematic enough. To write poetry without being able to draw on these capacities would seem even harder, because they appear to be necessary tools of the poet's trade. Yet it might in principle be possible for a piece of writing to meet the minimal requirements of poetry without possessing qualities such as imagination and reflexivity that we normally expect of it. Such work would display formal characteristics of poetry while lacking typically "poetic" content. In a recent discussion of what constitutes a poem (as distinct from a piece of prose) Christopher Ricks argues that the key defining feature of a poem is the way the lines are arranged on the page: "in poetry, the line-endings are significant, and they effect their significance—not necessarily of rhythm, and whether of force or of nuance—by using their ensuing space, by using a pause that is not necessarily a pause of punctuation and so may be only equivocally a pause at all. Lines of prose end with a soft return; lines of poetry end with a hard return" (14).

This definition, which emphasizes that poetry is characterized above all by its use of space, pertains to the present discussion, because individuals with autism are often good at processing and imitating spatial patterns. Poetry written by people with autism might well emulate the physical appearance of poetry, or embrace obvious or conventional stylistic features such as rhyme and rhythm, while reflecting content devoid of the other expressive qualities we usually associate with the art.

It is possible, then, for some sort of poetry to be written according to a formula or set of rules. If so, poems by people on the autistic spectrum might not be such a surprising achievement after all. Baron-Cohen has argued that people on the spectrum have an accentuated capacity for systematizing—for ordering their thoughts and behavior according to rules of the kind that govern physical systems (*Essential* 133–54). Perhaps, then, autistic poets have internalized a set of formal rules in order to write their poetry. If so, we need to consider the possibility that their poetry is published not because it is particularly good but because it is an intriguing oddity. It follows that we need to know not only *that* people on the autism spectrum can write poetry, but *what* their poetry is like.

Beate Hermelin and her colleagues have contributed some findings relevant to this question in a study analyzing the use of imaginative devices such as metaphor and a thematic focus on self in a single poet, Kate, with Asperger's syndrome (Dowker, Hermelin & Pring). However, we can draw no firm conclusions from this study. Kate suffered from profound cognitive and social disabilities and led a circumscribed and dependent life; by contrast, the "control" poet to whom her writings were compared, though physically disabled, was intellectually able, with a good university degree, a profession, an active social life, and many hobbies. Thus it is not possible to say how much the distinctive features of Kate's poetry are a specific consequence of her autistic spectrum condition and how much they are a more general effect of her cognitive and social impairments. Nor is it legitimate to generalize the findings to other autistic poets.

A SYSTEMATIC STUDY OF AUTISTIC SPECTRUM POETRY

The research described here was designed as a wide-ranging study of autistic poetry, involving the work of both male and female, young and mature poets, from different parts of the autism spectrum. The approach sought to integrate a scientific approach to the autistic mental world, via systematic analyses of its poetic expression, with an attempt to understand the autistic poets' points of view on their work.

To date we have studied work by five published autistic spectrum poets, each compared with a range of work by neurotypical poets, suitably matched in terms of sex, age and educational level. The ASD group includes two male poets, aged 11 and 20, both with diagnoses of autism, and three female poets, aged 24, 41 and 53, with diagnoses of Asperger syndrome, autism and Asperger syndrome respectively.

We analyzed the poetry using quantitative content analysis. Initially we devised a set of coding categories, refining them until they could be reliably and consistently employed by coders working independently of one another. We then coded global or whole-poem characteristics for each poem. These included the theme, which was coded according to the predominant focus into broad categories including self, "other," relationship, or nature. Global characteristics also included voice: whether the poet was writing from his/her own perspective, from another person's perspective, or from no particular perspective. We also coded the poetry line by line for its use of literary devices such as rhyme, rhythm and alliteration, imaginative devices such as metaphor and simile, and for the use of language referring to the writer's own mental states, and to the mental states of real or fictitious others mentioned in the poems. We found that the autistic poetry we studied shares many of the characteristics of non-autistic poetry, and appeared not to be a minimal interpretation of the craft, but an exploration of many of its stylistic, imaginative and expressive possibilities. In the following sections, I describe and illustrate some salient features of the results.

DOES AUTISTIC POETRY HAVE A UNIFIED STYLE?

Poetry written to a formula would likely conform to a narrow and predictable range of conventions. Instead, we found that the styles varied widely among the autistic poets, and that relatively little of it consisted of equal-lengthed stanzas or rhyming couplets, as might be predicted by a formulaic or systematizing approach. It is true that each poet had certain characteristic ways of filling the space in terms of the length and number of lines, stanzas and verses. For instance, Tito Mukhopadhyay's poems often consist of an unbroken sequence of shorter and longer lines, as in the example at the beginning of this chapter. However, he also experiments with longer lines and lengthier poems, and with both free verse stanzas and verse. Donna Williams's poetry is also diverse in format, including poems of a handful of lines and multiple stanza works, and using both rhyme and free verse.

By contrast, Jennifer Fan's poems usually consist of five or so stanzas of free verse:

> I bought a bottle of champagne to celebrate
> "Celebrate what?" You may ask.
> "Life," I reply.
> I bought a bottle of champagne to taste
> "Taste what?" you may wonder
> "Life again," I reply.

> From "A brighter tomorrow" (Fan 3)

IS AUTISTIC POETRY DOMINATED BY CONVENTIONAL LITERARY DEVICES?

In this context, "literary devices" denotes phonological and structural features such as rhyme and rhythm. If the autistic poets relied on such physical attributes to the exclusion of devices such as metaphor, then we would expect to find a preponderance of the former in their works. In fact, we found that both autistic and non-autistic poets employed rhyme, rhythm, refrain and modified repetition in moderation and to an approximately equal extent. Wendy Lawson's poetry, however, makes more use of rhyme and rhythm than that of the other autistic poets, though she also occasionally experiments with free verse.

> 'Wendy, Wendy' I hear the teacher say.
> 'Wendy, Wendy please look this way.'
> 'Wendy, Wendy' I hear the children say.
> 'Wendy, Wendy, please come and play.'
> I hear the words that come each day,
> 'What do the mean' I hear me say.
> Words without pictures simply go away.
> I turn my head and look instead
> All that glitters; blue, green and red.
> 'You'll like it here,' Father speaks,
> 'Come and play with Billy'
> Inside my head my brain just freaks
> 'How can they be so silly?'
> Why would I want to do this thing?'
> My mind can find no reason.

'Please leave me with the sparkly string.
This gives me such a feeling.'

("What is Play?," Lawson 19).

Both autistic and neurotypical poets used alliteration and assonance, though the autistic poets employed considerably less of both. The reasons for this statistically significant difference are not yet clear. Mukhopadhyay employs these devices least of all, and because speech is not his principle medium of communication, we might speculate that he does not use implicit speech to "hear" how his poetry sounds as he writes it. Yet his capacity for rhyme is inconsistent with this suggestion. And although we found the overall frequency of alliteration and assonance to be lower in the autistic poetry, there were also some highly accomplished celebrations of the sound properties of words, such as this extract from a poem by Craig Romkema:

Ghana caught my attention first,
Panama, Zambia, Corsica,
Then Kayla, Jessica, Erica, Elena,
Iowa, South Dakota,
And best of all,
Mozzarella,
Lovely sibilance of sounds.

(From "The Search," Romkema 53)

DO AUTISTIC POETS EMPLOY IMAGINATIVE LANGUAGE?

In terms of global or whole-poem characteristics, we found that the autistic poets differed somewhat from the neurotypical poets in their handling of imaginative subjects and language. Fantasy was infrequent in their poetry, though they also contributed a number of markedly surreal works, such as the following extract from one of Williams's poems:

Standing on the edge of black inspiration night,
Lure of Strawberry Fields for ever,
Backed up in a duel,
Against a knight of the night in shining armour
Life behind glass, a living death made tolerable,
Pure fear of the one touching touch which could shatter the glass forever,
And send the tightrope walker plummeting from her tightrope,
Into the knowing of the unknown

From "Becoming Three-Dimensional" (*Not Just Anything* 72)

Line-by-line analysis reveals that all but one of the autistic poets made substantial use of metaphor, and their overall rate of metaphor use was similar to that for the non-autistic poets. The autistic poets also showed some capacity to sustain metaphors across a number of lines or stanzas, which suggests a relatively sophisticated grasp of this trope. Nonetheless, the autistic poets' metaphor use was distinctive in some respects. They provided fewer "creative" metaphors—that is, figures of speech that bring together images in an exceptionally original or imaginative way. More of their metaphors were standard or idiomatic figures of speech, such as "bright new worlds" or "pompous talking heads." However, Williams offers a substantial number of idiosyncratic metaphors—figurative phrases with a complex or ambiguous relationship to what is represented. Though difficult to understand, such metaphors cannot be said to lack originality, as the extract just discussed shows.

Given the autistic poets' relatively liberal use of metaphor, it was surprising to find that they used significantly fewer similes than the non-autistic poets. Happé's studies of figurative language understanding in people on the spectrum demonstrates a hierarchy of difficulty in which simile is the most accessible form of figurative language, with metaphor being more difficult and irony even more so. Perhaps constraints on the capacity to understand figurative language do not work the same way when the autistic individual is generating the examples him- or herself. Composing a successful simile may require a tighter control on language than composing a reasonably convincing metaphor, and the distribution of metaphor types in the autistic poets' writings we studied is consistent with this claim.

DO AUTISTIC POETS WRITE ABOUT THE SELF?

The most strikingly distinctive feature of the autistic poets' work was their pronounced focus on the self. Their themes mostly concerned the self or relationships between the self and others, whereas the non-autistic poets also wrote frequently about philosophical, political or fantastical topics, as well as favoring poems about nature, places or events. The autistic poets also mostly wrote in their own voice or perspective, whereas the non-autistic poets also used other voices, took the perspective of others, or talked about others from a neutral stance. Quite a few of the neurotypical poets' works, especially those with a philosophical, political or fantastical theme, had no discernible or specific perspective, indicating the capacity to transcend or step back from the world of their own immediate experience.

Some of these differences are illustrated by the following poem extracts. From the first, written by a neurotypical poet in the 15–18 age group, we can infer the attitudes of the poet towards the events she describes, but she is not a central presence in the poem:

A greater world; a stronger race;
A new regime for them to face
A wholesome land the future sees;
Filled with horror and atrocities,
His plan to rid his world of them;
The ethnic cleansing starts again.

From "Divided Nation—A Greater Serbia,"
by Nikola Bunyon, from *Boom boom BANG!* (37)

The second, from a poem by Craig Romkema, deals with a theme that must figure centrally in the experience of many with autistic difficulties—disability. The markedly personal voice and language are characteristic of many of the autistic poems:

From the beginnings of my differentness, I remember doctors, students,
    therapists measuring my head, the tightness of my muscles, the
    tracking of my eyes, the dysfunctions of my stomach. Some were
    stiff and cold, others blessedly kind,
others not acknowledging I understood every word
they said,
so freely did they label me retarded, or some other variant, equally
    untrue.

From "Perspectives" by Craig Romkema (22)

Notably, in this poem, Romkema uses a selection of mental state words: "remember," "acknowledging," "understood." An important finding from this study is that the autistic poets made significantly more use of language referring to their own thoughts, emotions and desires than did the neurotypical poets. In contrast, their use of comparable language to refer to the mental states of others was significantly less frequent than that of the neurotypical poets. It follows that, contrary to the predictions of the theory-of-mind approach, levels of self-awareness in people with autism cannot be assumed to follow from their levels of other-awareness. We cannot judge autistic people's capacity for self-insight from an apparent inattention to the thoughts and feelings of others.

Despite the overall bias towards self-related works, it would be misleading to suggest that the autistic poets do not step back from the self to write evocatively about natural and other themes, as this early example of Tito Mukhopadhyay's poetry shows:

The brow of evening
Gold and red,
In the wait for

Sun to set,
The earth at peace

Asks for rest,
With fading lights
Of the west

An untitled poem (Mukhopadhyay 48)

IS AUTISTIC POETRY A DISTINCT GENRE?

The picture of the autistic mind suggested by these data seems far from the
rigid, repetitive, rule-bound thinking and lack of reflexivity of the autistic
stereotype. The autistic poetry we studied shares many characteristics with
non-autistic poetry, and appears not as a minimal, formulaic interpretation
of the craft, but as an exploration of its stylistic, imaginative and expressive
possibilities. Yet this poetry did present distinctive features, and may indeed
differ from neurotypical poetry in ways that our techniques of coding and
content analysis cannot capture. For instance, because some research suggests that people with autism have difficulty understanding humor (Emerich et al.), it would be interesting to look at this dimension. We have not
attempted to code the poems for humor, because it is difficult to define it
in a sufficiently objective way for content analysis. However, lines such as
Donna Williams's "Some people are stormy weather" surely have universal appeal. Similarly, we could not objectively assess qualities such as the
emotional impact of a poem on the reader, though there may be differences
along this dimension. The evaluation of these less tangible qualities of the
poetry by alternative techniques is in progress and will be reported in future
papers.

The subtle and varied ways in which poetry may achieve its impact on
others is well demonstrated by the work of Wendy Lawson, whose poetry
is relatively lacking in figurative language such as metaphor and simile, and
therefore scores relatively low on our indices of imagination. However, I
have recently had the privilege to hear Lawson recite her poetry, and the
beautiful cadence and expressive range of her voice imbues it with qualities
of performative imagination not apparent on the page.

To gain a deeper understanding of autistic poets' imaginative world and
the markedly personal focus of their work, it is necessary to know more
about how and why the poets go about their task, and what it means to
them. Not only is this of interest in its own right, but it may highlight distinctive features of the autistic approach to poetry not apparent from the
works themselves. For instance, Beate Hermelin has suggested that autistic
artists may create works more as a means of self-expression than as a form
of communication (62). If so, perhaps the intense focus on self manifested in

poems by the autistic writers reflects an inattention to real or imagined audience: their work is essentially soliloquy. The implicit assumption that neurotypical artists create principally or exclusively with an audience in mind is, of course, a simplistic view of the many-faceted nature of the artistic impulse. A closer look at such questions requires a move from the perspective of content analysis to a consideration of the poets' own reflections on the process and purposes of their writing.

POETS' REFLECTIONS ON THEIR WORK

Poets whose works we explored in the content-analysis study were invited to complete a questionnaire about their perspectives on their work. Of course, asking the poets to reflect on their work does not guarantee that their response is an authentic reflection of why and how they write. However, such responses at least tell us something about the individual poet's stance towards being a poet: for example, how they construe their relationship to the sources and purposes of their creativity.

To date, the basis for a full comparison of the autistic and neurotypical poets' reflections is not available. However, some intriguing contrasts between the responses of the adult autistic poets—Donna Williams and Wendy Lawson—and those of the adult neurotypical poets merit discussion. In addition, some fascinating reflections came from a female poet who reported some autistic-like traits in her own make-up. Because the content-analysis study required poets who could be clearly categorized as either autistic spectrum or neurotypical, we were not, unfortunately, able to include her poetry in that stage of the research.

Of course, seeking the autistic poets' reflections via questionnaire assumes that they have just those qualities of self-awareness that have been considered lacking in those with ASD. Hence, the fact that they provided coherent and informative answers for all the questions is quite significant. The two adult poets with ASD indeed furnished some of the most expansive and telling answers of all those who participated. They were clearly adept at reflecting on these aspects of themselves and their experiences. I can include only a small selection of the material here.

EARLY BACKGROUND INFLUENCES
AND THE ROLE OF TEACHING

Most of our participants indicated that external influences, such as school, home or radio, had stimulated their initial interest in poetry, and reported that they had learned to write poetry partly or substantially with a teacher, parent or other mentor. These answers suggest familiar, even conventional formative experiences. In contrast, Williams and Lawson both offered highly idiosyncratic responses that disavowed external influences and mentors. Lawson stressed that "words and rhyme intrigue me. I think in rhyme (most of the time)." Williams further emphasized that she did not consciously teach herself poetry, or even discover it within herself. Rather, the poetry spoke "through her" and used her as an outlet: "Had it been a conscious process involving thought and trying I'd say I taught myself . . . but it had none of this; my job was to let it out and not tear it up, no more, no less." Similarly, Lawson emphasized that she didn't need teaching because her poetry "came instinctively."

These claims parallel evidence that autistic talents in visual art and music are autodidactic. For example, Stephen Wiltshire's skills initially appeared spontaneously and without tuition, and later efforts to develop and diversify his skills through tuition when he was a teenager were only partially successful (Pring and Hermelin). Noel, a savant musician studied by Hermelin, had no musical instrument at home, and was never taught. When he had access to a school piano, he would play what he had heard during hours listening to the radio (157). Williams denies that she even heard poetry before she started writing, describing how "I first wrote letter strings when I was nine, then word strings, then word columns. Out of these eventually came poetry by the time I was about eleven." According to this account, the process was one of spontaneous experimentation with the properties of language, which she only later realized was poetry.

INSPIRATION

Would the intensely personal focus of the autistic poetry, established in content analysis, be matched by distinctive claims about the poets' sources of inspiration? Asked where the ideas for her poetry came from, Lawson stated, "From ME. My thoughts. My experiences." In contrast, neurotypical poets listed a range of both internal and external influences. This representative neurotypical answer combines autobiographical and emotional aspects of the self with ideas drawn from events in the wider world: "childhood experiences"; observations on the world; newspaper/media stories; intense emotional experiences/responses. One or two neurotypical poets mentioned creative writing classes or online writers' groups as an external source.

Williams listed sources that were external, but elemental rather than social. Her first poetry used sensory and perceptual qualities such as "dark, light, wind, rain, holes, glass, mirrors to capture more concrete experiences it couldn't express." She described a powerful sense of acting as a "conduit" for thoughts and words emanating from somewhere beyond the conscious self, an idea also expressed by the one poet who had reported borderline autistic traits: "When I write really well and without much effort it feels like the words are coming from outside of myself, that I am only the channel for them."

The experience of a hypothetical voice speaking through the artist is akin to one that many writers report (Taylor, Hodges, and Kohanyi). Yet in our admittedly small sample, all of the poets describing this experience were on or close to the autistic spectrum; the insight would seem to require heightened powers of self-reflection and an imaginative attribution of activities of the self to something beyond the self as consciously experienced.

THE INFLUENCE OF OTHER POETS

The notion that autistic poetry might be executed primarily as a form of self-expression, or "for its own sake," raises the question of whether the ASD poets are at all interested in or influenced by other poets. Holcombe points out that "writing calls on and borrows from other pieces of writing, establishing itself within a community of understandings and conventions." One neurotypical respondent answered thus: "you're not really a 'proper' poet unless you are aware of your contemporaries and what they are writing." Thus, all the neurotypical poets listed a substantial number (minimum: eleven) of favorite, oft-read poets.

Lawson acknowledged reading a small number of poets, including others with ASD, suggesting, perhaps, that it is with this community of poets that she feels most connection. Williams had briefly encountered poetry by Sylvia Plath, Emily Dickinson and T. S. Eliot's *Four Quartets* when younger, but of these only Eliot had had any impact, because "it was far more 'intangible' than Plath or Dickinson and hence could only be heard without analysis to be felt so fully, . . . so it spoke to me in the right place." Yet this seems to indicate resistance, rather than indifference, to other poets' works, and may perhaps reflect Williams's difficulty in processing incoming language for meaning, which, she says, impedes reading for pleasure.

POETRY AS SELF-EXPRESSION AND COMMUNICATION

Pursuing her claim that the primary motive for autistic art is self-expression, Hermelin argues that autistic spectrum artists may have little interest or investment in its communicative function, and therefore little motivation to revise their works with the interests of an audience in mind (61–2, 176). However, the desire for self-expression and for communication are not mutually exclusive: poets may write for both these reasons and for others not consciously articulated. Equally, the impulse to rework one's poetry may stem from a personal standard rather than a desire to tailor it to an audience.

Both neurotypical and autistic poets mentioned the importance of self-expression, and some poets in both groups stated that they wrote both for themselves and others. The need to unite self-expression and communication emerged in this neurotypical poet's account of how her poetry evolved over time: "Early poems tend to be personal 'outpourings' following intense/

difficult experiences. . . . [Later] you still use your experience as a starting point but learn how to include others in a way which allows them to identify and recognize the experience you are trying to convey."

Donna Williams's answers to these questions were once again idiosyncratic. She claimed not to write for anyone in particular, and was the only poet who usually did not revise her work. Her response alone was consistent with the notion of art for its own sake that Hermelin considers a special characteristic of autistic creativity, but that is not, of course, without precedent in the history of art and artists.

Finally, all the poets listed a range of outlets for their work. These included books, magazines and Web sites, and for several, including both Williams and Lawson, public readings. In this regard, the autistic poets' take on being a poet was no different from those of the other poets.

CONCLUSION

This chapter set out to consider the work of autistic poets as a test-case for some influential claims about the mental world of people on the spectrum. The first of these—the belief that creativity and other forms of imagination are difficult or impossible for the person on the spectrum—has meant that autistic output within creative domains has tended to be dismissed as falling below the accepted neurotypical criteria for creative work. Of all the creative media in which examples of autistic talent might challenge this claim, probably the best is poetry, with its dependence on intensely abstract, symbolic, and free-flowing forms of expression. Yet even here there was the possibility that the poets might simply emulate the craft of poetry while failing to attain any of its more obvious artistic qualities. But our comparisons between the autistic and comparable non-autistic poets in terms of indices of literary and imaginative content do not clearly support this claim: the autistic poets used all the poetic techniques that the non-autistic poets used. Even when they used them to a lesser extent, as in the case of exceptionally creative metaphor, it was not an all-or-none distinction.

Turning to self-awareness, this too has been seen as deficient or even non-existent in people on the autistic spectrum. Yet, if anything, our findings suggest just the opposite: that autistic poets reflect extensively on themselves, somewhat to the exclusion of an interest in other themes. Of course, the fact that the autistic poets write poetry about themselves does not conclusively prove that they have self-insight. That is, their preoccupation with self-related themes and language does not constitute evidence for true self-knowledge. Further work is needed, both to investigate the kinds of self-attributions these poets make and to analyze the self-reflections of other autistic persons. Nonetheless, the present results are consistent with considerable self-insight, a claim supported by the autistic poets' extended and thoughtful responses to our questionnaire.

These questionnaire responses helped to contextualize the distinctive and shared features identified within the autistic and non-autistic poetry, adding some glimpses of individual poets' perspectives. Though it would be quite inaccurate to characterize the autistic poetry as having been written purely for its own sake, or the non-autistic poetry as purely communicative, there are indications that for poets such as Wendy Lawson and Donna Williams poetry represents a profoundly personal and individual voyage from initial experimentation with sounds and words, to later explorations of the self.

A limitation of the findings outlined here is that they are not representative of autism: after all, few autistic individuals have these poets' literary talent. But it does not necessarily follow that others on the autism spectrum have no imagination or self-awareness, because they may have these faculties but be unable to express them in words. If so, then these autistic poets may represent the tip of an iceberg that merits further investigation.

Indeed, poetry may be particularly suited to the autistic cognitive style. To write successfully in prose may require cognitive capacities that are impaired in people with autism: for instance, sustaining control over sentence structure and over the continuity and unity of narrative may require efficient executive function and/or a cognitive processing bias toward wholes rather than parts. Both of these areas are thought to be compromised in autism (Pennington and Ozoff; Happé and Frith). In contrast, some fragmentation of language and images is not only permissible in poetry, but may add to its appeal, its leaps from one idea to another tantalizing and intriguing the reader.

Further, the possibility of reflecting on thoughts and feelings quietly at one's own pace, rather than under the pressure of spoken interchange, may involve a grasp of complex mental events that seems to be lacking when rapid processing is called for. If these claims are correct, then poetry may offer a powerful outlet for imagination and self-expression in those autistic people who have not yet found their voice.

> On paper thought can't drift away
> Emotions and memory from here do not stray
> On paper is safe and shared and real
> From paper my thoughts give me feedback with feel
> On paper my life finds order and sense
> Continuity, security for just a few pence.

> From "Notes," by Donna Williams (*Not Just Anything* 96)

ACKNOWLEDGMENTS

I would like to thank: Alison Sillence who, as research assistant, has contributed so much, both practically and conceptually, to the studies described in this chapter; the Open University for funding pilot work and the British Academy for funding the research described in this chapter; the poets and their publishers for permission to quote from their works; all poets who completed the questionnaire, and especially Wendy Lawson and Donna Williams for permission to quote them. The interpretations are mine, and therefore any errors are also my responsibility. My gratitude also to Tom Sillence, for specialized computation support; and to Daniel Nettle, Sophie Read, and Elizabeth Archibald for helpful suggestions.

"What is Play" is quoted from *ASPoetry, Illustrated Poems From an Aspie Life*, copyright © 2006 by Wendy Lawson. Reproduced by permission of Jessica Kingsley Publishers.

Excerpts from *The Mind Tree* by Tito Rajarshi Mukhopadhyay are reprinted by permission of the National Autistic Society.

WORKS CITED

Baird, Gillian, Anthony Cox, Tony Charman, Simon Baron-Cohen, Sally Wheelwright, John Swettenham, Auriol Drew and Natasha Nightingale. "A Screening Instrument for Autism at 18 Months of Age: A Six-Year Follow-up Study." *Journal of the American Academy of Child and Adolescent Psychiatry* 39 (2000): 694–702.

Baron-Cohen, Simon. *The Essential Difference* London: Penguin, 2004.

———. "Theory of Mind and Autism: a Review." Special Issue of *The International Review of Mental Retardation* 23 (2001): 169.

Boom boom BANG! An Anthology of Poetry from Teesside for Children by Children 1996. Middlesborough: Writearound, 1996.

Bruner, Jerome, and Carol Feldman. "Theories of Mind and the Problem of Autism." *Understanding Other Minds: Perspectives from Autism*. Ed. Simon Baron-Cohen, Helen Tager-Flusberg, and Donald J. Cohen. Oxford: Oxford UP, 1993. 267–91.

Craig, Jaime, and Simon Baron-Cohen. "Creativity and Imagination in Autism and Asperger Syndrome." *Journal of Autism and Developmental Disorders* 29 (1999): 319–326

———. "Drawing Ability in Autism: A Window into the Imagination." *Israel Journal of Psychiatry* 38 (2001): 242–253.

Craig, Jaime, Simon Baron-Cohen and Fiona Scott. "Story-telling Ability in Autism: A Window into the Imagination." *Israel Journal of Psychiatry* 37 (2000): 64–70

Decety, Jean, and Jessica A. Sommerville. "Shared Representations between Self and Other: a Social Cognitive Neuroscience View." *Trends in Cognitive Science* 7.12 (2003): 527–533.

Dowker, Ann, Beate Hermelin, and Linda Pring. "A Savant Poet." *Psychological Medicine* 26 (1996): 913–924.

Emerich, David M., Nancy A. Creaghead, Sandra M. Grether, Donna Murray, and Carol Grasha. "The Comprehension of Humorous Materials by Adolescents With High-Functioning Autism and Asperger's Syndrome." *Journal of Autism and Developmental Disorders* 33.3 (2003): 253–257

Fan, Jennifer, and Autumn Fan. *Cinderella with Wrong Shoes: Poems by a Young Woman with Autism*. Lincoln: Writer's Showcase, 2001.

Fitzgerald, Michael. *Autism and Creativity: Is there a link between autism in men and exceptional ability?* Hove and New York: Brunner-Routledge, 2004.

Fodor, Jerry A. *Modularity of Mind*. Cambridge, MA: MIT P, 1983.

Frith, Uta. "Asperger and His Syndrome." *Autism and Asperger Syndrome*. Ed. Uta Frith. Cambridge: Cambridge UP, 1991. 1–36.

———. *Autism: Explaining the Enigma*. Oxford: Blackwell, 1989.

———., and Francesca Happé. "Theory of Mind and Self-Consciousness: What is it Like to be Autistic?" *Mind and Language* 14.1 (1999): 1–22.

Garrard, Peter, Lisa M. Maloney, John R. Hodges, and Karalyn Patterson. "The Effects of Very Early Alzheimer's Disease on the Characteristics of Writing by a Renowned Author." *Brain* 128 (2005): 250–260.

Glastonbury, Marion. "'I'll Teach you Differences': On the Cultural Presence of Autistic Lives." *Changing English* 4.1 (1997): 51–65.

———. "A Stain upon the Silence: Samuel Beckett 1906–1989." *Asperger Syndrome Support Network Newsletter*. February, 1991. N.p.

Grandin, Temple. *Thinking in Pictures: and Other Reports from My Life with Autism*. New York: Doubleday, 1995.

———., and Margaret M. Scariano. *Emergence: Labeled Autistic*. Novato, CA: Arena, 1986.

Happé, Francesca. "Communicative Competence and Theory of Mind in Autism: A Test of Relevance Theory." *Cognition* 48 (1993): 101–119.

———., and Uta Frith. "The Weak Coherence Account: Detail-focused Cognitive Style in Autism Spectrum Disorders." *Journal of Autism and Developmental Disorders* 36.1 (2006): 5–25.

Hermelin, Beate. *Bright Splinters of the Mind: A Personal Story of Research with Autistic Savants*. London: Jessica Kingsley, 2001.

Holcombe, C. J. 20 July 2007. http://textetc.com/theory/aesthetics/html.

Klein, Stanley B., Leda Cosmides, Emily R. Murray, and John Tooby. "On the Acquisition of Knowledge about Personality Traits: Does Learning about the Self Engage Different Mechanisms than Learning about Others?" *Social Cognition* 22. 4 (2004): 367–390.

Lawson, Wendy. *ASPoetry: Illustrated poems from an Aspie Life*. Illustrated by Alice Blaes Calder. London and Philadelphia: Jessica Kingsley, 2006.

McGeer, Victoria. "Autistic Self-Awareness." *Philosophy, Psychiatry and Psychology* 11.3 (2004): 235–251

Mukhopadhyay, Tito Rajarshi. *Beyond the Silence: My Life, the World, and Autism*. London: National Autistic Society, 2000.

Pennington, Bruce, and Sally Ozonoff. "Executive functions and developmental psychopathology." *Journal of Child Psychology and Child Psychiatry* 37 (1996): 51–87.

Pring, Linda, and Beate Hermelin. "Native Savant Talent and Acquired Skill." *Autism* 1. 2 (1997):199–214.

Ricks, Christopher. "All Praise to Proper Words." *Times Literary Supplement* 25 February 2005. 13–15.

Romkema, Craig. *Embracing the Sky: Poems beyond Disability*. London: Jessica Kingsley, 1996.

Simonton, Dean Keith. "Creativity." *Handbook of Positive Psychology*. Eds. C. R. Snyder and Shane J. Lopez. New York: Oxford UP, 2002. 189–201.

Tager-Flusberg, Helen. "Language and Understanding Minds: Connections in Autism." *Understanding Other Minds: Perspectives from Autism*. Ed. Simon Baron-Cohen, Helen Tager-Flusberg, and Donald J. Cohen. Oxford: Oxford UP, 1993. 138–57.

Taylor, Marjorie, Sara D. Hodges, and Adèle Kohanyi. "The Illusion of Independent Agency: Do Adult Fiction Writers Experience Their Characters as Having Minds of Their Own?" *Imagination, Cognition and Personality* 22 (2003): 361–368

Treffert, Darrold A. *Extraordinary People*. London: Bantam, 1989.

Williams, Donna. *Nobody Nowhere: The Extraordinary Autobiography of an Autistic.* New York: Doubleday, 1992.

———. *Not Just Anything: A Collection of Thoughts on Paper.* London and Philadelphia: Jessica Kingsley, 2004.

Ziatas, Kathryn, Kevin Durkin and Chris Pratt. "Differences in Assertive Speech Acts Produced by Children with Autism, Asperger Syndrome, Specific Language Impairment, and Normal Development." *Development and Psychopathology* 15 (2003): 73–94

8 Human, but More So
What the Autistic Brain Tells Us about the Process of Narrative

Matthew K. Belmonte

NARRATIVE AS DEFENSE AGAINST DISORDER

The human mind occupies a unique status in nature, able to contemplate the eternal and the absolute, and yet bound within a mortal animal and a mutable world. This juxtaposition of mental and physical existence creates a tension fundamental to human psychic development that Becker has labeled "the denial of death." As Becker describes, this denial can be more generally construed as an aversion to direct experience of disorder and impermanence—the death of the self being an ultimate, personal manifestation of this universal tendency. Psychic life requires the construction of defenses, albeit temporary and in a sense ultimately futile ones, against this disorder. Both the implicit, mental narrative that implements human perception and cognition and the explicit, written narratives of literature can be read as the mechanism of this defense. A fear of death drives us to become narrators, to transform the disconnected chaos of our sensorium into representative mental texts whose distinct scenes contain recognizable characters that act in coherent plots and evince meaningful themes. This capacity to project the concrete and intractable complexity of direct experience onto abstract and predictable scripts is fundamental to human cognition: in this sense there is no thought without narrative, and in fact, a strong argument has been made for the genesis of language as an externalized representation of the narrative structure of human thought (Turner). As long as we're able to keep up this substitution of perceptual representation for sensory referent, we maintain cognition and forestall death.

This narrative denial of death, though, produces its own reactive fear, which may be described as a denial of life. In projecting particular elements of sensory experience onto mental representations, the process of narrative inevitably discards many more elements for which no projection can be formed. Thus in constructing abstract or global meaning, the process of narrative destroys, according to Lacan (or rather excludes from higher order representation), concrete or local detail. Which details are so elided depends on the narrative frame onto which experience is being projected, and the authorial decision as to what frame to apply thus carries life-or-death responsibility. This responsibility is a heavy burden, and in order to avoid bearing it humans look to parents, deities, ideologies, or other externalized authorities. In short, we seek escape from the status of being a narrator into that of being narrated. In Freud's Oedipal frame, we want to displace the father who dictates narrative order but at the same time to be dominated by the mother who protects us from unnarrated chaos. Or as Thomas Szasz frames this conflict, "man's [sic] need for rules and his propensity to follow them is [sic] equaled only by his burning ambition to be free of rules" (179). Others too have induced that the human tendency to ritualized behavior is a manifestation of the desire to be protected by rules (Werner 131; Bettelheim 83), and from this perspective we may discern that ritual operates to relieve not just the pathological anxieties of psychiatric conditions but also the everyday anxieties of healthy human life.

These construals in terms of the denial of death, the Oedipal conflict, rule-following, and the narrative nature of human thought all are statements of the same observation, and rather than arguing over which terms ought to be treated as primary we may do well, for the moment, to accept that all these formalisms are theoretical projections of one and the same phenomenon of narrative organization—an activity that simultaneously permits and limits cognitive life. In neuropsychological terms, narrative organization is implemented by interacting and not entirely separable processes of perceptual organization, attention and memory. Perceptual organization is the process that binds separate stimuli into coherent higher order objects, replacing, for example, a horizontal plane and four perpendicular posts with the single entity of a table. Attention, a group of many subprocesses, focuses processing on those parts of a scene judged relevant to the current script or story. And memory, by holding in mind the higher order representations of what one has seen before and what one expects to see next, informs attention and perceptual organization with the context of this story (see Gerrig and McKoon). It is only after treatment by these processes of cognitive organization that one attains conscious perception. This distance between sensory input and narrative consciousness is the root of Proust's insight that events are most real not when they are experienced, but when they are remembered or imagined.

The tension between self and environment that gives rise to narrative structure, scripts, and rituals is particularly close to the surface of the psyche during the early years of human development, and indeed children's rituals bear great similarity to behaviors that in older individuals would qualify as pathologically obsessive-compulsive (see Evans, "Rituals, Compulsions" 53). Lacking as yet a large and flexible repertoire of scripts onto which phenomena can be projected, and lacking efficient cognitive mechanisms with which to implement such projections, children attempt the converse solution to the problem of psychic life: they try, through rituals, to constrain experience to fit their limited repertoire of scripts. We may glimpse a clue to the origin of such rituals as a consequence of the denial of death (or more generally as a consequence of narrative organization) in the trait-based correlation of typically developing children's fear of death with their repetitive behaviors and compulsive arrangement of objects (see Evans et al., "Rituals, Fears"). A crucial corollary for autism research is that repetitive behaviors, despite their diagnostic validity, are etiologically not a primary symptom and should not be studied as though they were. They are, rather, an adaptive strategy aimed at rendering the environment tractable enough to be modeled by a severely restricted process of narrative organization.

PHYSIOLOGICAL CAUSES OF
NARRATIVE IMPAIRMENT IN AUTISM

In addition to their role in normal child development, ritualistic and compulsive behaviors are one of the three broad diagnostic symptoms of autism. This similarity between autistic and typical development becomes comprehensible in light of recent evidence that autistic neurophysiology may impair the processes subserving narrative organization. We may construe autism's other two diagnostic symptoms, impairment in communication and impairment in social interaction, even more immediately as consequences of disrupted narrative. To understand this relationship between autistic behavior and narrative disruption, we need to know something about autism's atypical neurobiology, and about the atypical psychology that develops around it.

Rather than a single mutated gene or a single atypical region of the brain, recent theoretical syntheses of the neurobiology of autism have focused on interactions among many genes that produce abnormal neural connectivity within and between many brain regions (see Belmonte et al., "Autism and Abnormal Development," and "Autism as a Disorder" 647; Courchesne and Pierce). By altering connectivity within local groups of neurons, a synergy of genetic and environmental factors may sabotage a neural network's ability to represent information. In the same way that a pen and paper may be just as useless when the ink bleeds as they are when the ink won't flow at all, pathologies involving either unusually strong or unusually weak connections can evoke the same impoverishment of representational capacity within local networks, and may prevent long-range transfer of information between networks (Belmonte et al., "Autism and Abnormal" 9228). The result would be a collection of brain regions each of which may be more or less intact by itself but in which regional activities are not coordinated or modulated in response to cognitive demands. This pattern is, in fact, exactly what is observed in neurophysiological studies of autism (Belmonte and Yurgelun-Todd).

This deficit at the network level impairs the associative processes essential to narrative thought (Gerrig and McKoon), those that automatically and fluidly extract structural similarities and draw attention to those features most relevant to the scene and the story. Since there is no neuroanatomical

Cartesian theater wherein all the separate elements of the perceptual scene are integrated, narrative organization must depend on coordination of activity among widely separated brain regions (Tononi et al., 330–332)— exactly the capacity that seems impaired in autism. Narrative connectivity therefore depends on corresponding functional connectivity between all the brain regions and subsystems that participate in perceptual and cognitive experience; disrupted neural organization implies disrupted narrative organization.

Autistic people's characteristic pattern of impairment in cognitive tasks that demand contextual processing, coupled with their superiority at tasks that demand piecemeal processing of individual features, has been described as "weak central coherence" (Frith, *Autism* 124; Happé)—that is, an atypically weak tendency to bind local details into global percepts. An ostensibly competing neuropsychological theory of autism is that of executive dysfunction, an impairment in coordinating and sequencing cognitive activities (see Ozonoff et al.; Pennington et al.; Russell). The idea of impaired neural connectivity and disrupted narrative organization reveals weak central coherence and executive dysfunction to be two sides of the same coin, describing the effects of narrative disruption on perception and on action, respectively.

PSYCHOLOGICAL CONSEQUENCES OF NARRATIVE IMPAIRMENT

When narrative is so disrupted, what fallback cognitive strategies can be substituted as ways of finding learnable associations in one's environment? One possible understudy for narrative organization is the simpler sort of associative learning that underlies behavioral conditioning. Indeed, a learning style founded on statistical association rather than on instructive focus on relevant stimuli well describes autistic cognition and behavior, in which both essential and accidental correlations amongst perceptual inputs are learned equally strongly (Belmonte and Baron-Cohen). Others (e.g., Evans) have noted that ritualized behavior is associated with an excessively perceptual (rather than conceptual) style of interaction with one's environment— another indication of poor narrative organization.

Although autism is not the only neuropsychiatric disorder featuring repetitive and ritualistic behavior, autistic rituals and preoccupations are distinguished by their frequent focus on mechanical or other deterministic systems (Baron-Cohen and Wheelwright). This cognitive style in which mechanistic details are elaborated into complex preoccupations contrasts with that of schizophrenia, in which preoccupations most often derive from social stimuli such as gaze or voice. Schizophrenic ritual centers on elaborate beliefs about other minds that conspire against one, whereas autistic ritual centers on elaborate beliefs about impersonal systems. If schizophrenic ritual is mentalism run amok, autism is mechanistic explanation run amok (see Badcock 107). Or, if in Werner's terms, schizophrenia is an animistic de-differentiation of self and other, autism is if anything a solipsistic hyper-differentiation of self and other: precisely because the narrative defense against sensory chaos is so impaired in autism, people with autism are unusually sensitive to the problem of constructing this defense, and their solutions to this problem tend to be more deliberate and explicit than those the rest of us implement (see Belmonte, "The Yellow Raincoat"). This meticulous, systematic engineering approach to making sense of the world gives rise to a fundamental difference in the quality of autistic thought and the process by which autistic people establish abstract or global relationships: where others may begin with the concept and work down to the details, people with autism study each local detail in isolation, and work up through interactions to the concept (Baron-Cohen and Belmonte 112).

In understanding the role of ritual in the autistic defense against disorder, we may find useful the metaphor of film. Imagine that your life is a film being screened in some Cartesian cinema (a metaphorical one, to be sure, since no such Cartesian representation exists neuroanatomically). The trouble is that this film is being shown by an incompetent projectionist. Perhaps the aperture is wrong, so that you can see only a small corner of the image at a time, or perhaps the sound track is absent, or distorted, or out of synchrony with the picture. In any case, you can glean only disconnected fragments. Everyone around you is talking about this film, and you'd very much like to understand it. So you ask the projectionist to rewind the film and play it again and again. Keeping this one film in the Cartesian projector serves two purposes: it allows you to build an understanding of the story (deliberately, meticulously) by picking up new fragments each time the film is screened and, perhaps even more importantly, by monopolizing the projector it prevents any new, unpredictable and incomprehensible film from being introduced. When people with autism replay films in the Cartesian cinema, we say that they are engaging in repetitive or ritualistic behaviors.

We have seen how we may understand repetitive and ritualized behavior in autism as an adaptive response secondary to a neurobiologically based impairment in narrative organization. Szasz contended that we should understand all abnormal behaviors this way, as rational responses to abnormal experience. He took as his example the case of hysteria, a socially constructed disorder that was not supposed to have any concrete and definite biological foundations (100). However, his reframing of abnormal behavior as a product of rationality applies equally to disorders involving psychological response to abnormal neurobiology. Szasz wrote that "the sociohistorical context of the learning experience must not be confused with the history of the subject" (11). This insight can be extended: the perceptual and cognitive context of the learning experience must not be confused with the (rest of) the history of the subject. This realization is crucial to understanding the atypical psychology of autism and of developmental disorders in general:

much of autism's "abnormal" psychology arises not directly from abnormal neurobiology but from the interaction of a normal human mind with an abnormal perceptual and cognitive environment. Such psychobiological interactions can produce developmental outcomes as deterministic as those produced by direct biological causation. Thus autism's core symptoms of repetitive and ritualized behaviors, impaired communication, and impaired socialization, though diagnostically valid, clinically significant, and psychologically informative, are unlikely to be etiologically primary (Belmonte, et al., "Autism as a Disorder" 658).

Ironically and tragically, this psychological nature of certain aspects of autistic development was touched on by the person whose work did the most damage to autism research and autism families: Bruno Bettelheim. His utterly false description of autistic social withdrawal as a reaction to the mother's rejection of her infant was responsible for a generation of suffering during which medical authority blamed parents for causing their children's autism. As with so many arguments within the autism research community, Bettelheim's error lay in setting his own and other theories against each other instead of seeking synthesis. Bettelheim actually was correct in characterizing autistic withdrawal as a consequence of rejection, but wrong in assuming that this rejection was a social phenomenon originating with the parent. Combining part of Bettelheim's autistic psychology with what we now know about autistic neurobiology reveals autistic withdrawal as a response to rejection by one's own internal cognitive and perceptual environment, an environment whose limited capacity for narrative modeling often cannot encompass the complex and incompletely scripted phenomena of social interaction (see Greenspan, "The Affect").

THE NARRATIVE BASIS OF SOCIAL COMMUNICATION

Social interaction depends on the ability rapidly to update and apply one's mental representations of others' beliefs and intentions, to place oneself within the context of a developing social story. This capacity is known as "theory of mind." Although impairment in theory of mind has been read as a cardinal or even a primary cognitive symptom of autism by Baron-Cohen et al. ("Does the Autistic"), the framework of narrative organization supplies a deeper interpretation, one that more effectively unifies autism's social and nonsocial atypicalities. In this view, impaired theory of mind (or, as it has been more recently and more generally construed, impaired empathizing [see Baron-Cohen, "Extreme Male"]) is but one of many specific abnormalities that arise from a general disruption of narrative organization, and stands out as an especial deficit only because it is so frequently applied during normal social interaction (see Herman). We might characterize the effect of this narrative disruption on social cognition as a deficit in allocentric (other-centered) perspective, the social analogue of the distinction between object-centered and viewer-centered spatial perspective (Frith and de Vignemont); its effect on the sequencing and coordination of cognitive activities is compatible with a deficit in executive function.

As for the autistic impairment in communication, although the relationship between communication and narrative may seem trivial, there is some complexity to be explored because of the great variability in autistic communicative impairment. At one extreme is the person with "high-functioning" autism or Asperger's syndrome, in whom the mechanics of vocabulary and syntax are intact (and often superior) but whose pragmatic application of language is impaired (see Bishop & Baird); at the other extreme is the person with "low-functioning" autism who may entirely lack the ability to speak. Pragmatic language, like social interaction, depends on rapidly updating mental models and translating those models into external speech. Although the vocabulary and syntax are scripted and static, the pragmatic application of these capacities can overwhelm a severely limited mechanism of narrative organization, leaving the person with autism to cobble together rote phrases. We may thus straightforwardly explain the pragmatic language impairment in "high-functioning" autism as a consequence of disrupted narrative organization.

What about the case of the "low-functioning" person with autism, in whom the communicative impairment lies not merely in the pragmatic application of narrative but in the very articulation of speech sounds? Though long ignored in favor of autism's more socially debilitating, cognitive symptoms, motor impairment seems a common feature of autism and is perhaps its earliest behavioral sign in the developing infant (Teitelbaum et al.). Speech articulation is among the most complex of motor tasks, demanding rapid translation of words into sequences of coordinated movements of the vocal tract. This physical ordering and coordination of movements shares a great deal of computational structure with mental ordering and organization of ideas, both of which depend on an ability to connect emotions and intent to plans and sequences (Greenspan & Shanker 260–272). Thus, the same computational disconnection that makes the translation of events into narrative such a deliberate effort may likewise complicate the translation of emotion and intent into movement—a translation which, as any dancer or gymnast can attest, is far from trivial. We thus take an expansive view of "narrative," one that includes any facility of structuring and sequencing representations, whether these representations are cognitive, perceptual, or motor.

VIRTUE OF NECESSITY IN AUTISTIC COGNITIVE SKILLS

In responding psychologically to the constraints of atypical neurobiology, the developing autistic mind makes virtue of necessity. Social interactions are difficult, so the child replaces them with self-directed activities such as parallel play, in which (s)he stands at the edge of a group and mimics its activities without engaging in its social give-and-take. Pragmatic communication is difficult, so the child replaces it with rote phrases and with self-directed discourses on topics that (s)he knows well. Unscripted phenomena are difficult, so the child replaces them with ritual. In general, intact cognitive capacities are developmentally redirected towards nonsocial (and therefore more easily scriptable) phenomena, rather than being applied in a narratively coordinated and flexible manner (Gerrans). People with "high-functioning" autism, Asperger's syndrome, and the broader autism phenotype which occurs in many autism families are of particular interest in this regard because, although their impairment in the narrative organization of experience requires them to work harder at defending against perceptual disorder, their intact speech skills allow them in the end to succeed in rendering such defenses explicit. This extraordinarily effortful, unusually intense, and atypically deliberate process of narrative organization can also produce unusually deep insights, as exemplified in the developing genre of autistic memoir. The narrator who is more conscious of the effort of narration can, almost paradoxically, in the end achieve a deeper understanding of the characters and events around him or her precisely because (s)he is so impaired at automatic social perception and must concentrate harder to construct a theory of reality, to piece it together from perceptual fragments. A case in point is the work of Sean Barron, who writes retrospectively and introspectively about his mental life before he developed speech. In this regard, people with autism can be described as "human, but more so": confronted by the same fundamental problem of organizing perceptual experience into coherent stories that confronts all of us, they must overcome greater fragmentation of perceptual and cognitive experience to solve this problem.

This description of autistic cognition as "human, but more so" may seem contrary to Temple Grandin's view of autistic cognition as similar to animal cognition—as human, but less so (57). The contradiction evaporates when one examines the specific comparisons on which these ideas are based: Grandin's view takes its impetus from the piecemeal and fragmented nature of autistic perception and cognition, an absence of narrative order that she argues is part of what distinguishes human cognition from animal cognition. It is precisely this narrative disruption that elicits an unusually deliberate effort to construct reality—narrative deliberation that has been characterized as an egocentric attempt to mimic allocentric perspective (Frith & de Vignemont). Thus, although absence of narrative organization may seem to make people with autism neurobiologically human, but less so, the deliberate ordering strategies and the consciousness of representation evoked by this absence make people with autism neuropsychologically human, but more so.

Support for this concept of autism as in some sense an exaggerated state of humanity comes from psychometric findings of autistic traits within the larger population. Autistic social traits are in fact continuously distributed within the normal population (Constantino et al.), making the exact point of discrimination between normal and autism-spectrum behavior somewhat arbitrary. (This is not to diminish the validity of autism as a diagnosis, nor to make light of the severe hardships faced by people with autism; it is, rather, only to state that the exact, quantitative boundary of the broader autism spectrum diagnosis is open to interpretation.) Especially at the ages of two through four years, typical children often manifest repetitive behaviors, sensory preoccupations, and particular sensitivity to environmental change (Evans et al., "Ritual, Habit"). They are upset when their routines are disrupted or when their environments are rearranged—behaviors common in kind albeit not in degree to autism (and to other neuropsychiatric disorders with obsessive-compulsive features). The very fact that we view such sensitivities as normal childish behavior says a great deal about the psychological continuity between some aspects of typical and disordered development. Indeed, the developmental timing with which such behaviors resolve in normal children correlates strongly with the development of frontal white matter and the refinement of synaptic connectivity (Gogtay et al.), neurobiological hardware essential to theory of mind (Giedd) and to mature narrative organization in general. Further support for this relationship between autism and neurotypicality arises from the observation that compulsive-like behaviors in typical children correlate positively with performance on measures of perceptual coherence such as the Embedded Figures Test (Evans et al., "Visual Organization"), at which people with autism excel, and negatively with measures of executive function (Evans et al., "Role"), at which people with autism do poorly. Even in adults, the content of culturally normative rituals resembles that of childhood rituals, suggesting that all such behaviors may be manifestations, pathological or not, of a human disposition to perform socially meaningful rituals—a disposition that in autism is redirected away from social phenomena (Fiske & Haslam; Gerrans).

Such comparisons between autistic and neurotypical behavior raise the possibility that a liability to autism may be inevitable in a species whose brain is complex enough to implement narrative organization. In contexts in which attention to detail rather than to theme confers cognitive advantages, people with autism-spectrum conditions and people with the broader autism phenotype tend to excel (see Belmonte et al., "Autism as a Disorder" 648–649, 657), suggesting that pseudo-autistic qualities in moderate measure may be adaptive. It is hardly a surprise, given autism's cognitive profile, that first-degree relatives of people with autism are over-represented in engineering occupations and, conversely, the incidence of autism is heightened in family members of engineers, mathematicians, and physicists (Baron-Cohen et al., "Is There a Link?"; Baron-Cohen et al., "Autism Occurs"). The genetic influence on autism is multifactorial, arising not from any single gene but rather from interactions among a large number of genes whose point of convergence may consist in their effect on neural connectivity (Belmonte & Bourgeron). This multifactorial convergence may well produce within the population a continuous distribution of neural organization, and by extension a continuous distribution of narrative organization. From a genetic viewpoint as well as from behavioral and neurophysiological perspectives, then, autism can be construed as an extreme case of normality.

AUTISM AND SELF-CONSCIOUS NARRATIVE

We've seen how narrative impairment in autism leads to a more deliberate consciousness of the problem of narration. Literature, as the externalization of thought into text, shares this high level of deliberation. So we ought to be able to glimpse in literature the same attention to ritual and awareness of narrative defense that characterize autism. This defensive nature of narrative has been made plain by literary criticism in the wake of psychoanalytic theory, and inheres in every narrative, from the mythic to the preliterate to the modern. A few brief examples may serve to illustrate this theme.

In the Judeo-Christian creation myth, the Tree of Knowledge tempts with its representational power, promising that Eve and Adam will become like angels—that they will achieve mental existences distinct from their physical circumstance and comprehend abstract distinctions such as good and evil. Satan functions as the archetype of the trickster, the agent who steals the power of the gods and bestows it on humans. In other variants of this myth the nourishing tree or plant is actually part of the trickster's body; transitively, therefore, the trickster embodies knowledge itself. Genesis reminds us that the very power of narrative abstraction, in banishing chaos by substituting the mental for the physical, divorcing thought from action, symbol from referent, renders us susceptible to death in the ultimate resurgence of that chaos. It is no surprise, then, that the first action of Adam and Eve after eating from the Tree of Knowledge is to clothe themselves against the impermanence of flesh, a response that can be read as a physical metaphor for narrative defense against disorder.

In *Beowulf*, the Danes implement this same narrative defense in another physical boundary, the walls of the mead-hall, which separate an interior space of warmth, nourishment, and safety from the chaos outside (Earl 53–54). (The importance of the Anglo-Saxon hall as defense against the environment is expressed perhaps nowhere as vividly as in Bede's account of the conversion of King Edwin, in which the brevity of human life is compared to that of a sparrow's transit through the hall: "swylc swa þu æt swæsendum sitte mid þinum ealdormannum ond þegnum on wintertide, ond sie fyr onælæd ond þin heall gewyrmed, ond hit rine ond sniwe ond styrme ute; cume an spearwa ond hrædlice þæt hus þurhfleoh, cume þurh oþre duru in, þurh oþre ut gewite" ["as though you're sitting at a feast with your aldermen and thanes in wintertime, and the fire's kindled and your hall warmed, and it's raining and snowing and storming outside; in comes a sparrow and swiftly flies through the house, arriving in through one door, departing out through the other" Miller 134, 136; my translation.])

Grendel's nightly attacks threaten this boundary, penetrating the interior with the chaos and death of the outside. Ironically, even antinarrative chaos, in order to be brought within the Beowulf narrative, must be crystallized in the persona of Grendel the monster—a telling example of the symbol's killing of the thing, if there ever was one. Grendel represents an objectification that aids narrative comprehension but belies the chaos that he's meant to represent; in order for the fight to be staged, Grendel must enter the interior space of the hall just as he must enter the narrative. Beowulf's real test, therefore, cannot come until he immerses himself in the overwhelming flood of the mere, the space of raw, chaotic sensation that lies outside the protection of the hall and outside narrative order. As we are reminded both by Hroðgar (Zupitza 76–81; lines 1724–69) and by the Last Survivor (Zupitza 104–07; lines 2246–67), any victory in this struggle against entropy can be no more than temporary.

If old stories such as those in Genesis and *Beowulf* establish the universality of narrative as defense, it is left for new stories to connect this function to our present-day terms of discourse. Pynchon's *Gravity's Rainbow* is a particularly illustrative example because Pynchon is very much aware of what he is trying to do as he interposes lines between order and chaos (Hite 37–38, 96), divisions signified in human constructions of sexuality, race, religion, clothing, and naming; and also in impersonal artefacts such as maps, chemical lattices, manufacturing and supply chains, transport grids (tunnels, railways, canals), electric power supply grids, and of course toilets, sewers and waste treatment streams—implements of order with which autistic people become desperately obsessed. The scientific terms and metaphors with which these boundaries are constructed lead us especially close to the autistic mode of thought because Pynchon makes their authority seem non-agentive: instead of Jehovah, Hroðgar, or the Last Survivor warning us of the inevitability of death, it is the Second Law of Thermodynamics. Antihero Tyrone Slothrop spends most of the book trapped in the Zone, a series of scripts, roles, and costumes that orders his existence, and without which he will dissolve. Slothrop's extreme of desperate scriptedness holds up a mirror to our own narrative modes of coping, as does autism's concrete extreme of scripts and rituals. Slothrop's urge to be ruled by scientific law, to become part of the rocket's Laplacian, ballistic arc, is the same as that which drives all of us, autistic or not, to live in terms of scripts, rituals, systems and rules.

In autism, when failures of neural connectivity impede narrative linkage, when each element of a scene or a story exists in isolation, the surrounding world can seem threateningly intractable. We may read autistic withdrawal into repetitive behaviors and scripted interactions as an effort to gain control over such arbitrariness and unpredictability. In this regard, people with autism differ from other human beings only in the degree of concreteness with which they approach this problem of control: the tension between our mortal nature and our capacity to contemplate the eternal makes us desperate to impute narrative order and authorial intent in a universe where there may be only chaos and arbitrariness, and drives us as artists and scientists to construct themes within which our observations and experiences can be represented and therefore realized. In this regard, we may describe people with autism as human, but more so—for we all are driven by the same desperation to control or at least to predict what is going to happen to us, to keep chaos, entropy, and death outside our walls. The study of autism has much to tell us about theories of typical neural and psychological development, and about the nature of human cognition and literary representation in general.

WORKS CITED

Badcock, Christopher. "Mentalism and Mechanism: The Twin Modes of Human Cognition." *Evolutionary Psychology, Public Policy and Personal Decisions*. Ed. Charles Crawford & Catherine Salmon. Mahwah, NJ: Lawrence Erlbaum, 2004. 99–116.

Baron-Cohen, Simon. "The Extreme Male Brain Theory of Autism." *Trends in Cognitive Sciences* 6 (2002): 248–254.

———., and Matthew K. Belmonte. "Autism: A Window onto the Development of the Social and the Analytic Brain." *Annual Review of Neuroscience* 28 (2005): 109–126.

———., Patrick Bolton, Sally Wheelwright, Victoria Scahill, Liz Short, Genevieve Mead, and Alex Smith. "Autism Occurs More Often in Families of Physicists, Engineers, and Mathematicians." *Autism* 2 (1998): 296–301.

———., Alan M. Leslie, and Uta Frith. "Does the Autistic Child Have a 'Theory of Mind'?" *Cognition* 21 (1985): 37–46.

———., and Sally Wheelwright. "Obsessions in Children with Autism or Asperger Syndrome: a Content Analysis in Terms of Core Domains of Cognition." *British Journal of Psychiatry* 175 (1999): 484–490.

———., Sally Wheelwright, Carol Stott, Patrick Bolton, and Ian Goodyer. "Is There a Link between Engineering and Autism?" *Autism* 1 (1997): 153–163.

Barron, Judy, and Sean Barron. *There's a Boy in Here*. New York: Simon & Schuster, 1992.

Becker, Ernest. *The Denial of Death*. New York: Free P, 1973.

Belmonte, Matthew K. "The Yellow Raincoat." *Evocative Objects: Things We Think With*. Ed. Sherry Turkle. Cambridge, MA: MIT P, 2007. 70–75.

———., Greg Allen, Andrea Beckel-Mitchener, Lisa M. Boulanger, Ruth A. Carper, Sara Jane Webb. "Autism and Abnormal Development of Brain Connectivity." *Journal of Neuroscience* 24 (2004): 9228–9231.

———., and Simon Baron-Cohen. "Small-World Network Properties and the Emergence of Social Cognition: Evidence from Functional Studies of Autism." *Proceedings of the 2004 International Conference on Development and Learning*. Ed. Jochen Triesch and Toni Jebara. La Jolla: UCSD Institute for Neural Computation, 2004. 268.

———., and Thomas Bourgeron. "Fragile X Syndrome and Autism at the Intersection of Genetic and Neural Networks." *Nature Neuroscience* 9.10 (2006): 1221–25.

———., Edwin H. Cook Jr., George M. Anderson, John L.R. Rubenstein, William T. Greenough, Andrea Beckel-Mitchener, Eric Courchesne, Lisa M. Boulanger, Susan B. Powell, Pat R. Levitt, Elaine K. Perry, Yong-hui Jiang, Timothy M. DeLorey, Elaine Tierney. "Autism as a Disorder of Neural Information Processing:

Directions for Research and Targets for Therapy." *Molecular Psychiatry* 9 (2004): 646–663. Unabridged edition at http://www.cureautismnow.org/conferences/summitmeetings/

———., and Deborah A. Yurgelun-Todd. "Functional Anatomy of Impaired Selective Attention and Compensatory Processing in Autism." *Cognitive Brain Research* 17 (2003): 651–664.

Bettelheim, Bruno. *The Empty Fortress: Infantile Autism and the Birth of the Self.* New York: Free P, 1967.

Bishop, Dorothy V., and Gillian Baird. "Parent and Teacher Report of Pragmatic Aspects of Communication: Use of the Children's Communication Checklist in a Clinical Setting." *Developmental Medicine and Child Neurology* 43 (2001): 809–818.

Constantino, John N., and Richard D. Todd. "Intergenerational Transmission of Subthreshold Autistic Traits in the General Population." *Biological Psychiatry* 57 (2005): 655–660.

Courchesne, Eric, and Karen Pierce. "Why the Frontal Cortex in Autism Might be Talking Only to Itself: Local Over-Connectivity but Long-Distance Disconnection." *Current Opinion in Neurobiology* 15 (2005): 225–230.

Earl, James Whitby. *Thinking about Beowulf.* Stanford: Stanford UP, 1994.

Evans, David W. "Rituals, Compulsions, and Other Syncretic Tools: Insights from Werner's Comparative Psychology." *Journal of Adult Development* 7 (2000): 49–61.

———., Julie Marie Elliott, and Mark G. Packard. "Visual Organization and Perceptual Closure Are Related to Compulsive-Like Behavior in Typically Developing Children." *Merrill-Palmer Quarterly* 47 (2001): 323–335.

———., F. Lee Gray, and James F. Leckman. "The Rituals, Fears, and Phobias of Young Children: Insights from Development, Psychopathology, and Neurobiology." *Child Psychiatry and Human Development* 29 (1999): 261–276.

———., James F. Leckman, Alice Carter, J. Steven Reznick, Desiree Henshaw, Robert A. King, and David Pauls. "Ritual, Habit, and Perfectionism: The Prevalence and Development of Compulsive-Like Behaviors in Normal Young Children." *Child Development* 68 (1997): 58–68.

———., Marc D. Lewis, and Emily Iobst. "The Role of the Orbitofrontal Cortex in Normally Developing Compulsive-Like Behaviors and Obsessive-Compulsive Disorder." *Brain and Cognition* 55 (2004): 220–234.

Fiske, Alan Page, and Nick Haslam. "Is Obsessive-Compulsive Disorder a Pathology of the Human Disposition to Perform Socially Meaningful Rituals? Evidence of Similar Content." *Journal of Nervous and Mental Disease* 185 (1997): 211–22.

Freud, Sigmund. "The Interpretation of Dreams." *The Standard Edition of the Complete Psychological Works of Sigmund Freud.* Ed. James Strachey. 8/e, vol. 4. London: Hogarth P, 1953. 1–630.

Frith, Uta. *Autism: Explaining the Enigma.* Oxford: Blackwell, 1989.

———., and Frédérique de Vignemont. "Egocentrism, Allocentrism and Asperger Syndrome." *Consciousness and Cognition* 14 (2005): 719–738.

Gerrans, Philip. "The Norms of Cognitive Development." *Mind and Language* 13 (1998): 56–75.

Gerrig, Richard J., and Gail McKoon. "Memory Processes and Experiential Continuity." *Psychological Science* 12 (2001): 81–85.

Giedd, Jay N. "The Anatomy of Mentalization: A View from Developmental Neuroimaging." *Bulletin of the Menninger Clinic* 67 (2003):132–142.

Gogtay, Nitin, Jay N. Giedd, Leslie Lusk, Kiralee M. Hayashi, Deanna Greenstein, A. Catherine Vaituzis, Tom F. Nugent III, David H. Herman, Liv S. Clasen, Arthur W. Toga, Judith L. Rapoport, and Paul M. Thompson. "Dynamic Mapping of Human Cortical Development during Childhood through Early Adulthood."

Proceedings of the National Academy of Sciences of the United States of America 101 (2004): 8174–8179.

Grandin, Temple, and Catherine Johnson. *Animals in Translation: Using the Mysteries of Autism to Decode Animal Behavior*. New York: Scribner, 2005.

Greenspan, Stanley I. "The Affect Diathesis Hypothesis: The Role of Emotions in the Core Deficit in Autism and the Development of Intelligence and Social Skills." *Journal of Developmental and Learning Disorders* 5 (2001):1–45.

———., and Stuart G. Shanker. *The First Idea: How Symbols, Language, and Intelligence Evolved from Our Primate Ancestors to Modern Humans*. Cambridge, MA: Da Capo, 2004.

Happé, Francesca. "Studying Weak Central Coherence at Low Levels: Children with Autism Do Not Succumb to Visual Illusions. A Research Note." *Journal of Child Psychology and Psychiatry* 37 (1996): 873–877.

Herman, David. "Stories as a Tool for Thinking." *Narrative Theory and the Cognitive Sciences*. Ed. David Herman. Stanford: Center for the Study of Language and Information, 2003. 163–192.

Hite, Molly. *Ideas of Order in the Novels of Thomas Pynchon*. Columbus: Ohio State UP, 1983.

Lacan, Jacques. "Fonction et champ de la parole et du langage en psychanalyse." *Écrits*. Paris: Éditions du Seuil, 1966. 237–322.

Miller, Thomas, ed. *The Old English Version of Bede's Ecclesiastical History of the English People*. Early English Text Society #95. London: N. Trubner, 1890.

Ozonoff, Sally, Bruce Pennington, and Sally J. Rogers. "Executive Function Deficits in High-Functioning Autistic Individuals: Relationship to Theory of Mind." *Journal of Child Psychology and Psychiatry* 32 (1991): 1081–1085.

Pennington, Bruce F., Sally Rogers, Loisa Bennetto, Elizabeth McMahon Griffith, D. Taffy Reed, and Vivian Shyu. "Validity Test of the Executive Dysfunction Hypothesis of Autism." *Autism as an Executive Disorder*. Ed. James Russell. Oxford: Oxford UP, 1997. 143–178.

Piven, Joseph, Pat Palmer, Dinah Jacobi, Debra Childress, and Stephan Arndt. "Broader Autism Phenotype: Evidence from a Family-History Study of Multiple-Incidence Autism Families." *American Journal of Psychiatry* 154 (1997): 185–190.

Pynchon, Thomas. *Gravity's Rainbow*. New York: Viking, 1973.

Russell, James. "How Executive Disorders Can Bring about an Inadequate Theory of Mind." *Autism as an Executive Disorder*. Ed. James Russell. Oxford: Oxford UP, 1997. 256–304.

Szasz, Thomas. *The Myth of Mental Illness*. New York: Hoeber-Harper, 1961.

Teitelbaum, Philip, Osnat Teitelbaum, Jennifer Nye, Joshua Fryman, and Ralph G. Maurer. "Movement Analysis in Infancy May Be Useful for Early Diagnosis of Autism." *Proceedings of the National Academy of Sciences of the United States of America* 95 (1998): 13982–13987.

Tononi, Giulio, Olaf Sporns, and Gerald M. Edelman. "Reentry and the Problem of Integrating Multiple Cortical Areas: Simulation of Dynamic Integration in the Visual System." *Cerebral Cortex* 2 (1992): 310–335.

Turner, Mark. *The Literary Mind*. New York: Oxford UP, 1996.

Werner, Heinz. *The Comparative Psychology of Mental Development*. Chicago: Follett, 1948.

Zupitza, Julius, ed. *Beowulf: Autotypes of the Unique Cotton MS*. Vitellius Axv in the British Museum. Early English Text Society #77. London: N. Trubner, 1882.

Part III

Autist Biography

9 Crossing Over
Writing the Autistic Memoir

Debra L. Cumberland

What I first recall is the head-pounding. We were sitting at the dinner table and Lawrence rose, his head thrust forward, and bolted for the wall, banging his head against it as hard as possible. My father flung down his fork and rushed toward him, pressing his hand up against the wall to cushion the blow, begging him to stop, but Lawrence didn't stop, couldn't stop. Memories like this one, precise and often painful, always remind me of how central my life with Lawrence is to my own work and identity as a writer, a daughter, and a sister. Writing is a way of entering into the human experience, understanding the self, and, for many, a way to heal. I observe this in my own writing, as I continue to explore my relationship with my brother and my mother's pain at the hands of the psychiatric profession, and I have observed it countless times in reading memoirs about autism and those by people outside the mainstream. My notions of selfhood have surely been affected by living with a disabled sibling. My own understanding of language and identity grew hand in hand with watching him attempt to construct his.

When I was growing up, there were few accounts of autism, and thus, little perspective from which to evaluate our own experiences; now there are hundreds. And when I was growing up during the seventies, memoir itself was a small and ignored genre, unless the memoir was written by white men like Benjamin Franklin. However, the genre has grown, partly because it has made room for voices from outside the mainstream: women and other minorities, the disabled—although often these memoirs are viewed as "confessional" and taken less seriously. Yet there has recently been a healthy explosion of such memoirs, in large part because these voices have been silenced for so long. Ironically, it is these memoirs—written by mothers of disabled children—that have often enabled women to "cross over": to write memoirs in which women act as heroic figures in a manner similar to those in the male "quest narrative," as explored by Carolyn Heilbrun in *Writing a Woman's Life*. As Heilbrun explains, autobiographies of famous women such as Margery Kempe and Jane Addams follow the pattern of reporting "the encounters with what would be the life's work as having occurred by chance" (24–25). The women depict their lives as passive until they are "called" to fulfill their mission, their quest. Women memoirists traditionally do not represent their lives as pre-ordained scripts the way male memoirists often do; for women memoirists, life is something that happens to them, rather than something they create (Heilbrun 22).

Mothers of autistic children complicate our notion of this quest narrative through the ways gender affects their memoirs. The mother of a disabled child may be damned by society because she is perceived as the cause of her child's disability. But in writing the memoir, she has the chance to redeem herself, to show that she is in fact the agent of the child's salvation. Thus mothers, as agents of the child's salvation, enact the "heroic" script often found in male memoirs. Society wants these scripts of heroism, and the mother, in writing it, also knows that she is writing to redeem both herself and her child. As Barbara Hillyer notes, writing a memoir is "an act of controlling, delimiting, and shaping one's emotional expression" (35). However, in writing such a memoir, the mother may, perversely, write herself back into the script from which she was trying to escape. For if autism, as we now understand it, is biogenetic, or the result of neurochemistry, scripts of the "saved" child may simply feed the idea that the mother has the power to save because she also, by implication, has the power to damn.

My parents first realized that something was wrong when Lawrence was three years old. My father met my mother in Germany when she was 24 and he 30; they married and came back to the United States to Storm Lake, where he had a job teaching history at the local college. Lawrence, a beautiful blond-haired baby boy, was their first child. Things were not right with Lawrence, although they didn't realize it at the time. In later years, when Lawrence was grown, my father speculated that the delivery may have affected the baby: my mother was kept waiting while the doctors in the small hospital finished working on another patient. Recent studies cited in Uta Frith's *Autism: Explaining the Enigma* indicate a high incidence of birth complications with autistic children. At the time, of course, no one knew of this. What was known were Leo Kanner's theories: how, after interviewing countless parents, he had decided that they were responsible for the children's condition. Kanner classified autism as an emotional withdrawal from the world, noting that the parents of autistic children were by and large professional, highly educated men and women. My parents fit this classification. Bruno Bettelheim also believed that parents (particularly the mothers) of autistic children were cold and intellectual, and that their inability to love had caused their child's emotional isolation.

But when they first drove Lawrence to Iowa City, when he was five or six, wondering why he didn't talk like other children but simply repeated what was said to him, my parents didn't think of autism. Few people did at the time. Autism then meant being relegated to a mental institution for a lifetime.

Being Lawrence's sister made me feel protective towards my mother. As I sat in the chair, large green clinical book in my hands, and read about how she may have caused his condition, I slammed the book shut. I knew who she was, and I knew that this simply was not true. I skimmed a few of the personal accounts they had on their shelves, such as Clara Claiborne Park's *The Siege*, Copeland's *For the Love of Ann* and Barry Kaufman's *Son Rise*. I started writing then as a way to escape, and a way to understand our situation. I often tried to think of my life in fictional terms, painting everything that happened around me as a story: *the young heroine rose in the morning and ran toward the bus stop, swinging her lunchbox*. Doing so detached me from all the strange and confusing events around me. However, my parents kept knocking on the door, giving me books to bring me back to reality—books about kids learning to cope with their mentally retarded siblings, as well as books such as *For the Love of Ann*, because they were the only stories available close to my experience. I kept trying to think of my life as a fiction, while they tried to make me understand the true story we were living.

And yet the early books on autism, such as *The Siege* and *For the Love of Ann*, did indeed follow the trajectory of our lives: the sense that something clearly wasn't right, the struggle to find an answer, the psychiatric profession as antagonist, the incredible sense of being blamed, and then, usually, small victories offering hope for the future: not what other people would define as a normal life, but at least a sense of connection with the child that had not been there before, a connection with the child's spirit and an opening into a new world of possibility.

Clara Claiborne Park's *The Siege: The First Eight Years of an Autistic Child*, one of the earliest memoirs recounting a parent's experience and still a classic, is particularly notable for its meticulous attention to detail in relating the strategies the Park family used to break through to Jessy, their youngest child (called Elly in the memoir). Clara Park devoted her life to her autistic daughter and the family underwent great sacrifices, including uprooting and living in England, so that Jessy could be a patient of Anna Freud.

Park's memoir follows the form of a quest for salvation. The male script she adopts is clearly evident in the title, *The Siege*, with its martial implications. Only this battle takes place on domestic turf, and Park stresses both her and her daughter's places in the family, making the writer/mother rather than the husband the repository of its accomplishments. The story recounts Clara Park's days with her child, the vast array of notebooks she filled with Jessy's words and Jessy's progress toward language. Park also devotes considerable space to accounting for her gifts in raising her three older children and the domestic well-being in which she enshrined them.

Establishing the home as healthy is important for Park, for in 1967 the mother was still viewed as responsible for the child's disability. Park's memoir commences with a strong testament that both reinforces this notion and defies it. As she writes,

> I set down only what is obvious, what is attested by teachers, friends, and neighbors. Our children were intelligent, responsive, and adaptable. They were also—quite irrelevantly—beautiful, with a pink and

gold beauty which seemed to belong not to the real world but to the illustrations of old-fashioned storybooks. . . . It shone around them, an astonishing, almost palpable fact, as if to symbolize their less superficial successes—their intelligence and their affection. (16)

She feels both proud of and responsible for her children's beauty, intelligence and happiness. As Helen Featherstone notes, "The whole culture supports a mother in the opinion that her children are what she has made them" (71). Yet "if a mother takes full credit for the toddler's glowing smiles and precocious syntax, whom does she blame for the schoolboy's nightmares and inefficient study habits?" (71).

Park attempts to establish that she has done a good job with her other children, and therefore cannot be responsible for "Elly's" disability, for she raised her just as she raised the others, and her child-rearing methods were not unusual. "Within two hundred yards of our house were fifteen or twenty children for Sara and Becky and Matt to know," Park explains. "A selection of these streamed steadily through our house . . .; our children streamed correspondingly through the houses nearby. These children were attractive and alert, brought up with care and considerable success by mothers like me, the mothers of the forties and fifties for whom Dr. Spock had replaced the conventional wisdom. . . . [M]ost of us . . . had made motherhood our profession" (14). Chronicling their community interconnectedness is important, for it testifies to the sheer normality of the Parks' lives: they were parents like every other parent on the block, reading the same books, operating according to the same scientific discourse of motherhood. As a result, the book's meticulous detail attests not only to the Parks' heroic efforts, but also to the triumph of the mother as a force in the home, where Park put all of her intelligence and love.

The home symbolizes the mother's ability to establish domestic health and harmony and becomes the repository of her identity: although Park yearns to teach part-time and to have time to read and write (which she eventually does), it is the home she creates, and her gifts as a mother, that enable her to break through to her daughter and help her emerge as a self. She is not the bad mother so often blamed for what is wrong with her child; she is the good mother who will do whatever it takes to "save" her children. This is the only role she can play in the public eye, for "mothers of disabled children are held more accountable than others to an externally defined concept of adequate mothering" (Hillyer 11). Unlike many other memoirs written by parents of autistic children, Park's adopts the cool, calm rational voice of science. Yet when she does eventually become a full-time teacher, she is careful to note that this is not a symptom of cold intellectualism, but a part of her identity that enables her to be a happy, loving, well-functioning mother.

However, it is clear from the memoir that this is the mother's story, for although Park mentions her husband David (an academic), and often refers to "we," he is not a clearly defined figure. His absence implies that only the mother can "save" her child, and this emphasis on the mother's role actually places Park back in the position that the memoir strives to release her from: she is responsible. In Park's case, this responsibility manifests itself as a concern to assert the virtues of the mother in opposition to the medical establishment's mother-blaming. But the emphasis in *The Siege* falls on the woman writer's accomplishments as a model daughter, wife, and mother, and how these are interpreted and assessed by the outside world that so often judges her.

Clara Claiborne Park acknowledges her temporary guilt feelings for wanting to return to work when she becomes pregnant with "Elly":

> I had the stirrings of a vocation. . . . My days would be my own again; I could have again the forgotten experience of being alone. I would have time to read, to bring my knowledge up to date. I could perhaps write. I could locate a school where I could teach part-time.
>
> It was in this forward-looking state of mind that I learned I was pregnant for the fourth time and that the job was to be done all over again. (17)

Acknowledging her depression here is of course important, for the prevailing theory was that the child became autistic because he/she could sense that the mother did not want her or him. Park must acknowledge her guilt. Yet by giving scientific, objective accounts of her day-to-day activities with her daughter, she indicates that yes, indeed, she and her husband were intellectuals; yes, they were objective and capable of detachment; but she also delineates how these very qualities labeled as pathological served, along with their great love, to enable her daughter, in the sequel, *Exiting Nirvana*, to paint and hold a steady job in the post office at the college where her parents teach. If the public will damn her as a woman, she will prove as rationally as possible that she can save through the power of her love turned into science.

My mother also stayed home with her children until she, too, taught part-time. But unlike Clara Claiborne Park, she did not escape feelings of guilt, for Lawrence was her first-born, and she did not grow up with a great deal of experience with babies. My parents often stood around the crib in terror, wondering what they could do to quiet his screaming, then hoping they were doing the right thing. If a shoestring was out of place, Lawrence screamed. If his blanket was not positioned exactly the right way, Lawrence screamed. He rocked in his crib, he rocked out of his crib, he howled if there was any change in his routine. When he was three, they took him to the local doctor, who said he was simply slow. They took him to the specialist in Spencer, Iowa, who flung up his hands and said Lawrence might be retarded. The specialist at Cherokee thought he might be schizophrenic.

The specialist at the hospital in Iowa City simply didn't believe anything my parents told him.

"Be careful," my father warned him. "if anything is out of place, he'll scream."

The specialist smiled coolly.

"Okay," said my father. "Pull his shoestring."

The specialist pulled the shoestring and placid, blond and beautiful Lawrence shrieked.

"Okay," said the specialist, hurriedly retying the shoe. "I see you're right."

But Lawrence was again diagnosed as retarded and my parents were told that their son—who eventually graduated from college with a B.A. in accounting—would not make it beyond the third grade. Years later, my mother told me of her despair at that moment: watching, through a glass partition, her baby boy methodically stacking blocks in the intricate patterns he loved, feeling that there was nothing she could do to reach him, no way to help him, and then hearing the words she would cling to throughout the later years: "There is more to your son than they have told," said a nurse who had worked with him.

Like my parents, this woman did not believe that Lawrence was mentally retarded. My father, not the professional psychiatrists, diagnosed him. He spent weeks plowing through the stacks in the college library, and finally came home to announce that he knew what was wrong: Lawrence wasn't mentally retarded, he was autistic. My mother responded with joy: he's *artistic*, how wonderful. Imagine her slow, sinking feeling on realizing her mistake, knowing that now nothing would ever be the same. There is something so quaint, so lovable, in that mistake: of course someone with an acute artistic sensibility would be hauled at an early age from psychiatrist to psychiatrist to be diagnosed with a mental disability rather than appreciated for what he was—a spirit set apart, with a heightened vision that can tell us something of who we are. This is the tension that so many autism memoirs increasingly explore: the concept of normality and the manner in which an autistic child can make us more careful about defining it. The autistic child such as my brother, such as the Parks' Jessy, does have profound limitations, yet those very limitations also force us to address what is missing in our own so-called normality. Although my mother's response was wrong, in another sense, she was right, for the very reason that society shuns the disabled is a fear of being different, of being vulnerable, perhaps even a fear of spirit itself.

Whereas Park's memoir roots itself in the sanctifying power of the domestic space, Jane Taylor McDonnell's memoir focuses on the struggle to escape what she sees as the confining world of domesticity in order both to have a fulfilling professional career and to be a good mother. McDonnell's memoir, published in 1993, is as much about a woman struggling to fulfill herself professionally as it is about the enormous struggles she and her husband endured in raising a son with autism and a daughter with cerebral palsy. As a result, it is a Bildungsroman—an account of her attempt to grow as an artist and intellectual—loosely modeled on the traditional male quest narrative; only in this instance the quest is the mother's attempt to help her son create a fulfilling life for himself.

My mother, unlike Jane Taylor McDonnell, was not a highly ambitious woman struggling to balance her role as a wife, mother, and career professional. Nor was she like Clara Claiborne Park, who wanted to teach part-time and hired a series of helpers to enable her to do so. My mother hated having to go into the classroom and teach German. She wanted to stay home. She wanted to bake cookies. She wanted to knit sweaters, afghans, baby blankets: in short, to be a traditional mother. Despite her desire not to be what psychiatrists called "a cold female intellectual," she had already, somehow, failed, according to the family therapists we regularly saw: she had failed simply because she was female.

Anger at such sexism in the professions—both psychiatric and academic—fuels McDonnell's memoir. She does not have the flights of carefully controlled, beautiful and precise language that characterize Park's memoir. McDonnell's narrative is far more complicated, for her relationship to the domestic is more tenuous. As a professional woman, she yearns to escape domesticity. But the attempt to balance a career with mothering two disabled children, coupled with her guilt feelings, engenders the burden of her narrative and her life. Fighting for the child becomes a socially acceptable quest: she must become a "supermom" both to compensate for her guilt and to prove that the domestic space can heal, rather than harm, her child.

McDonnell's memoir begins as so many others do—with the beautiful baby and the subsequent nagging doubt that something is wrong that must be discovered and remedied. In recounting this time in the wilderness, her story bears a striking resemblance to the spiritual memoir discussed in this volume by James Fisher, in which the soul is lost and ultimately becomes whole again through the power of divine love. In this family's case, of course, the fractured soul becomes restored through human love: Jane's for her husband Jim, which helps to give Paul the promise of a college degree, and, astonishingly, a wife and child. The transference from the wilderness to salvation is again ironically achieved by the previously demonized figure of the mother, who saves others through her own suffering, subsequent enlightenment, and love.

McDonnell's memoir thus does not attempt to redefine normality, or address what might be missing in our so-called normality; she is determined to view her son Paul *as* normal, no matter what the cost. And the cost for her is profound emotional and intellectual isolation. The isolation at first comes through her own ignorance of the condition that makes her son so different. Like Park, and like my own parents, the McDonnells had no idea initially of the nature of autism, and their child is repeatedly misdiagnosed by uncaring and or willfully ignorant professionals who variously believe Paul to be deaf or retarded. As an intellectual, McDonnell must deal with her horror at the thought of something being wrong with her son's mind: that, for her, would be the worst realization possible. But her conflict is compounded by her growing drinking problem, as well as by her sense of inadequacy in the academy and her desire to hide this at all costs. While on sabbaticals, for instance, her desire to finish her dissertation and work on her classes always comes second to her husband's work and her own role as Paul's primary caretaker.

The struggle to articulate what this experience means as a woman, an academic, and a mother is particularly agonizing for McDonnell. Ironically, Paul is as isolated in his ability to articulate his own meaning as his mother is. The title of *News from the Border* not only refers to an old Irish legend of the child switched in the crib by the fairies, but also serves to illustrate the difference and the distance that she feels from others—that she exists on the margins, and her and her son's lives are relayed in dispatches. If she dared to articulate her reality, she feels intuitively she would be misunderstood or condemned. And she is condemned, repeatedly, by people who don't understand and who inform her, time and again, that she is what she fears: a bad mother. While she and her husband are on sabbatical in England, for instance, the daycare center informs her that she is not disciplining her son properly, and women in the grocery store cast disapproving glances when Paul shrieks (36).

McDonnell's role as a professor necessitates weaving the elaborate illusion of a woman carefully balancing motherhood and career. When a student interviews her on the college radio station, McDonnell quickly concludes, as her colleague in religious studies chatters on about how easy it is to combine work and family, that she cannot tell the truth about the life she lives. As she notes when interviewed on radio:

> Lilly announced that she kept the crib in her office, that the baby slept there peacefully. . . . Her two older children went to an after-school program where they painted the most marvelous pictures, or made potholders and paperweights as little gifts to present to her later. . . . I sat there . . . my hands sweating against the microphone. What could I say . . . ? How could I say that Paul would never be happy in an regular after-school program, nor would they be happy with him. . . . How could I tell the listeners that Kate had been expelled from her first regular nursery school because she wasn't potty trained . . .? The world wasn't set up for children like Paul or Kate, but sitting there in the radio station I could only think that it was my fault for not training them better. (161)

Unlike Park, McDonnell does not enjoy the luxury of having three older, successful, well-adjusted children to lessen her guilt; instead, she gives birth to another child with a disability, a fact that initially nearly does her in. But unlike Paul's disability, cerebral palsy can't be blamed on the mother: it has a definite cause, and Kate's ability to overcome her cerebral palsy and dance in their small town's ballet becomes a saving grace for Jane McDonnell, for now people point to her second child and remark on what a good job she has done with her.

Throughout *News from the Border*, McDonnell deals with the categories outsiders fling out so easily—good mother/bad mother—categorizations enforced by "psychiatrists" such as Bruno Bettelheim, who denounced female intellectuals for their children's problems. In *The Empty Fortress* he compared autistic children to victims of torture and of war, linking the emotional trauma of concentration camp victims to those of children raised by emotionally scarred parents—particularly mothers—who could not love their children and whose children, therefore, could not love. McDonnell includes a passage in *News From the Border* in which she reads Bettelheim in the library and is haunted by the image of other women reading him and taking him seriously: "this book, three copies of it, was in the library. Lots of people had checked it out" (136). All of these conflicting emotions highlight her feelings of fragmentation and guilt, feelings that make her as isolated as her child.

McDonnell's memoir does not so much question what it means to be human as it challenges the sexism and classism in the definition of disability and in the treatment of the disabled. As she notes, nothing she could do, nothing she could achieve, could ever make up for the fact that her disabled child would always be treated as a second-class citizen. And this she cannot accept, just as she cannot accept her own second-class citizenship as a woman in the academy. McDonnell's desire for acceptance and validation in her career become inexorably linked with the protectiveness and love she feels for her child. Her love comes, however, from wanting to see Paul become like other children. She calls parents on the phone and yells at them to play with her son, though she realizes that she should not; yet she cannot bear to see him not have a friend.

Jane McDonnell, like her son Paul, seeks an experience of wholeness, of healing, alongside her son's struggles to find intimacy: first, with a friend, and then, later in life, with a girlfriend. McDonnell's isolation as an academic ultimately denied tenure and as a mother, combined with her drinking problem, also create a marital rift that is not healed until the end of the memoir, when Paul emerges as a remarkably self-sufficient adult who not only marries and has a child, but also goes to college and serves on the board of the Autism Foundation in the Twin Cities. The journey in the wilderness is over, and salvation again comes through loving sacrifice on the part of the family, but particularly on the part of the mother who, contrary to prevailing opinion, saves her child rather than destroying him. Interestingly enough, the role of the father is not questioned, nor does anyone in the book feel concern over the father's influence. Although the title clearly states that this is *A Mother's Memoir*, both the book itself—its existence as a challenge to prevailing opinion on the role of the mother—and the reactions of professionals and family members to Paul reinforce the stereotype that McDonnell seeks to avoid. The mother, with the power to damn, also, perversely, has the power to save. Whatever happens, she is responsible.

Like the McDonnells and the Parks, my parents refused to put Lawrence into an institution and instead kept him busy, giving him work that followed an established routine, something that he craved. Living in a small town, they too suffered isolation from not having the support groups many have today; but that did not stop them. They found outlets for Lawrence within the community. In the summers he de-tasseled corn and "walked" beans and throughout the year delivered newspapers. In our small town of Storm Lake, Iowa, Lawrence had the biggest paper route in the Des Moines *Register*'s history, and his papers were always placed at approximately the same time on people's front steps, rain or shine.

Small-town life can be difficult for those outside the norm. Lawrence was viewed as a freak, an oddity. The public school system wasn't eager to take him. But Lawrence wasn't mentally retarded, so my parents fought to get him into class. This was before the days of handicap-accessible classrooms. The teachers eyed him warily, trying to ignore him as best they could. Lawrence was like a space alien, sitting with his square sixties glasses, twirling his pen in the middle of class, laughing oddly while solving math problems. There was no telling what triggered his odd responses, quirks, and tics: someone may have looked at him strangely, a sound may have frightened him. He often developed strange obsessions and as he grew older sat in his room and cut articles out of the paper about shooting and crimes committed in the community; sometimes my mother and father would lie awake at night and wonder what had provoked this fascination, and whether he'd grow up to be one of those people you read about in the newspaper who suddenly snap.

For me the hardest moments were not defending him at school against taunts and jeers, or even the nights around the family dinner table when he would try to hurt himself. The hardest times were the family therapy sessions. I was eight when we started going to Cherokee for these sessions, and I remember clutching my mother's hand tightly as we walked up the sidewalk into the brown brick building with the bars on the windows. I remember hearing screaming in the foul-smelling corridors, and the squeak of rubber-soled shoes; smelling the strong institutional stink and squinting in the harsh fluorescent lights. I remember hating the psychiatrist as he sat there with his clipboard, asking me whom I loved more, my mother or my father, asking me to walk over and sit beside my favorite parent. I knew that he was out to get my mother, to prove she was responsible for Lawrence's condition. I knew nothing of Kanner and his theories. I didn't really understand what was wrong, but I could sense his feelings toward my mother. I don't remember how I knew, but I hated him, and refused to say anything. My mother left the sessions with her eyes dim and red-rimmed and I held her hand even tighter.

Years later, after the Freedom of Information Act was passed, Lawrence requested his files from Cherokee and read the doctor's report. When Lawrence announced that he had requested those records and read them my mother's face blanched. She knew what was in them; she knew what he had read. But he patted her on the shoulder and said in his big, booming, awkward way, "I know it's not your fault, mom, they said it was your fault, but I know it wasn't your fault." And her eyes filled with tears.

My family's experience with mother-blaming made me curious to read memoirs of autistic children written by men. Would they follow the same path as those by women? Indeed, neither Paul Collins's *Not Even Wrong* nor Josh Greenfeld's *A Child Called Noah* follows the traditional plot we might expect from a memoir written by a man: a male quest narrative, with the hero as the agent of his destiny. Greenfeld's book, for instance, is written in the form of a journal, which reflects the "female tradition" of memoir, according to critic Estelle C. Jelinek, who writes that such "discontinuous forms have been important to women because they are analogous to the fragmented, interrupted, and formless nature of their lives" (19). Greenfeld, the father of an autistic child, focuses in his narrative on fragmentation, chaos, a loss of identity, and the structure of his narrative reflects this chaos and fragmentation as he chronicles the first five years of his child's life. *Noah*, first published in 1970, is particularly poignant, for Noah is a child who does not improve. He does not, like Jessy/Elly and Paul, become an adult able to hold down a job; instead, in the third volume, *A Place for Noah*, the Greenfelds struggle with the realization that he must be institutionalized. Thus Greenfeld's narrative does not follow the traditional trajectory of the male quest narrative, with heroic triumph in the end. Instead, he focuses on the quest's interruption. Each diary entry reflects on the work not done, the books not written, the paintings his Japanese wife, Foumi, does not have the time to paint, the energy drained, the life interrupted as a result of raising a disabled child, the anger he and his wife feel that is so often left out of memoirs.

Indeed, Greenfeld's memoir seethes with anger. He and his wife lash out at each other and despair over the future of their son. "I realized how hard a day Foumi has every day," Greenfeld writes (104), only later to paint a scene in which his wife Foumi packs her suitcase, crying that she "doesn't see the point of throwing her life away" (119). "I've leafed through three books, chronicles by parents of severely disturbed or brain-damaged children," Greenfeld notes in one entry. "None of them palpitated with truth for me. The parents didn't burn with enough anger; they were all too damned heroic for me. Because one must be angry about all of the technology and all of the science that does not go into researching what the hell is wrong with a Noah" (126).

Anger is of course an emotion largely left out of Clara Claiborne Park's carefully constructed memoir; Jane Taylor McDonnell feels more despair, more helplessness, more guilt, more self-recrimination than she does anger—or she finds herself unable to share her feelings at all. Her anger is more often directed at the shunning of her son than at institutions. But the Greenfeld diary entries, although acknowledging guilt, more often speak of anger, particularly at the institutions and at the racial and economic inequities that compound the difficulties in dealing with those like Noah—a name that ironically means "hope."

As Carolyn Heilbrun notes, in writing autobiography, "what has been forbidden to women is anger" (13). In contrast, as a male and father of an autistic child, Greenfeld is free to feel this anger and write of it, for his emotions are not on trial by the psychiatric profession or the public who will read his memoir. He lacks the defensiveness that so often marks women's memoirs of disabled children. And when Greenfeld feels guilt for Noah's condition, he does not feel it because of his gender or his intellect; he feels it because of his genes: "If it is my lousy genes," he asks himself, "how could I have known my genes were that lousy?" (76). He also spends a moment considering that neither he nor Foumi wanted Noah, and that perhaps Noah "sensed chemically in the womb that he wasn't welcome" (19). However, the more Foumi and Josh Greenfeld research the problem, the more they accept biochemical causes and reject theories that blame the parents: "Freudian-oriented psychiatrists and psychologists, if ill-equipped to deal with the problems of those not verbal, tried to inflict great feelings of guilt upon us all-too-vulnerable parents" (91). As Greenfeld implies, it is easier to assign guilt than to solve problems.

Although Park's and McDonnell's stories focus on the domestic, Greenfeld's narrative ponders the social and economic conditions that complicate disability, as well as on race. Greenfeld observes that "Noah removes me from the world of wars, yet at the same time enhances my understanding of Vietnams. I can easily see how a nation which so cruelly treats its own 'gooks,' its own second-class citizens, its own smitten children, can lack all compassion for any people or land that is foreign and alien, different and deviant" (169). Vietnam becomes the logical outcome for a society with no compassion for its most vulnerable citizens—the disabled. But Greenfeld consistently resists easy answers, and consistently shows how his love for Noah is only a step away from his rage: "I must confess something: sometimes I hope Noah gets sick and dies painlessly" (139). Love, for Greenfeld, is not the answer; and it certainly is not all you need: only the righting of economic and social injustice will help solve the problem of the Noahs of the world.

Greenfeld's memoir cannot be read as a traditional quest narrative, for that requires a sense of agency, an ability to create the self and to view the world as a privileged terrain for the enaction of desire. Noah's life demands a different reading. Where once Greenfeld "believed in the institutions of organized medicine, private philanthropy, and public programs"—institutions that represent easy patriarchal privilege, institutions to which he might very well have had access—he now sees them as representations of social, racial, and economic inequities, as shutting out children such as Noah and all too often blaming the mother (91). Having a disabled child, for Green-feld, should lead one to read the world from the vantage point of those on the margins. As Greenfeld observes:

> I've been thinking about the irony of Noah. I was glad when Karl was born that my son was of the future, the mixed race bag of the future. But perhaps Noah in his way is the real grim example of the future, the schizophrenic future.
>
> Meanwhile, though, we still have to face the prejudicial present. Foumi still finds it almost impossible to get help. Both black and white domestics and mothers' helpers do not like to work for an oriental woman. And Noah's condition just compounds the problem. No one likes to take care of a problem kid. (77)

Whereas Clara Claiborne Park lives in an all-white, suburban neighbor-hood, and easily finds a string of domestic helpers, Noah's condition as a mixed-race child adds to the problem of isolation so often felt by parents with disabled children. (As Greenfeld asks: how can you travel with a men-tally disabled kid?) The Greenfelds must not only deal with society's fear of and hostility toward the mentally ill, but also its profound racism. What Greenfeld once saw as a sign of hope—a mixed-race child—becomes now a representation of the ills of a world that harms the vulnerable.

In the late seventies, when Lawrence was a teenager, my father and mother took us to Germany to visit my aunts, uncle, and cousins. Lawrence loved reading about Hitler and asked in his obsessive way everyone he met what he or she thought of the *Führer*. It was one thing to do this in Storm Lake, but quite another in Germany. My father said: "Don't ask the Germans about Hitler." Lawrence said, "No, sir, I won't ask anyone about Hitler." When we got on the German tour bus, Lawrence sat next to an elderly Ger-man man behind my father and promptly asked him, "So what do you think about Hitler?"

Now that I am older, there seems something fitting about this story. Law-rence knows love and joy and defiance, those qualities that make us human. On that same tour, he grinned and—despite the huge towers across the bor-der with armed men standing on patrol, ready to shoot anyone who crossed over—took a tiny step, putting his foot on Czech soil.

It is all too easy for us to stay on our own side of the fence, trapped on our own soil, either high up in towers and ready to shoot at those who cross over, or on the other side of the fence, fearful of life on the other side. There often are no happy endings, only daily struggles. And those stories, the stories of daily, never-ending struggles, matter too, even if they do not always fit the pattern of the salvation story our society craves. Perhaps it might be better to ask why those salvation stories are so much in demand, why those are the texts so often written, when in reality those stories are the exception rather than the rule. Perhaps it would be better to focus more on our definition of what it means to be human than to create texts that all have the same endings.

My brother Lawrence was willing to step on the dangerous soil, take that risk, and his life, and the life of those unspoken for, asks us to do the same.

WORKS CITED

Bettelheim, Bruno. *The Empty Fortress: Infantile Autism and the Birth of the Self.* New York: Free P, 1967.

Collins, Paul. *Not Even Wrong: Adventures in Autism.* London and New York: Bloomsbury, 2004.

Copeland, James. *For the Love of Ann.* London: Arrow, 1973.

Featherstone, Helen. *A Difference in the Family: Life with a Disabled Child.* New York: Basic Books, 1971.

Frith, Uta. *Autism: Explaining the Enigma.* Oxford and Cambridge: Blackwell, 1989.

Grandin, Temple. *Thinking in Pictures And Other Reports from My Life with Autism.* Foreword by Oliver Sacks. New York: Vintage, 1995.

Greenfeld, Josh. *A Child Called Noah: A Family Journey.* New York: Holt, Rinehart and Winston, 1970.

———. *A Place for Noah.* New York: Holt, 1978.

Heilbrun, Carolyn. *Writing a Woman's Life.* New York: Ballantine, 1988.

Hillyer, Barbara. *Feminism and Disability.* Norman and London: U of Oklahoma P, 1993.

Jelinek, Estelle, ed. *Women's Autobiography: Essays in Criticism.* Bloomington: Indiana UP, 1980.

Kaufman, Barry N. *Son Rise.* New York: Warner, 1976.

McDonnell, Jane Taylor. *News from the Border: A Mother's Memoir of Her Autistic Son.* Afterword by Paul McDonnell. New York: Ticknor and Fields, 1993.

Park, Clara Claiborne. *The Siege: The First Eight Years of an Autistic Child. With an Epilogue, Fifteen Years After.* Boston: Little, Brown, 1982

10 (M)Othering and Autism
Maternal Rhetorics of Self-Revision

Sheryl Stevenson

> What is it to acknowledge one's cognitive ability/privilege? How can the "mentally accelerated" be disloyal to their cognitive privilege while acknowledging the significance of their own identity? (Carlson 142)

In medical and popular representations over the last half century, the mother of the autistic child has emerged as a contentious figure, a magnet for blame and admiration. At first blamed for her child's condition, the unfeeling "refrigerator mother" appears today, in myriad counternarratives, as an exposed illusion that reveals fundamentally flawed, outmoded understandings of autism, as well as widespread patterns of mother-blame. Like a demonic transformation of the Angel in the House that haunts Virginia Woolf until the writer "kills" her, Bruno Bettelheim's pathologized maternal specter keeps returning, and whether she materializes in women's life stories, in documentaries like *Refrigerator Mothers*, or in histories of autism, she is roundly attacked as a harmful, though historically revealing, social construction (see, e.g., Nadesan 1, 97–99). Current cultural understandings of the mother in relation to her autistic child are also reflected in popular narratives such as Temple Grandin's autobiographical story in *Emergence: Labeled Autistic* and Mark Haddon's fictional autistic autobiography, *The Curious Incident of the Dog in the Night-Time*. Commonly seen as portraying the perspective of an adolescent with Asperger's syndrome, Haddon's phenomenally popular novel constructs a boy's coming-of-age narrative that hinges on his successful search for his mother; meanwhile, readers discern, as the adolescent narrator does not, the nearly muted story of the overwhelmed woman herself, almost defeated by her intensely emotional, traditional, but misguided approach to mothering. Oddly similar in effect to the loving but strong maternal figure who fosters Grandin's story of triumph, Haddon's realistic portrait may sound the death knell of the refrigerator mother, even if this cultural archetype is one of those phantasms that Woolf observes are "far harder to kill . . . than a reality" (286).

Yet the fantasy of the autistic child's lethally detached mother is perhaps being buried under the sheer weight of mothers' diverse experiences, conveyed in the outpouring of women's autobiographical essays, memoirs, advice books, literature for children, and Web sites that play a significant role in the contemporary cultural construction of autism. For example, by documenting and reflecting on day-to-day realities of raising an autistic son, Kristina Chew's blog *Autismland: The Autism Reality Show Starring Charlie* implicitly challenges expectations that a family's experience of autism will be packaged in a totalizing narrative of tragedy or recovery, an expectation stemming from the "cognitive ableism" that treats the "'cognitively disabled' . . . as a homogeneous group."[1] With a more overt revisionist focus, mothers dealing with their own autism also address the assumption that the autistic person is a disabled "other" whose life will fit a predetermined cultural script. Examples of autistic women's reconstructions of motherhood can be found in Jean Kearns Miller's collection *Women from Another Planet?: Our Lives in the Universe of Autism*, where essays like "Mother at Odds" and "Mommie Wyrdest" employ personal experience to defend a less emotional (and less emotionally demanding) form of mothering, which the writers see not only as highly suited to their autistic children, but also as fostering the strengths of children who fall within developmental norms. This polemical use of autobiography brings into question what one autistic mother calls "the cultural belief in a socially sentimental and intuitive form of loving as the single, legitimate source of parenting," excluding more rational forms that preserve clear boundaries (Miller 195). Through such narratives, readers glimpse possible modes of nontraditional mothering in which the mother–child bond, rather than being assumed and culturally prescribed, is rationally constructed to fit the strengths and needs of specific women and children.

However, my analysis focuses on another type of maternal narrative, the non-autistic mother's memoir of her autistic child. This focus highlights strategies of narrative representation adopted by women who negotiate contradictions of motherhood in the dual context of autism and their own cognitive ableism—a limiting perspective that is hard to escape entirely for the neurotypical. Against expectations hallowed by images of Madonna and Child, these mothers reconceive their own maternal role to fit an individual child who may have profound difficulties understanding emotion and responding to eye contact, touch, play, and other prescribed modes of mother–child relationship. Yet these women join other mothers of children with diverse disabilities in experiencing a need for narrative described by anthropologist Gail Landsman: the pressure to construct the child's life in ways that counteract pervasive devaluation of the very "personhood" of the disabled person ("Emplotting" 1949–50). As Landsman asks, "How do mothers of children with disabilities define their children in relation to their disabilities?" (1948). To what extent is the mother situated "at the center of a great paradox," both "defending the child's potential to be nondisabled" while also "defending her child's right to be permanently disabled *and* valued in a nondisabled world" (1949)? I argue that this paradox becomes especially intense and culturally significant when the nondisabled mother of an autistic child adopts a deconstructive, self-revising rhetoric that discloses her own cognitive ableism—the bias that evaluates both child and mother by dominant norms of cognitive and emotional ability. Strategies of self-revision that focus on irreconcilable dilemmas and paradoxical identities become a way for the mother to mitigate her ableism, to promote the mutual empowerment that, as Joey Sprague and Jeanne Hayes argue, should characterize relationships between the cognitively privileged and people with developmental disabilities (683). Memoirs by two gifted writers provide revealing subjects for analysis of maternal rhetorics: Clara Claiborne Park's *The Siege*, her sequel *Exiting Nirvana*, and Jane Taylor McDonnell's *News from the Border*. These texts allow us to explore how mothers who are writers use rhetorical strategies to negotiate contradictions of motherhood that are exacerbated by autism and their own privileged abilities.[2]

Research shows that being a parent remains a highly gendered experience and that contradictory views of motherhood put specific demands on women—demands that may contribute to the higher rates of stress and depression reported by mothers than by fathers of autistic children (Little 568; Gray 636). In *The Cultural Contradictions of Motherhood*, sociologist Sharon Hays provides an influential analysis of contradictions arising from the contemporary "ideology of *intensive mothering*" (x). Reinforcing assumptions that the mother is "the central caregiver," this ideology also defines appropriate child rearing as requiring that the woman "put her child's needs above her own," foster "every stage of the child's emotional and intellectual development," and do so under the guidance of expert knowledge (x, 8). Such assumptions, especially for mothers who work outside the home, tend to conflict with dominant Western values that favor "the efficient, impersonal, competitive pursuit of self-interested gain" (Hays 10). Because Hays does not explore how a child's disability may enhance these conflicting pulls between self-sacrifice and self-interest, her model needs to be supplemented by work in feminist disability theory.

Barbara Hillyer, both a feminist scholar and the mother of a child with cognitive and physical impairments, argues that demands posed by a disability highlight the often unquestioned primacy given to productivity. In *Feminism and Disability*, she observes that "society's labeling of disabled people as incompetent or unproductive makes conformity to the ethic of productivity almost a prerequisite to self-esteem for them" (68). And the mother of a disabled child faces similar pressures, says Hillyer, to attain the status of a "superwoman" who is simultaneously a figure of supreme self-sacrifice (52–53). Such parents "are expected to increase their productivity by providing educational and rehabilitative services, medical therapies, and so on in addition to their own normal work loads" (69). Yet, as Landsman notes, through our culture's conflation of reproduction and production, "mothers of children with disabilities are the producers of defective merchandise," their motherhood tainted by failure ("Reconstructing" 77; cf. McDonnell, *News* 110). Seen in this light, when mothers use autobiographical representation to portray how their families' lives are affected by autism, their texts offer crucial insights into ways women cope not only with a specific disability but with pressures exerted by irreconcilable conceptions of a productive/ unproductive, enabling/disabled motherhood.

The memoirs of Park and McDonnell reveal that a primary dilemma stems from the mother's need to represent the child whose autism impedes his or her own autonomous self-representation. Given the prevailing cultural belief that females possess strengths in empathy and relationships, the mother's role as communicator, both with and for her child, is often assumed; the prevalence of this assumption is apparent in Sharon Hays's analysis of the most popular child-rearing manuals, those of Benjamin Spock, T. Berry Brazelton, and Penelope Leach (55–59). Yet contradictory social prescriptions frequently cast guilt and suspicion on the "oversolicitous or overprotective mother," as Molly Ladd-Taylor and Lauri Umansky note (13). For the mother of a child with autism, a disorder that profoundly affects communication abilities, telling the child's story may seem to involve a questionable projection of her own views that would create only an illusion of communication. The tension between facilitating and usurping the child's discourse recalls the early 1990s debate over "facilitated communication," brought to the general public's attention through the 1993 *Frontline* documentary "Prisoners of Silence." Park reflects this tension through the regret she repeatedly expresses about intervening in her daughter's slow, continuing acquisition of more normal speech, a laborious process that she views as curbing Jessy's modes of expression—the "telegraphic speech" of her idiosyncratic pidgin and what Oliver Sacks calls "the strange, mad poetry of Jessy's own words."[3] Writing in *The Siege*, when her daughter is eight, Park laments the fall "from our ideal of education" in "this supplying of conventional patterns into which thought . . . is to be poured" (229–30), just as she remarks thirty-four years later, in *Exiting Nirvana*, "Of course I would rather not teach Jessy language. To impose forms of language is to impose forms of thought" (51). But because "Jessy cannot tell her story for herself" (as the final paragraph of *Exiting Nirvana* states), how is her mother to tell that story without imposing her own forms of thought?

As though responding to a charge of eclipsing the autistic child's efforts to communicate, both Park and McDonnell find ways to include their children's discourse and modes of self-representation. For example, McDonnell's book, subtitled *A Mother's Memoir of Her Autistic Son*, concludes with a fifty-page Afterword by her son Paul, giving his version of his life story (an account that emphasizes his attempts to find and keep a girlfriend). Park's subtitle for *Exiting Nirvana*—*A Daughter's Life with Autism*—notably distracts attention from the mother's story, a move consistent with her more frequent and pervasive strategies of incorporation, such as her use of Jessy's phrases, in quotation marks, for the book's chapter titles (except for the framing chapters, "Introductory" and "Valedictory"). Both of her memoirs also incorporate facsimiles not only of her daughter's artwork, but also of handwritten items such as Jessy's journal writings and descriptions of her paintings, because the distinctive, child-like cursive script graphically represents Jessy Park.

A contrasting, and more extreme, effort by a mother to give her child a voice can be found in Karen L. Simmons's *"Little Rainman": Autism— Through the Eyes of a Child*. Written in the format of a children's book, this text offers the story of Simmons's son in "his" first-person perspective: "My name is Jonathan. I have autism (aw-tis-um)" (9). Simmons claims in her preface that Jonathan is *"indirectly"* the book's author, for as she says, "I felt like I was literally inside of his head and writing what he truly feels" and "I know this is how he felt at the time as any mother knows her own child" (2, 3; emphasis in original). McDonnell's narrative rarely suggests such certain maternal knowledge of her autistic child, and though Park seeks to explain aspects of how Jessy thinks, her narrative distinctly sets off her daughter's verbal and pictorial self-representation. Undermining any comforting impression of maternal understanding, one chapter of *Exiting Nirvana* delves into Jessy's creation of "books"—"hundreds of them"—reflecting her many obsessions through her own acts of authorship (97). In the same chapter, Park repeats the words "strange" or "strangeness" with striking frequency, to convey "the strangeness of that busy mind," an uncanny "strangeness that infused our family's every day" (97; see also 115). Indeed, *Exiting Nirvana* opens with this sense of otherness, with a self-referential query: "How to begin? In bewilderment, I think—that's the truest way" (3). Park places herself, not her daughter, in the uncomprehending position as she tells an anecdote from that very morning, when Jessy reacted to the word "remembrance" by exclaiming, "A new fluffy-in-the-middle! Found in the newspaper!" (3).

This Jessy embodies the pure, eerie otherness of cognitive difference. Michael Bérubé suggests that such figures "haunt narrative" precisely because they draw attention to "a form of human embodiment that cannot narrate itself but can only be narrated" ("Disability" 572). Park's "Epilogue" in *The Siege*, published fifteen years after the first edition, captures a terrific image of this human condition when she depicts Jessy as the uncomprehending typist for the book's Spanish translation (280–81). Reinforcing the estrangement of the young woman from the narrative purporting to represent her life story, Park comments on the choice to call her daughter "Elly" in the first edition: "Fifteen years ago I gave her that name, in case—could I actually have thought it?—she would someday read this book and be embarrassed. I need not have worried. Jessy likes coming across her book name. She likes coming across an extra space between paragraphs, too, or unusual punctuation" (*The Siege* 281). Jessy's relationship to "her" story reveals her difference in self-awareness, while also suggesting cognitive requirements for narrative self-representation.

Bérubé elaborates on this idea, showing that numerous depictions of cognitive difference in fiction and film provoke recognition of the "[m]indedness" that seems to be "a necessary condition for self-representation and narration" ("Disability" 572). He notes that many narratives develop strategies of incorporation, attempting to include perspectives shaped by cognitive disability, as we see in popular films depicting short-term memory loss such as *Memento*, *Fifty First Dates*, and *Finding Nemo*. This trend reveals an impulse toward the "democratization of narrative representation," an effort of empathy and inclusion that will give a voice to those "who cannot represent themselves" due to their neurological difference (575, 572). Yet Park's and McDonnell's memoirs show that when maternal narratives include their autistic children's writings or artwork, the resulting hybrids reveal how the gendered role of mother-the-communicator places a pressure on women that is intensified by autism. For even as these mothers try to allow the child's voice and story to emerge, their texts clarify the gulfs that separate mother and child, hence also stressing the cognitive difference that separates many readers from the autistic subject and that may preclude understanding. This situation is encapsulated in Park's recursive image of Jessy at twenty-three, an image from the epilogue of *The Siege* that deliberately evokes the eighteen month old of the book's opening page: "She still flips through books, as that golden baby did, and smiles her secret smile, only now she is looking for spaces, or irregular quotation marks, or the longest sentence she can find" (281). Does this passage reflect a mother's cognitive ableism, an othering of the autistic child? We could put such descriptions (including Park's many references to Jessy as an unworldly "fairy") to the test articulated by Susan Wendell: "When we make people 'other,' we group them together as the objects of *our* experience instead of regarding them as fellow *subjects* of experience with whom we might identify" (271; emphasis in original).

In a chapter called "The Others," Park ends the first edition of *The Siege* with words that might seem to fail Wendell's test. After telling of an unknown young man's suddenly offered tribute to "Elly's" beauty, she writes, "It helps to know that a stranger, seeing Elly, can look beyond her embarrassing defects to sense something of her strange integrity, and it helps more deeply than anything else can to know that stranger can touch stranger, in gentleness and love" (277). Laced with "strangeness," "strangers," the "strange" (Park's favored word, in all its morphological variations), her narratives at times draw out the writer's, and perhaps the reader's, cognitive ableism. However, we can take an alternative view of this rhetorical strategy of encapsulating cognitive difference by considering the mother's memoir as a complex performative utterance. Bérubé highlights this concept in "Autobiography as Performative Utterance," his contribution to an *American Quarterly* forum, "The Empire of the 'Normal': A Forum on Disability and Self-Representation." As the author of *Life As We Know It*, about his son who has Down syndrome, Bérubé emphasizes that his own book "is *not* an autobiography" but instead part of "the genre of life writing about disability" (339), like the memoirs of McDonnell and Park. He focuses his essay on emerging autobiographies by people with cognitive or developmental disabilities, arguing that such writing may necessarily be highly mediated: brought to publication, introduced, and even "authenticated" (as the disabled person's own words) by nondisabled others, just as slave narratives were similarly mediated.[4] And yet, for "a person with a cognitive or developmental disability . . ., the act of self-authorship performs the same performative function it did for Frederick Douglass and Harriet Jacobs . . .: it establishes the life writer as, at bare minimum, someone capable of self-reflection and self-representation" (341). Viewed in this light, we may see Park's and McDonnell's memoirs as acts of mediation that frame, and publicly disseminate, the self-representations of their autistic children, incorporated in their texts. Though not autobiographies of disability, the mothers' memoirs are performative in that they enact the very difference between themselves and their children that make mediated representation necessary. By reflecting the writers' own dominant perspective, including their cognitive ableism, the texts disclose their own inherent limitations.

Another contradiction arising from the mother's gendered role as communicator is that the condition that impedes the child's self-representation also gives the woman a voice, a compelling purpose, and an audience. Autism refigures the mother's traditional role as protector of her children, intensifying the demands for a parent (typically the mother) to perform specific types of advocacy for the child with special medical and educational needs. As the older brother of a young man with autism comments in the documentary *Refrigerator Mothers*, "My brother needs a protector, and I think that my mother feels like she's his protector in this life." The study Landsman conducted, in which she observed and interviewed numerous mothers of children with an array of disabling conditions, substantiates the pivotal role played by mothers as advocates for their children's welfare. Landsman (herself the mother of a child with cerebral palsy) finds that women formulate empowering narratives particularly in developmental evaluation sessions, when they seek the most nurturing services available by constructing their children's lives "within a story of developmental delay, in competition with the physician's story of disability" ("Emplotting" 1950). We can compare this pragmatic use of narrative with Nadesan's differing constructions of her child's autism, which she strategically tailors to audiences ranging from social service providers to teachers to other parents (2).

Mothers of autistic children have also taken on more public roles of communication and advocacy. Though activists like the "Mercury Moms," with their high-profile, controversial agenda, may gain extensive media coverage (as chronicled in David Kirby's *Evidence of Harm*), women more typically seek to educate the public and promote better services for their autistic children through local parent support groups. Writing in 1967, in her chapters of *The Siege* dealing with how parents' abilities were often discounted by physicians and psychiatrists, Park argues for exactly the parental training and outreach—in which experienced parents then help educate other parents (191)—that has since evolved through the Autism Society of America.

Another form of public advocacy, mounted from within the academy, can be seen in McDonnell's 1990s feminist essays, "Mothering an Autistic Child: Reclaiming the Voice of the Mother" and "On Being the 'Bad' Mother of an Autistic Child," both appearing in prominent academic essay collections dealing with motherhood. Park and McDonnell, as academic women, have forged a path mapped by Celest Martin, who writes of facing her own need to connect her academic work (in university teaching, research, and writing) with her work, including research, as the mother of an autistic son. But if an academic woman recognizes, as Martin says, that her child "provided the subject matter for [her] writing" (168), she may face the question of how a mother can play the role of communicator or advocate without drawing attention to the "crippled" or "damaged" child.

This question is one of the appropriate rhetorical stance for the mother-writer who wishes to portray, but not betray, her autistic child. Rosemarie Garland-Thomson outlines several possible stances by categorizing "visual rhetorics" in photography representing disabled people. The memoirs of Park and McDonnell avoid any taint of the "exotic" rhetoric that "presents disabled figures as alien, often sensationalized, eroticized, or entertaining in their difference" (Garland-Thomson 343). But in a chapter each calls "The Changeling," each mother conveys the uncanny sense of her child's difference by describing Irish folklore of the "fairy child left behind in the cradle when the real child is stolen away" (McDonnell, *News* 54; 325–26; Park, *The Siege* 5–6, 12). Aside from Jessy's "strangenesses"—her obsessions, compulsions, and amazing feats of memory—it is an ageless quality that impresses her mother as peculiarly belonging to the Irish fairyland, "the Land of Youth" (*The Siege* 5). It is for this quality that "people love her," Park says near the end of *Exiting Nirvana*, "for her otherworldliness, her simplicity, her utter incapacity for manipulation or malice" (204). Using Garland-Thomson's taxonomy, we might place such representations into the "wondrous" mode, which leads the audience to view "the disabled figure as the exception to human capability rather than the rule" (341). Because Jessy's autistic behaviors, as well as her mathematical and artistic gifts, are more pronounced than Paul's, it is not surprising that Park's memoirs draw on this rhetoric of defamiliarizing wonder much more pervasively than does McDonnell's *News from the Border*.

However, both mothers try to balance the impression of wondering estrangement with the realistic mode that, according to Garland-Thomson, "minimizes distance and difference," encouraging the audience's identification with the disabled person (344). Park thus fills her final chapters of *Exiting Nirvana* with anecdotes that present the "unromanticizable" ordinariness that she sees as a major achievement of her adult daughter's life (202), just as McDonnell concludes her memoir with incidents that convey the typical, late-teenage aspects of Paul's day-to-day life, with friends dropping by, part-time work, and community college courses. Capturing "an increasing, precious ordinariness"—Park's words in the final sentence of *Exiting Nirvana* (208)—this combination of rhetorics, juxtaposing the strange with the everyday, claims the ordinary world for the person with autism.

Garland-Thomson's fourth category, the "sentimental" rhetoric that portrays "the sympathetic victim" (341), clarifies why both mothers only sparingly elicit pity for their children's pain. Yet it is in their portrayal of suffering that the two memoir writers differ decisively, in that McDonnell bares much more of her own grief, guilt, and depression, especially through her struggle with alcoholism. Her journal-like narrative strongly contrasts with Park's more conceptually organized, emotionally restrained, and self-effacing narration, which often employs first-person plural pronouns (she even uses "Ourselves" as the second chapter title in *The Siege*, to introduce the rest of the family besides "Elly"). *The Siege* and *Exiting Nirvana* convey a mother's life absorbed in her daughter's progress and in keeping extensive records, a total-immersion ethnography carried out over more than four decades. As Oliver Sacks notes in his foreword to Park's second memoir, this commitment to detailed, daily documentation has produced, perhaps, "more 'data' on Jessy . . . than on any other autistic human being who has ever lived" (x). In contrast, McDonnell rejects pressures to devote her whole life to her son, showing that her husband and daughter both have problems that demand her attention, as does her teaching and research—work that does not focus on Paul or autism. In this way, *News from the Border* resists autism's pressures on mothers to adopt an intensified version of "intensive mothering."[5] As a feminist scholar, McDonnell develops broader contexts for understanding her maternal experiences through research and teaching on motherhood; her memoir demonstrates how her professionalism—her role as a public intellectual—finally gives her the necessary distance to understand the debilitating "overresponsibility" that had led her to blame herself for Paul's limitations and suffering (325). Her "adult life" situated in "an academic environment" (324) helps to foster both her autonomy and her son's, exemplifying Barbara Hillyer's view that mothers of children with disabilities can work against maternal codependence by seeking mutual "interdependence," connecting two individuals, mother and child, with sources of fulfillment outside their relationship (193–94, 216–17).

The arc of belated understanding that McDonnell traces at the end of her memoir is embodied in the more experimental, self-revising narrative form of *The Siege* and *Exiting Nirvana*. The remainder of this chapter explores how these two joined but conflicting narratives—through their shifting structures, concepts, and positions—consummately represent the mother's evolving understanding not only of her autistic child but of herself, as she becomes decentered by her daughter's strange, estranging perspective. This destabilizing evolution is textually figured in the unpredictable relationship between the two memoirs. Rather than forming a two-part chronicle, the memoir published in1967 (when Jessy was eight) is even more complexly related to the 2001 text by the lengthy chapter, "Epilogue, Fifteen Years

After," added to the 1982 edition of *The Siege*. The epilogue not only summarizes the progress 23-year-old Jessy has made, but shows the mother's
possible need to abandon and progress beyond the fundamental, organizing
conceptions of her own text. Like the narrator of a self-deconstructing meta-
fictional novel, she describes "reread[ing] the pages of this book . . ." (305).
And what sticks out for her is the text's emphasis on Jessy's many "willed"
deficiencies—"Willed Weakness," "Willed Blindness," "Willed Deafness,"
"Willed Isolation"—each a chapter title of *The Siege*. This conception of her
daughter's "emotional orientation to the world" (not her cognitive impairment) pervades the first memoir, starting from the initial elaboration of the
siege metaphor: "She dwelt in a solitary citadel, compelling and self-made
. . . [,]" requiring that others overcome "a tiny child's refusal of life" (303,
12). The writer of the 1982 epilogue finds that she can no longer accept
her earlier, foundational assumption, as she sees the misperceptions of cognitive impairments that in 1967 she could not understand, perhaps could
not accept. "I thought I had seen these things; I had made them central to
the story," she writes, disclosing her narrative's unwilled deficiencies (305).
Attempting to update the story after fifteen years leads to the discovery that
she may have to "reconceptualize everything" (305). This radical rethinking
involves not simply rejecting a past concept, but rather perceiving a paradox: "Cognitive or emotional? We have seen both play their part. . . . It is
not only unnecessary to choose between them; it is impossible" (306).

Querying her terms but not rejecting them, allowing contradictions to
stand and alternative views to emerge—these strategies become even more
pronounced in *Exiting Nirvana*. Many of the narrative's contradictions
concern differing conceptions of Jessy's understanding. For example, Park
claims that her daughter does not think of herself within "the vocabulary of
handicap," even though elsewhere she quotes her as saying, "I had a speech
handicap a long time ago" (188, 178). The writer expresses a similar view
when discussing her self-conscious choice to end both the first edition of
The Siege and its 1982 epilogue with the same word: "Love, ours and other
people's, is the condition of Jessy's life, little as she would be able to understand that" (205). Though Park goes on to assert that "love" is "not part of
[Jessy's] effective vocabulary," she immediately refutes this notion, through
quotations and dramatized incidents demonstrating that her daughter uses
the word, feels the emotion, and comprehends love (205–07).

The paradoxical, shifting conception of Jessy's ability is perhaps most
striking when *Exiting Nirvana* portrays her as "a busy, useful member of the
household and community" (204). Through details that accumulate over the
course of the memoir, the daughter is shown as achieving many outcomes of
the "success story" that Park initially rejects as an oversimplified and misleading cultural script (24; cf. *The Siege* 319). Clearly, Jessy *is* successful—in
holding her longtime job, in creating friendships at work, in putting away
"more money than any of her siblings," in earning recognition and additional income through her paintings, and in assuming the caretaking role

for her "aging parents," performing many of the domestic tasks that were her mother's (24–25). Park's text thus exemplifies ideals of empowerment and full inclusion by depicting interdependence between people with differing cognitive abilities, mutually involved in a relationship characterized by reciprocity, "in which inequality is not fixed but dynamic" (Sprague and Hayes 683; cf. Rohrer 47). Yet *Exiting Nirvana* does not allow the picture of Jessy's competence, her "tremendous achievement," to stand unqualified; instead Park switches tacks, declaring that it is not her daughter's "usefulness" but her difference that is the "future's best guarantee," because it is for "her otherworldliness" and "childlike purity" that she is loved (204). These contradictions do not simply betray the mother's cognitive ableism, her clinging to a bias that equates difference with a less developed being. Instead, Park refuses to leave an impression that Jessy "is really just like other people" (204); the mother defends cognitive difference through contradictions that highlight the daughter's paradoxical identities: strange/ordinary, able/disabled, like/unlike others.

In Park's contradictory narratives, even the writer's goals shift, as shown in the ways she qualifies, if not abandons, her texts' organizing metaphors. Near the beginning of *Exiting Nirvana*, she reiterates how her title for *The Siege* encapsulated the seemingly dire necessity to penetrate the citadel of autism that also appeared to be a Nirvana for her child, who had to be forced out into "our common world" (10). Yet toward the end of the first memoir the mother already has seen the need to transcend this conception, to focus instead on "work" and "our motion forward," which the daughter shares (*The Siege* 271–72). The texts' organizing metaphors continue to shift in ways that suggest the mother's increasing ability to get past the ableism that assumes a one-way growth—Jessy's movement forward into her parents' world. This shift is foreshadowed in the 1995 edition of *The Siege*, in which the subtitle changes from *The First Eight Years of an Autistic Child* to *A Family's Journey into the World of an Autistic Child*. Implications of this revision emerge in two passages of *Exiting Nirvana* that develop the journey metaphor in a typically self-revising way. Early in the memoir, Park defines "the experience of autism that I can write about" as one of gradual learning, in which "strangers" like Jessy "challenge us to perceive differently, . . . to stretch our imaginations to apprehend, even appreciate, an alternative world" (24). For Jessy's "journey . . . out of that world" required that "we too had to travel, as best we could, into experience as foreign to us as ours was to her, learning different things, but learning them together" (24). Though this statement qualifies the rescuer mentality expressed in the siege metaphor, Park goes further near the end of *Exiting Nirvana* when she seems to accept more fully Jessy's alternative world, "the emotional intensity of her secret life," a "life that is so much more thrilling than our own" (201). Recognizing that her daughter's art connects directly with the "private universe" of her obsessions, yet also benefits her day-to-day existence, Park says, "we realize that as we no longer even dream of a triumphant emergence into normality, we no longer even want her to exit Nirvana all the way. In a development we could never have envisaged, it looks as if she, and we, can have it both ways" (201).

This unforeseen development of the writer's understanding, delayed until the final pages of her text, suggests a repositioning of the mother's and daughter's worlds of experience. Park reinforces this altered relationship in her narrative's final words, describing how "Jessy enters, more and more fully, yet never entirely, the world in which we live, all of us, together" (208). Through variations of the diagram that Elaine Showalter uses to analyze men as the "dominant group," women as the "muted group" (199–200), we can visualize the non-autistic mother's shifting spatial conception of the increasing overlap between her own and her daughter's worlds, from their early position of contiguous separateness to the increasing shared space that still grants Jessy, in the end, the crescent of her secret, private realm:

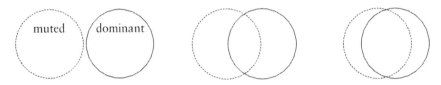

Park reflects the views of the dominant group, those in the empire of the "normal" for whom the realm of the muted other remains an inaccessible "wild zone" outside language itself (Showalter 200; cf. *Exiting Nirvana* 201). But the shifts in the mother's spatial metaphors chart how others within the dominant culture can also move beyond a conquering, siege mentality. This mindset is expressed in the conversion narratives that James T. Fisher, in his chapter, incisively analyzes, in which the autistic individual is cured, transformed, no longer autistic—the latter a claim Park makes about Jessy in her 1982 epilogue (286), a claim so utterly absent from *Exiting Nirvana* that its abandonment indicates the mother's progress. And it is through such progress that Park makes herself a type or guide for her culture, like Bunyan's classic protagonist. Her use of "we" thus comes to include the reader in her narrative's journey, as is especially clear in her final descriptive claim, her vision of "the world in which we live, all of us, together."

Park's evolving, self-revising narratives fully capitalize on the rhetorical power of the non-autistic mother's position as a writer. For in chronicling her own developmental delay, she brings out the "slow growth" of a "partial understanding" of autism, for herself and her culture (*Exiting Nirvana* 24). Revising both her own guiding concepts and various cultural misconceptions (like the refrigerator mother she helped to banish), Park uncovers through her story the dominant culture's need to accept its own position of limited comprehension, restricted in part by forms of cognitive ableism that can be mitigated, even overcome. Her remarkable narratives invite readers to celebrate the shared space of cultural understanding made possible by empowering autistic individuals, while also appreciating the wild zones, the alternative worlds of cognitive difference.

ACKNOWLEDGMENTS

I would like to acknowledge colleagues whose experience and insight have greatly contributed to this chapter: Marjory Payne, Kristina Chew, Karen Coen Flynn, Julie Drew, Kathryn Feltey, and Mark Osteen.

NOTES

1. Carlson 141. James T. Fisher notes, in this volume, the avoidance of pre-scripted trajectories for the autistic subject and the writer herself, achieved through the "phenomenological" approach of mothers' accounts like Chew's and the memoirs of Park, which are central to my study.
2. Further examples in this genre of maternal narrative include memoirs by Maurice, Paradiž, Harland, and LaSalle.
3. Park, *Exiting Nirvana* 50; Sacks x. Park's words reveal what McDonnell describes as autism's "almost unresolvable contradiction for the mother," between the need "to normalize her child" and to "appreciate her child's difference" ("Mothering" 66). Sacks's phrase risks conflating autism and "madness," perhaps evoking an earlier period's medical confusion, which Park depicts by showing the faulty diagnoses that labeled the young Jessy as "psychotic" and related her condition to childhood schizophrenia (*The Siege* 124). In contrast to Sacks, Chew's illuminating analysis in this volume proposes a way of understanding the discourse of Jessy Park and other autistic individuals by comparing their language to that of poets like Gerard Manley Hopkins ("Fractioned Idiom").
4. Bérubé, "Autobiography" 342. Contrastingly, in Park's *American Scholar* essay "Exiting Nirvana" (which won the National Magazine award for feature writing), two of Jessy's paintings, with the facsimile of her description of each, frame the essay. This structure reverses the daughter's and mother's positions in the 2001 book: Jessy Park's writing frames and authenticates Clara Park's essay, and in this way Park deconstructs roles described by Bérubé.
5. Debra Cumberland, in her chapter in this volume, points out contrasting representations of the domestic sphere in *News from the Border* (which finds the traditional female space confining) and *The Siege* (which celebrates, in a quasi-Victorian way, the nurturing and transforming power of the female space).

WORKS CITED

Bérubé, Michael. "Autobiography as Performative Utterance." *American Quarterly* 52 (2000): 339–43.
———. "Disability and Narrative." *PMLA* 120 (2005): 568–76.
———. *Life as We Know It: A Father, a Family, and an Exceptional Child.* New York: Pantheon, 1996.
Carlson, Licia. "Cognitive Ableism and Disability Studies: Feminist Reflections on the History of Mental Retardation." *Hypatia* 16.4 (2001): 124–46.

Chew, Kristina. *Autismland: The Autism Reality Show Starring Charlie*. 12 Dec. 2005. http://www. kristinachew.com/

Garland-Thomson, Rosemarie. "Seeing the Disabled: Visual Rhetorics of Disability in Popular Photography." *The New Disability History: American Perspectives*. Ed. Paul K. Longmore and Lauri Umansky. New York: New York UP, 2001. 335–74.

Grandin, Temple, and Margaret M. Scariano. *Emergence: Labeled Autistic*. Novato, CA: Arena, 1986.

Gray, David E. "Gender and Coping: The Parents of Children with High Functioning Autism." *Social Science & Medicine* 56 (2003): 631–42.

Haddon, Mark. *The Curious Incident of the Dog in the Night-Time*. New York: Doubleday, 2003.

Harland, Kelly. *A Will of His Own: Reflections on Parenting a Child with Autism*. Bethesda, MD: Woodbine, 2002.

Hays, Sharon. *The Cultural Contradictions of Motherhood*. New Haven: Yale UP, 1996.

Hillyer, Barbara. *Feminism and Disability*. Norman: U of Oklahoma P, 1993.

Kirby, David. *Evidence of Harm: Mercury in Vaccines and the Autism Epidemic: A Medical Controversy*. New York: St. Martin's, 2005.

Ladd-Taylor, Molly, and Lauri Umansky. Introduction. *"Bad" Mothers: The Politics of Blame in Twentieth-Century America*. New York: New York UP, 1998. 1–28.

Landsman, Gail. "Emplotting Children's Lives: Developmental Delay vs. Disability." *Social Science & Medicine* 56 (2003): 1947–60.

———. "Reconstructing Motherhood in the Age of 'Perfect' Babies: Mothers of Infants and Toddlers with Disabilities." *Signs: Journal of Women in Culture and Society* 24 (1998): 69–99.

LaSalle, Barbara. *Finding Ben: A Mother's Journey Through the Maze of Asperger's*. New York: McGraw-Hill, 2003.

Little, Liza. "Differences in Stress and Coping for Mothers and Fathers of Children with Asperger's Syndrome and Nonverbal Learning Disorders." *Pediatric Nursing* 28 (2002): 565–70.

Martin, Celest. "Silver Linings: Forging a Link between Mothering a Child with Autism and Teaching/Scholarship." *The Family Track: Keeping Your Faculties while You Mentor, Nurture, Teach, and Serve*. Ed. Constance Coiner and Diana Hume George. Urbana: U of Illinois P, 1998. 167–72.

Maurice, Catherine. *Let Me Hear Your Voice: A Family's Triumph Over Autism*. New York: Knopf, 1993.

McDonnell, Jane Taylor. "Mothering an Autistic Child: Reclaiming the Voice of the Mother." *Narrating Mothers: Theorizing Maternal Subjectivities*. Ed. Brenda O. Daly and Maureen T. Reddy. Knoxville: U of Tennessee P, 1991. 58–75.

———. *News from the Border: A Mother's Memoir of Her Autistic Son*. New York: Ticknor & Fields, 1993.

———. "On Being the 'Bad' Mother of an Autistic Child." Ladd-Taylor and Umansky 220–29.

Miller, Jean Kearns. "Mommie Wyrdest." Miller 191–95.

———, ed. *Women from Another Planet?: Our Lives in the Universe of Autism*. Bloomington, IN: AuthorHouse, 2003.

Nadesan, Majia Holmer. *Constructing Autism: Unravelling the "Truth" and Understanding the Social*. London and New York: Routledge, 2005.

Paradiž, Valerie. *Elijah's Cup: A Family's Journey into the Community and Culture of High-Functioning Autism and Asperger's Syndrome*. New York: Free P, 2002.

Park, Clara Claiborne. "Exiting Nirvana." *American Scholar* 67.2 (1998): 28–43.

———. *Exiting Nirvana: A Daughter's Life with Autism*. Boston: Little, Brown, 2001.

———. *The Siege: A Family's Journey into the World of an Autistic Child*. 1967. Rev. ed, 1982. Boston: Little, Brown, 1995.

"Prisoners of Silence." *Frontline*. Dir. Jon Palfreman. PBS. 19 October 1993.

Refrigerator Mothers. Dir. David E. Simpson. Fanlight Productions, 2002.

Rohrer, Judy. "Toward a Full-Inclusion Feminism: A Feminist Deployment of Disability Analysis." *Feminist Studies* 31 (2005): 34–63.

Sacks, Oliver. Foreword. Park, *Exiting Nirvana* ix–xiv.

Showalter, Elaine. "Feminist Criticism in the Wilderness." *Critical Inquiry* 8 (1981): 179–205.

Simmons, Karen L. *"Little Rainman"*: *Autism—Through the Eyes of a Child*. Arlington, TX: Future Horizons, 1996.

Sprague, Joey, and Jeanne Hayes. "Self-Determination and Empowerment: A Feminist Standpoint Analysis of Talk about Disability." *American Journal of Community Psychology* 28 (2000): 671–95.

Wendell, Susan. "Toward a Feminist Theory of Disability." *The Disability Studies Reader*. Ed. Lennard J. Davis. New York: Routledge, 1997. 260–78.

Woolf, Virginia. "Professions for Women." *Collected Essays*. Vol. 2. New York: Harcourt, 1967. 284–89.

11 Urinetown
A Chronicle of the Potty Wars

Mark Osteen

Only the young are allowed to suffer
openly. Adults go to a punishment room

with water but nothing to eat.
They lock the door and suffer the noises

alone. No one is exempt
and everyone's pain has a different smell.

Craig Raine, "A Martian Sends a Postcard Home"

Not long after we learned that my son Cameron had autism, my wife Leslie attended a workshop led by a psychologist who called himself "Mr. Potty." The man boasted that he could toilet-train a kid in one day. He'd taken his methods from a book by Nathan Azrin and Richard Foxx, who tell parents to give their child copious quantities of liquids and confine him or her to the bathroom. When the child appears ready to urinate, you place him or her on the toilet. With nowhere else to go, the child quickly learns where to deposit the waste. We figured this method might be effective, but it seemed cruel, and we were confident we wouldn't need to resort to such harsh tactics. We'd take Cam's cues, and when the time was right, gently teach him to urinate and defecate in the toilet.

At the time—Cam was about three—we were still fairly ignorant about autism. But at the workshop Les heard disturbing toilet-training tales from the other parents:

"My son was toilet trained, and then it was as if he forgot everything he'd learned. He would always go in the toilet, and then suddenly he started spraying it everywhere. He was trained, and then he wasn't trained."

"My son smears his feces. If he wakes up early and has to go and we don't catch him in time, he spreads poop all over his bedroom walls."

"My daughter still wears diapers at age eight. I'm desperate for a solution."

These horror stories scared Les, but I brushed them aside, rationalizing that these parents had probably done something wrong or that their children were more severely impaired than our boy. I've been amply repaid for my hubris: we battled with Cam for almost nine years over toilet training.

BASIC TRAINING

We made a few desultory attempts to train Cam when he was three and four, but he wasn't ready, so we abandoned the idea. In the summer of 1994, when he was turning five, he started grabbing his crotch when he had to pee, and no longer liked to wear diaper pants. We took off his diaper for portions of the day and watched him closely. When he began to urinate or defecate, we rushed him to the toilet and said, "Go in the potty." After a few weeks he made the connection. He was trained for bowel movements by the time he was five, and has almost never had an accident since.

Urination was another story—a long and painful one.

When we were first training him—at three and four—sometimes he'd give signs that he had to go; other times he'd simply stand on the rug and, gazing curiously at his penis, let it flow. He liked to watch the water, but didn't seem fully to grasp—as it were—that it was coming from himself. As for getting out of bed to urinate, forget it. We began to worry: he was supposed to start preschool in the fall, and the school stipulated that every child be toilet-trained. It was now or never.

I went to the Johns Hopkins University library and checked out Azrin and Foxx's book *Toilet Training in Less Than a Day*. After our months of struggles, their procedures no longer seemed cruel. In fact, they're geared to children who need constant repetition to get the picture, so they were tailor-made for Cam. We subjected him to the method for most of one Saturday.

As the day passed, I recalled those lines from Craig Raine's "Martian" poem, and wondered if Cam shared the alien's perception of toilet habits. Whatever the case, my son learned how to "suffer the noises" pretty quickly: by mid-afternoon, he was voluntarily peeing in the toilet. Before the day was over, his basic training was nearly complete.

For the rest of the summer his understanding of the process got better and better, and by the time school started that fall, we had a toilet-trained kid. He was still inconsistent, but over the next year he learned to recognize the signals and usually made it to the bathroom, where he'd pee somewhere near the toilet.

That was the rub: he didn't always go in the toilet. In fact, he seemed to take great delight in peeing everywhere *but* there. He'd let fly toward the corner between bathtub and toilet, or hose down the toilet seat (it took years to teach him to raise it). His favorite ploy was to aim directly at the raised seat and then stare in furrowed-browed fascination as the urine trickled slowly into the water. Of course, not all of it made its way into the toilet, and what didn't left a yellow trail and a pungent scent.

Was he just careless? Or had he simply found something fun to do and enjoyed the variations on this liquid theme? We tried following him and gently reminding him, "Put the pee in the potty, bud." That worked some of the time, but when nobody was watching, he'd sneak into the bathroom and spray wherever he felt like spraying. It was as if his penis was a new toy he'd found—and look, the stream goes wherever you point it! I figured that as long as he urinated somewhere in the bathroom, we should probably be satisfied; he'd get the aim thing down eventually. I also remembered my own early childhood, when I was sometimes so thrilled by my ability to control the pressure and direction of the flow that I'd forget to aim. Anyway, what male doesn't urinate on the floor occasionally?

GOING TO BATTLE

By the end of the summer of 1995, when Cam turned six, he was so well trained that even at night he'd dutifully arise from bed, pad into the bathroom, and pee near the toilet. We were finally able to take him out of diapers and put real sheets on his bed. There were occasional boo-boos, and when we paid a lot of attention to his urination, he used it as a tool. For example, that October Les reported to his teacher that he'd wet the bed the last few nights. In response to their queries about his spraying, the next day she wrote that he'd been methodically urinating on the back of the toilet seat. We removed the toilet seat and he stopped doing it.

But as the months passed the ubiquitous odor of urine began to get under Les's skin, and she started scolding him whenever she caught him missing the toilet. She thought we should make him sit down to pee, but when she did, he refused to go. During this time, things were degenerating in so many other aspects of our life that we vowed to hold the line on this: "He *will* pee in the toilet. For God's sake, we've got to have some semblance of civilization around here," we'd say. But soon urination came to represent how autism controlled our lives: it epitomized our failure to *make* Cam get better.

And so the bathroom became a battlefield, with Cam determined to make water wherever he wanted to make water, and the two of us equally determined to make him put it in the toilet instead of on the floor, in the sink, bathtub, or behind the commode.

We began following him to the bathroom, reminding him, "Put the pee in the potty." Even then, he'd first irrigate the back of the toilet before tilting down toward the basin. Sometimes he'd stand on the bathtub and shoot from there. Once I caught him happily peeing into the bathtub.

"Cameron! What are you doing?!" He flinched, which of course made him spray on the floor.

"Heeka, deeka," he said.

I lifted him from the tub and plumped him down in front of the toilet. "Now put your pee in the potty!" Of course, then he couldn't go at all.

With shame, I recall another time when I grabbed him by the shoulders and shook him after he'd repeatedly urinated all over the floor.

"God damn it! That's the third time you've done that today!" I yelled, shoving my flushed, grimacing face next to his. "Put it in the potty!" The quivering child fled the bathroom, and for the rest of the day peed *only* on the floor.

The tougher we got, the more erratic he became. We didn't understand then that once a behavior gets entrenched, it demands inordinate effort to dislodge it, that you're better off ignoring it and letting it pass on its own. Nor did we understand how Cam's mind works. For example, even the most stubborn neurotypical people (I count myself in this group) are not in the same class as a person with autism. We're not even in the same school district. When it comes to fixations, Cam—like many other autistic people—doesn't respond to logic; or rather, he responds only to a private logic of strict rules and compelling obsessions.

"Where does the pee go?" we'd ask, coaxingly, pleadingly, angrily, repeatedly. "In the potty," he'd answer. But though Cam could *say* it until he was red-faced and bawling, he wouldn't or couldn't consistently *do* it.

No doubt he was confused: first we told him to go to the bathroom, and then we shouted and got all worked up about it. "Am I supposed to go in here or not? How come when I do they start yelling? What's the right thing to do?"

For Cam, the bathroom really had become a punishment room.

During these first Urine Wars my son learned a lesson he never forgot: he could make us instantly angry or happy simply by withholding or giving up his urine. Denied normal ways to wield power, he clung to those he could control, and for years brandished this one like a sword. And we were so immersed (almost literally) in the problem that we couldn't see the connection between our heightened vigilance and his defiance—that the more attention we paid to it, the more he used it.

Before long he used the "potty" request to delay or avoid doing any unpleasant task. By 1996 he commenced every home teaching session by announcing, "Potty!" The shrewd little dude had figured this much out: that word gets you a few minutes off. We could have ignored the requests, but believed we should honor them because it had taken him so long to start making them. We instructed the therapists to take him to the bathroom after the first request, but ignore his pleas after that. That meant he wet his pants frequently, even when he'd apparently emptied his bladder only ten or fifteen minutes earlier.

So it wasn't always easy to tell when he was just delaying and when he really had to go. Cam had figured out how to hold some back, to save some for the proverbial rainy day. And once he'd learned that, we were at his mercy.

In early 1996 Cam's sleep problems—which we had banished the previous year after several months of struggles—returned, and this time they coincided with (and may have been caused by) his toilet-training regression. A typical night went like this.

At 3:34 a.m. I hear clapping. I think, "He peed the bed again. Damn it!" I jump out of bed and stomp into Cam's room. My son is standing on the floor, pretending to ignore the drenched blankets and yellowish puddle on the mattress cover. He looks up fearfully at the red-eyed ogre who has barged into his room. I seize him by the shoulder. "Do you need to go potty?"

"Potty."

"Then get your butt in there!"

I hustle him into the bathroom. Cringing and anxious, he can't urinate.

"Pee, damn it." Cam understands what I'm saying, but my threatening tone only makes him more fearful. We wait five minutes, as he stands, bare feet on the cold tile floor, dutifully trying to void an already empty bladder. He gazes up, his brown eyes for once looking directly into mine, seeking approval or comfort. I can't give it to him. Hands shaking, he gazes back at the toilet.

The light is on, but I'm so tired I can barely see. At length I hear a fine stream of urine trickle timidly into the bowl. "Is that all?" I say.

"Ah."

I squat down next to him. "Look at me."

His wandering eyes briefly rest on mine. "When you have to go potty, get out of bed!"

As soon as I say it, I realize how absurd I sound: he *is* getting out of bed. I doubt he even understands what he's done wrong; all he knows is that Dad is very mad.

Back in his bedroom, I pull away Cam's wet blankets and cover him with clean ones. "Now get back in bed and go to sleep." I tuck him roughly between the covers and pull the door closed with a not-quite slam.

And that's a good night.

Of course, now he lies awake, petrified he'll wet the bed again and arouse his angry father. A half-hour later he arises, and either walks into the bathroom and urinates or, more often, pees on the floor of his room or on the living room rug. Then he dashes around the living room clapping his hands, turning on lights, slapping the walls. Leslie and I wait each other out. After several minutes one of us gets up and puts Cam back to bed. Not gently.

Before long Les and I are fully trained to get up every night.

The next school year—1996–1997—brought near-total devolution in his toilet training. At school they put him on a timed bathroom schedule, but he refused to go at designated times; instead he'd hold it in and pee on the playground or at his study cubicle.

Things were no better at home: he was not only wetting the bed almost every night, sometimes more than once, but seemed to be peeing everywhere, all the time. It was as if all of his dammed-up play instincts had been rechanneled to his urinary tract. He delighted in urinating on the floor, on the living room chairs or sofa—anywhere but in the toilet. When he was four we'd bought a large plastic climber for his room. He didn't explore its many nooks and crannies; his favorite activity was to find a secure perch and urinate down onto the rug: our own little gargoyle fountain. Of course, we cleaned up each time, but eventually the smell became so powerful that we had to discard the rug. Doing so uncovered a large patch of permanently discolored floorboards.

Cam loved carpets. Often he'd enter the living room with the clear and sole purpose of urinating on the rug. This habit was infuriating, because although it's easy to clean up urine on a hardwood floor (and it leaves no mark as long as it doesn't remain for long), rugs soak up the liquid and let the smell linger. Why rugs? Maybe because the liquid makes no sound and then seems to vanish: "Look! It comes out of here and then it goes there but then it just goes away. Cool!" Or maybe my son agreed with autistic author Donna Williams, who loved to urinate on carpet because "[t]he more I covered the carpet, the more of a 'me' in the world there was. . . . The smell belonged to me and closed out other things" (61). In other words, perhaps Cam was claiming the house for himself. A vinegar/water mixture will dry the stain and mask that "me" smell, but the scent of so much urine never fades entirely.

Our living room couch was another favorite target. For a long time we dutifully tried to scour away every stain, but eventually the sheer volume of liquid overwhelmed our puny efforts to staunch it. What had been an off-white couch was now pintoed with pee stains.

We tried everything we could think of to change this behavior. On weekends we put him on a twenty-minute schedule, setting an egg timer on the living room table that chimed when the interval ran out. Then we'd say, "Cam, do you need to go potty?" Usually he'd decline, but we'd make him go into the bathroom anyway. The idea was to keep his bladder empty. Other times we'd ignore his urinating, reasoning that he was doing it only to get our attention. If we stopped noticing it, maybe he'd stop doing it. But after three days we had to give up this tactic or face death by inundation.

Our ears became minutely attuned to a myriad of liquid sounds: the melodious splash of water in the toilet; the soft, spattering drizzle when urine hits the floorboards; the squish of feet on a soaked rug; the "eek" heard after one of us sat on an invisible damp sofa patch.

Not only were the toilet seat and floor becoming sticky and discolored, but the bathroom reeked, because urine had seeped into the floorboards and the tiny cracks around the bathtub. In fact, the smell of Cam's "pain" was so pervasive that you could detect it the moment you entered our house.

So it was that we came to live in the village called Urinetown. Mayor Cameron had ringed the village with an ammoniac aroma every bit as effective as a moat. This watery barrier kept all but the most intrepid visitors far away.

Urinetown was a confining place for all residents. Not only couldn't we invite guests to our place (who can enjoy a meal when enveloped by the stench of urine?), but for years one of us had to be in the room with Cam at all times so he wouldn't urinate on the furniture. At the end of one particularly trying Sunday in 1997, for example, Les and I slipped into the den to watch *The Simpsons* (Cam's vocalizing and clapping made it impossible to watch TV in the living room). After a blessed half-hour of amusement we emerged to discover an unholy trinity of new wet spots—one each on the floor, rug and sofa: our penalty for having fun.

Car rides have always been one of Cam's favorite activities. He loves looking out the window, gazing at the houses and cars streaming by as the sights constantly change. He'll sip a Coke, crunch ice, sway to music, and vocalize his comfort sounds—"ooh wee looee, awee." Occasionally he'll giggle, as if watching his own private movie. He's master of the world, safe in his climate-controlled bubble. You'd think, then, that he'd be placid and pee-free on rides. You'd be wrong.

Motor vehicles were for Cam mobile toilets. By 1997, he habitually peed his pants on any ride longer than fifteen minutes. Perhaps he figured that if he told us he had to go potty, we'd rush back home, thereby ending the ride and dampening his fun. So he usually stayed mum and let it flow into his pants and onto the seat. We learned to prepare for such incidents by placing a thick towel beneath him, but some urine inevitably oozed into the upholstery. Sam, our Corolla, now permanently wore Cam's smudge and shared Cam's smell—the same pungent tang that perfumed our home.

Urinetown had expanded, colonizing the world beyond its walls. It was becoming Urine-Nation.

We had to do something. So that December we visited the Behavioral Clinic at Callaway Carver Institute, where they assigned us a doctoral student named Lisa Finch. A slender, attractive woman with jet black hair and a sharp gaze, Lisa listened attentively to our tales of woe, then crisply assured us that she could help, but warned that the therapy would require a lot of work and persistence.

She asked us if he still wore diapers at night.

"Yeah, he wears pull-ups. We got so tired of getting up in the middle of the night to change the bed that we put them back on him a few months ago."

"I understand. But the pull-ups could be confusing him. He might not understand that it isn't okay to urinate in the bed."

Leslie and I exchanged uneasy glances. We knew what was coming next.

"I recommend that you throw away the diapers."

"Oh, God! We put him back in them because we were getting no sleep at all!"

"I'm sure that must have been tough," said Lisa. "But he's got to learn that the only place you urinate is in the toilet, whether you're in bed or walking around."

She then asked if he went sitting down or standing up.

"He used to stand up, but his aim was so bad that we've been having him sit down."

"Why don't you try getting him to stand up?"

"How come?"

"Well, he's gotten into a bad pattern. Along with the confusion there might be a sensory problem—he isn't sure when he needs to go. So getting him to stand up will help jolt him out of the pattern, and it might also reassure him to actually see the urine flowing into the water."

That made sense, and so did the final portion of the plan: record each time he urinated—both appropriately and inappropriately—noting antecedents and consequences. That way we could discover if he was having "accidents" more frequently at certain times of day, or at stressful moments; we could also determine if our responses were helping or hindering.

The first result of these measures was, of course, constant bedwetting. To our surprise, however, he no longer woke up, but slept right through the deluge. The data showed that his urination increased after meals and during high-demand periods. Lisa recommended that we put him back on a twenty-minute schedule.

Over the next three months the problem gradually improved. Standing up to urinate did seem to assure Cam that his body was working fine and that he'd actually done the deed. Taking off the pull-ups did end some of his confusion. This is not to say that the problem dried up.

For example, during this period they came up with a new protocol at school to combat his frequent bouts of aggression. When he had a tantrum, they put him in a "time-out" room, where he was supposed to calm himself before returning to the group. But they gave this up after two days. Why? Because Cam enjoyed this punishment room! As soon as the door closed, he'd strip off his clothes and happily urinate on the floor. "Whee! I'm free to pee!" Hell, it's probably what we'd all do if we could.

By late February of 1998 he was down to a ten-minute interval, which meant that he was almost constantly being prodded to go potty. His bathroom schedule now controlled our lives. Les or I would set the timer and sit down just long enough to read part of a magazine article or watch one segment of a TV show. At the signal, Les would retrieve Cam from his room, or stand by the couch and hold his hand. "Okay, Cam, the timer went off, time to go potty."

"No, okay!"

"Yes. You need to go so you don't pee on the floor."

He preferred not to.

I'd come over to help him up and herd him into the bathroom. Sometimes he'd urinate, sometimes not.

With our days broken into tiny portions, it was like living in one of those psych experiments in which researchers ring a bell every few minutes. Your day is parceled out into short waiting periods punctuated by ugly confrontations. The hours crawl by.

Cam fought the schedule tenaciously. He'd go into the bathroom but refuse to urinate, and then as soon as he left the room he'd let fly on the floor. Or he'd refuse to get off his knees, which meant we had to carry him into the bathroom, wailing and flailing. He put five new stains on the sofa in two days. We were in despair: the new protocols seemed to be making things worse. What should we do?

Just as the rope of our nerves was ready to snap, Cam apparently decided that all this surveillance took the fun out of it. The next weekend we had nary an accident, though he was still on a twenty-minute interval. Hope arose like a tattered flag. Had we finally won the Potty Wars?

LIQUID LANGUAGE

I wish I could say we had. But actually we continued to live in Urinetown for several more years, though the wars evolved from a *blitzkrieg* into frequent guerrilla skirmishes and sniper attacks. Our tactics? One: constant monitoring in public. Take him to the bathroom first on every outing and thereby stave off most accidents. Two: hawk-eyed vigilance at home, thereby preventing further furniture blemishes. Thus did we confine Urinetown to a few toxic sites.

Motor vehicles were one of them: Cam still thought of cars and buses as large, comfortable Porta-potties. During 1998 and 1999 he arrived at school most days with wet pants. Then he reversed the habit to wetting on the way home. Between 1998 and 2001, Cameron wet his pants on the ride home from school virtually every day.

He also continued to wet his pants on even the shortest car trips. It seemed as if the little internal timer that we had finally, with such trouble, taught him to hear, went offline as soon as our son entered a car. But he didn't seem to mind wetting his pants, and seldom made a peep before or after he peed. Short of banning rides—one of Cam's few pleasures—we saw little recourse but to ignore the wetting and quietly mop up.

Nor did the bedwetting go away: with occasional exceptions, he wet the bed every night between 1998 and 2001. Believe me, we did everything we could think of to wipe out this habit. We tried keeping him up as late as possible, cutting out fluids after 7 p.m., making him visit the toilet frequently before bedtime. Occasionally these tactics worked, but mostly they just made him testy. Theorizing that a sensory issue was involved, we employed various combinations of sheets, blankets and comforters. But those experiments ended when he started shredding his bedclothes. The sheets were the first to go, followed by the blankets. Beneath them was the ever-present slick plastic sheet covering the mattress. Cam tore that up too. We learned to leave on even torn plastic covers until they became unuseable, but he developed an uncanny knack for divining the one spot where the mattress was exposed. The result was a permanently smelly bed. Yet it seemed foolish to spend money on a new mattress as long as the bed-wetting continued.

We also tried to catch him in the act, and discovered that he usually wet the bed just as he fell asleep: it was too much trouble to rise from the warm bed and walk to the "punishment room." Once he'd peed, he'd immediately bounce out of bed, with a clap that meant either "Yay for me," or "Yoohoo, I did it again" or "Dang it, I really meant to get up this time."

No doubt he enjoyed the feeling of urine oozing into the bedclothes. I'd often ruefully recall the beginning of James Joyce's *A Portrait of the Artist as a Young Man*, when young Stephen Dedalus reminds himself, "When you wet the bed first it is warm then it gets cold" (7). Cam luxuriated in that liquid warmth, and the clamminess that inevitably ensued didn't outweigh the pleasure of that initial womblike wetness.

Then, sometime in 2000, he began to climb quietly out of bed in the morning and pee on the floor. One of us would spring up at his first sound and hustle him into the bathroom. But he was too quick. One morning we both heard Cam stirring and scurried into his room to find him poised on the edge of the bed, a puddle at his feet.

"Buddy! Don't pee on the floor; look what a mess you made!"

He looked up at us—a boy who almost never said anything intelligible or appropriate—blinked and replied clearly, "I didn't know." Leslie and I exchanged wide-eyed looks.

She answered, "You did too know. We've only told you that a hundred times."

For a moment it was as if we had a regular kid, and without thinking we'd responded as though he were one. Was he just giving the kind of lame excuse other kids give when they do something they know they shouldn't have? Was he trying to explain that he'd been half asleep? Did he really not recall the countless reminders we'd given him not to urinate on the floor? Why, then, did he act so guilty whenever we caught him doing it?

Maybe he meant exactly what he'd said: he hadn't even realized he'd urinated. For a moment a light shined onto the dark battlefield: was it possible that Cam didn't recognize the connection between his action and the consequences? Surely, we thought, that couldn't be.

If we had set the alarm for 5 a.m. and forced him to go to the bathroom, we may have solved the problem, but years of sleep deprivation still loomed large in our minds, eliminating that gambit.

What remained of the viable bed clothes were five or six comforters too thick for him to rip into bits. We had to launder these heavy comforters almost every day for several years, a practice that, by 1999, wore out our washer and dryer. We used up a gallon of detergent every week, and God knows how much water and electricity, because the comforters usually needed at least three cycles to get fully dry.

In 2001 Leslie offered a new strategy: instead of lecturing or yelling at him, why not give him lots of hugs and comfort? Her theory was that his urination was related to anxiety: reduce the anxiety—make him feel secure, loved, content—and end the problem. Alas, this strategy, which wrought wonders in other aspects of our son's life, worked no better than the other measures we'd tried; in fact, it seemed to reassure him that peeing anywhere was okay with us.

Eventually we just threw up our hands and made do. Cam was going to wet the bed, and we were going to wash comforters every day. And so we arrived at a truce: we said nothing when he peed in the car or in the bed, but kept the flow in check everywhere else. We bought a new living room rug and sofa and, through constant vigilance, managed to keep them nearly stain-free.

Why was this habit so hard to wipe out? Clearly there was something deeply gratifying to Cam about the act of urinating. But the problem was knottier than that. People with autism often have neuromotor problems: they can't make their muscles obey them and sometimes don't recognize the signals their bodies send. Maybe Cam couldn't always sense that it was time to urinate until the feeling was so urgent that he couldn't restrain himself. And just as certain sounds that wouldn't bother you or me seem unbearably loud to him, perhaps his system intensified the full bladder feeling so much that he couldn't endure it even for a moment.

Then there's the sequencing problem. When you stop to think about it, learning to urinate in a socially acceptable way involves a whole lot of motor planning. First you feel the sensation, and then you walk (or run) to the bathroom, where you pull down your pants, stand in the right place, aim carefully, and finally whiz into the water until you're finished. But you're not really finished: now you must pull up your pants, flush the toilet, wash your hands, dry them, put the towel back and leave the bathroom. Cam has a severe executive planning dysfunction—an inability to sequence and execute multiple-step actions.[1] Many times I watched him walk into the bathroom and then stand there as if he couldn't remember what to do next; sometimes he'd start peeing before he had dropped his pants. Afterward, he'd sometimes try to walk away without pulling them back up, or flush the toilet before urinating and leave without flushing again, or dry his hands before washing them. This set of tasks seemed impossibly complicated, as if he had to relearn them every day. Just imagine if going to the toilet was like learning a new set of dance steps. Would you perform them successfully every time? Would you bother trying?

But even his sensory and executive functioning problems don't tell the whole story. Throughout his life Cam has been forced to find ingenious ways to compensate for his inability to speak. And he learned very early that when you let that pee go, adults snap to attention. "So what if they're yelling? At least they're looking at me!" Urination gave him power he couldn't gain any other way.

Sometimes he exercised this power blatantly—"If I pee the bed, then I get to get up!"—but often he was more subtle. For example, on arriving at his weekly gymnastics lesson, the first thing we'd do is go to the bathroom. The main reason, of course, was to prevent accidents, but retreating to this quiet place before we started also gave Cam a moment to get his bearings and separate himself from the disorienting buzz and blur of the busy gym. In this case his urination "problem" was also a way to calm himself and prevent blowups.

More often, however, peeing was a way to communicate. And he learned to say many, many things in this tongue, ranging from "I'm so anxious that I can't stand it," or "I'm confused and hurt," or "I'll show you!" to the obvious—"Boy, am I pissed off!" Alas, the flexibility of this liquid language was also its fatal flaw: because peeing could mean so many things, we never knew exactly what he was saying. Often we concluded that it didn't mean anything, except that we *weren't* communicating. And it sometimes seemed that urinating had become an autonomous entity separate from him, that whatever message it conveyed wasn't even Cam's, but that of the urine itself, speaking through him: "I'm peeing because that's what I do!"

But certain messages were hard to misinterpret. For instance, one August day in 2000 Cam and I spent virtually the entire day together, and it was a good day. We visited the mall together, rode the escalators, then ate two small cones at Dairy Queen. After that he was calm enough to sit in his room and listen to music.

I couldn't believe my luck, and was reluctant to bother him. But after forty-five minutes of tranquility, I entered his room, only to discover that he'd wet the bed and tossed the soiled comforter onto the floor. This was his little nudge to Dad: "You weren't noticing me; remember what I can do?" A little later he peed on the living room table and rug—just in case I'd forgotten.

Other times the message was clear only after the fact. For instance, one day he got off the school bus wearing long, baggy (urine-damp) sweat pants I'd never seen before, which meant he'd had a very wet day at school. During his after-school work session, he wet his pants three more times. Twenty minutes after we put him down for the night, he wet the bed. I tried for the three-hundredth time to explain.

"Cam, you need to get up BEFORE you pee the bed. When you wet all the time, it makes the blankets yucky, and Mom and Dad have to wash them over and over."

He looked at me soberly for a few seconds until his brown eyes began their usual wandering. Did he understand? Or was I missing the point: he knew what he was supposed to do; he just didn't want to do it?

"Anyway, wetting your pants and bed is what babies do. You're way too big for that. When you have to pee, GET OUT OF BED. You can do it, 'cause you're a big boy." I patted his head and left the room, pleased with the way I'd handled it and confident he wouldn't wet the bed again. Heck, we might even have a dry night.

Les and I settled in to watch a hospital documentary. Engrossed in the moving true-life tales, we forgot about Cam for a few minutes. Then we heard telltale thumping from his room. Les walked him into the bathroom, and then looked at his bed.

"He peed the bed again!"

So much for my theories. But then I remembered that the school nurse had informed me that one of Cam's classmates had hit him during recess. Perhaps Cam had been saying in Urinish, "Mom and Dad, I'm scared 'cause a boy at school was mean to me." He'd been seeking our attention and sympathy the only way he knew how.

But what about the hundreds of other days?

Most often his emotions were clear, but his motives obscure. For instance, one Saturday that same year (Cam was eleven) we did our usual things—grocery shopping, drives, the playground—and then, on the way back from a drive around the reservoir, Cam got very agitated and started shouting, "Hone, hone!" Dismayed that we didn't immediately transport ourselves to our driveway, he started kicking Leslie's seat and my shoulder, then pinched her arm hard enough to break the skin. Blood trickled out of the wound as she tried to soothe him: "Okay, honey, we're on the way home. Just hang on!"

As my son rocked, growled, and kicked my shoulder, I gunned the car, ran stop signs and broke speed limits, barely managing to hold onto the wheel and prevent the car from sliding into the ditch. Les and I were literally sitting on the edge of our seats. By the time we pulled into the carport fifteen minutes later, Cam was shrieking and thrashing like a man riddled with electric shocks. Then he wouldn't get out.

"Get out of the car," I commanded in my most authoritative voice. "You were BAD, so you need to go to your room."

Right: if you knew you were going to be punished, would you cooperate?

I pulled him out of the seat; he went to his knees in passive resistance. I managed to lift him by the shoulders and march him toward the front door, but after a few strides he collapsed again. A neighbor living a few houses up the road stopped mowing his grass and gaped at the drama unfolding in our carport: Was this child abuse? Some bizarre game?

We stood uncertainly for a few minutes, waiting for Cam to calm down. Suddenly he sprang up, bellowed, slapped Leslie's head, and fell to his knees again. We could wait no longer: Les picked up Cam's feet, I grabbed him behind the shoulders, and we hauled him into the house like a casualty of war, then tossed him onto his bed and slammed and locked his door.

There we stood, our faces flushed, our hearts thumping, Leslie's arm bleeding, my shoulder aching from Cam's kicks. I stumbled into the den and stared at nothing for several minutes. The white walls seemed to pulsate. I felt as if I were about to suffocate.

As Cam shouted wordlessly, pounded on his door and stomped his feet, Leslie came into the den, sat on the dark red love-seat and began to weep softly.

"How long can we keep this up?" she asked between sobs.

"I don't know. As long as we have to, I guess."

After Cam grew quiet, I entered his room: he'd urinated all over the floor. That explained his agitation. But was he mad *because* he'd needed to pee, or had his anger caused him to pee? Had he, for some reason, *not* wanted to urinate in the car, and then become upset because he couldn't make us go faster? Or was he already mad about something and using urine as an exclamation point?

For many minutes I sat mulling over these questions. I made no headway. I did know three things: a) my son felt imprisoned by his disorder; b) Les and I were prisoners too; c) we all felt like warm piss.

But if Cameron was at the mercy of his excretory functions, the opposite was also true: he used urination to assert his will. He was determined to pee at particular times and places, to demonstrate that he could do it if he wanted to and that we couldn't stop him. Urinating gave him control not only over us but over a body that refused to obey his other commands. No wonder he cleaved to it like a security blanket. And he had created his own liquid language. Caught up in our own expectations and anxieties, determined to make him change, we couldn't comprehend his meaning. Perhaps, in this way, we were as autistic as he was.

But though Cam was fluent in Urinish, it was a language restricted to his tiny domain—the village called Urinetown. Even its other residents didn't understand it. And if this habit further separated us from friends and neighbors, it isolated my son most of all, leaving him alone in a world of singular sensations and private meanings that nobody could share, not even those who loved him most.

Yes, the Martian is right: everyone's pain has a different smell.

NOTES

1. For discussions of executive dysfunction as a core deficit in autism, see Russell.

WORKS CITED

Azrin, Nathan H., and Richard M. Foxx. *Toilet Training in Less Than a Day*. New York: Simon and Schuster, 1974.

Joyce, James. *A Portrait of the Artist as a Young Man: Text, Criticism and Notes*. Ed Chester G. Anderson. New York: Viking, 1968.

Russell, James, ed. *Autism as an Executive Disorder*. Oxford and New York: Oxford UP, 1997.

Williams, Donna. *Nobody Nowhere: The Extraordinary Autobiography of an Autistic*. New York: Times Books, 1992.

Part IV

Popular Representations

12 Recognizing Jake

Contending with Formulaic and Spectacularized Representations of Autism in Film

Anthony D. Baker

THE DEFINITIONAL POWER OF FILM

When the public has no direct experience with a disability, narrative representations of that disability provide powerful, memorable definitions. In films, novels, plays, biographies, and autobiographies that depict a character with a disability, the character comes to exemplify people with that particular disability—demonstrating how individuals with that disability behave, feel, communicate, exhibit symptoms, and experience life. In short, a character with a disability serves as a lens through which an audience can view and define that disability.

Rain Man (1988) serves as the public's primary definitional text for autistic spectrum disorders. People now use the term "rain man" to describe individuals who exhibit autistic characteristics; the term indexes autism in general. Several other films have echoed and reinforced Dustin Hoffman's characterization of autism—notably, *Mercury Rising* (1998), *Bless the Child* (2000), *Molly* (1998), *Stephen King's Rose Red* (2002), and *Cube* (1997). Together these films construct a composite definition of autism that includes these features: extreme discomfort with the unfamiliar, echolalic and monotonic speech, difficulty understanding social cues, unusual preoccupations, pronounced lack of affect, and auditory hypersensitivity. Additionally, autistic characters in films possess spectacular powers. For audiences who have no experience with autism, characters in such films map the unknown territory of autistic spectrum disorders. In Rosemarie Garland Thomson's terms, such texts offer audiences a "discursive construct of the disabled figure" (9).

What happens, however, when the viewers of films that depict autism already possess working definitions of autism? How do audiences who have direct experience with autism read the discursive construct of the disabled figure? What happens if representations of autism counteract or fail to match viewers' direct experiences with the disability? Because experiences with autistic spectrum disorders range so widely, answers to these crucial questions must vary widely among audience members. To explore the disparity between autism as it is represented in feature films and the experiences of individuals living with autism, this chapter illustrates ways that popular depictions of autism spectacularize the disability, identifies troubling themes regarding the families of autistic characters, and explains how cinematic representations of autism may be reconciled with the realities of living with autism. My critique of films about autism is rooted in a personal subject position that must contend with the problematic elements of screen representations of autism, while simultaneously striving to identify features in these films that validate and inform my own experiences as a parent of a child with autism. As a parent, I am simultaneously repulsed by and desperately drawn toward movies and other representations of autism. Watching a film about autism is a personal investment for me: the definitional power of film depictions competes with the certainties of my experiences with my eight-year-old son, Jake. Although there's nothing inherently wrong with the phenomenon of films shaping and defining disabilities for the general public, the plots of films about autism tend to mislead audiences about the disability; such films misdefine autism in ways with potentially detrimental consequences.

Films, of course, have no monopoly on sensational media presentations of autistic individuals. Neither, of course, is autism the only disability displayed sensationally in films or other media. Autism, however, is a disability that lends itself particularly well to sensationalism. In Robert Bogdan's history of carnival freak shows, *Freak Show: Presenting Human Oddities for Amusement and Profit*, he divides sensationalism into two distinct modes of presentation. Although Bogdan is writing primarily of individuals with physically visible disabilities, the "major patterns by which exhibits were presented to the public" clearly apply to representations of autism: "the exotic, which cast the exhibit as a strange creature from a little-known part of the world; and the aggrandized, which endowed the freak with status-enhancing characteristics" (97). In representations of autism, the individual with autism is usually exoticized, depicted as otherworldly or in his or her own world, separate from the normal world. Such otherworldliness is expressed even in titles of films and texts about autism: for example, *Autism is a World*, Gerardine Wurzburg's 2005 award-winning documentary, and *Women from Another Planet*, Jean Kearns Miller's 2003 collection of writings by women with autism. *Time*'s May 6th, 2002, cover story employs the same rhetorical construction: the title "Inside the World of Autism" is printed in all caps across the torso of a beautiful blond boy with his eyes closed, frozen in the middle of an otherworldly dance. Autism is thus constructed as ontologically different from the realm of the typical. Because there is no known etiology or cure, because no treatment regimen has proven to be consistently successful, and because so many individuals with autism are unable to communicate fully or effectively about the behavioral traits that earned them the diagnosis, autism is indeed an exotic disorder. And individuals with autism portrayed in public narratives such as films, novels, or human-interest media texts are therefore unknowable; they are mysteries on display. When an autistic character is additionally endowed with uncommon skills or talents, the exhibition of autism is stretched to include both the exotic and the aggrandized. With the combination of the autistic character's mysterious idiosyncrasies and special talents, autism becomes a spectacle. No wonder Hollywood is attracted to it.

THE AUTISTIC FORMULA

Feature films tend to define autistic behaviors consistently. The actors who portray autistic characters usually do their homework, the producers usually hire expert medical consultants, and the behavioral quirks that signify autism are generally performed accurately. However, feature films also employ autism as a strikingly consistent, formulaic plot device, and these devices are the primary targets for my critique. The formula for a feature film about autism spans a variety of film genres: action/thriller (*Mercury Rising*, *Bless the Child*), drama (*Molly*, *Rain Man*), horror (*Stephen King's Rose Red*), and science fiction (*Cube*). The following description of the formulaic components illustrates that, whatever the film genre, the recipe for including an autistic character remains unfortunately limited. My description of the formula is followed by a critique of two of its primary themes.

Introduce a Protagonist Who Is Not Autistic

Bruce Willis plays a renegade FBI agent in *Mercury Rising*. Kim Basinger plays a benevolent nurse in *Bless the Child*. As a selfish salesman in financial trouble, Tom Cruise plays a less-than-heroic protagonist in *Rain Man*. In *Molly*, Aaron Eckhart portrays a busy professional. Both *Cube* and *Stephen King's Rose Red* employ an ensemble of protagonists; a cop, a doctor, an architect, and a mathematician find themselves imprisoned in *Cube*, and in *Rose Red* a group of paranormals with different specialties are recruited by a psychology professor played by Nancy Travis to explore a haunted mansion.

Introduce a Character Identifiable as Autistic

Frequently, the autistic individual is a prepubescent boy or girl. *Mercury Rising*'s nine-year-old Simon, played by Miko Hughes, has slow and limited speech, avoids direct eye contact, and requires strict routines for entering his house and going to sleep. *Bless the Child*'s five-year-old Cody, portrayed by Holliston Coleman, rocks back and forth, spins plates, and has limited speech. Kazan, the adult with autism in *Cube*, played by Andrew Miller, rocks and flaps his hands. In *Molly*, Elisabeth Shue's 28-year-old character speaks in limited monotones, and *Rose Red*'s Annie, played at the beginning by Kristen Fisher and as a five-year-old by Kimberly J. Brown, is nearly nonverbal. In each of the movies, the individual is labeled as autistic, usually in an early conversation between the protagonist and a doctor, with the autistic character in the next room. The autistic characters in each film tend to walk atypically, hold themselves with odd postures, and avert their eyes either heavenward or downward.

Make the Autistic Character Cute, Endearing, Innocent, or Attractively Quirky

Cute children such as Simon, Cody, or Annie are automatically innocent, attractive, and endearing. As an adult inmate in *Cube*'s deadly Rubik's-Cube-type prison, Kazan isn't cute, but his actions construct him as childlike and innocent: he urinates without shame or malice in front of other characters in the cell, communicates his fear through tantrum-like behaviors, and is motivated by gumdrops to help his group escape. *Rain Man*'s Raymond Babbitt is attractively quirky, due in part to his comic use of echolalia and verbal repetition; several of Raymond's utterances even became popular catch phrases: "K-Mart sucks," "Four minutes to Wapner," and "I'm an excellent driver." And Elisabeth Shue's Molly exhibits a fascination with shoes and strings and is distracted by beautiful aspects of the mundane such as shiny refrigerator magnets and her reflection in a toaster. Hers is an engagingly blissful innocence (the movie's tagline is "Innocence is bliss").

Establish the Autistic Character's Vulnerability by Depicting Reliance on Parents or Caregivers

In *Mercury Rising*, Simon needs his mother's assistance to enter his own house and to prepare a cup of cocoa, and needs his father to rock him to sleep. Both *Bless the Child* and *Mercury Rising* depict their autistic characters attending special schools that can accommodate their exceptional needs. In *Rose Red*, Annie's older sister facilitates Annie's communication, even within the family. Raymond Babbitt's and Molly's respective rituals in their residential institutions have obviously been in place for years. As the inmates form a group in *Cube*, Kazan is immediately assisted and defended by the only doctor in the group, and he relies on her to help him climb from cell to cell. These extremely vulnerable autistic characters rely on others (the children on family members, the adults on institutional employees and healthcare providers) for their physical, psychological, and emotional safety.

Endow the Autistic Character With Savant Skills or Superhuman Powers

The special powers of autistic characters in films come in a limited variety of flavors. Superhuman mathematical ability seems to be the power of choice for filmmakers. For example, Raymond's card-counting feat at a Vegas blackjack table is rendered humanly impossible when viewers are privy to the conversation between two casino employees who are watching Raymond from the casino's surveillance room:

Casino Employee 1: I don't see him using a computer.

Casino Employee 2: He's not, but something's not right. We know there's no one in the world who can count into a six-deck chute.

In another famous scene in *Rain Man*, Raymond—in a single glance—accurately counts 246 toothpicks a waitress has dropped on the floor. In *Cube*, Kazan calculates factors of complex numbers, which just happen to be the keys to predicting the complicated arrangement and movement of rooms in the prison. According to the mathematician in the group, Kazan's immediate answers would take weeks of calculation with a supercomputer. *Mercury Rising*'s Simon cracks the government's allegedly uncrackable new encryption code at a single glance. The audience hears a digital-computational sound effect to complement the close-up of Simon's eyes as he effortlessly and automatically decodes a document. In some films, the autistic character's powers are even more supernatural. In *Bless the Child*, Cody's touch is curative and resuscitative: she brings a dead pigeon back to life in the schoolyard, sends a fellow diner's cancer into remission, and heals Kim Basinger's fatal bullet wounds in a cathedral. In *Rose Red*, Annie has telekinetic powers and the ability to conjure objects and spirits. As a child, she incites a rock storm on her neighbor's house by drawing it with heavy crayon strokes, and her powers are later enlisted to awaken the dormant spectral inhabitants of a haunted mansion. In *Molly*, the autistic character's powers are of a different nature. When Molly becomes "normal" temporarily, thanks to an experimental medical procedure, her non-autistic persona possesses an uncanny zest for life, free from the social constraints under which typical individuals must operate.

Separate the Autistic Character from the Parents or Caregivers

Once an autistic character's support system and vulnerability are established in a film, removing the character from the safe situation is a seemingly inevitable plot feature. In *Mercury Rising*, Simon's parents are murdered at home by a government agent in an attempt to eliminate anything that might render the secret code vulnerable. In *Bless the Child*, Cody is abandoned by her drug-abusing mother and raised instead by her loving aunt, played by Kim Basinger. Then Cody's birth mother—now married to a satanic cult leader—returns, claims custody rights, and abducts the child. Raymond Babbitt is abducted from his institutional home by his long-lost younger brother, Charlie. In *Molly*, the residential institution loses state funding, forcing the patients to scatter either to other institutions or to family members. In *Cube*,

Kazan, like the doctor and other inmates, has been abducted from his home and imprisoned, and then, when another prisoner kills the doctor, must fend for himself. Abduction and custody are major themes in films about autism.

Endanger the Autistic Character

Removing the vulnerable autistic character from his or her safe environment certainly endangers the character. Additionally, though, danger arises when a villainous character desires the autistic character's special powers. *Mercury Rising*'s Simon is hunted by NSA agents who intend to kill him so that the encryption code will remain inviolable. In *Bless the Child*, the cult leader wants either to exploit Cody's direct connection to God for the forces of evil or to kill her. Raymond Babbitt's ability to count cards and inability to keep a secret make him vulnerable to detection by authorities. In *Rose Red*, Annie's risk is heightened as the haunted mansion kills off some of the other paranormals, and the psychologist is willing to use Annie's supernatural powers even if the girl must die in the process. At the very least, autistic characters are endangered when they are removed from their safe environments, as is the case when Molly must move in with her reluctant, uncaring brother.

Allow the Hero to Save and/or Bond With the Autistic Character, Perhaps Even Replacing the Parent

Although Cody's birth mother is presumably no longer a cult member at the end of *Bless the Child*, Maggie (Kim Basinger) retains custody. After the adventure is over at the end of *Mercury Rising*, Simon and Bruce Willis's character share a *Rain Man*-like hug. In *Cube*, with the help of another inmate, Kazan is saved from an evil inmate and becomes the only character who escapes from the Cube. In *Rose Red*, Annie finds a boyfriend among the psychics who survive the haunted house. The title character in *Molly* regresses to her former autistic self and moves in with her formerly intolerant and impatient brother. The sibling dynamics at the end of *Molly* are nearly identical to those in *Rain Man*, where Tom Cruise's character has learned important lessons about love and acceptance, although it's clear that Raymond will remain institutionalized.

AUTISM SPECTACULARIZED

The most troubling feature embedded in this formula is the spectacularization of autism. Plots hinge on the way that some other character can use the autistic character's special powers. Autism is a viable plot device—and autistic characters are viable characters—only if a spectacular skill or power is among the character's defining traits. Autistic characters are in the movies only because they have spectacular powers. Remove the savant or supernatural power, the film loses its plot, and the autistic character loses his or her raison d'etre.

After abandoning Cody to Maggie's care in *Bless the Child*, Cody's birth mother wants custody of her daughter only so that the cult can use the girl's supernatural powers. Cody's spectacular powers are the only trait her birth mother values. Similarly, in *Mercury Rising* Simon's superhuman deciphering skills are the sole reason he becomes endangered. Without his savant ability to crack the government's encryption code, Simon would not be targeted by NSA henchmen or need Bruce Willis's character to protect him. In both films, the discovery of the autistic character's spectacular powers sets the entire plot into motion. If Cody and Simon were merely autistic, there would be no motive for the villains to pursue the children, and no occasion for the children to meet the protagonists.

The same is true in *Rose Red*. The obsessed psychology professor has heard about Annie's telekinetic powers, perhaps in a newspaper account of the rock storm, and invites her to join a team of psychics. Annie's powers are clearly far more potent and pure than those of the other psychically gifted but non-autistic members of the group. Not unlike Simon cracking government code, Annie uses her spectacular powers to unlock secret passages of the haunted house, to make the hidden visible.

According to director and co-writer Vincenzo Natali, *Cube*'s autistic character is the least human of all the inmates: "Kazan is essentially a computer." He's "their portable pocket calculator," their "reward for taking him along" as they work toward their escape. Kazan's non-savant autistic traits—his inability to control his speech and fear, his need for assistance—severely annoy three of the four other members of the group. But Kazan's spectacular skills are the only way that the group can decipher the Cube's arrangement of cells; even the mathematician in the group is unable to calculate in ways that begin to approach Kazan's skills. His savant skills are his only use to the group; without his phenomenal factoring abilities, the group would likely have ditched him in one of the safe cells and proceeded without him, thereby sentencing him to death, because no food or water is available in the Cube. Without his savant skills—as a character with mere autism—Kazan would be worthless, disposable.

In *Rain Man*, abducting and spending time with Raymond and his autistic traits is a real drag for Tom Cruise's character, until Raymond's savant mathematical skills redeem him to his greedy brother. Without Raymond's spectacular ability to count cards, he is a burden to his brother, necessary only as an annoying means to extort his share of an inheritance from Raymond's institution. In *Molly*, Molly's estranged brother desires to spend time with her only after she has undergone the miraculous medical procedure that reveals her irrepressible *joie de vivre*. Only with the removal of her autism is she a useful, viable, worthy sister. It's clearly her autistic traits that make her unlovable to her brother.

By spectacularizing autism and featuring savant or supernatural powers as an essential component of the disability, these films misrepresent autism to the general public. According to Darold A. Treffert, a psychiatrist specializing in savant syndrome and expert consultant for *Rain Man*, the estimated incidence of savant skills among individuals with autism is ten percent. Yet these films present this minority as the norm for individuals with autism. Through these films, the general public learns that all autistic individuals have savant powers or even supernatural abilities. The composite definition of autism that includes savant skills, however, is neither helpful nor productive; indeed, such a definition is potentially harmful in several ways.

First, the value of autistic characters in these films is located exclusively in their savant powers, which renders all of their other autistic or non-autistic characteristics worthless or undesirable. According to the formula constructed by these films, only autistic individuals with savant abilities serve any function in society. Such a limited model of existence and interaction with the world perpetuates the most negative and inaccurate stereotypes surrounding autistic spectrum disorders. Defining autism primarily as a savant disorder places unreasonable expectations on individuals with autism. For older children and adults with nonsavant autism—that is, most people with autism—popular conflation of autism with savantism can damage self-esteem and foster feelings of inadequacy. Additionally, such a conflation raises unrealistic expectations in the minds of parents and the general population. As Jonathan Mitchell notes, parents' expectation of savant abilities for their autistic children "provides fodder for the special educators, special education attorneys, ABA therapists etc., to legitimize their profits and to encourage the false hope ... that so many parents of these children have." By over-representing savant skills as a defining trait of autism, film and other media contribute to an illusion that savant skills are far more prevalent than they actually are.

When spectacular abilities serve as the sole quality that marks autistic characters as useful or desirable to the non-autistic characters in these films, audiences may conclude that people with autism who are not savants are not acceptable or desirable in the neurotypical world. Parents and others close to autistic people must contend with the definition of autism that includes spectacular or savant powers as a crucially requisite feature, even when this definition fails to match their lived experiences. Hence, individuals with autism and no savant skills—that is, ninety percent of individuals with autism—are constructed as savant-deficient, as lacking the key, redeeming feature of cinematic autism.

Second, these films propose a simplistic model of autistic thought processes. With Raymond's innate card-counting abilities, Kazan's factoring abilities, and Simon's code-breaking abilities, *Rain Man, Cube,* and *Mercury Rising* propose a computational, nonhuman model of the autistic brain. According to this model, individuals with autism process information and stimuli much like a computer—mathematically, consistently. And these skills are not learned but innate, pre-encoded. Such a model helps to perpetuate several dangerous myths that construct individuals with autism as robotic. Robots, after all, are unable to learn the way typical humans learn, unable to express emotions, and unable to think for themselves. In order to function, computers and robots need programming by experts.

The cinematic proposition that autistic individuals think like computers is not only inaccurate, but dangerous. The savant skills for which the characters are so valued are innate abilities, not skills developed through any kind of thinking or learning or intentionality. No autistic character in these films is depicted in an act of synthesizing knowledge or thinking critically. The problems that autistic characters resolve in these films—puzzles, codes, equations, calculations of odds—are all prefigured problems. Onscreen autistic characters do not make decisions or choices, nor do they think through scenarios or problems in context; their responses to the world around them are instead automatic and prefigured. And although they have savant skills, they are unable to deploy these skills toward any benefit on their own; villains or heroes from the neurotypical world exploit these skills to destructive or productive ends. The savant skill—and the autistic character—is thus objectified and stripped of any agency.

This stripping of agency freezes autistic characters developmentally. Indeed, portrayals of autism in these movies involve no change over time, no development of new interests or difficulties, no learning of new skills or knowledge. The adults with autism in these films are locked into their child-like obsessions: Raymond Babbitt sorts and displays Dodgers baseball cards from his youth, Kazan assesses the value of his mathematical prowess in terms of gumdrops, and Molly twists shoestrings around her fingers. The films fail to depict the origins of these behaviors, and viewers see no evidence that these behaviors have evolved from other behaviors. Neither do the children with autism in these films develop as characters. The autism portrayed in these films is monolithic, unchanging, reified. We viewers see no indication that these individuals used to be any different or are about to change in any way. Such a simplistic conception of autism offers viewers the idea that individuals with autism do not grow, do not learn, do not change over time, do not develop. By portraying autistic characters exclusively as vulnerable savants incapable of agency or growth, these films offer a harmfully reductive definition of autism as a pitiful, exploitable, and inhuman condition.

PARENTAL ABSENCE

Another troubling component of the formula for films about autism is the role of the parent and family. Parents and family members either lack a strong bond to the autistic character or are removed from the plot, either of which makes the autistic individual more vulnerable, more pathetic. Parents of children with autism are sometimes also portrayed as insufficiently compassionate. The birth mother in *Bless the Child* abandons Cody at nine days old, and it is suggested that the mother's drug use and lack of compassion for Cody are partly responsible for his autism: thus does Kanner's refrigerator mother rise from her grave. In *Rose Red*'s first scene, four-year-old Annie's telekinetic powers escalate as her parents' argument about her disability grows louder downstairs. Judging from their argument in this sole scene from her childhood, neither parent accepts Annie and her disability. The infuriated father shouts, "She can't think!," and after the rock storm has subsided, the tearful mother doesn't even go to Annie's room. Instead she looks helplessly out the window and says to herself, "Oh Annie, what have you done?" It's Annie's sister, not a parent, who later serves as her guardian in the haunted mansion.

In both *Rain Man* and *Molly*, the adult characters with autism have been living in institutions for most of their lives. Parents in these films have chosen to institutionalize their autistic child; subsequently, in both cases the parents died, leaving estranged brothers as the closest family members. In *Cube*, all characters, including Kazan, have been abducted in their sleep and imprisoned in the Cube. The audience gains no information about Kazan's pre-cube life, except that he has earned gumdrops for solving math problems in the past. In *Mercury Rising*—the only feature film in this group that actually depicts parents loving their autistic child—the parents are quickly and brutally executed in their own home by a government agent.

The absence or removal of strong familial bonds in these movies certainly serves to intensify the autistic characters' vulnerability and endangerment. The autistic plot is basically a fish-out-of-water plot, the water being the safe environment created—through much trial and error, love and acceptance, joy and pain—by caring families or specialized institutions. But by neglecting to explore the home environment of the autistic individual and how it has been constructed, these films miss the chance to tell a different kind of story. The building of trust, the creation of rituals, the development of quirks—aspects of an autistic individual with which family members and caregivers have experience and familiarity—are all erased in films about autism that give short shrift to the home environment or remove it altogether. As Thomson explains, such erasures oversimplify characters with disabilities:

> Characters are thus necessarily rendered by a few determining strokes that create an illusion of reality far short of the intricate, undifferentiated, and uninterpreted context in which real people exist. . . . [T]extual descriptions are overdetermined: they invest the traits, qualities, and behaviors of their characters with much rhetorical influence simply by omitting—and therefore erasing—other factors or traits that might mitigate or complicate the delineations. (10)

The erasure of parents, families, and homes in films with autistic characters is a simplistic shortcut; with the absence of a loving family, the autistic character is alone, pitiable, vulnerable, in need of a protector or savior. Unfortunately, this shortcut has a potentially high cost.

Although parental absence is a reliable, bankable plot element, the consequences of removing parents are very serious. Parents—particularly mothers—have worn the mantle of guilt for their child's autism ever since Kanner defined the disorder in 1943. Given the medical community's history of publicly blaming uncaring mothers for their children's autism, parental absence in films with autistic characters presents an unfortunate opportunity for an audience to perpetuate parental culpability for the child's disability. And when films about autism offer no alternative etiologies for the disorder, parental absence serves to maintain the myth that autism is caused by poor parenting. Additionally, the removal of the parent or family may suggest to audiences that parents and families aren't the best caretakers for autistic individuals. Films usually fail to depict emotional connections between autistic characters and their parents or caregivers. Instead, the autistic character usually experiences some sort of unique connection with the film's protagonist. In *Rain Man*, for example, Raymond Babbitt leans his head toward his self-centered brother—whom he's only known for a week—for a hug. These films suggest that a wide range of inexperienced strangers with no training or qualifications can step in to care for an autistic individual, perhaps even facilitating a breakthrough in communication. The protagonists' methods for dealing with the autistic individual are represented as more effective than any of the methods or techniques practiced (although not portrayed) by the parents, caregivers, or qualified institutions. According to depictions in these movies, forcing the autistic individual into the real, albeit dangerous, world is a more effective treatment for autistic behaviors than any parent-sanctioned or medically-sanctioned strategy. Such a notion is extremely dangerous, considering that funding for institutions, insurance coverage for various therapies, and educational accommodations for autistic individuals are already always at risk.

RECONCILING PORTRAYALS OF AUTISM

For most audiences, the composite definitions of autism offered by feature films and other popular texts are challenged or replaced only when new public narratives or private experiences render them insufficient or inaccurate. People who live with autism—autistic individuals, their families, caregivers, friends, and the professionals who work with them—inhabit an alternative subject position when viewing films or reading other popular representations of autism. We enter a movie with preconceived, experience-based notions about autism through which we read the movie's version of the disability. As a parent of a child with autism, I experience these portrayals of spectacularized autism and parental absence in extremely personal ways, even as I intellectualize them as problems. When Simon's loving parents are murdered in *Mercury Rising*, I am frightened for my own son Jake. What if I were murdered? I check the door locks. More realistically, what if I were killed in a car wreck? How vulnerable is my son? I wonder quickly how much life insurance we have. What would Jake do without his parents? How would he fare if we were removed from his life? Who would take care of him? I think of our wills and wonder where I filed them. When films fail to depict strong relationships between autistic individuals and their families, the stories of parents are ignored. My experiences with my son are neglected, even erased. When I see autistic characters performing wondrous feats of the mind onscreen, I wonder if my son has savant skills that I just haven't recognized yet. Maybe I should look harder. What if Jake isn't good at math? Or worse: what if math is his worst subject? What if he shows no aptitude or interest in playing a musical instrument? What if he's just normally autistic? Will people besides his family and friends value him? How? Why?

When my son Jake was diagnosed as autistic in 1999, he was just shy of his second birthday. On several occasions when I've shared news that my son is autistic, I've heard, "I saw a movie with Bruce Willis that had this genius kid with autism," or "I saw this autistic kid on the news who played concert piano." I've been asked if Jake is good at math, as if being good at math were a consolation prize for being autistic. I've heard, "Autistic? Oh yeah, like Rain Man." No, not exactly. Not like Rain Man. Although Jake and Raymond Babbitt share a diagnostic label, unlike Raymond, Jake can't count toothpicks at a glance, is only eight, has never lived in an institution; his parents aren't dead, he doesn't have a brother who kidnaped him, has never been to Las Vegas, and doesn't care where his underpants were purchased, although he does not particularly care for K-Mart. He does, however, really like his Spider-Man and Hulk underpants. Sometimes he strips down to his underpants, flexes his skinny arms, growls, and says, "I'm Hulk. Rrrrr!" I can't picture Raymond playing Hulk. And if Jake were to visit Las Vegas, he'd be much more interested in the roller coasters than in the casinos. It would be an understatement to say that Jake likes roller coasters; he once rode thirty-one times in less than four hours. If not quite spectacular, it was nonetheless a feat of endurance, even on a slow day at the amusement park. Jake also demonstrates impressive mastery of the remote control: he can stop a DVD on precisely the same frame of film with remarkable accuracy many times in a row. Impressive, perhaps, but not classifiable as a savant skill.

Over the last two summers, Jake has learned to swim, although not with any stroke officially recognized by an Olympic committee. Jake can eat a plate of waffles with maple syrup in less than a minute. During the fall of his first-grade year, he aced six spelling tests in a row, although he's also failed his share since. He can express his basic needs and preferences, but can't describe how his day at school went. Jake can't tell us when he feels sick, but can recite stretches of dialogue from his favorite videos, including sound effects. Although his elocution may not always be intelligible to the uninitiated, we can easily tell that he's trying to deliver Buttercup's lines from a scene in *The Princess Bride*. Sometimes he's upset, sometimes he's euphoric, and sometimes we can discern why. I could go on, but suffice it to say that Jake's autism differs significantly from spectacularized versions depicted in feature films.

Although onscreen representations of autism trouble me both as an academic and as a parent, I find ways to reconcile onscreen depictions with my own personal definitions of autism. I try to recognize moves, rituals, quirks, and details that can redeem a film's spectacularized portrayal of the disability and validate my own experiences with autism. I look for and usually find ways to recognize Jake and our own personal narratives. One basic mode of recognition is in a film's portrayal of an autistic character. For example, in *Molly*, Elisabeth Shue eerily nails the precise intonation of Jake's emphatic "no" in her performance. It trails off in volume—NOOoooooo—and its duration persists in direct relation to the level of protest. In *Cube*, Kazan negotiates with another character for the precise promise of 27 bags of gumdrops in a way that evokes for me Jake's tendency to negotiate for five more times down the slide before we leave the park. These tiny character traits resonate for me because they fit into my own autistic schema; I recognize bits and pieces of my son's particular brand of autism in these characters.

Much less frequent in films about autism, however, are narrative moments that depict real, rich, intensely human components of living with autism. *Mercury Rising* offers a few examples early in the film, before the formula requires Simon's parents to be murdered. On his bus ride home from school, Simon flips ritualistically through his picture booklet of friends' faces and familiar places. The audience sees that he needs this booklet. Simon uses it to trace what's happening around him and what to expect next; it's a way to organize his experiences. I recognize Jake in Simon's behavior. Jake uses a pictorial activity schedule at school to help him know what to expect next. Like Simon, Jake always takes a set of his favorite pictures with him to look through in the backseat of the minivan. Jake's pictures are usually of his favorite roller coasters or videogame characters, and they provide him with a way to pass the time, or a positive emotional anchor during transitions into the unfamiliar. He studies them, colors them, talks about them, and creates verbal scripts that dramatize them. The audience understands that without his picture booklet, Simon might have difficulties. In the film, Simon gets off the bus and, according to the usual routine, his mother greets him at the door. As he enters the house, her glance lingers for a moment on the typical neighbor kids playing baseball in the street. I recognize the look on the mother's face: that feeling, that guilty and selfish wish that my own child might want to join the other kids in their game. A similar moment touches me when Simon's father comes home from work and rocks Simon to sleep. The father kisses and caresses his son in so tender a way that he seems to say, "I know you, my son. I accept you as you are. I'm with you wholly. I love you." Simon, in turn, is so safely immersed in familial love that he immediately falls asleep in his father's arms. I recognize this moment; I aspire to it with my own son, and sometimes it happens. These elements in the film aren't spectacular moments. For audience members who are not intimate with autism, these moments are merely exposition to establish the autistic character as different from other characters and to evoke pathos for the vulnerable autistic individual. From my subject position as an audience member close to autism, however, these moments are poignant, resonant, and profound: they identify and distill my own experiences. I am rewarded by these moments because they capture some element of my life with a son who is autistic.

Unlike the spectacularized plot elements, these cinematic moments help to deepen the general audience's understanding of disabilities. They construct a mundane but meaningful subnarrative of what it might be like to live with autism. Although I recognize these rich little moments as familiar reminders or validations of my own experience, the general audience might incorporate them into an enriched, more humane definition of autism that could help mitigate or complicate films' spectacularized representations of the disability. Given the power of films to shape the public's understanding of differences and disabilities, such subnarratives are crucially important. Michael Bérubé argues that disabilities demand their own narratives: "Whether the disability in question is perceptible or imperceptible, a matter of a congenital illness or of a degenerative disease, an effect of aging or the object of the inconceivably rude query *How did you get that way?*, disability, too, demands a story" (570). Films tend to tell spectacularized, reductive, misleading stories about autism. Yet in spite of these troubling plot elements, audience members can find some value in these representations of autism. When I watch movies about autism, I look for recognizable glimpses of Jake, of myself, my wife, my life; I look for ways to understand better my son and my life. I look for autism as I know it so that I can know that other viewers may better understand my son and better understand some of the nonspectacular, everyday realities, complexities, and even joys of living with autism.

WORKS CITED

Bérubé, Michael. "Disability and Narrative." *PMLA* 120.2 (2005): 568–576.
Bless the Child. Dir. Chuck Russell. Perf. Kim Basinger, Jimmy Smits, Rufus Sewell, Ian Holm, Angela Bettis, Christina Ricci, and Holliston Coleman. 2000. DVD. Paramount, 2000.
Bogdan, Robert. *Freak Show: Presenting Human Oddities for Amusement and Profit.* Chicago: U of Chicago P, 1988.
Cube. Dir. Vincenzo Natali. Perf. Nicole DeBoer, Nicky Guadagni, David Hewlett, Andrew Miller, Julian Richings, and Wayne Robson. 1997. DVD. Lions Gate, 2003.

Mercury Rising. Dir. Harold Becker. Perf. Bruce Willis, Alec Baldwin, Chi McBride, Kim Dickens, and Miko Hughes.1998. DVD. Universal, 1999.

Mitchell, Jonathan. "Undiagnosing Gates, Jefferson and Einstein." *Jonathan Mitchell.* 2004. Jonathan Mitchell.10 June 2006. http://www.jonathans-stories.com/ non-fiction/undiagnosing.html.

Molly. Dir. John Duigan. Perf. Elisabeth Shue, Aaron Eckhart, Jill Hennessy, and D. W. Moffett. 1998. DVD. MGM, 2000.

Natali, Vincenzo. Director Commentary. *Cube.* DVD. Lions Gate, 2003.

Rain Man. Dir. Barry Levinson. Perf. Dustin Hoffman, Tom Cruise, and Valeria Golino. 1988. DVD. MGM, 2004.

Stephen King's Rose Red. Dir. Craig R. Baxley. Perf. Nancy Travis, Matt Keeslar, Kimberly J. Brown, David Dukes, Judith Ivey, Matt Ross, Julian Sands, and Kevin Tighe. 2002. DVD. Lions Gate, 2002.

Thomson, Rosemarie Garland. *Extraordinary Bodies: Figuring Physical Disability in American Culture and Literature.* New York: Columbia UP, 1997.

Treffert, Darold A. "The Savant Syndrome: Islands of Genius." *Wisconsin Medical Society.* 2005. Wisconsin Medical Society. 10 June 2006. http://www.wisconsin medicalsociety.org/savant/islands.cfm.

13 Hollywood and the Fascination of Autism

Stuart Murray

Mainstream American commercial cinema does not have an especially good heritage of portraying the disabled. As Martin F. Norden makes clear in *The Cinema of Isolation*, his history of physical disability in the movies, the representation of a number of different disabilities in Hollywood features bears little relation to the actual experiences of those living with the disabilities in question. Norden notes that "the movie industry has perpetuated or initiated a number of stereotypes over the years . . . stereotypes so durable and pervasive that they have become mainstream society's perception of disabled people and have obscured if not outright supplanted disabled people's perceptions of themselves" (3). He generally damns an industry that finds disability most useful as a narrative vehicle for telling stories of the nondisabled and that displays little conscience when engaged in such misrepresentation.

Norden's anger is justified, though the situation is not especially surprising. The commercial and narrative formulae driving Hollywood have produced multiple Others characterized by their misrepresentation. As E. Ann Kaplan has observed in relation to issues surrounding feminism and the imperial gaze, Hollywood's insistence in its imaginary self-construction as representing "all human life and behavior," as opposed to that which comes from a limited and bounded culture, has always flattened out the specificities of minority communities (57). In truth, Hollywood's misrepresentation should probably be taken as a given. As Richard Maltby has written, Hollywood "functions according to what we have called a commercial aesthetic, one that is essentially opportunistic in its economic motivation. . . . Hollywood movies are determined, in the last instance, by their existence as commercial commodities" (7). Such commercial opportunism will always, we can presume, involve transforming its subject matter to fit the need for a certain kind of product, and the perceived enigmatic status of many disabilities offers ample opportunities for such a process.

Nevertheless, even within such a paradigm of (mis)representation, there are reasons to view Hollywood's recent fascination with conditions of cognitive impairment, and autism in particular, with a sharp critical eye. Here we find ourselves in a space largely free of substantive criticism. Cognitive impairment itself still occupies a relatively peripheral space within disability studies, of course, like a stray family member who is wished well but whose habits are not understood; and the critical treatment of the cinematic representation of such impairments equally lacks rigorous theorizing or discussion. Although there is clearly something we might identify as a "disability film," it is still often absent from most wide-ranging contemporary critical studies of Hollywood. Steve Neale's *Genre and Hollywood* (2000), for example, contains no discussion of disability film (as opposed to, say, detective or disaster movies), despite the clear interrelation between filmic representations of disability and well-defined and discussed genres such as melodrama. Equally, Neale and Murray Smith's 1998 collection *Contemporary Hollywood Cinema* explores, under the heading of "Audience, address and ideology," issues involving the women's picture, the family picture, the relationship between Hollywood and independent black cinema, and the yuppie horror film, but makes no mention of disability movies (intriguingly, *Rain Man*—the foundational text in cinematic representations of autism— has a single entry in the volume, where it is described by Barry Keith Grant as a "bland yuppie movie" [289]). There is no room for disability of any kind in Trevor B. McCrisken and Andre Pepper's *American History and Contemporary Hollywood Film* (2005), and even a subtle and sensitive reader of Hollywood such as Maltby finds interest in *Rain Man* only as a "female-oriented picture"(9) in the 1999 collection on Hollywood and its audiences he co-edited with Melvyn Stokes.

Disability is absent, then, from the major book-length critical studies of Hollywood where we might hope to find its presence, and the often puzzling ways that disability films are glossed in these works (as with the *Rain Man* examples just noted) makes such an absence only more telling. Equally we might note that a number of critics who have produced studies of disability in film (often as articles or essays) have used methodologies derived from disability, as opposed to film, studies. Writers such as Paul Darke, Tom Shakespeare, and Michael T. Hayes and Rhonda S. Black have published in journals and collections primary aimed at disability studies audiences. Even within this community, however, there are barriers to a full understanding of how autism features in narrative film. That some disability scholars (and indeed wider contemporary culture as a whole) seem to think disability is primarily oriented around questions of physical impairment adds an extra obfuscatory layer to any desire to look at representations of the condition. Norden's concentration on physical impairment has a perfect logic to it, yet in *his* passing reference to *Rain Man*, he terms Dustin Hoffman's character in the film "mentally impaired" (309). Although this is not technically wrong, and the approach of Norden's study means *Rain* Man is not a film he will treat in detail, the lack of specificity here, particularly the absence of the word "autism" itself, is somewhat surprising. What is it about the condition that people do not know?

And yet, we can see—especially from *Rain Man* onward—that Hollywood has frequently returned in differing ways to depictions of autism. The use of autism as a point of focus for film narrative, or the deployment of autistic characters within films, is relatively recent. It is, however, possible to find films from the 1970s and even before in which characters have clear autistic tendencies, even if they are almost never termed "autistic."[1] In the 1980s, films emerged in which autism occupies a clearer narrative focal point and which have a clearer understanding of autism due to increased medical discussion of it. The success of *Rain Man* in 1988 prompted a breakthrough into wide public consciousness, but the film's public impact also inspired a specific development in terms of a disability film *narrative*, with a new avenue for a particular "commercial aesthetic" of the kind Maltby describes.

From the 1990s to the present there have been numerous examples in visual media such as film and television of narratives concerning autism operating within a discourse of knowledge of the condition, precisely because this period saw the subtleties of the autistic spectrum receive further definition and neuroscientific research begin to understand more fully its biogenetic aspects. The majority of these narratives, however, lack any real exploration of the complexities of autistic agency or subjectivity. Rather, their representations share a number of key issues. The first is a clear fascination with the condition as way of being that appears to defy categorization and invites speculation in terms of the "enigmatic." The second is an issue peculiar to film, namely the opportunity to develop a specifically *visual* dimension to frame autism—the attraction of *witnessing* the condition performed in a feature film. Third, the films focus on ideas of ontological difference provided by the presence of the person with autism.[2] Typically, this involves placing the autistic individual in relation to supposedly typical neurological behavior, and then mediating an idea of the human by a refractive comparison between the two. This frequently takes the form of a concentration on the perceived savant abilities of the autistic, read especially in terms of creativity and exceptionality, which are seen to inform and enrich the nonimpaired/non-autistic world. In effect, within the films discussed here, and as a consequence of the intersection of the issues just described, autism creates a specific space, figured in primarily visual terms and articulated through an apprehension of how the condition is perceived to function. Yet this process rarely allows for presentation of autism within the terms of the individual with autism or through any autistic logic; more commonly such a space reflects back on the details of the non-autistic world and its concerns. Such a method resembles what David T. Mitchell has noted about the deployment of disability within narrative generally: that it "hinges on the identification of physical and cognitive differences as mutable categories of cultural investment" (16). With autism, the categories of investment are mutable in the extreme, precisely because of the perceived narrative openness resulting from the manner in which the condition is seen and represented.

The issues of representation just outlined frame the presence of autism in a number of high-profile Hollywood feature films, starting with *Rain Man*, which feature autistic or Asperger's characters in a variety of narratives.

These include *House of Cards* (1993), *Silent Fall* (1994), *Cube* (1997), *Molly* (1998), *Mercury Rising* (1998), *Bless the Child* (2000), *Punch-Drunk Love* (2002) and *Snow Cake* (2005). Other features, such as *What's Eating Gilbert Grape* (1993), *Benny & Joon* (1993), *Forrest Gump* (1994), *Nell* (1994), *Shine* (1996), *I Am Sam* (2001) and *The United States of Leland* (2003), contain characters, often with complex and overlapping disabilities, that it is *possible* to read in terms of autistic presence.[3]

These films move through a spectrum of concentration on autism: in some, such as *Rain Man* and *House of Cards*, the condition is ostensibly central to the narrative; in others we might call autism narratively enabling, driving the plots of genre pieces such as *Silent Fall*, *Cube*, *Mercury Rising* and *Bless the Child*. To a degree, then, these latter narratives exemplify the point made by many scholars working in disability studies that disability and impairment often animate narrative while rarely being at its center, and that, as Mitchell and Sharon Snyder put it, "[w]hile disabled populations are firmly entrenched on the outer margins of social power and cultural value, the disabled body also serves as the raw material out of which other . . . communities make themselves visible" (6). However, all the films discussed here are in some way animated by an apprehension of autism and cognitive difference, and share a desire at least to structure some aspect of narrative through a specific *use* of the condition. It is the terms of such usage that warrant investigation, as they point to the *desire* of commercial contemporary culture both to be fascinated by the appeal of autism and to fit it into generic, pre-existing narrative concerns. The shifting scale of focus of these various films, their differing emphases, is itself a phenomenon inviting critical conclusions, as it clearly speaks of a *range* of potential subject positions for autism within contemporary narrative. As a consequence, of course, it also speaks of the degree to which autistic presence is (mis)understood within contemporary cultural practice.

To raise such an issue as this last one is to think of autism within the logic of a cultural majority. Such logic is clearly contained within Hollywood's contemporary presentation of the condition, and is the reason why we might accept misrepresentation as a guiding baseline. What is most noticeable here, however, is that even as a number of the films that represent autism try to make diverse points about the place of autism within a spectrum of humanity (often, as we shall see, by focusing on ideas concerning relationships, masculinity and family), they frequently do so through a politics of display that enacts the fascination of the medium (and audience) for the condition, and also through using specific genre-based narratives. The films under discussion here concentrate, in highly visual ways, on the *presence* of the person with autism. In this sense, characters with autism in film enact the codes of display and spectacle that are central to the visual apprehension of disability in the general cultural sphere and not just in narrative. Rosemarie Garland-Thomson's work on the modes of representation in American freak shows and in popular photography outlines a set of processes in which "staring at disability choreographs a visual relation between a spectator and a spectacle" (56), and precisely this relationship constructed by the staring gaze places autism on display for a cinematic majority audience.

In their display of the condition, *Rain Man, House of Cards, Silent Fall* and *Mercury Rising* all use the potential for visual eruption within autism. The autistic body, unlike certain physically impaired bodies, frequently does not signal its disabled status. It can, however, suddenly move from such a situation to generate—through excessive physical movement—an obvious behavioral difference. In manipulating the potential uses of such visual excessiveness within their plotlines, all four films use the refraction narrative of paired impaired/non-impaired characters to provide a fascination based on difference, and to illuminate for majority audiences questions of individual responsibility, behavior and knowledge. The most obvious example of this enforcement of "normalcy" (to use Lennard J. Davis's term) is probably *Rain Man*'s juxtaposition of the way Raymond Babbitt (Dustin Hoffman) humanizes his isolated, dysfunctional brother Charlie (Tom Cruise); but psychiatrist Jake Rainer (Richard Dreyfuss) in *Silent Fall*, mother Ruth Matthews (Kathleen Turner) in *House of Cards*, and FBI agent Art Jeffries (Bruce Willis) in *Mercury Rising* are all portrayed as dysfunctional characters who require interaction with an autistic presence in order to change. If this observation makes it appear that the films in question focus on clearly delineated characters *as individuals*, I should add that all four are structured with clear generic patternings and concerns: *Rain Man* is a melodrama and buddy road movie; *House of Cards* is a family melodrama; *Silent Fall* is a routine crime genre picture requiring Rainer to use his maverick skills with young autistic children to solve a murder; and *Mercury Rising* is a technology-based thriller in which Jeffries's outsider, renegade status affords protection for Simon Lynch (Miko Hughes), the autistic nine year old who has cracked the government's new, top secret, Mercury defense encryption code. In this film, Simon first recognizes the code buried within the pages of an everyday puzzle magazine, and to represent this moment of exceptional ability the camera comes in to an extreme close-up on his eyes, before zooming in on the close type of the puzzle laid out on the page. The clear invitation for the audience to conjecture on the workings of the autistic mind (i.e., that which is beyond neurotypical comprehension and, indeed, cinematic representation) is obvious here, and heightened because of the medium's visual nature.[4]

Similarly, the other feature films in which autism is less obviously a narrative concern also use genre conventions. For all of its off-beat concentration on the social impairments of lead character Barry Egan (Adam Sandler), *Punch-Drunk Love* plays out as a variation of the romantic melodrama. As Barry negotiates his way through a world that offers endless problems for all aspects of his life, the manner with which he pursues Lena (Emily Watson) recalls Hollywood's screwball comedies of the 1930s, though seen through an Asperger's filter. In *Cube*, the hand flapping and repetitive verbal utterances of Kazan (Andrew Miller) clearly mark him as autistic, though the narrative never labels him as such. Yet the film uses Kazan's exceptionality to render him one of a group chosen for unexplained reasons to try to escape a deadly cube-like structure in a science fiction format with antecedents in a films such as Ridley Scott's *Alien* (1979). For its part, *Bless the Child* employs both a thriller format and the classic horror convention of the innocence of the child (interestingly here—as with *House of Cards*—a girl, unusual in autism narratives) in a battle against satanic evil.

This prevalence of autism's characterization within standard generic narratives points (again) to a narrative space where the condition's inherent difference animates an idea of absence/presence that refracts back into more conventional narrative development. What is crucial to note about the features discussed here is the ways in which this point is frequently reinforced by a focus on the characters' savant qualities. Hollywood narratives indulge in a clear fascination with the supposedly exceptional skills of the autistic individual in a process that both creates and responds to the popular media construction of the condition. Raymond's card-reading skills in Las Vegas in *Rain Man* lead to a succession of scenes in the later films that center key plot developments on such abilities. In *Silent Fall*, the mimicking abilities of young autistic boy Tim Warden (Ben Faulkner) ultimately lead to the discovery of the truth about his parents' deaths. In *Cube*, Kazan's mathematical skills allow the imprisoned group finally to escape the complexities of their entrapment, though (intriguingly) he is the sole survivor. In *House of Cards*, Sally's (Asha Menina) ability to build an impossibly complex tower of playing cards leads to her mother's attempts to reproduce the tower in a larger form and to a final reconciliation on the structure itself. In *Bless the Child*, the girl Cody (Holliston Coleman) comes to personify an angelic innocence that reveals her to be the chosen child of the second coming who can defeat the presence of the satanic Eric Stark (Rufus Sewell). And in *Mercury Rising*, as we have already noted, Simon's skills with mathematics and word puzzles permit him to break the Mercury encryption code and then to help Jeffries search for justice.

This fascination with the savant figure needs proper understanding and contextualizing. Ultimately it signifies a fundamental misapprehension of the true nature of autism. Rates of savantism in the autistic population are in the region of 10%, and only marginally higher than in the majority population. Hollywood's concentration on savant skills actually exemplifies a tangential and misguided understanding of cognitive difference, and betrays the use of such difference for fictional ends. Autism does often produce islanded knowledge and differential abilities across a range of activities, but there is no causal connection between this and savant skills. Instead, in the films under discussion the savant figure becomes a peculiarly *narrative-driven* phenomenon, often an opportunity to modify plot or character relations. This sense of narrative then combines with the invited stare of the majority audience to create a visual spectacle of wonder at the cognitive difference that could produce such exceptionality. This wonder can take differing forms, though Hayes and Black characterize it ultimately as a "discourse of pity" through which Hollywood uses actual impairments to construct cultural signs (114).

This idea of a narratively constructed presentation of autism allows an entry into ideas about autistic characters and the levels of *performance* by the actors who play them. Upon *Rain Man's* release, Hoffman's performance as Raymond Babbitt gathered numerous critical accolades, including an Academy Award, and his portrayal became a key selling point of the film. In the same way, both Sean Penn's performance in *I Am Sam* and that of Sigourney Weaver in *Snow Cake* seem to be natural (complex, challenging) roles for such talented actors. Here the actors in question become the focal point for the wonder produced by the "enigmatic" status of autism and disability, especially that of savant ability. The question of how much research the actor in question undertook, the extent to which he or she had to perform a "different" humanity, become issues for public debate. Yet similar responses are not, on the whole, extended to child actors such as Ben Faulkner, Asha Menina, Miko Hughes and Holliston Coleman, whose performances in the films under discussion are often underplayed, frequently featuring a lack of speech and expression, as if they have been directed *not* to act. The range of portrayals here, from award-winning performances to inert, motionless representations, underscores the presence/absence continuity so central to the representation of autism. It is also further proof of the complex narrative space the condition inhabits, precisely because of the numerous points within this continuum that can provide the starting place for fiction.[5]

The concentration on individuals with savant skills might invite a further conclusion. Hollywood's fixation on autistic savant ability is clearly part of the wider emphasis on individual worth operating in mainstream US cultural production. The "ability" of the disabled figure to overcome (or, in the case of *House of Cards*, to come back from) adversity, and to take part in the key organizational formations of relationship, family, community, etc., is part and parcel of the kind of narrative prosthesis of which Mitchell and Snyder write. Autism seems to encourage a peculiar form of this, in which savant ability underscores a disabled individual's worth. Its status as a "special" skill provides, so the films suggest, a suitably compensatory element that offsets the actual impairment. For the majority nondisabled audience of a mainstream Hollywood feature, such logic is in keeping with the wider cultural politics that uses an idea of the "benevolent good" to connect individuals to communities and to the State.

The striking consistency in contemporary representations of autism ultimately makes a point both about autistic presence and about the construction of the condition in contemporary culture and society. In visual terms, autism is both visible and invisible. As with other cognitive impairments, it carries no obvious set or fixed marker that signals it. So, in the majority of the narratives just discussed, the autistic characters (especially the children) alternate between the twin poles of absence and presence, where the exceptionality that dominates certain narrative elements can suddenly become a passivity that offers no narrative at all. It is no coincidence that, in *Mercury Rising*, Simon escapes the government-hired contract killers who murder his parents by hiding, and remains hidden even as the police investigate the scene, only to be finally found by Jeffries. Equally, for all of the interest placed on Sally's withdrawn passivity in *House of Cards*, she is frequently at the periphery of both image and narrative as the film concentrates on the trauma of her mother Ruth, who has lost both a husband (killed in an accident, the event that "prompts" Sally's autism) and now a daughter. The exception to such shuttling between absence and presence is *Punch-Drunk Love*, where Barry's Aspergic subjecthood dominates the film. It is telling, however, that by far the majority of the reviews of the film fail to mention autism/Asperger's at all; rather, Barry is personified as sad, lonely or awkward, and the potential to see *Punch-Drunk Love* as an autistic narrative can become lost as it is pulled towards a non-autistic sense of what constitutes character.

Such notions of the active and passive constitute a peculiarly narrativized account of autistic presence, and hence form part of the ways in which the condition has become written in contemporary culture. Majia Holmer Nadesan has shown that, despite its clear status as a neurological impairment, and without denying its biogenetic origins, autism in the contemporary world still frequently operates as a *constructed* idea. As she writes, "perhaps autism is not a *thing* but is a nominal category useful for grouping heterogeneous people all sharing communication practices deviating significantly from the expectations of normalcy" (9; emphasis in the original). Filmic narratives like those discussed here are clear contributors to such a construction and category, and they inflect the condition with specific terms. The films "produce" an idea of autism, and are themselves part of the wider production practiced by medical, social and cultural institutions, which offers a version of the condition for the consumption of a majority audience which has the interest to speculate on, but not the time to know about, the ontological questions that autism raises. In an era of vaccine scares and exponentially increasing diagnoses, themselves events that contribute to a changing idea of autism, Hollywood's narratives add to the idea that we live in the time of an "epidemic," an autism "age," through stories only tangentially related to the actual condition.

Ideas of autistic presence suffuse the films discussed here, making the condition central in terms of both image and narrative at key moments in their fictional constructions. At the same time, the ontological questions central to any representation of autism remain as a surplus in these fictions. The films present a constant invitation to look at the autist (and it is noticeable that a number of them contain scenes set in schools or hospitals in which we see non-acting children and adults who *are* autistic, whereby the films aim to establish credentials) and this look is, ultimately, a moment in which the audience is encouraged to speculate on the human condition. At the points when these invitations occur, however, the films become formless and any meaningful comment on the actuality of autism collapses. The formlessness here is largely rescued by generic patterning or by an overt move towards sentimentality as the narrative redirects the issues of humanity it has raised into more familiar codifications. The majority of the films under discussion have sentimental endings: Jeffries visits Simon in school at the end of *Mercury Rising* and in response to his demand, "Look in my eyes," achieves both eye contact and a hug that are totally out of character with Simon's behavior up to this point. In *Bless the Child*, following her abduction Cody is reunited with her caring aunt Maggie (Kim Basinger), who plans to adopt her. *Rain Man* and *Cube* contain the most ambivalent endings. In the former, Raymond returns to Wallbrook, the institution from which Charlie originally took him, and the film avoids an overtly sentimental conclusion, though Charlie's education in humanity makes up for his loss of the custody battle concerning his brother. In *Cube*, Kazan is the only character to escape from the cube, though the "outside" into which he might venture is never shown in the film, and he is left on the threshold of safety, a survivor of the horror within. The very lack of any attempt to display the world outside the cube reinforces the idea that, for all his mathematical genius, Kazan's place within the narrative is merely to solve the problem of how to escape. He is, first and foremost, a function.

For its conclusion, however, *House of Cards* should receive the final comment here. Sally's "return" from her autism is seen as deriving from her mother Ruth's expression of an appropriate degree of love and understanding, a process that dumbfounds psychiatrist Jacob Beerlander (Tommy Lee Jones) and in effect negates all of his professional work, something we have seen a lot of in the film. This conclusion's structure, its emphasis on autism as (first) a condition that is *not* neurological but rather behavioral, and (second) as vehicle for the mobilization of other, non-autistic, sentiments, completely evacuates any idea of autism as it really exists. The drive to make the Matthews family cohesive once again (and it is clear that there is a space for Beerlander to replace the absent father) becomes the conclusion's ultimate logic. Autism here is simply another occasion to remind parents to love their children properly.

In terms of the kinds of melodrama Hollywood practices with regard to autism, this focus on family is typical. The strength of the family unit, with all its perceived moral good, becomes central in a number of these films. In both *Rain Man* and *Molly*, a sibling must learn the power of family love through an encounter with an autistic individual, and both narratives have nearly identical conclusions regarding the family dynamic produced through such a "learning" process. Sibling relationships are also central to *Silent Fall*, where sister Sylvie (Liv Tyler) supports Ben following the murder of their parents, whereas familial dysfunction dominates *The United States of Leland*, where the gruesome murder of young autistic Ryan Pollard (Michael Welch) by protagonist Leland Fitzgerald (Ryan Gosling), after he establishes a relationship with Ryan's sister Becky (Jena Malone), prompts a narrative inquiry into the dynamics of the American middle-class nuclear family. The murder of Simon's parents is also central to *Mercury Rising*, and in both this film and *Silent Fall* the adult male hero becomes a surrogate father figure and protector. Maggie's adoption of Cody at the end of *Bless the Child* displays a narrative institutionalization of this impulse. The otherness of autism, it is implied, can be most negated, made most familiar, by incorporating it within the family structure. In being made to function in such a way, autism becomes just another element (like crime, or drugs, or any number of perceived individual "abnormalities") to be characterized and thematized in Hollywood's dominant drive to create normative narratives of social relations.

Presence is the key category in discussing contemporary representations of autism. Hollywood's continual need to portray the condition responds to the increased presence of autism in the contemporary world and the variety of stories such presence might allow. At the same time, the representation of autistic presence in the films described here constitutes a misreading of autistic agency and a wilful recontextualization within the logic of majority nondisabled storytelling. An idea of autistic presence animates any number of narrative possibilities in these films. From the championing of an individual's right through the law, the salvation of a trapped community, a resistance to a repressive government, to the love of a mother for her daughter, autism provides the raw material for a seemingly endless range of complex fictions, yet any greater understanding of the presence of autism in contemporary culture eludes the films' audiences. Despite the fascination that prompts Hollywood's continual return to the autistic figure, we are unlikely to find in these stories any sense of a productive disabled agency. The drive of the industry's commercial aesthetic, and the desire for conformity on issues of social relations (such as the family), is too overpowering to allow audiences to move beyond the parameters offered by genre and sentiment. But if we cannot necessarily regulate such cultural power, we can at least learn how to read it; and even when we feel ourselves within a system as powerful as Hollywood, we can nevertheless challenge its authority. Mainstream cinema audiences may never choose to watch in huge numbers the 485 minutes of Andy Warhol's *Empire* (1964), a film that—with its continual and unedited focus on the Empire State Building—might qualify as a genuine autistic narrative, but they can and, one hopes, will, come to recognize images and stories that offend in their misrepresentation. Reaching such a position is ultimately a job for educators in the widest sense of the word, and for those, autistic and not, who are currently working to break down the barriers of misunderstanding and prejudice. We will know the good films when we get to see them.

NOTES

1. William A. Graham's 1974 television film for CBS, *Larry*, is one such film. Centered on the true story of Larry Herman, a man confined to a Nevada institution for much of his early life, it discusses in depth a number of the recognizable traits of autism but never mentions the condition
2. In this chapter, I deliberately alternate between using the phrasing "autistic person" and "person with autism." Though the former is more contentious, suggesting to some that the person is defined by autism, I use it in a sense of optimism, convinced that to be autistic is to be part of the perfectly acceptable spectrum that makes up humanity. In addition, "person with autism" does potentially suggest that the condition might somehow be removable, like a disease, and I remain extremely wary of such an idea.
3. Dating from roughly 1969 to the present, there are approximately 50 feature and short films with narratives that either focus on autism or contain characters who are identifiably somewhere on the autistic spectrum. Before this date, it is difficult to distinguish elements of the condition from a generic portrayal of "idiocy."
4. This scene is very similar to one in Ron Howard's biopic of mathematician John Nash, *A Beautiful Mind*, in which Nash (Russell Crowe) is asked by the military to decipher an intercepted code. Here, too, the extreme close-up on the face, and the subsequent camera play on the coded numbers themselves (to a suitably charged soundtrack), is an attempt to enact the workings of the exceptional mind. Though *A Beautiful Mind* is largely about Nash's schizophrenia, it is clear from early scenes in the film in which he displays dysfunctional social skills that the Nash character is seen to have autistic tendencies. The close-up on Simon's eyes also parallels a number of the photographs of children with autism in Thomas Balsamo and Sharon Rosenbloom's *Souls*, another text that invites a non-autistic audience to speculate on the nature of the condition through a specifically visual medium.
5. It is noticeable that a number of the characters with autism under discussion here are children, and that the representation of autistic characters in film features as many children as adults. This observation lends support to the idea that the films reduce the actuality of autism to the periphery of their narratives, given that the children are not the films' major characters. It could also signal a desire to contain the condition, with childhood autism aligned with an idea of "childhood behavior," something understood to be regulated by adults.

WORKS CITED

A Beautiful Mind. Dir. Ron Howard. Universal/Dreamworks SKG/Imagine Entertainment, 2001.
Alien. Dir. Ridley Scott. Twentieth-Century Fox, 1979.
Balsamo, Thomas and Sharon Rosenbloom. *Souls: Beneath and Beyond Autism*. New York: McGraw-Hill, 2004.
Benny & Joon. Dir. Jeremiah S. Chechik. MGM, 1993.
Bless the Child. Dir. Chuck Russell. Icon Entertainment/Paramount, 2000.
Cube. Dir. Vincenzo Natali. Trimark Pictures, 1997.
Darke, Paul. "Understanding Cinematic Representations of Disability." *The Disability Reader: Social Science Perspectives*. Ed. Tom Shakespeare. London and New York: Continuum, 1998. 181–97.
Davis, Lennard J. *Enforcing Normalcy: Disability, Deafness and the Body*. London and New York: Verso, 1995.

Empire. Dir. Andy Warhol. Prod. Andy Warhol. 1964.

Forrest Gump. Dir. Robert Zemeckis. Paramount, 1994.

Garland-Thomson, Rosemarie. "The Politics of Staring: Visual Rhetorics of Disability in Popular Photography." *Disability Studies: Enabling the Humanities*. Ed. Sharon L. Snyder, Brenda Jo Brueggemann, and Rosemarie Garland-Thomson. New York: MLA, 2002. 56–75.

Grant, Barry Keith. "Rich and Strange: The Yuppie Horror Film." *Contemporary Hollywood Cinema*. Ed. Steve Neale and Murray Smith. London and New York: Routledge, 1998: 280–93.

Hayes. Michael T., and Rhonda S. Black. "Troubling Signs: Disability, Hollywood Movies and the Construction of a Discourse of Pity." *Disability Studies Quarterly* 23 (2003): 114–32.

House of Cards. Dir. Michael Lessac. A&M Films/Penta Pictures/Miramax, 1993.

I Am Sam. Dir. Jessie Nelson. New Line Cinema, 2001.

Kaplan, E. Ann. *Looking for the Other: Feminism, Film and the Imperial Gaze*. New York and London: Routledge, 1997.

Larry. Dir. William A. Graham. Tomorrow Entertainment Inc., 1974.

Maltby, Richard. *Hollywood Cinema: An Introduction*. Oxford: Blackwell, 1995.

McCrisken, Trevor B., and Andre Pepper. *American History and Contemporary Hollywood Film*. New Brunswick: Rutgers UP, 2005.

Mercury Rising. Dir. Harold Becker. Imagine Entertainment/Universal, 1998.

Mitchell, David T. "Narrative Prosthesis." *Disability Studies: Enabling the Humanities*. Ed. Sharon L. Snyder, Brenda Jo Brueggemann, and Rosemarie Garland-Thomson. New York: MLA, 2002. 15–30.

———., and Sharon Snyder. "Introduction: Disability Studies and the Double Bind of Representation." *The Body and Physical Difference*. Ed. Mitchell and Snyder. Ann Arbor: U of Michigan P, 1997: 1–31.

Molly. Dir. John Duigan. MGM, 1998

Nadesan, Majia Holmer. *Constructing Autism: Unravelling the "Truth" and Understanding the Social*. London and New York: Routledge, 2005.

Neale, Steve. *Genre and Hollywood*. London and New York: Routledge, 2000.

Nell. Dir. Michael Apted. Twentieth-Century Fox/Polygram,1994.

Norden, Martin F. *The Cinema of Isolation: A History of Physical Disability in the Movies*. New Brunswick: Rutgers UP, 1994.

Punch-Drunk Love. Dir. Paul Thomas Anderson. New Line Cinema/Sony Pictures, 2002.

Rain Man. Dir. Barry Levinson. The Guber-Peters Company/Mirage Entertainment/United Artists/MGM,1988.

Shakespeare, Tom. "Art and Lies? Representation of Disability on Film." *Disability Discourse*. Ed. Mairian Corker and Sally French. Buckingham: Open UP, 1999. 164–72.

Shine. Dir. Scott Hicks. Australian Film Finance Corporation/Film Victoria/Momentum Films. 1996.

Silent Fall. Dir. Bruce Beresford. Kouf/Bigelow Productions/Morgan Creek Productions/Warner Bros., 1994.

Snow Cake. Dir. Marc Evans. Revolution Films/Rhombus Media, 2006.

Stokes, Melvyn and Richard Maltby, eds. *Identifying Hollywood's Audiences: Culture Identity and the Movies*. London: British Film Institute, 1999.

The United States of Leland. Dir. Matthew Ryan Hoge. MDP Worldwide/Media 8 Entertainment/Thousand Words/Trigger Street Productions, 2003.

What's Eating Gilbert Grape. Dir. Lasse Hallström. Paramount, 1993.

14 Film as a Vehicle for Raising Consciousness among Autistic Peers

Phil Schwarz

INTRODUCTION

In 2004–2005 I organized a film series at the Asperger's Association of New England (http://www.aane.org) for my peers on the autism spectrum and their families, friends, and supporters. The goal was more than simply getting people together to socialize. The films were chosen because they highlight critical issues affecting living fully as a person on the autism spectrum: identity and self-esteem, membership in a community with a history and culture, and the realities and possibilities of interaction with the majority non-autistic population. After screening each film, we opened the floor for discussion of the issues each film touched on.

This chapter illustrates the ideas behind the film series through exploring the four films we screened the first season. It is not a full analysis of the films; rather, it is a narrative of the purpose, process, and outcomes of the films, and of the discussions that ensued.

HISTORICAL, BIOGRAPHICAL AND POLITICAL CONTEXTS

AANE was founded in 1995 by a clinician, a social worker, and a small group of parents of children diagnosed with Asperger's syndrome (AS), at that time a new diagnostic category unfamiliar to most clinicians and educators. The parents were at a loss for finding resources and support. There was little awareness of the very existence of high-functioning forms of autism, much less of AS. AANE sought to provide that support, to identify and provide access to those resources, and to educate school systems and clinicians. It succeeded in doing so—and in the process discovered that its initial glimpse of the affected population was the tip of an iceberg.

In particular, as awareness of AS and high-functioning autism spread, surprising numbers of *adults* who fit the diagnostic profiles (and sometimes their spouses and family members) began showing up seeking support and resources. And every bit as much as the families of AS children, if not more so, they came seeking contact with fellow travelers.

My own journey parallels and intersects with this history. The diagnosis of our son Jeremy with autism in 1994 led my wife and me into a course of reading that produced an unexpected side-effect: the recognition and eventual diagnosis, ten months later, of my own AS. Soon thereafter, I joined the fledgling AANE, coordinated the development of its first Web site, and eventually joined its board of directors.

Jeremy's and my diagnoses gave us two points of reference along what we discovered to be a wide spectrum of ability and disability—his point, when he was diagnosed at age three, being more toward the classical definition of autism, mine at the mild end of the spectrum. We discovered that it is a dynamic spectrum whose inhabitants can move from point to point within it as they gain abilities and mitigate handicaps.

As we read more, and met more people whose lives had been touched by autism, particularly other adults on the spectrum, it became clear to me (as it is to most people on the spectrum of all degrees of ability who have expressed themselves on the subject) that autism is still terribly misunderstood by the mainstream population, and even by many professionals who deal with autism, and therefore also by many parents and families of autistic children and adults.

On the one hand, the future holds hope: the more society takes seriously what people on the spectrum have to say about the reasons behind our divergences in behavior, sensory needs, cognitive styles, aesthetic sensibilities, and intuitive social and emotional responses, the more that understanding will improve. On the other hand, there remains a stark division between mainstream attitudes and responses to autism and those of people on the spectrum. The mainstream speaks of autism primarily in the medical language of deficit, and cannot see, as many of us on the spectrum do, that once the right kinds of support, accommodation, and mitigation of specific handicaps are available, there are *desirable* aspects to autism that we would not want to live without, and without which we would no longer be ourselves.

The mainstream sees autism as a monolithic disease, as something extrinsic to the self, like paraplegia or cancer, which can be turned into "the enemy," fought and eradicated. But they ignore the pervasive nature of autism: a set of differences in the architecture of the brain and central nervous system with a range of effects, some overt and intrinsically disabling, and some subtle, producing divergences from the norm that are often disabling only because they are devalued or not accommodated by mainstream society. These subtle effects extend deep into areas of identity, personality, and sensibilities.

Once the grossly disabling effects are properly identified and accommodated or mitigated, we begin to notice those subtle effects more and more, and the medical model that posits a discontinuity between "ill" and "well" begins to break down. Questions begin to arise about whether the remaining disabilities are symptoms of an individual impairment, or rather of the inflexibility or intolerance of the society and its ergonomic, economic, political and social landscapes.

Unfortunately, the two sides of the division in attitudes towards autism are far from equal in power, resources, media presence, and mindshare. Consequently, many people who are diagnosed, particularly those diagnosed in childhood, receive such a surfeit of the negative, deficits-only image of autism that they internalize those images at the expense of their self-esteem. The drumbeat of messages that autistic people are damaged goods unless they are somehow "recovered" or "cured" is insidious and pervasive.[1] Even those diagnosed as adults generally come into a clinical or support-provider purview as a result of negative experiences and failures that they often have thoroughly internalized.

Many peers come to AANE with debilitating quantities of such negative internalization, but with no appreciation for their *positive* autistic attributes, no community of peers and allies to bolster and internalize those positives, and no perspective from which to ask challenging questions about their situation: no way to ask which parts of their handicaps, setbacks, and struggles are due to intrinsic *individual* impairment, and which parts are due to economic, ergonomic, social, or political elements of the status quo that can be scrutinized and changed.

And that is where the film series comes in.

THE GOALS OF THE FILM SERIES, AND THE FILMS CHOSEN

I had several goals in mind for the film series. I wanted to inspire the audience to think, as well as to socialize. I wanted to prompt people to ask questions that would enrich their perspectives and their perceptions of themselves and of others like them. Hence, the primary goal was to find films that would spark discussion of topics that would lead to strengthening self-esteem and sense of identity.

I chose four films. Two were biographies of historical figures who were very likely AS. A third was a fictional story with a protagonist/narrator who shares many traits with AS folks; the fourth seemed to have very little to do with autism, but could be interpreted as a powerful metaphor for constructive family responses to autism.

By intention, none of the four displays a character's autism as a novelty, such as it is in *Rain Man, Mercury Rising,* or *Silent Fall.* In fact, none of the films mentions autism or AS explicitly. Yet each is an antidote to the *misrepresentation* of autism in the more widely publicized films that overtly feature autism as a plot novelty.

The four films chosen, in the order we screened them during the year, were:

- *32 Short Films About Glenn Gould*, the Canadian pianist (1932–1982).
- *Smoke Signals*, screenplay by Sherman Alexie.
- *Breaking the Code*, about the British mathematician Alan Turing (1912–1954).
- *The Secret of Roan Inish*, screenplay by John Sayles.

I discuss the four films in the order we screened them in order to represent the journey we took together as series organizer and audience—a progression through several stages in the development and expression of positive identity and self-awareness.

The first of these stages is learning to identify and deem positive some traits we share with fellow travelers; *32 Short Films* helps us do that by portraying famous fellow traveler Glenn Gould, and perhaps more importantly, in portraying the world from Gould's perspective. The second stage is gaining awareness of the extent to which we have internalized the majority's negative characterizations of us, and learning how to counteract that internalization. That is a major theme of *Smoke Signals*. The third stage is recognizing the contexts in which it is safe or unsafe to assert our identity, and determining what to do about the latter. *Breaking the Code* portrays another famous fellow traveler's struggles in that vein. The fourth stage is conveying our positive self-awareness to those who should be our natural allies—parents and family. *Roan Inish*, viewed as metaphor, helps us do that.

Before we begin the journey through the four films, let me address a question that arises regarding the biographical films: if a subject was never formally diagnosed as autistic or AS, can we validly claim that he or she is "one of us"? And by extension, is it valid to include the biographical films?

Neither film identifies its subject as autistic or AS, but both are portrayed as having many AS traits. Both have been posthumously "diagnosed" by members of our community (in Gould's case, also by his biographer). In fact, I chose both films in part to focus on questions about the posthumous diagnosis of historical figures. This phenomenon is not unique to the autism community: it has an analogue in the gay community—in the posthumous outing of historical figures. In both cases, the primary motives are to turn the historical figures into role models, and to make the community less subject to marginalization.

Claims about the sexual orientation of historical figures can be supported by a relatively narrow range of historical fact, and homosexuality has been a known variant in the human condition for a long time. But in the case of autism, we are dealing with traits recognized as such only within the past sixty years, and that have undergone a number of revisions since then, and are still problematic and incomplete.[2] So in identifying historical figures who might have been on the autism spectrum, there are questions not only of applying debatable criteria, but also of applying these modern criteria across significantly different historical, cultural, and societal contexts. And yet there is a clear resonance among many of us on the spectrum when we see or hear descriptions of people like us. Gay people speak of "gay-dar," the intuitive sense that another person is gay; among folks on the autism spectrum, there seems to be just as strong a phenomenon of "A-dar" about fellow travelers.

It is this sense of identification with others like us that resonates. And ultimately it doesn't matter, for the purposes of the film series, whether a rigorous clinical diagnosis of a particular biographical figure is or would have been possible. Rather, it is the combination of values, choices, actions, reactions, and sensibilities that the figure exhibits *as portrayed* that we look to, identify with, and aimed to think about, because *those* things are what we share, whether or not the clinicians or the general public agree about attributing an autism spectrum condition to the historical figure.[3]

The same can be said of fictional characters as well. Thomas Builds-the-Fire, the narrator/protagonist of *Smoke Signals*, is never identified as autistic or AS, but he is depicted as having many AS traits. These traits are what draw us fellow travelers in and invite us to examine other questions that the story and the character's role pose for us.

Film #1: *32 Short Films About Glenn Gould*

This film was the ideal starting point for the series, because it addresses the primary level of connection I was seeking to foster: identification of familiar experience in a positive, holistic, non-devaluing light, in this case through the life story of a well-known fellow traveler.

32 Short Films builds its picture of Glenn Gould from the bottom up, illustrating and amassing a wealth of details to arrive at a gestalt, which is exactly the cognitive style of many folks on the spectrum. Many of our viewers identified with little things scattered throughout the film: Gould's sensory sensitivities; his dietary penchants; his love for animals; his yearning for solitude; his late rhythm of wake and sleep; the body language in the segments "Practice" and "Passion According to Gould." Many viewers' "A-dar" pegged not only Gould, but also the piano tuner interviewed in "Crossed Paths," who seems to represent a different archetype within the spectrum.

Gould's statements in "Lake Simcoe" about his precocious musical aptitude and his mind for minutiae, and his unanswered question about what might have become of him if not for music and his mother's early nurturing of his talent, gave rise to a discussion about the mainstream's greater tolerance of eccentricity in those it perceives to be geniuses.

Many viewers singled out "Truck Stop," the segment in which Gould (to the beautifully comic strains of Petula Clark singing "Downtown") drives up-province to an Ontario truckers' restaurant he regularly frequents, and sits at his table alone amid the crowd. Here the camera and microphone begin to meander, creating a fugue of faces and voices. This scene strongly resembles how many of us manage to stay afloat when awash in sensory input that exceeds our available bandwidth or capacity to process. This fugue-of-voices structure in "Truck Stop" is followed by a similar fugue-of-voices in the segment "The Idea of North," only this time Gould is "conducting" as he cues in each voice; such control over the wash of sensory input through our limited real-time bandwidth is precious and often desperately sought.

Some viewers were surprised at Gould's astuteness as an investor, as portrayed in "The Tip," perhaps assuming that market savvy involves social skills we are supposed not to possess. There is a significant difference, however, between the powers of observation and reasoning required to anticipate the statistical behavior of a market, and those required to anticipate and meet the expectations of specific people with a variety of mainstream personality and interaction styles: split-second reasoning that must be intuitive, or as-fast-as-intuitive if in fact deductive. Playing a market may be fast-paced, but it is fundamentally asynchronous and not quite in real time, and thus amenable to the heuristic thinking that good chess players develop.

In the segment "Hamburg," Gould sits an anonymous chambermaid down with him to listen to a recording of the scherzo of the Op. 27 #1 Beethoven sonata, which turns out to be a new recording he has made that he is hearing for the first time. The scene sums up much about him: intense focus coupled with near-obliviousness to the expectations or needs of others; his belief that recording can replace the concert experience; his simultaneously awkward, intimate and anonymous attempt at sharing.

Discovering and recognizing kinship with those who share traits, sensibilities, and struggles is one way to affirm identity. These discoveries also help build a sense of community: the knowledge that there are others out there who understand one's situation and perspectives better than the mainstream does, others one might turn to for advice, moral support, friendship. Yet recognizing kinship with historical figures is not just about finding role models; it also establishes a history, a community-through-time, and permits the reclamation of a shared cultural heritage.

Is there such a thing as "autistic culture"? Yes, as much as there is a Deaf culture or gay culture: a population of fellow travelers who, despite wide diversity, share experiences, values, sensibilities, sensitivities, struggles, a growing lexicon, and an emerging history.[4] The coping strategies many of us develop to leverage the limited real-time bandwidth we have available for processing sensory input lead, as Bruce Mills suggests in his contribution to this volume, to a distinct aesthetic sensibility that is an integral aspect of that culture: an affinity for structure and patterns, for repetition and for variation-within-repetition. It is no accident that Gould so strongly identified with the richly structured music of Bach. Even the humor that appeals to many of us on the spectrum, such as puns, involves the extrapolation, juxtaposition, or breakage of patterns.[5]

The emergence of community and recognition of shared elements leading to a cultural identity is perhaps easier to see among so-called "high-functioning" or AS people. But it is really full-spectrum: it is also voiced by the more severely disabled who are fortunate enough to use keyboarding or other assistive technology and who have contact with other fellow travelers through the Internet.[6] This commonality is borne out by many of the scenes in *32 Short Films*, thus providing sensory and nonverbal touchpoints of identification.

Film #2: *Smoke Signals*

With *Smoke Signals*, we move to the next stage in the journey. As with Glenn Gould in *32 Short Films*, we found elements of positive self-recognition in one of protagonists in *Smoke Signals*. But *Smoke Signals* moves us beyond self-recognition into new territory: a heightened awareness of how we internalize majority attitudes.

The film is about two young men from the Coeur d'Alene American Indian nation, Victor Joseph and Thomas Builds-the-Fire. They are total opposites: Victor is athletic, stoic, hip, and socially dominant; Thomas is small, clumsy, talkative, socially awkward and dreamy, written off or patronized by Victor and his peers—except in his capacity as storyteller. A weaver of idiosyncratic stories, Thomas is the film's narrator/protagonist. He and Victor are bound together by tragic circumstances: when they were infants, Thomas's house burned down during a drunken Fourth of July party. His parents were trapped in the house but, just before they died, threw him to safety. Victor's father Arnold caught Thomas, who lionizes him for that. But Arnold's drinking made him unpredictable, and his mercurial temperament ultimately precipitated his estrangement from Victor's mother Arlene. Victor has grown up stoic and bitter, resenting his father's abandonment and the dysfunction he sees all about him. News comes from Phoenix, Arizona, where Arnold had been living, that he has died. Victor needs to travel there to take care of Arnold's personal effects, but he and Arlene don't have the money for a bus ticket to get him there. Thomas offers to pay for the trip, on the condition that they travel together. At the end of their road trip, these strange partners meet Suzy, Arnold's neighbor/friend/confidante, who presents them with Arnold's ashes, opens Arnold's trailer for them, and shares memories. Victor makes discoveries about his father and the house fire and its aftermath that begin a process of transformation and healing. Thomas too grows in the course of the journey, ultimately gaining the confidence necessary to challenge Victor about his bitterness and emotional detachment and to earn his respect.

Our audience included some non-autistic people and an AS woman who is part Chippewa. Hence, we got a fascinating triplet of perspectives on the film: those of mainstream viewers, of one Indian viewer, and those of autistic viewers. Mainstream viewers seemed to focus on the classic themes of father–son tension, the journey, obscured truth and its discovery, personal growth, and the dynamics of the personal relationships in the film. For Indian viewers, the film's in-jokes and historical and situational ironies—and the character types that populate the film, including those of Victor and Thomas—are likely familiar dimensions. More important, this is a film in which real Indian characters and real Indian cultural and social contexts are matter-of-factly placed front-and-center, neither as a novelty, as a set of stereotypes (though plenty of stereotypes are skewered: it is a good day to be an indigenous filmmaker), nor as the be-all and end-all of the film, but as a living stage on which the personal and dramatic themes play out and with which they interact. The Indians in this film are fully round characters.

Viewers on the autism spectrum found many aspects of Thomas appealing and familiar. Though Thomas is identifiably a fellow traveler, his "autistic" traits do not render his role one-dimensional; rather, they are an integrated part of a round character. It is just as important for *autistic* identity and self-esteem for autistic folks to see such positioning and development in characters they identify with as it is for *Indian* identity and collective national self-esteem to see the corresponding breakthrough in Indian presences.

That Thomas's storytelling is valued in his community and culture struck our audience strongly and led to a stimulating discussion. We made comparisons with other societies and the valued roles within them toward which folks like us have gravitated and through which we have sought fulfillment: the monastic life, for example. Or in scholarship: three hundred years ago, within my own Jewish religious and cultural tradition, I would have most likely been a student of sacred texts—certainly a prestigious role in that society.

But perhaps the thing that struck me most, as an autistic viewer of the film (perhaps paralleling an Indian viewer's perspective on the film), is the depth and entrenchment with which negative self-imagery and attitudes can take hold internally, and how liberating to one's self-esteem gaining awareness of that internalization can be. For example, sitting in Suzy's trailer as the TV plays a Hollywood western, Thomas says, "You know, the only thing more pathetic than Indians on TV is Indians watching Indians on TV." Thomas's narration and Alexie's script capture the pervasive dysfunction in their situation, as well as the everyday lives of the Coeur d'Alenes, with sometimes-comic, sometimes-tragic understatement that drives home the ubiquity of these conditions.

Frybread, the quintessential contemporary pan-tribal Indian food, is a symbol of cultural identity in the film. In one scene, Thomas, goaded by Victor into updating his attire and hair, comes out of a clothing store wearing a t-shirt emblazoned with the slogan "Frybread Power." One of Thomas's whimsical stories is about Arlene feeding the whole community with her world's-best frybread. But there is a darker side to frybread. Made from refined white flour, sugar, and lard—surplus commodities with which the U.S. government fed Indian populations once they had been relocated to reservations and stripped of their hunting, fishing, and farming lands—frybread is about as unhealthy a food as one could concoct as a dietary staple. Suzan Harjo writes in "No More 'Fat' Indian Food" of Indians referring to other Indians rendered unhealthy by such a diet as having a "commod bod." It is very much (to borrow an annually visited catch-phrase from my own cultural tradition) "bread of affliction." Yet, ironically, it has become a thoroughly entrenched aspect of modern Indian identity. Just as Native Americans have consumed and converted frybread, so they consume and internalize unhealthy images of their own cultural identity.

There has been an equally massive internalization of negatives and low expectations on the part of autistic people, with few stereotypes as alternatives (e.g., heroism in living a "normal" life despite ever-present handicaps, or being an eccentric genius). So much of our definition as an autism community is generated by parents, professionals, clinicians, and researchers who are not autistic themselves but who hold all the cards when it comes to resources, media access, and public mindshare, that many of us are not even aware of its pervasiveness. By drawing parallels with Indians' internalization of negatives, we may begin to identify and ask questions about the origins and power base of the similar phenomenon in our experience.

Film #3: *Breaking the Code*

Breaking the Code moves us to the next stage in the journey of self-awareness: to considering the issues of disclosure and assertion of our identity and, conversely, to issues surrounding attempts to navigate intolerant social contexts.

Breaking the Code is British playwright Hugh Whitemore's television adaptation for *Masterpiece Theatre* of his play of the same name, which in turn was based on the book *Alan Turing: The Enigma*, by Andrew Hodges. Turing was a principal contributor to the mathematical field of automata theory, the foundation for modern computer science. During World War II, he worked for a top-secret cryptographic unit of the British intelligence agency, helping to crack the German navy's cryptographic codes, and developing programmable mechanical calculating tools that paved the way for the design and construction of the first electronic digital computers in the following decade. After the war, Turing continued to do cryptography for the British government, though neither his wartime nor his postwar work were matters of public knowledge for many years to come (Hodges, parts 3–5, 8).

Turing was gay when homosexuality was illegal in Britain, and in 1951 had a liaison with a young man he had met on the street who later conspired with a friend to burglarize Turing's home. Turing went to the police to report the burglary, in the process revealing that he and the young man had had a sexual encounter. This revelation prompted his arrest and a public trial and conviction on a morals charge. To avoid prison, Turing submitted to a year of estrogen injections, ostensibly to curb his libido; nevertheless, the public trial and conviction resulted in his being stripped of his security clearances and dismissed from his cryptographic work—homosexuality in that era being an immediate disqualifier for security-sensitive work. Moreover, Turing traveled abroad and had liaisons with foreign sexual partners, inducing the government's external security agency to tail him and subject him to searches. In the eyes of the government, Turing regressed from a wartime intelligence asset to an intelligence liability. Ultimately, this harassment and virtual imprisonment pushed Turing to commit suicide, in June 1954, at the age of 41 (Hodges, part 8).

Whitemore portrays Turing as intellectually brilliant yet socially naïve. Whitemore's version of the romantic liaison's beginning takes place in a pub where Turing has gone after seeing a movie (*Snow White*, which figures further in the plot, as in real life: his means of suicide was an apple laced with cyanide). Following a brief conversation that establishes Turing and the young man as coming from different planets socially and intellectually, Turing nonetheless invites him over for dinner and discloses his home address— before they have even exchanged names! It turns out that the young man, whom Whitemore names Ron, is unemployed and somewhat of a grifter; he has spotted Turing coming out of the movie theater, sized him up as an easy mark, followed him into the pub from the theater, and initiated the encounter.

At the police station after the burglary, Whitemore's Turing shows a striking myopia about what to say to the detective and what the consequences might be. Writing years before AS became well known, Whitemore gives us an uncanny depiction of higher order difficulties in theory-of-mind reasoning quite typical of a gifted AS adult. For example, Turing is in far over his head attempting to make partial disclosures and not get himself or Ron, about whom he still has conflicting feelings, into trouble; Turing's initial complaint is so poorly constructed that the detective thinks he's hiding something, and visits Turing's house to follow up. In this second exchange, Turing's story collapses. He admits to fabricating his initial story and, when pressed about why he tried to conceal Ron's identity, admits that he is having an affair with him. When told that their physical intimacy is illegal, Turing acts much like a child playing chess—making wrong moves and wanting to take them back.

Our viewers felt kinship with this character. They picked up on the homophobia and its consequences, comparing mainstream misperceptions and stigmas regarding homosexuality with those regarding autism. They also remarked on the parallels between Turing's enforced estrogen treatments and the "cures" that autistic people have been (and continue to be) subjected to in ill-begotten attempts to make them "normal"; and they noted parallels between coming out gay and disclosing an autism spectrum condition.

Things have certainly improved regarding homosexuality since Turing's time, but there is still a long way to go, and many ingrained stigmas to dispel. There is a long way to go for us too: many misconceptions about autism and people on the autism spectrum still need to be corrected, and strong enough stigmas surround autism that those who can "pass" tend to do so, rather than identify and share strength with the autistic community. Disclosure is still often too risky a business in employment, education, and elsewhere.

Yet there is another potential parallel we autistic self-advocates can draw on to help change these conditions: the gay community's very successful model of educating and empowering straight allies to help dispel stigma and bigotry and open doors in education and employment. We would do well to foster such dialogue and consider how such a model of identifying, educating, and empowering non-autistic allies could further our own efforts in individual and collective autistic self-advocacy.[7]

Film #4: *The Secret of Roan Inish*

The Secret of Roan Inish is about homecoming—and it represented a homecoming for the film series itself, for the idea of presenting the film series derived from a prior experience with this very film. At Autreat[8] 1999, a Canadian autistic woman named Kim Duff led a workshop on representations of autism in folklore. I had serendipitously packed *Roan Inish* to watch with the family on our trip, and because it seemed to fit so well after Kim's workshop, I suggested that several of us get together that evening to watch the film. Afterward, we discussed the film as, among other things, a metaphor for constructive family responses to autism; that conversation germinated the idea for the film series. And as a metaphor for such constructive family responses, *Roan Inish* opens the door to the final of the four stages in developing positive identity and self-awareness: outreach and dialogue with our natural allies issuing from a positive sense of self.

Roan Inish is based on western Irish folk legends about selchies—half-seal, half-human creatures who on rare occasions are said to have mated with humans. The film centers on a small island community off the coast of County Donegal, which is evacuated during World War II. The evacuation hits home hard for ten-year-old Fiona Coneelly and her family: as they are loading the boat to head to the mainland for the last time, her dark-haired little brother Jamie, in his wooden heirloom cradle, is carried out to sea by the advancing tide. Soon their mother Brigid dies and is buried back on the island. Their father moves to the city to work and can't care for Fiona, so she goes to live with her and her cousin Eamon and grandparents Hugh and Tess, who have settled in a cottage on the coast facing the island.

Eamon tells Fiona that Jamie has been seen around the island, traveling in the wooden cradle. On a visit to the island, she explores the abandoned cottages where their families lived and finds fresh green ferns on the floor, still-warm coals in the fireplace, shells of eaten shellfish, flint firestones—and a child's footprints: someone has been there very recently.

Soon after, a shopkeeper introduces Fiona to Tadgh, another Coneelly cousin, dark-haired like Jamie, at work cleaning fish. The shopkeeper says of Tadgh, "He's a bit special, if you know what I mean," pointing to his head. Tadgh abruptly asks her, "You know why I'm dark?" and proceeds to tell her the story of how their ancestor Liam Coneelly captured a selchie's seal-skin as she lay sunbathing and then took her as a wife. "She called herself Nuala. When it was time for their baby to be born, Nuala told Liam she needed a cradle carved of a seagoing vessel." But Nuala eventually found the seal-skin and disappeared back into the sea as a seal. Tadgh says, "Once a selchie finds her skin again, neither chains of love nor chains of steel can keep her from the seas. . . . The Coneellys would see her. The cradle was passed on. And every so often one would be born with dark hair of the selchie, and they be good fisherfolk."

On a second visit to the island, Fiona sees a little boy by the shore who spots her and jumps into a tiny cradle-like boat and paddles off. Subsequent sightings end the same way. She asks Tadgh, "Why must he [Jamie] always run from me?" He replies, "Why do you chase him?" Fiona: "He's lost out there." Tadgh: "He's just with another branch of the family." Fiona: "I don't know whether to believe you. Have you seen him?" Tadgh answers: "I may be daft, but I'm not blind."

Fiona becomes determined to reclaim Jamie by getting her grandparents and Eamon to move with her back to the island. Initially they resist, but Eamon helps Fiona fix up the cottages on the island, and when Hugh and Tess learn that their landlord plans to evict them, Fiona and Eamon convince the grandparents to move. After Hugh and Tess find the cottages Fiona and Eamon have restored, a climactic reunion takes place as the seals gather to turn Jamie out of his cradle-boat and back into the arms of his (own branch of the) family.

Taking up the film's descriptions of the "dark-haired ones," our audience explored what happens if we interpret "selchie blood" as a metaphor for the genetics of autism. Autism tends to run in families, and along with individuals who come under clinical purview, other family members often exhibit some autistic traits—a little like the "dark ones" among the Coneellys. These "dark ones" are a diverse lot, but share some characteristics: some are brilliant; some are "daft, but not blind"; some are wild and given up for lost, like Jamie.

Many family members also testify to feeling they have "lost" their autistic children. In the past, many families were told there was no hope for their autistic child, and even after the Bettelheim era of blaming "refrigerator mothers," families were advised to institutionalize their autistic children, to forget about them and have another child—much as Hugh and Tess put the island behind them and resign themselves to the conclusion that Jamie is gone.

Fiona discovers that Jamie has never left. But he is elusive, fleeing anything that might thrust him into the unknown. Fiona therefore makes the critical leap of reasoning that he can't be yanked out of his world into the family's world: instead, they must move into his world. The irony, of course, is that his world *is* theirs—just a part of it that they have abandoned. And so the family reunites with him, moving back onto the island and learning to recognize and work with, rather than against, the forces that have kept Jamie there.

Would that we parents similarly learn to recognize how to work *with* our children's autism: to recognize aspects that might lead us to untapped motivators and alternative ways of learning and doing. Would that we find a way to get autistic traits destigmatized, so that the fair-haired Coneellys among us can allow themselves to live comfortably and confidently alongside the "dark ones," now comfortable in their own skins, and fully embracing a lineage that includes the traits that make the "dark ones" who they are.

PARTING THOUGHTS

The four films we screened brought us through several stages in the development of positive identity and self-esteem, from initial self-identification all the way to the threshold of turning our identity outwards and engaging those who should be our natural allies. *Roan Inish*, with its metaphorical message to families about returning to roots and rediscovering what was really never lost, about working with rather than against, brings us full circle to where we started with *32 Short Films*: to rediscovering and affirming shared aspects of ourselves. *Smoke Signals* and *Breaking the Code*, each in its own way, add dimension to the circle by illuminating how to create a positive identity in the face of adversity. All four films teach us about constructing identity and self-awareness in positive ways, without sensationalizing, romanticizing, or demonizing autism or autistic people.

What we did with the film series involves such a simple idea, and is so easy to replicate. I'm convinced that such programs can inspire more of us—and our allies in the non-autistic majority—to think about ways to transcend our version of Indians watching Indians on TV, and to gain the insight and perspective necessary to advocate more effectively for ourselves, individually and collectively.

NOTES

1. Sue Rubin, author of the film *Autism Is A World*, wrote about "killing autism" in her 1995 essay of the same name. Her handicaps must loom large enough to render moot for her most questions about the positive, subtler aspects of autism. But it is also clear that she has fully internalized the equation of autism with individual impairment, and the false dichotomy that exists in mainstream conventional wisdom about the supposed discontinuity between low-functioning and high-functioning autism ("Acceptance vs. Cure"). I know many people whose very existence and developmental histories refute that dichotomy. See

Montgomery for one such person's eloquent thoughts on the matter, and follow the links in that article for more. Also see the "Getting the Truth Out" Web site, and follow its links at the end; they offer a good syllabus of writing in the autistic self-advocacy movement.

2. For example, nearly all people on the autism spectrum capable of doing so will acknowledge sensory issues to be a major factor in their lives, an integral part of their being autistic, and a dimension in which they diverge from the mainstream; yet sensory issues are nowhere present in the *DSM–IV* or *ICD–10* clinical definitions of autism. They are the elephant at the cocktail party that none of the guests seems willing to talk about—at least the cocktail party of clinicians who write the diagnostic manuals.

3. Valerie Paradiž explores some of the issues around identifying historical figures who may have been on the autism spectrum in "Outing Andy Warhol."

4. See, for example, Sinclair.

5. Regarding puns: when my son Jeremy was four years old, one day amid the eleventy-third repetition of his favorite Raffi tape, which features the lyric "I love to ate, ate, ate, ayples and banaynays" (it cycles through the long vowel sounds—"eat, eat, eat, eeples and baneenees," etc.), Jeremy sang along with "I love to ate, ate, ate, ayples and banaynays," and then grinned slyly at me and sang, "I love to seven, seven, seven. . . ."

6. I saw this in action recently at the self-advocacy session of the 2005 conference of the Autism National Committee (http://www.autcom.org).

7. I have written and spoken more extensively on this topic elsewhere (see Schwarz).

8. Autism Network International's annual conference/retreat; see Sinclair.

WORKS CITED

Breaking the Code. Dir. Herbert Wise. Perf. Derek Jacobi, Alun Armstrong, Richard Johnson, Harold Pinter, Amanda Root, Prunella Scales. *BBC/Mobil Masterpiece Theatre*, 1996.

"Getting The Truth Out" Web site. 2005. 26 December 2005. http://www.gettingthetruthout.org.

Harjo, Suzan Shown. "My New Year's resolution: No more fat 'Indian' food." *Indian Country Today*, 20-Jan-2005. *Indian Country Today Magazine*. 26 December 2005. http://www.indiancountry.com/content.cfm?id=1096410209.

Hodges, Andrew. "Alan Turing: a Short Biography." 1995. *The Alan Turing Homepage*. 26 December 2005. http://www.turing.org.uk/bio.

Montgomery, Cal. "Defining Autistic Lives." *Ragged Edge Online*. 26 December 2005. http://www.raggededgemagazine.com/reviews/ckmontrubin0605.html.

Paradiž, Valerie. "Outing Andy Warhol." *Disclosure and Asperger's Syndrome: Our Own Stories, proceedings of the Asperger's Association of New England Conference on Disclosure, Waltham, MA, March 2000*. Watertown, MA: Asperger's Association of New England.

———. *Elijah's Cup: A Family's Journey into the Community and Culture of High-Functioning Autism and Asperger's Syndrome*. Rev ed. London: Jessica Kingsley, 2005.

Rubin, Sue. "Killing Autism Is A Constant Battle." *Facilitated Communication Digest*. 4. 1 (November, 1995). 26 December 2005. http://soeweb.syr.edu/thefci/4-1rub2.htm.

———. "Acceptance versus Cure." *CNN Presents*. 26 December 2005. http://www.cnn.com/CNN/Programs/presents/shows/autism.world/notebooks/sue/notebook.html.

Schwarz, Phil. "Building Alliances: Community Identity and the Role of Allies in Autistic Self-Advocacy." *Ask and Tell: Self-Advocacy and Disclosure for People on the Autism Spectrum*. Ed. Stephen Shore. Shawnee Mission, KS: Autism Asperger Publishing, 2004. 143–76.

Sinclair, Jim. "Autism Network International: The Development Of A Community And Its Culture." 26 December 2005. http://www.jimsinclair.org/History_of_ANI.html.

Smoke Signals. Dir. Chris Eyre. Perf. Adam Beach, Evan Adams, Irene Bedard, Gary Farmer, Tantoo Cardinal. Miramax, 1998.

The Secret of Roan Inish. Dir. John Sayles. Perf. Jeni Courtney, Mick Lally, Eileen Colgan, Richard Sheridan, John Lynch, Susan Lynch, Cillian Byrne. Sony, 1994.

32 Short Films About Glenn Gould. Dir. François Girard. Perf. Colm Feore. Rhombus Media/National Film Board of Canada, 1993.

15 Alterity and Autism

Mark Haddon's *Curious Incident* in the Neurological Spectrum

James Berger

PRIME NUMBERS

Christopher Boone, the fifteen-year-old narrator and protagonist of Mark Haddon's *The Curious Incident of the Dog in the Night-Time*, likes prime numbers. Christopher has Asperger's syndrome and is a mathematical savant, and for him "prime numbers are like life. They are very logical but you could never work out the rules, even if you spent all your time thinking about them" (12). A prime number, of course, is a number divisible only by two integers—itself and one. Thus, 2, 3, 5, 7, 11, 13, 17, 19 and so on are prime numbers, whereas 4, 6, 9, 12, 15, 16, 18, 20, and so on, are not. As Christopher remarks, "[p]rime numbers are what is left when you have taken all the patterns away" (12).

Haddon's presentation of Christopher's thoughts on prime numbers suggests that they can serve as figures for the autistic subject: prime numbers do not mix; they are singular, indivisible, unfactorable. Their numbers are small in relation to the total number of integers, and yet there are an infinite number of them. Moreover, they are not alien to the overall number system, but intrinsic to it. Mathematics could not exist without these singular entities that, like inert elements in chemistry, are only apparent anomalies. A similar understanding has emerged with regard to autism. The *Diagnostic and Statistical Manual of Mental Disorders* (*DSM–IV*) emphasizes the isolation experienced by people with Asperger's, the "impairment in reciprocal social interaction"—the degree to which people with Asperger's "lack understanding of the conventions of social interaction" (82). *DSM–IV* also refers to restricted and repetitive patterns of behavior and interests, although noting that, unlike more severe forms of autism, people with Asperger's show normal cognitive and language development. At the same time, however, many writers on autism criticize what they regard as the "categorical approach" of the *DSM–IV* and speak instead of a "spectrum" of autistic features. There seems at present to be a broad consensus that, as Lorna Wing writes, "autism is not, as Kanner first thought, a unique or separate condition . . . but is closely related to a range of developmental disorders" (312). Further, this spectrum may not simply link diagnosable disorders, but extend through the whole human population. Temple Grandin, the noted animal scientist and memoirist with Asperger's, argues that highly talented people in many fields share certain autistic traits, so that "the genes that produce normal people with certain talents are likely to be the same genes that produce the abnormalities found at the extreme end of the same continuum," and thus "there is no black-and-white dividing line between normal and abnormal (179, 186). Oliver Sacks describes the extraordinary mimetic powers of the autistic artist Stephen Wiltshire as perhaps an evolutionary legacy of a part of the human mind that preceded symbolic and linguistic thinking (Sacks, *Anthropologist* 240–41); speaking of Temple Grandin, he describes an even vaster autistic continuum "extending from the animal to the spiritual, from the bovine to the transcendent . . . which we may call 'primitive' if we wish, but not 'pathological' " ("Foreword"16).[1]

The notion of an autistic spectrum has far-reaching significance for how we regard autism culturally and how we read Haddon's novel about a teenager with Asperger's syndrome. Because autistic disorders are (at least partly) genetic and neurological, our understandings of these disorders have changed with the rapid expansion of genetic and neurological knowledge over the past twenty years. The idea of a genetic-neurological spectrum of autism re-emphasizes and transforms Sacks's, Grandin's, and other writers' more humanist and spiritual suggestions of links between the autistic and the normal. Recent research in genetics and neurology shows both the almost unimaginable complexity of the physical workings of the brain and the minuteness of the differences that lead to what seem such different outcomes. Thus, longstanding philosophical and theological concepts of otherness have difficulty when confronted with contemporary neurology.[2] Sacks, for example, searches for alterity and transcendence through his narratives of neurological impairment and finds, rather, that alterity is not "other" at all—that radically different modes of consciousness and perception are parts of ordinary experience simply made more visible in moments of neurological impairment. This realization, grounded in genetics and neurology, makes clearer as well how the impairments of neurological conditions such as autism can also be linked to enhanced powers of memory, organization, and expression. If the mind is physical, biological, and closely related to the minds and neurological systems of animals, then we need not think of any mental process, product, or relation in terms of alterity or transcendence— unless we conclude that the mind contains and produces its own alterities and that the experience of otherness is not just a phenomenological, but a neurological reality, and so, in every sense, is not other at all.

Haddon's portrayal of Christopher falls within these clinical, neurological, philosophical, and popular frames. Haddon shows in great detail Christopher's difficulties with social interactions. His manner with others is wooden; he cannot stand to be touched and sometimes screams when someone touches him. He tells us that he feels more comfortable with animals than with people. His condition makes even his family relationships difficult, and the novel suggests that Christopher's autism was at least a partial cause of the failure of his parents' marriage. Christopher is extremely orderly: he must know at all times exactly what time it is; he knows precisely the contents of his pockets; he enjoys maps, diagrams, and lists. He is, in addition, extremely gifted in mathematics: though only fifteen, he is preparing to take the A-level exams in math, which lead to university entrance in England. All these features can be found in the clinical and popular literature on autism and Asperger's. Perhaps most significant, and encompassing these other traits, Christopher has enormous difficulty deciphering what other people are thinking or feeling. He cannot read body language or facial expressions. Christopher relates how his teacher showed him simple sketches of faces bearing schematic expressions, and that although he could interpret the basic "happy" and "sad" faces, any further complexity baffled him (2–3). As some writers on autism/Asperger's have put it, Christopher lacks a "theory of mind" and so has difficulty conceiving that others have feelings and perceptions different from his.[3]

Haddon, who has experience working with autistic people and clearly is familiar with the clinical and popular literature, has created a character who, unlike modernist and postmodernist antecedents, exhibits a clinically distinct neurological impairment rather than a more vague conceptual alterity. I am not arguing, of course, that this form of representation is an advance over the earlier ones, but it is certainly different and must be approached in different terms—in particular, with more attention to its clinical and scientific models. At the same time, Christopher is not simply a "case" in this novel. He is both the protagonist and narrator, and so Haddon engages here in imagining an Asperger's language, consciousness, and literary style.

ASPERGER'S AND NARRATIVE

Christopher strives for an absolute literality in language. He cannot understand, and so tries always to avoid, metaphors, jokes, and lies. When his mother calls him a good boy because of his honesty, he tells us that he is not honest because he is good, but because "I can't tell lies" (19): he is cognitively incapable of lying. As he says earlier, explaining why his narrative must be nonfiction, "I find it hard to imagine things which did not happen to me" (5). Metaphors and jokes are incomprehensible to him because, like facial expressions, they have multiple meanings. For this reason, he dislikes his own name which, as he tells us, is a metaphor: to carry Christ, or the bearer of Christ. Christopher does not want a name that means something else, he says: "I want my name to mean me" (16). Every case of figurative—that is, counterfactual—language seems to lead to more cases, unceasingly, leaving Christopher "shaky and scared," with a case of cognitive vertigo, and this is why he dislikes "proper novels" (20, 19). On the couple of occasions when Christopher does employ a figure of speech, he quickly informs us that he has used a simile and not a metaphor. Thus, when he writes that a policeman's hairy nose "looked as if there were two very small mice hiding in his nostrils" (17), he assures us that this is indeed what the man's nose looked like. Similes can be true, whereas metaphors—and jokes and novels—are always lies.[4]

Language, as Christopher perceives, threatens always to veer out of control. Even when referents are particular, the signs for them must always be general, and so the name can never mean only the thing; as Kenneth Burke puts it, the thing is the sign for the word rather than the other way round (361). The world, for Christopher, is a world of things, and there are so many of them but so few words. How then can language adequately organize reality? Christopher prefers maps, diagrams, algorithms—stable forms that represent the world in ways that slippery words cannot. Words, evidently, refer in large part only to themselves, and clearly are in league with the impossible, shifting meanings of human faces and with a social world whose most prominent traits are concealment and untruth.

Christopher objects to language *per se* insofar as it is figurative and thus false, or at least ambiguous. It is an inadequate tool to organize the world as he perceives it, and in this conclusion Christopher joins Temple Grandin, one of whose chief themes is the predominance in autistic people of visual over verbal thinking.[5] He objects also to narrative, which we know as the most characteristic mode of organizing and giving meaning to human experience and action over time. Time is a topic that preoccupies and troubles Christopher. The problem with time, he tells us, is that it is the universal mechanism of change and unknowability. "[T]ime is not like space," in which positions and relationships remain constant. One can construct a physical or mental map of an area of space that is a true representation; if "you put something down somewhere, like a protractor or a biscuit," the object will not change its position on its own, and your map will remind you of its position and its relation to other objects (156). With an adequate map, you can always find yourself in space.

Time, however, cannot be mapped in this way, for a great part of its terrain—the future—cannot be known. To become lost in time, then, is a real possibility for Christopher. This anxiety explains Christopher's preoccupation with knowing exactly what time it is, and his obsessions about personal daily schedules and railway timetables. "[T]his is why I like timetables," he explains, "because they make sure you don't get lost in time" (158). And yet, the timetable or schedule is not like a map of space, for it does not represent an actual, current reality, but is more like a preliminary sketch of circumstances that may or may not ultimately come to pass. And Christopher, as an outstanding student of modern physics, is aware as well that mapping relationships in time depends on the position and relative speed of the observer, and therefore, "because nothing can travel faster than the speed of light, this means that we can only know about a fraction of the things that go on in the universe" (he provides a helpful diagram to illustrate his point: 157).

But why not narrative, for narrative is precisely the mode of knowledge that, in general, situates the human subject in time? Christopher is, after all, composing the narrative that is the text of this novel. However, he makes clear that in composing this narrative he is not writing "a proper novel," but rather a mystery novel, which in his view is quite different. A mystery novel is a puzzle, and resembles an algorithm more than it does a chronological narrative encrusted in figurative language. A neighbor's dog has been murdered. Christopher himself came upon the dog's body. Having located the body in space, it remains for him to locate the murderer and place murderer and victim in a mappable spatial relation. A mystery, for Christopher, exists to be solved, for the crime has already been committed and its effects have been discovered. All that remains is the missing piece of a contemporaneous spatial puzzle, to which temporal narrative may be of assistance but is not essential.

Christopher's idea of the mystery novel differs significantly, and obviously, from most contemporary narrative theory. For Gary Saul Morson, the essential quality of narrative lies in its emphasis on the unknowable possibilities inherent in any present moment, and thus the contingency of all events. An actor may do one thing, or he may do another, and there is no law of narrative physics or chemistry that finally will determine his act. Time, Morson argues, must be "open" in order for a moment fully to be present, and for it to have significance, and so "for a present moment to matter, to have real weight, more than one thing must be possible at the next moment. . . . In open time, at least one thing that did not happen could have" (62). Time's motion, insofar as it enters narrative, is not mechanical: it requires consciousness and willed interventions, and "*now* is not just yesterday plus one unit of time" (64). The world described by narrative is not a puzzle lacking a single piece, or an algorithm all of whose variables will ultimately be identified. Contingency is at the center of human conscious experience, and narrative, in Morson's view, is the most accurate depiction human beings have devised for portraying and analyzing it. "One needs story," Morson concludes, "because the world is imperfect. One needs story because there is no goal. And one needs story because things do not fit" (66).

Christopher would share Morson's premise—that narrative is the verbal expression of the contingency of human actions and relations in time—but reject his conclusion that this expression represents a form of knowledge that is both true and edifying. Christopher wishes for a form of knowledge and expression that is spatial, not temporal, and that therefore can be certain, not contingent. Christopher's attitudes toward language and narrative appear to place him in the tradition of longing for a perfect, Adamic, Cratyllic, pre-Babel, pre-Saussurean language of pure correspondence in which signifier, signified, and referent merge, and all slippage and ambiguity are banished. Christopher lives, or would like to live, in a world of physical objects located in space, in a present that does not change significantly from moment to moment. It would be a world of routine and habit, of problems or puzzles that need to be solved, but not of personal growth or of life-changing decisions.

EVOLUTIONARY NEUROLOGY, THE
AUTISTIC SPECTRUM, AND LANGUAGE

And yet, as biological anthropologist Terrence Deacon argues, we may see Christopher's approach to language as neither alien nor mystical but, rather, as part of the human evolutionary legacy. Deacon adapts Charles Saunders Peirce's analysis of the sign in terms of icon, index, and symbol to describe the concurrent and mutually reinforcing evolutions of human language and brain physiology. An icon, as Peirce defines it, is a sign that stands for itself, or that *is* the thing it represents. The icon exists "such as it is, positively and without reference to anything else" (Peirce 383) and is determined "by virtue of its own internal nature" (391). A mathematical diagram whose logic and references all are internal would, for Peirce, be an icon. The icon of a deity is understood by a believer not to represent, but to *be* the deity. For Deacon, any animal, however primitive its nervous system, must have iconic recognition. It must be able to recognize a thing as itself: an object as an object, food as food, a predator as a predator. Iconic recognition is, Deacon writes, the "default position" of consciousness (76), "the base on which all other forms of representation are built . . . the bottom of the interpretive hierarchy" (77). The index, in Peirce's thinking, is a sign that points to an object or to another sign. A proper name is an index, as is a symptom of a disease (Peirce 391). A flash of lightning would be an index of an atmospheric condition; smoke might be an index of fire. Whereas with an icon there is an identity between sign and thing and thus no need for interpretation, an index relies on contiguity or causation: as Deacon explains, there must be a physical association between the indexical sign and its referent (82). Deacon cites as an example in animal behavior the cries of vervet monkeys, in which a particular utterance indicates the approach of a particular predator (leopard, snake, or eagle). Such indexical reference, Deacon argues, is not language proper because it is based on a "necessary association"; the vervet cries "rely on a relatively stable correlation with what they refer, in order to refer" (67). Genuine linguistic or symbolic reference, conversely, is not based on direct association or contiguity, but on more general, systemic relationships. For Peirce, use of the symbol requires always a third term—not just sign and referent, but also an "interpretant," a sign that governs the interpretation of the relation between sign and referent, and subsequently itself requires an interpretant to facilitate its own interpretation. Thus, the use of symbols, in Peirce's view, can be understood only in the context of a universe of symbols, each requiring the others to achieve its meaning. Deacon, echoing Peirce, asserts that the relation between symbol and object relies on the "complex function of the relation the symbol has to other symbols" rather than simply to the object to which it refers (83).

For Deacon, all animals with relatively complex nervous systems, certainly all mammals, are capable of indexical thinking. They can see objects not simply as themselves but in relation to others. A dog or cat knows the meaning of the sound of a can being opened, for the sound is consistently followed by a meal. Indexical thinking, Deacon observes, is an enormously effective evolutionary adaptation. For every animal but ourselves, it has served admirably, and for our primate ancestors was the only form of thinking until about two million years ago. The evolution of human language, Deacon argues, is in essence the shift from indexical to symbolic thinking, a gradual "restructuring event" in which, over the course of nearly two million years (our current linguistic abilities were achieved between 200,000 and 100,000 years ago), "we let go of one associative strategy and grabbed hold of another, higher order one" (93). In Deacon's theory of co-evolution, language and the brain evolved together, and "symbol use itself must have been the prime mover" for extraordinary development of the human brain. "Language has given rise to a brain which is strongly biased to employ the one mode of associative learning that is most critical to it" (336). Human beings are, Deacon concludes, "incarnations, so to speak, of the processes of using words" (322).

This process of incarnation, however—this shift from indexical to symbolic thinking—was lengthy and difficult for, as the animals around us demonstrate, indexical, associative thinking is quite effective. Moreover, as Deacon argues, the two types of thinking are in certain ways incompatible. In order to learn to use symbols—that is, to work with signs whose meanings are general, abstract, unstable, and dependent on a system of signs—the use of indices, with their invariable, associative meanings, must be unlearned or suppressed. Although symbolic thinking depends on indexical thinking for its most fundamental sense of reference (as pointing toward, or immediate association of one thing with another, just as indexical thinking depends on iconic perception for its ability to identify a thing as such), as we learn to think in symbols and use the conceptual flights and shortcuts that symbols provide, we must forget the potential infinitude of one-to-one concrete correspondences in which (living in a world of language) we would drown were our thinking to remain indexical.

This potential drowning in indices seems to describe life with autism. Deacon refers to autism as an instance of genetic damage to symbol-using capacities, citing the often extraordinary abilities of people on the autistic spectrum for memory, mathematical calculation, and mimesis, and their difficulties in matters of social and linguistic interpretation. Deacon notes that although people marvel at these "savant" skills, non-autistic people, without realizing it, are themselves savants and prodigies at *language*, miraculously acquiring entire languages as children in just a few years, and thereafter, like autistic savants, applying "our one favored cognitive style to everything"

(416). People on the autistic spectrum are, for Deacon, people whose thinking is more indexical and less symbolic.

THE ASPERGER'S DETECTIVE,
GENRE, AND "SOCIAL AUTISM"

The Curious Incident of the Dog in the Night-Time is more than a fictional case study or a contribution to literary theory. It has a plot and a genre, and to understand this book more thoroughly, it is necessary to explore how its view of autism and its thinking about language intersect with its generic status as a detective novel.

As the novel opens, Christopher goes for a walk at night and discovers that a neighbor's dog, a poodle named Wellington, has been murdered, stabbed with a garden fork. He had been fond of the dog, and so decides to find out who killed him. The novel is Christopher's narrative of his search, which he regards as a mystery novel, with the added feature that his novel is true.

As a person with Asperger's syndrome, Christopher makes an excellent detective. He notices things: when a teacher compliments him on being clever, Christopher replies that he is merely "observant" (25). His powers of observation, moreover, rely on precise spatial memories: they are associative, indexical, and made far more difficult by social interaction. As he says, "when I am in a new place and there are lots of people there it is even harder because people are not like cows and flowers and grass and they can talk to you and do things that you don't expect, so you have to notice everything that is in the place, and also you have to notice things that might happen as well" (143). His indexical mode of thinking is confused and threatened when it enters a world of symbolic action, and yet his observant, associative mind gives him advantages in activities that require logical thinking within strict regulations. "[T]hat is why I am good at chess and maths and logic," Christopher explains, "because most people are almost blind and they don't see most things and there is lots of spare capacity in their heads and it is filled with things which aren't connected and are silly, like 'I'm worried that I might have left the gas cooker on'" (144). Christopher's Asperger's mind focuses on a particular task to the exclusion of all others, notices everything relevant to that task, but is overwhelmed if faced with too much information on other matters. Christopher surely would have noticed at once Poe's purloined letter sitting openly on the table.

Christopher's ratiocinative abilities and social inabilities are functions not only of his status as a person with Asperger's but also of his generic status as detective in a detective novel, for the detective is generally both an acute observer and a social outsider. Furthermore, the crime he initially investigates often opens the way to deeper and more dangerous inquiries into underlying social disorder and corruption. What Christopher discovers—or, more accurately, what readers discover through Christopher's investigation—is that the social order is itself on the autistic spectrum. That is, his society is characterized by its members' isolation and inability to communicate with each other. He finds this first in his family. His mother is frustrated to the point of despair by her inability to have a normal maternal relationship with Christopher, and her marriage suffers, especially because her husband often blames her for her problems with their son. She leaves with her neighbor Roger Shears, but judging from what we see in the novel, this relationship does not seem especially close. Christopher's father then embarks on a failed relationship with Mrs. Shears, and their emotional and communicative impasse leads to the murder of the dog. Christopher's father seems a solitary, brooding man given to violent outbursts. Rather than explain his separation from his wife to Christopher, he ends her existence as a member of the family by telling Christopher she is dead.

The novel's depiction of social isolation extends beyond the family. As Christopher walks through his neighborhood, knocking on doors and interviewing neighbors about the dog's murder, we find that the neighbors barely know each other. The first person Christopher talks to wears a T-shirt that thematizes a lack of social connection: "Beer—Helping Ugly People Have Sex For Over 2,000 Years." Christopher asks him, "Do you know who killed Wellington?"

> I did not look at his face. I do not like looking at people's faces, especially if they are strangers. He did not say anything for a few seconds.
> Then he said, "Who are you?"
> I said, "I'm Christopher Boone from number 36 and I know you. You're Mr. Thompson."
> He said, "I'm Mr. Thompson's brother."
> I said, "Do you know who killed Wellington?"
> He said, "Who the fuck is Wellington?" (36).

Christopher has better luck with his two succeeding interviews. One woman, whose name he doesn't know, greets him, "It's Christopher, isn't it?" (37); and the next, whom he knows as Mrs. Alexander, says, "You're Christopher, aren't you?" (39). These neighbors know who he is—the kid down the street with some kind of disability—but clearly have never spoken to him. Christopher tells Mrs. Alexander, "I don't like talking to strangers," but apparently no one in the neighborhood likes talking to strangers much, and everyone is more or less a stranger to each other. And yet, the people are not unfriendly to Christopher, and try to be helpful. The unnamed woman warns Christopher, "You be careful, young man"; the man with the unusual T-shirt asks, "Look son, do you really think you should be going around asking questions like this?"; and Mrs. Alexander wants to converse with Christopher and goes inside to prepare a soft drink and cookies for him though he leaves before she returns. Their desire for connection conflicts with a broader inhibition that appears to arise from social and economic factors.

Christopher's family and neighbors are working class. His father runs a small home heating repair service with one employee, and his mother is a secretary who cannot spell very well (as we see from her letters to Christopher) and who has worked only at temporary jobs. The city where they live, Swindon, lies seventy miles west of London and has a population of about 180,000, with significant south Asian and Caribbean communities. Since the 1980s, although its traditional manufacturing sector has declined, Swindon has developed thriving mid- and high-tech industries. Unemployment on the whole, however, has risen, wages have been flat, and affordable housing remains scarce.[6] Haddon portrays Swindon as exemplary of a post-Thatcher England characterized by vibrant high-tech industries coexisting with declining social services and education, rising unemployment and homelessness. It seems to lack social networks and civic, community, and class organizations of the sort that E. P. Thompson described as helping to form a distinct working-class culture in England from the eighteenth through the mid-twentieth centuries.[7] Nor do we see any evidence of extended families: the small detached houses of Swindon are inhabited only by nuclear families, or fragments of them. This is a social world that, for reasons Haddon does not investigate, has been flattened, atomized, each household an isolated and fragile entity.

By means of Christopher's role as detective (a generic role strongly marked by autistic qualities), Haddon depicts a pervasive social autism. The administrative bureaucracy of this society is not malign; Christopher does not uncover the sorts of corruption and police violence found by hard-boiled detectives such as Sam Spade and Philip Marlowe, or to a lesser degree by his model Sherlock Holmes. The police, in fact, are always patient, helpful, and reasonable in *Curious Incident*. But the police and the contracting welfare state can do nothing to address the weakening of social and family bonds that Christopher's investigation reveals. At the same time, however, although Christopher can be read as a figure for a broader social autism, this novel is not primarily a work of social or political critique. Its political points are not developed, and the extended metaphor of a social autism is offered but then withdrawn. The novel's focus returns, at last, to the family, to human emotion, and to difficulties in personal relationships that appear to go beyond or beneath any particular social structures. In spite of his apparent critique of a specifically post-Thatcher social fragmentation, Haddon's deeper explanation of social dysfunction seems to rely more on neurology and notions of the autistic spectrum than on politics. In this reading, Christopher, as a person with Asperger's, is not a trope for a social autism that has political or economic causes; rather, the novel's instances of social disconnection, anomie, and violence are products of autistic tendencies that are wired, in some degree, into all human neural systems. Christopher—with his resistance to symbolic thinking and ambiguity, his abhorrence at being touched, his difficulties in understanding others' thoughts and feelings—is an extreme example of qualities possessed in lesser amounts by everyone.

"... A LOUD WAILING NOISE, LIKE AN ANIMAL ON A NATURE PROGRAM ..."

Christopher acknowledges that he has trouble with what philosophers and, more recently, writers on autism call "theory of mind"—the ability to conceive of other people possessing separate minds and imagine what they might be thinking or feeling. Christopher remembers his teacher telling his parents that he would always find this skill very difficult, but Christopher reframes his limitation as a puzzle, for "[i]f something is a puzzle," Christopher tells us, "there is always a way of solving it" (116). His solution, however, consists of regarding other minds as he regards his own. People's minds, he concludes, are like computers, and consciousness is a picture on a screen—without, he cautions us, any subject of consciousness there to watch it. What we may regard as the subject watching the screen is merely another picture. Even emotion, for Christopher, does not distinguish human consciousness from computer cognition: "feelings are just having a picture on the screen in your head . . . and if it is a happy picture [you] smile and if it is a sad picture [you] cry" (119).

But, significantly, Christopher provides these thoughts on theory of mind just after the most intense emotional and linguistic event in the novel to that point: his discovery and reading of the letters from his supposedly dead mother that his father had hidden from him. In these letters we witness for the first time a voice, a mind, unmediated by Christopher's consciousness, and the mother's voice breaks the novel apart. These letters show an extreme instance of another cognitive and emotional mode of being, and Christopher's Holmesian, Asperger's puzzle-solving method of apprehending this other mind proves inadequate.

Christopher's mother's letters are extraordinary. Their sudden shift in voice and sensibility brings to the novel the complexity of adult emotions and social and sexual relations. They clearly contrast both with the autistic tone and sensibility of Christopher's narration and with the broader social autism the novel portrays. Simultaneously chatty and emotionally intense, the letters tell Christopher of the deterioration of her marriage and her decision to leave the home, relating the mother's frequent rages as she reaches "the end of [her] tether" (107) or has "lost [her] rag" (108) at some action of Christopher or her husband. She "cried and cried and cried" (107) after one incident, and her decision to leave "broke my heart" (109). She tells of household violence, of hitting her husband and of throwing food during a failed attempt to get Christopher to eat, and of her sorrow over these actions: "he told me I was being stupid and said I should pull myself together and I hit him, which was wrong, but I was so upset" (107). Christopher, however, cannot understand these emotions. He responds physically. "It was like the room was swinging from side to side, as if it was at the top of a really tall building and the building was swinging backward and forward in a strong wind" (112). This vertigo is the same feeling he described earlier when he wrote about his physical reaction to false statements. Thinking of things that aren't true, he wrote, "makes me feel shaky and scared, like I do when I'm standing on the top of a very tall building" (19). Apparently, his pain results from a terrible cognitive disruption: his mother is not dead; his father has lied to him. The stability of clear, unambiguous signification has been blown away by the winds of an emotional life that is steeped in, and can only be expressed in, the dangerous ambiguities of language. Christopher's difficulties in constructing a theory of mind with regard to other people is, as Haddon portrays it, entirely of a piece with his difficult relation to language.

The emotional climax of the novel, however, involves a moment of linguistic breakdown on the part of Christopher's mother: her reaction to the news that her husband had told Christopher she was dead.

> And then Mother said, "Oh my God."
> And then she didn't say anything for a long while. And then she made a loud wailing noise like an animal on a nature program on television.
> And I didn't like her doing this because it was a loud noise, and I said, "Why are you doing that?" (193).

Christopher's mother's response is nonlinguistic and nonsymbolic, an immediate outburst of feeling. It could be called "indexical," in that it points toward or bears a causal relation to an emotion although it does not, in any general, symbolic sense, represent the emotion. As Christopher notes, it links her to animals. In literary terms, her wailing places her in the lineage of William Faulkner's Benjy and Don DeLillo's Wilder, whose cries reinforce their separation from the symbolic realm.[8] But in this case, the nonlinguistic outburst is uttered by the character in this novel most thoroughly immersed in language, whose letters serve as counterpoint to Christopher's hostility to the resources and perspectives of language. Unlike Benjy or Wilder, Christopher's mother is not some "other," outside of language. She is both a competent, indeed enthusiastic, user of language and a person capable of an emotional loss of language that connects her with animal behavior—and also to her son, who is prone to screaming tantrums. Christopher's mother's "loud wailing noise" as an emotional center for the novel indicates powerfully that, for Haddon, all symbolic and emotional activity falls on a broad spectrum of neurological response, with no clear break between the linguistic and nonlinguistic. And the mother's wailing, we should note, is in response to a quintessential symbolic act: the father's lie, his denial of her existence.

Yet Christopher cannot understand his mother's wailing. He regards it in terms of animal behavior, does not see it as similar to his own emotional outbursts, and, sadly, rejects the emotional connection it invites. Immediately after her wailing, Christopher's mother asks him if she can hold his hand, "[j]ust for once. Just for me. Will you? I won't hold it hard." He refuses: "I don't like people holding my hand" (194). It is Christopher's affliction that, in a sense, *everyone* is other to him; every experience that is not his is other. The ambiguities, imprecisions, and necessary generalizations of symbolization are partly what make possible human contact and understanding, together with the emotional, physical forms of connection we share with animals. Christopher's failure to understand his mother's wailing—a failure of empathy—lies along the same neurological spectrum as his inability to understand her letters (or, indeed, to catch the most ordinary linguistic nuances).

Christopher's particular neurological constitution seems to restrict his symbolic actions to sophisticated forms of decoding and puzzle solving, and causes him to regard all others as other. This neurologically imposed auto-alterity reads partly as humor. Christopher's deadpan depictions of people's reactions to him frequently are very funny—as, for instance, when on a London subway, Christopher violently refuses a fellow passenger's offer to help him: "And I said, 'I've got a Swiss Army knife and it has a saw blade and it could cut someone's fingers off.' And she said, 'OK, buddy. I'm going to take that as a no'" (184). Overall, however, Haddon's depiction of Christopher's isolation, especially from his parents, seems intended to convey and produce an enormous, though complex, sadness. Even with the strengths and resources he displays throughout the novel, Christopher is terribly vulnerable; he is also desperately loved, but unable to return that love in recognizable ways. He needs protection, and can never be protected enough, can never be loved enough. He is always, irreducibly, strange, irreducibly himself—always a prime number. The novel ends with his triumph: having passed his A-levels with honors, he writes that now he will attend university. "And then I will get a First Class Honors degree and I will become a scientist. And I know I can do this because I went to London on my own, and because I solved the mystery of **Who Killed Wellington?** and I found my mother and I was brave and I wrote a book and that means I can do anything" (221). But this triumph, though genuine and impressive, does not obviate the sadness of his untouchability. At the same time, however, this sadness is not Christopher's. It belongs, rather, to his parents and, to generalize from my own reaction, to readers who do not have Asperger's.

ALTERITY IS RELATIVE

The novel places us, then, in a complicated situation. Christopher's social and emotional isolation reads as a terrible sadness, heightened by the irony of his incomplete awareness of it (which is, perhaps, what truly makes it isolation). This isolation, as a neurological given, can in part be ameliorated through education or medication, but can never be entirely overcome. At the same time, as this novel presents it, no person truly is other to another. We all are connected by nonsymbolic, indexical, and emotional bonds that we share with other animals, as well as by symbolic bonds. Moreover, our symbolic capacities are built on and cannot exist apart from the earlier, nonsymbolic cognitive structures; and all of us live, think, and interact along a spectrum of symbolic and nonsymbolic capacities. Yet, as this novel also suggests, this spectrum includes the autistic spectrum and its tendencies toward isolation.

This tendency toward isolation is social and political, as we observed earlier, a product of the late capitalist, post-Thatcher weakening of social bonds. In other forms of social life, the novel appears to imply, bonds would be stronger and tendencies toward isolation and anomie less pronounced. But, as Christopher's precisely observed neurological condition suggests, the tendency toward isolation is, finally, irreducibly neurological. Christopher is, on one level, a metaphor for the social autism that surrounds him. He is also and, for the purposes of this novel, more fundamentally an *instance* of an autistic tendency whose bases are biological and whose manifestations pervade individual and social life.

Shortly after his mother's collapse into wailing, Christopher describes his favorite dream. His mother's wailing, I want to stress again, is not an exit from the symbolic or the social realms. She had been banished by a symbolic act of betrayal: her *letters* had been hidden and she was narrated out of her son's life. Her wailing is her first utterance on returning to the social and symbolic realms, at least with regard to her family. This animal sound is her re-entry into a social-symbolic world from which she had been erased. Her cry, emerging from her deepest organic and cognitive being, protests and rejects isolation and silence. Thus, the close juxtaposition late in the novel of the mother's wailing with Christopher's favorite dream emphasizes unequivocally Haddon's view that alterity is relative, not absolute. Everyone desires connection, community, and love. Christopher, after all, searches for his lost mother and has ambitions to succeed in school and university. Yet everyone maintains a sector of self that rejects social-symbolic contact and is terrified of touch.

Christopher's dream is an apocalyptic vision in which nearly everyone on earth dies of a virus. This virus, however, is not biological, but semantic: "people catch it because of the meaning of something an infected person says and the meaning of what they do with their faces when they say it" (198). Because the virus can spread through televised images and dialogue as well as through personal contact, it spreads rapidly; soon, the only people left are people like Christopher who cannot understand facial expressions or the shifting meanings of symbols. In this new world, populated only by autistic people and devoid of ambiguities, Christopher feels liberated. He knows that "no one is going to talk to me or touch me or ask me a question" (199). He can eat whatever he wants, play computer games all day, drive cars, and when he goes home, "it's not Father's house anymore, it's mine" (200). When the dream is over, he says, "I am happy" (200).

Christopher's deepest wish, it seems, is that the world as a site of meaning—the social-symbolic world—be obliterated. He wishes a reversion to an indexical world consisting only of objects in which signs, presumably, would be either unnecessary or perfect, unvarying emblems for the things themselves. Perhaps, in this world, Christopher would lose his own false, metaphorical name and would discover his true one. In any event, through Christopher's dream, Haddon portrays the apocalyptic imagination as a violent opposition to ambiguity and symbolization—an interpretation very much in keeping with many of the central apocalyptic texts and commentaries.[9] Haddon further implies that the apocalyptic imagination is a form of autistic thinking, and that autistic thinking tends toward apocalypticism. The urge toward a symbolic reduction so complete that it requires global annihilation, in this view, is part of the human evolutionary-neurological inheritance. Just as (as in Christopher's mother's case), we can never be sufficiently emotionally and symbolically connected to others, Christopher's dream implies that neither can we ever be sufficiently alone. Both these tendencies and desires exist together, in all people, and in this sense we might read *Curious Incident* as a neurological *psychomacheia*, a drama of the struggle within every soul between opposing positions on the neurological spectrum. Once again, if this interpretation is valid, the social and political conditions depicted in this novel become secondary to, or particular manifestations of conditions and conflicts of, our neurology. The ideology of neurology trumps traditional ideology critique.

The problem with this interpretation and its corollaries, however, lies in the amount of *care* bestowed on Christopher, the avatar of isolation and apocalypse, by the other characters and, again to generalize from my own experience, by the novel's readers. Why should he be an object of care? And why especially should he be an object of care when he cannot reciprocate that care in expected ways? One cares, I think, for Christopher because of his vulnerability, his needs, his limits. The novel presents him continually in the context of this care, though Christopher seems oblivious to it. Haddon seems almost to present this care as a moral imperative. But rather than indicating reasons for this imperative, Haddon presents it as a fact: his parents care, and others who come in contact with him care, and the reader who encounters him, presumably, cares. One *must* care because one *does* care, rather than the reverse. His vulnerability, which manifests itself through his symbolic and social limitations, demands that one bestow care. Yet, as I have argued, these symbolic and social limitations—which constitute his vulnerability and thus the imperative to care for him—render him both different from and similar to others. His autistic qualities locate him on a neurological spectrum shared by all people: one empathizes with him, and empathizes even with his inability to empathize; one cares even for his inability to care. And this is because, I think, all of us share, in part, this lack of empathy and care, this wish for isolation, even the urge to annihilate the social and symbolic world. It is, perhaps, the absolute self-sufficiency and absolute vulnerability and need of the infant that ultimately demands this care.

But this care requires a social setting: families, communities, institutions. The urge to negate social and symbolic structures also has a place in those same structures. Although care for radical vulnerability may be based in our neurology, different social arrangements and institutions make possible different types and degrees of caring; and though the apocalyptic-autistic sensibility may be a neurological constant, again, different forms of social organization can channel urges toward social-symbolic negation in different directions and with different results—toward art, disciplined spiritual emptying, or other single-minded peaceful pursuits; or toward genocide, war, or greed-inspired destruction of the natural world. In this sense, Haddon's precise depiction of Christopher's social world may not be merely a realist red herring subordinated to implacable neurological foundations. Caring for the most vulnerable, fostering their gifts and their agency, and learning from them is more possible in some societies than in others, and to identify obstacles to caring is a beginning of social critique.

NOTES

1. Gyasi Burks-Abbott criticizes readings of *Curious Incident* that take Christopher as representative of all people with Asperger's. As he points out, the published work of Donna Williams, Dawn Prince-Hughes, and Temple Grandin demonstrates that people with Asperger's can indeed write books themselves, contrary to a comment made by Haddon in an interview. It is important to keep in mind that Haddon's character occupies a particular point on the autistic spectrum. He is not a synecdoche, nor I believe, meant to be. I argue that Haddon uses the autistic spectrum and Christopher's place on it to explore questions about language and social relations, and that the neurological grounding of our understanding of the autistic spectrum makes these inquiries possible in the particular ways that Haddon pursues them. Haddon *uses* the disabled character, and this use raises ethical questions central to the field of disability studies. I do not have space to address these ethical questions here, but an important conclusion of my argument is that in Haddon's understanding of human neurological features as a continuum, the presumed other is not other in any radical sense, which therefore mitigates the ethical problem of speaking for or about the other. This solution does not, of course, in any way fully address the problem of dominant groups' representations of suppressed or stigmatized subjects.
2. The other as wholly other—the sacred, the sublime, the abject, the Lacanian real, the Levinasian other, in some discussions the traumatic—must be, by definition, off the spectrum, inconceivable and unrepresentable. See my "Falling Towers" for a discussion of the relation between representations of linguistic impairment and notions of alterity.
3. See Baron-Cohen, Baron-Cohen et.al., and Frith for discussions of theory of mind in relation to autism. Although Grandin agrees with the thesis that people on the autistic spectrum lack, to some degree, an ability to grasp other people's perspectives, others with autism and Asperger's object to this position. See "A

Discussion About Theory of Mind: From an Autistic Perspective" for a selection of comments.

4. The philosopher Donald Davidson argues provocatively that metaphors do not have some hidden, alternative meaning that is either substituted for a surface meaning or links two previously unrelated meanings, or that radically disrupts an established meaning. Davidson argues instead that a metaphor simply means what it says—that there is no such thing as metaphorical meaning; there is only literal meaning. Therefore, for Davidson, as for Christopher, metaphors are lies. The only way to distinguish a lie from a metaphor is by understanding its use—that is, its place in a broader social context; and, of course, it is the realm of social understanding where Christopher's competence most falters.

5. This linguistic incapacity along the autistic spectrum varies. Prince-Hughes, in her memoir, stresses that social difficulties can coexist with verbal fluency, an observation supported by the research of Tager-Flusberg, who reports that autism's social and communicative impairments may "not have any identifiable influence on the course of grammatical development" (175).

6. For information on socio-economic conditions in Swindon, refer to *Swindon Borough Council Review of Homelessness Services*.

7. The decline of working-class social institutions and practices is portrayed compellingly in post-Thatcher films like *The Full Monty* and *Brassed Off*. See also sociologist Robert Putnam's analysis of the decline of comparable American social practices in *Bowling Alone*.

8. In *The Sound and the Fury*, Benjy's incomprehensible moaning is described as "hopeless and prolonged. It was nothing. Just sound. It might have been all time and injustice and sorrow become vocal for an instant" (288). In *White Noise*, after Wilder has cried continuously for seven hours, his father imagines he has "just returned from a period of wandering in some remote and holy place" (79), to say "nameless things in . . . an ancient dirge all the more impressive for its resolute monotony" (78).

9. The Book of Revelation contrasts the purity and incommensurability of the New Jerusalem with the economic and sexual exchanges that characterize Babylon. Žižek glosses the "second death" referred to in Revelation 20:6, 14 as the extinguishing of the symbolic order that completes the destruction of the physical world (*Sublime Object*, 132–34; *Looking Awry*, 22–23). See also Kermode and Berger (*After the End*) for interpretations of apocalyptic desire as a wish to end ambiguity.

WORKS CITED

Baron-Cohen, Simon. *Mindblindness: An Essay on Autism and Theory of Mind*. Cambridge MA: MIT P, 1995.

Baron-Cohen, Simon, Helen Tager-Flusberg and Donald J. Cohen, eds. *Understanding Other Minds: Perspectives From Developmental Cognitive Neuroscience*. Oxford and New York: Oxford UP, 2000.

Berger, James. *After the End: Representations of Post-Apocalypse*. Minneapolis: U of Minnesota P, 1999.

———. "Falling Towers and Postmodern Wild Children: Oliver Sacks, Don DeLillo, and Turns Against Language." *PMLA* 120 (2005): 341–61.

Brassed Off. Dir. Mark Herman. Miramax, 1997.

Burke, Kenneth. "What Are the Signs of What? A Theory of 'Entitlement.'" *Language as Symbolic Action: Essays on Life, Literature, and Method*. Berkeley: U of California P, 1966. 358–79.

DSM–IV: Diagnostic and Statistical Manual of Mental Disorders. Washington, DC: American Psychiatric Association, 1994.

Davidson, Donald. "What Metaphors Mean." *Inquiries into Truth and Interpretation*. Oxford and New York: Clarendon P, 1984. 245–64.

Deacon, Terrence W. *The Symbolic Species: The Co-evolution of Language and the Brain*. New York and London: Norton, 1997.

DeLillo, Don. *White Noise*. New York: Viking, 1985.

"A Discussion About Theory of Mind: From an Autistic Perspective." 26 July 2007. From Autism Europe's Congress 2000. www.autistics.org/library/AE2000-ToM. html.

Faulkner, William. *The Sound and the Fury*. 1924. New York: Vintage, 1990.

Frith, Uta. *Autism: Explaining the Enigma*. Oxford UK, Cambridge MA: Blackwell, 1989.

The Full Monty. Dir. Peter Cattaneo. Fox Searchlight Pictures, 1997.

Grandin, Temple. *Thinking in Pictures: and Other Reports from My Life with Autism*. New York: Vintage, 1996.

Kermode, Frank. *The Sense of an Ending: Studies in the Theory of Fiction*. London: Oxford UP, 1968.

Morson, Gary Saul. "Narrativeness." *New Literary History* 34 (2003): 59–73.

Peirce, Charles S. *Selected Writings: Values in a Universe of Chance*. Ed. Philip P. Wiener. New York: Dover, 1958.

Prince-Hughes, Dawn. *Songs of the Gorilla Nation: My Journey Through Autism*. New York: Harmony, 2004.

Putnam, Robert D. *Bowling Alone: The Collapse and Revival of American Community*. New York: Simon and Schuster, 2000.

Sacks, Oliver. *An Anthropologist on Mars: Seven Paradoxical Tales*. New York: Vintage, 1995.

———. Foreword. *Thinking in Pictures and Other Reports from My Life with Autism*. By Temple Grandin. New York: Vintage, 1996. 11–16.

Swindon Borough Council Review of Homelessness Services. May 2003. www.swindon.gov.uk/homelessness_review-March_2003-2.pdf

Tager-Flusberg, Helen. "Dissociations in Form and Function in the Acquisition of Language by Autistic Children." *Constraints on Language Acquisition: Studies of Atypical Children*. Ed. Helen Tager-Flusberg. Hillsdale NJ: Lawrence Erlbaum, 1994. 175–94.

Wing, Lorna. "Autistic Spectrum Disorders." *British Medical Journal* 312 (1996): 327–28.

Žižek, Slavoj. *Looking Awry: An Introduction to Lacan Through Popular Culture*. Cambridge, MA: MIT P, 1991.

———. *The Sublime Object of Ideology*. London: Verso, 1989.

16 Mark Haddon's Popularity and Other Curious Incidents in My Life as an Autistic

Gyasi Burks-Abbott

It's not just a book about disability. Obviously, on some level it is, but on another level ... it's a book about books, about what you can do with words and what it means to communicate with someone in a book. Here's a character whom if you met him in real life you'd never, ever get inside his head. Yet something magical happens when you write a novel about him. You slip inside his head, and it seems like the most natural thing in the world.

Mark Haddon, "Curiously Irresistible"

He presents an archetype, a distillation. . . . There are dozens of ways of having Asperger's or of being Aspergen. I don't think there is anything false or misleading here, but it can't represent the whole spectrum.

Oliver Sacks (qtd. in Gussow)

According to Mark Haddon, when he set out to tell the story of Christopher Boone, the mathematically gifted but socially challenged narrator of *The Curious Incident of the Dog in the Night-Time*, the author had no intention of writing a book about the autism spectrum. What galvanized Haddon's imagination was the image that opens the book—a dog impaled on a garden fork. What guided Haddon through the process of telling the story behind this bizarre image was the need to keep the reader interested in what the author himself considered mundane—a disabled teenager living with his father in Swindon, England. Despite his initial misgivings, Haddon not only succeeds in engaging the reader but also manages to appeal to a wide audience that includes fellow authors, critics, and even the noted neurologist Oliver Sacks, who confesses that he is not usually a fan of fiction.

Certainly, the increased public awareness of and interest in the autism spectrum can account for much of the attention *The Curious Incident of the Dog in the Night-Time* has received. However, most of the acclaim for *Curious Incident* has been for what the novel does as a novel. For instance, a number of critics have complimented Haddon for his skill as a storyteller and for his innovative approach to commonplace topics. Marketed to both children and adults, *Curious Incident* defies easy classification. After opening on a macabre note reminiscent of a gothic tale, the novel takes the reader on a light-hearted journey into the psyche of a narrator limited by his own narrow worldview. Along the way, the reader encounters a coming-of-age story, a murder mystery, a character study, and a soap opera. *The Curious Incident of the Dog in the Night-Time* also encompasses aspects of the picaresque in its focus on the adventures of a single character, the involuted novel in its description of its own creation, the realistic novel in its attempt at authenticity, the postmodern novel in its melding of several genres, and the anti-novel in its disruption of conventional literary expectations.

The novel's title calls attention to its attempt at literary experimentation. The title is lifted directly from "Silver Blaze," a Sherlock Holmes short story in which the master detective asks the inspector to consider "the curious incident of the dog in the night-time" (Doyle). Indeed, the "curious incident" is that the dog did not bark, which means that there was no intruder: a member of the household committed the crime. In other words, what did not occur is as important as what did occur. Similarly, what is absent from *The Curious Incident of the Dog in the Night-Time* is as important as what is present. For instance, the word "autism" is never mentioned, yet the disorder figures significantly in the plot. Equally important, autism is a literary device that enables Haddon to experiment with other absences; for instance, whether one can write a novel without the use of metaphor. Indeed, as Michiko Kakutani suggests, autism turns out to be the perfect vehicle for Haddon precisely because of what it allows him not to say:

> Christopher's inability to lie about the events he is recounting and his inability to sentimentalize his actions or the actions of others lend the story a visceral, stripped-down power, an understated precision that enables the author to talk about the big issues of love and mortality and loss without sounding maudlin or trite. (Kakutani)

As Polly Morrice points out in "Autism as Metaphor," autism has simply taken the place of other disorders that writers have historically used to tackle "the big issues":

> It's easy to see autism's appeal to storytellers. Even mildly autistic people have problems communicating and understanding social behavior; what's more, these difficulties remain tantalizingly unexplained in an era when medical advances have demystified so many other ailments. We now know too much about, say, cholesterol, for a writer to portray heart disease as metaphorically as Ford Madox Ford did almost a century ago in *The Good Soldier*. But writers can still turn to autism when they're looking for an ailment that can drive a plot and convey what English teachers once called "layers of meaning." (Morrice)

By making the narrator autistic, Haddon establishes dramatic irony and thus enriches his unlikely story about a Sherlock Holmes fan's investigation into the death of a neighbor's dog. Along the way, the reader is privy to the thoughts of someone Mel Gussow describes as "the most unusual adolescent one is likely to meet in or out of fiction."

Even though *Curious Incident* is not about autism *per se*—any more than *The Sound and the Fury* is about mental retardation—and Haddon himself disavows any conscious attempt to enter the flow of autism discourse (even going as far as to agree with one reader that *Curious Incident* is as much about a gifted boy with behavior problems as it is about anyone on the autism spectrum), the author's singular portrayal of autism, a portrayal that fails to capture the nuances and complexities of the autism spectrum, serves to perpetuate stereotypes. As Oliver Sacks suggests in the epigraph to this chapter, Haddon has invoked an archetypal image of autism—one so resonant, in fact, that readers can recognize Christopher as autistic even though, as mentioned earlier, the word "autism" never even appears in the book. A monolithic view of autism is evident in the choices made in constructing the character Christopher. As Haddon elaborates in an interview with Dave Weich of Powells.com:

> I wanted the whole book to be in Christopher's voice, but the paradox is that if Christopher were real he would find it very hard, if not impossible, to write a book. The one thing he cannot do is put himself in someone else's shoes, and the one thing you have to do if you write a book is put yourself in someone else's shoes. The reader's shoes. You've got to entertain them, and there's no way he could have done that. . . . The answer I came up with is having him be a fan of the Sherlock Holmes stories. That way, he doesn't have to put himself in the mind of a reader. He just has to say, *I enjoy Sherlock Holmes Stories and I'll try to do something similar to that* [emphasis in the original].

Christopher's inability to "put himself in someone else's shoes" refers to his lack of theory of mind, "the ability to attribute independent mental states to oneself and others, in order to explain behavior" (Happé 39), a liability that experts argue lies at the core of what makes autism a disabling condition. Cognitive psychologist Uta Frith suggests the following in *Autism: Explaining the Enigma*:

> Lack of a theory of mind makes sense out of the whole host of seemingly unconnected behavioral symptoms. . . . What often appears as a language problem can be better understood as a problem in the semantics of mental states. Similarly, what appears as a problem in affective relationships can be understood as a consequence of the inability to realize fully what it means to have a mind and to think, know, believe and feel differently from others. What often appears as a problem in

learning to become socially competent can be understood from exactly the same point of view: learning outwardly the forms of social rules is not sufficient—one needs the ability to read between the lines, and yes, to read other people's thoughts. (173)

As fundamental as the lack of theory of mind is as an autistic deficiency, most experts agree that not all autistics are affected by this lack to the same degree. Yet for Haddon, theory of mind is an all-or-nothing proposition that is as much of a given as the fact that Christopher dislikes fiction, distrusts metaphor, disdains touch, and does not appreciate humor.

Interestingly enough, Haddon's uncritical acceptance that Christopher lacks a theory of mind is not sustained while telling the latter's story. Not only does Haddon have Christopher state that he can learn theory of mind but he also has Christopher demonstrate theory of mind in the cat-and-mouse game he plays with his father. Christopher shows a particularly keen ability to infer another's intentions when he finds the manuscript that his father has hidden from him:

> I was happy because Father hadn't thrown my book away. But if I took the book he would know that I had been messing with things in his room and he would be very angry and I had promised not to mess with things in his room.
>
> Then I heard his van pulling up outside the house and I knew that I had to think fast and be clever. So I decided that I would leave the book where it was because I reasoned that Father wasn't going to throw it away if he had put it into the shirt box and I could carry on writing in another book that I would keep really secret and then, maybe later, he might change his mind and let me have the first book back again and I could copy the new book into it. And if . . . there were bits I wanted to check to make sure I had remembered them correctly I could come into his room when he was out and check. (93–4)

In addition to being able to understand that people can change their minds (something the theory-of-mind hypothesis suggests that autistics cannot comprehend), Christopher is able to separate what he knows (that the book has been discovered) from what his father knows (that the book has been hidden).

Showing a similar degree of social sophistication, Christopher sneaks past his sleeping father while wondering if the latter is setting a trap for him:

> Father's eyes were still closed. I wondered if he was pretending to be asleep. So I gripped the penknife really hard and I knocked on the doorframe.
>
> Father moved his head from one side to the other and his foot twitched and he said "Gnnnn," but his eyes stayed closed. And then he snored again.

He was asleep.

That meant I could get out of the house if I was really quiet so I didn't wake him up. (123)

Certainly, Christopher's fear of his father is exaggerated (the latter is deemed a potential threat after confessing to having killed the dog) and demonstrates a low level of social understanding; however, Christopher's ability to consider the possibility that someone is pretending in order to deceive displays a high level of social savvy that is assumed to be above the reach of most autistics.

In addition to his inadvertent refutation of the theory-of-mind hypothesis, Haddon also fails to confirm his assumption that autistics are literal thinkers. Christopher may eschew metaphor, but he clearly understands the concept and even knows the word's etymological roots. George Orwell, in fact, takes a stance similar to Christopher's in the "Politics and the English Language":

> When you think of a concrete object, you think wordlessly, and then, if you want to describe the thing you have been visualizing, you probably hunt about till you find the exact words that seem to fit it. When you think of something abstract you are more inclined to use words from the start, and unless you make a conscious effort to prevent it, the existing dialect will come rushing in and do the job for you, at the expense of blurring or even changing your meaning. Probably it is better to put off using words as long as possible and get one's meaning as clear as one can through pictures or sensations. (490)

Like Orwell, Christopher objects to "the existing dialect" because it fails to convey real meaning:

> [I]t should be called a lie because a pig is not like a day and people do not have skeletons in their cupboards. And when I try and make a picture of the phrase in my head it just confuses me because imagining an apple in someone's eye doesn't have anything to do with liking someone a lot and it makes you forget what the person was talking about. (15)

Indeed, although Christopher might disdain clichés like the ones just listed, he does not hesitate to use figurative language when he finds it appropriate. As he elaborates in a footnote to one of his analogies:

> This is not a *metaphor*; it is a *simile*, which means that it really did look like there were two very small mice hiding in his nostrils, and if you make a picture in your head of a man with two very small mice hiding in his nostrils, you will know what the police inspector looked like. And a simile is not a lie, unless it is a bad simile. (17)

Although Christopher shows remarkable insight for a fifteen year old into the nature of language, Haddon's parsing of metaphor and simile serves to downplay this precocity. Instead of recognizing that metaphor and simile are essentially the same, and that if you understand one you understand the other, Haddon tries to suggest that Christopher, and by implication all autistics, can only handle simile because he needs a prosthesis (such as the use of the words "like" or "as") when it comes to figurative language. By downgrading simile to what Thomas Jefferson calls "the level of plain narration," Haddon manages to move autistics the proverbial one step forward and two steps back by, on the one hand, making Christopher capable of using figurative language, but on the other hand, still leaving him able to engage only in literal thought.[1]

The Curious Incident of the Dog in the Night-Time has had a powerful and seductive effect on the popular imagination. In "The Remains of a Dog," critic Jay McInerney adumbrates the novel's wide-ranging influence:

> Haddon manages to bring us deep inside Christopher's mind and situates us comfortably within his limited, severely logical point of view, to the extent that we begin to question the common sense and erratic emotionalism of the normal citizens who surround him, as well as our own intuitions and habits of perception.

Moreover, just as Christopher's father temporarily adopts his son's disdain for yellow and changes the route of his evening walk to avoid three yellow cars that are perpetually parked in the same place, readers report thinking like Christopher several days after finishing *Curious*. I myself starting censoring my use of similes—I did not want to be complicit in upholding an old stereotype with a new twist—until I realized there are just some comparisons that convey meaning most effectively when phrased with "like" or "as." And I know for a fact that the charm of *Curious Incident* worked its magic on the Executive Director of the Asperger's Association of New England (AANE), Dania Jekel, before it wore off. On her first encounter with the novel, Jekel felt Haddon had succeeded in capturing Asperger's syndrome perfectly. On further reflection—and after discussion with AANE board member and Asperger's expert Dr. Daniel Rosen—Jekel concluded that Christopher is not Asperger's at all, but instead a high-functioning autistic. Contrary to the popular belief that autistics are automatically great in math, an overgeneralization supported by *Curious Incident*, Jekel has found that most of the members of AANE are far better with words and images than they are with numbers.

The Curious Incident of the Dog in the Night-Time is the new *Rain Man*, the new definitive, popular account of the autistic condition. Back in the early nineties when I was first diagnosed with autism, the only way I could counter the blank stares I would get when I disclosed my condition was to mention the 1988 movie *Rain Man*, which left a deep imprint on the popular psyche. I once told a Harvard student I was autistic, and he was about to tell me that he had had a friend with the same condition until he realized he was thinking about Dustin Hoffman. Less personal *Rain Man*-inspired reactions to my autism came from the people who wanted to know about my particular savant skills.

Today when I tell lay people that I am autistic, the first question they ask is, "Have you read *The Curious Incident of the Dog in the Night-Time?*" as if that were the best example of a book written about autism. And rather than recognizing and remarking on the actual personal accounts autistics have written—*Beyond the Wall: Personal Experiences with Autism and Asperger's Syndrome*, by Stephen Shore; *Songs of the Gorilla Nation: My Journey Through Autism*, by Dawn Prince-Hughes; *Nobody Nowhere: The Extraordinary Autobiography of an Autistic*, by Donna Williams; and *Thinking in Pictures: And Other Reports from my Life with Autism*, by Temple Grandin, just to name a few—critics focus on and derive insights about autism from Haddon's novel about an autistic person. The sentiment expressed by the Chicago *Tribune's* blurb on the inside of *Curious Incident*—that "facts alone don't add up to a life, that we understand ourselves only through metaphor"—might explain how fiction by a non-autistic could take precedence over nonfiction from autistics. Indeed, although the autistic Christopher is simply able to record what happens to him (even if he would like to believe he is writing a novel), the non-autistic Haddon can create a narrative that captures the reader's imagination. And there's the paradox. Although *Curious Incident* has generated widespread interest in the autism spectrum, an interest that could foster an increased demand for autistic perspectives, the author's conclusions and the book's reception actually militate against autistic self-representation. In declaring that people like Christopher are unfathomable unless written about, as Haddon does in the epigraph to this chapter, at the same time claiming that Christopher would have trouble writing for himself, Haddon has relegated the autistic to otherworldliness while establishing a non-autistic author like himself as the necessary medium between autistic and non-autistic reality.

NOTES

1. In *Notes on the State of Virginia*, Thomas Jefferson uttered the following statement about blacks' inability to use figurative language: "But never yet could I find that a black had uttered a thought above the level of plain narration" (140).

WORKS CITED

Doyle, Sir Arthur Conan. "Silver Blaze." *The Memoirs of Sherlock Holmes*. 24 Dec. 2006. http://etext.library.adelaide.edu.au/d/doyle/arthur_conan/d75me/silver.blaze.html

Frith, Uta. *Autism: Explaining the Enigma.* Cambridge, MA: Blackwell, 1989.

Grandin, Temple. *Thinking in Pictures: And Other Reports from My Life with Autism.* Foreword by Oliver Sacks. New York: Doubleday, 1995.

Gussow, Mel. "Novel's Sleuth Views Life From Unusual Perspective." *New York Times* 3 Aug. 2004. 30 August 2005. http://query.nytimes.com/gst/health/article-page.html?res=9F0DE4DD163CF930A3575BC0A9629C8B63

Haddon, Mark. *The Curious Incident of the Dog in the Night-Time.* New York: Doubleday, 2003.

———. "The Curiously Irresistible Literary Debut of Mark Haddon." *Exclusive to Powell's: Author Interviews.* June 2003. 8 October 2005. http://www.powells.com/authors/haddon.html

Happé, Francesca. *Autism: An Introduction to Psychological Theory.* Cambridge, MA: Harvard UP, 1994.

Jefferson, Thomas. *Notes on the State of Virginia.* Chapel Hill, NC: U of North Carolina P, 1954.

Kakutani, Michiko. "Books of the Times: Math and Physics? A Cinch. People? Incomprehensible." *New York Times* 13 June 2003. 30 August 2005. http://query.nytimes.com/gst/fullpage.html?res=9402E5DA1E39F930A25755C0A9659C8B63

McInerney, Jay. "The Remains of the Dog." *New York Times* 15 June 2003. 30 August 2005. http://query.nytimes.com/gst/fullpage.html?res=9905EED81E30F936A25755C0A9659C8B63

Morrice, Polly. "Autism as Metaphor." *New York Times* 31 July 2005. 30 August 2005. http://www.nytimes.com/2005/07/31/books/31MORRICE.html?ex=1129089600&en=a8f1c210814b7578&ei=5070

Orwell, George. "Politics and the English Language." *The Writer's Reference: A Pool of Readings.* Ed. Donald McQuade. New York: Bedford/St. Martin's, 2003. 481–496.

Prince-Hughes, Dawn. *Songs of the Gorilla Nation: My Journey through Autism.* New York: Harmony, 2004.

Shore, Stephen. *Beyond the Wall: Personal Experiences with Autism and Asperger Syndrome.* 2nd ed. Foreword by Temple Grandin. Shawnee Mission, KS: Autism Asperger Publishing, 2003.

Williams, Donna. *Nobody Nowhere: The Extraordinary Autobiography of an Autistic.* New York: Times Books, 1992.

Conclusion
Toward an Empathetic Scholarship

Mark Osteen

The October 2005 conference from which these chapters derive was among the most rewarding experiences of my professional life. Rarely does a conference generate such a feeling of community. This volume is the result of the intellectual excitement that conference created. Perhaps the main reason for that excitement was that the gathering enabled attendees to exercise our scholarly skills on a subject with enormous personal significance: most of us either have an autistic loved one or are ourselves on the autism spectrum. This convergence of the personal and professional, this blend of experiential knowledge and scholarly rigor, is what I am calling *empathetic scholarship*. This term emerged, along with several others, at the conference's wrap-up session, where we discussed the controversies and commonalities the sessions had exposed. Although, thankfully, we did not debate some of the other controversies that divide the autism community—neither vaccines nor facilitated communication came up—we congenially disagreed on many issues.

This diversity of opinions about and approaches to autism was fitting, for contrary to much popular opinion, autistic people and their loved ones are as different from each other as any other group of people on the planet. Yet, as I noted in the Introduction, all of us shared certain aims and motives: a desire to dispel misconceptions about autism and autistic people; a belief that autism already speaks in unusual and creative ways, and that both autistic and non-autistic people can benefit from learning about those ways; and a wish to create a community of autists and what Phil Schwarz calls fellow travelers—empathetic non-autists willing to speak with and, when absolutely necessary, for autists who can't speak for themselves.

Other common themes emerged from the conference that are also evident in the essays collected here. In what follows, I sketch a few of these themes and outline some avenues for future scholarship on autism and the humanities.

AUTISMS

The diversity of approaches and experiences our contributors represent suggests that understanding autism requires extraordinary flexibility and an

unusual willingness to accept atypical modes of communication and socia-
bility. After all, no two autistic people are exactly alike. That is not to dispute
the relevance or value of diagnostic categories or lists of deficits, differences
and abilities that mark what we call "autism." But it should remind us that
autistic people are not collections of symptoms but individuals with widely
disparate needs, interests and capacities. This fact may be one reason that the
autism community is so often swept by fads and furor over ill-understood
and overhyped treatments, and so riven by heated discussions and polar-
ized points of view. Therapies or accommodations suitable for one autistic
person may be unsuitable for another: some autists are skilled at math, but
others use words better; those who communicate well or who are socially
competent often have little in common with people on the less capable end
of the spectrum. Although many autism advocates scorn the low-function-
ing/high-functioning labels for stigmatizing autistic people and leveling their
complexity (many autists function well in some respects, but poorly in others), these terms do register an important fact: no one—neither autistic or
non-autistic—speaks for everyone in the autism community. Therefore, it is
essential to attend to a range of voices, not just the loudest ones, and, with
a skepticism tempered by tolerance, weed out the facts from the fictions. In
so doing, we may come to understand—as our conferees recognized—that
autism isn't one thing but many things, that there is no "autism," per se, but
autisms. To view autism as a monolith is, indeed, to perpetuate one of the
very misrepresentations we have tried to explode.

BANISHING THE SHADE OF BETTELHEIM

Though the refrigerator-mother paradigm of Bruno Bettelheim and Leo
Kanner has long-since been discredited in clinical circles, parent-blaming
persists in autism culture. In some ways, as our contributors show, it is even
more insidious today because it is so covert. Hints that bad parents cause
autism still appear in popular films (as Anthony Baker's chapter points out),
as well as in autism texts written by neurotypical (e.g., *The Curious Incident
of the Dog in the Night-Time, Girls of Tender Age*), and autistic authors (for
example, Donna Williams's *Nobody Nowhere*). Many parents of autistic
children can testify that parent-blaming also crops up in their daily lives—in
educators' innuendoes, for example, or in judgmental looks from the general public. Indeed, the enduring belief in parental guilt partially explains
the fury that fuels some current controversies about autism: because of the
condition's challenging and sometimes intractable manifestations, parents
of autistic children constantly feel guilty and inadequate; if they don't try
every possible therapy, diet or medication, they may believe they haven't
done enough for their child. This guilt not only makes them easy marks
for unscrupulous or careless practitioners; it also creates a need to point
fingers at others. Thus parental self-blame—itself a product of our society's

myth of the supercompetent parent—is easily transformed into a penchant to blame whatever scapegoat seems handy. Such finger-pointing sometimes consumes parents' lives and frequently does no real good; but it makes these parents feel they are doing *something*. Thus, our contributors agree, we must, at long last, forever banish the ghosts of Bettelheim's and Kanner's bad mothers and fathers. Good parents do their best for their children, but even neglectful, overwhelmed or dysfunctional parents do not cause autism. Further, autism culture needs to move beyond the discourses of blame that divide us and that preserve outdated and damaging views about autistic people and their families. To do so is the first step toward genuine empathy and community.

AVERSION TO CONVERSION

This phrase, coined by conferee Irene Rose during a comment on another panelist's paper, summarizes our contributors' collective stance toward the conversion or cure story that still dominates autism (and much disability) literature. Our aversion is not so much a comment on these stories' truth or untruth as a rejection of their detrimental power to create paradigms that push out other paradigms and stories. Our rejections, however, issue from different locations. Some autistic people don't believe they need to "recover," because they're fine as they are; these folks find such stories offensive and demeaning. Conversion or recovery stories play to the notion that autism constitutes their entire identity and that they are worthless unless they become or act "normal." Recovery stories also tend to pigeonhole autistic people and their parents as stereotypical victims or heroes, while diminishing both the positive and the negative aspects of living with autism. In addition, writers or artists wishing to tell other (often more representative) truths—for example, about the challenges *and joys* of life with more severely impaired autistic people—are forced to bend their experiences to fit the dominant paradigm, or be left without an audience. If, as James Fisher argues, the history of the conversion narrative is the history of autism in America, then this volume marks an attempt to start rewriting that history.

NORMALLY AUTISTIC

Anthony Baker uses this term in passing to refer to the sort of autistic people who do *not* appear in popular films. Instead, as he notes, popular cinema habitually portrays autists as savants or helpless victims. In different ways, our other contributors aim to describe and advocate for the normally autistic: that majority of autistic people who are not outstandingly gifted but possess a mixture of abilities and disabilities, strengths and weaknesses—like every other human being. To champion the normally autistic is again to recognize that autistic people, their loved ones and caregivers, must maintain flexible (but not low) expectations about behavior and achievements. The belief in the normally autistic, then, goes hand in hand with an aversion to conversion: together these attitudes promote skepticism about fad cures, and a resistance to sensationalizing autism and overgeneralizing about autistic people. Perhaps most important, to believe in the normally autistic is to accept that the norms, attainments and identities of individual autists must emerge not in spite of, but *because of and through* their autism. To endorse the idea of the normally autistic is to eschew applying neurotypical norms to autistic people; it is hence to recognize and respect *autistic agency and authority*.

RADIANCE IN DAILINESS

This term, which I've drawn from an interview with novelist Don DeLillo (DeCurtis 70–71), aims at striking a balance between viewing autism as either a disability or a gift. As our explorations of autistic creativity and autobiography demonstrate, the presence of an autist in a family almost always generates a peculiar intensity, an electricity or radiance, that pervades everyday life. The challenging behaviors I chronicle in my autobiographical excerpt show some of that negative intensity, while the diverse modes of autistic creativity and intelligence we've encountered—from David Karasik's *Superman* performances to Jessica Park's pictures, from Tito Mukhopadhyay's poems to Temple Grandin's chutes and doors—express a defiantly concentrated, radiantly energetic presence in the world. Those who hope to represent autism authentically must strive to capture but not dim this radiance.

EMPATHETIC SCHOLARSHIP

Above all, our contributors exemplify how a blend of experience and scholarly rigor, of intelligence and emotion, can engage scholarship in a true dialogue with disability and difference. Yet the shapes that empathetic scholarship may take are as varied as the essays in this volume. Hence, for instance, Kristina Chew melds her literary and linguistic training with her experiences as the mother of autistic child in her investigation of metonymy in autistic language; Bruce Mills delves into the history of aesthetics to comprehend the autistic imagination he finds in Jessy Park and Temple Grandin; Matthew Belmonte employs a wealth of neuroscientific scholarship to buttress a humane argument in defense of autistic agency; Anthony Baker furnishes a taxonomy of autistic characters in film to carve out a small viewing space for his own experience as the father of an autistic son; Gyasi Burks-Abbott compares a fictional autistic character to his own firsthand knowledge of autism, and so on. Empathy—the recognition of that "eudai-monistic" kinship between autists and non-autists—is therefore the keynote of this volume. It is also the reason we made it a point to incorporate work by both neurotypical and autistic authors: without such interaction, there can be no empathy or understanding.

AUTISM AND THE HUMANITIES

As the first collection devoted to autism and the humanities, this book is just a beginning. A great deal of work remains to be done. In the Introduction I argued that, despite its many important contributions, the field of disability studies has yet to make room for cognitive or intellectual disabilities such as autism. We now issue a call for more scholarship on autism within a disability studies framework. How, for example, can academia more success-fully accommodate cognitive difference? What does autism share with other disabilities, and how is it different from them? How does autism challenge the reigning paradigms of the field?

We also need more study of autism's languages from a humanist rather than a clinical perspective. Echolalia, verbal "stims," nonverbal modes of expression, collaborative or assisted forms of communication, the poet-ics of autistic language and its relation to figures of speech: these topics demand more attention from literary scholars and linguists. More broadly, we should continue to explore the similarities and differences between autis-tic and neurotypical brands of creativity. Is there, after all, a characteristi-cally autistic type (or types) of imagination, or is this concept, as Kamran Nazeer asserts, patronizing (86)? We await future conferences, monographs and gatherings on topics such as autism and the visual arts, autist music, architecture, and so on.

As Matthew Belmonte's chapter and my own Introduction suggest, autism's challenges to narrative constitute another underexplored topic. What innovative fictional and nonfictional strategies can authors—both autistic and non-autistic—use to represent autism *from within*? Is narrative even a suitable genre for autistry? If not, what is? How will authors tran-scend the recovery narrative, or at least transform it into a less conventional shape? A few texts discussed herein offer possibilities. Are there others?

Finally, we call on autistic people—from all ends of the spectrum, to the degree possible—to continue to represent themselves and their brothers and sisters candidly, without apology but also without minimizing the chal-lenges their condition presents. We must endeavor to hear and appreciate the words, thoughts and emotions of those with the most limited capacity to express them. Neurotypical parents, family members, clinicians and caregiv-ers must constantly strive to speak *with* autistic people rather than for them; those on the spectrum must continue to speak with neurotypical scholars, advocates and family members. Let us address each other with respect, not as means to some other end, but as human agents. Above all, let us keep listening.

WORKS CITED

DeCurtis, Anthony. "'An Outsider in This Society': An Interview with Don DeLillo." 1988. *Conversations with Don DeLillo.* Ed. Thomas DePietro. Jackson: UP of Mississippi, 2005. 52–74.

Nazeer, Kamran. *Send in the Idiots: Stories from the Other Side of Autism.* New York: Bloomsbury, 2006.

Contributors

James Arnt Aune is Professor of Communication at Texas A&M University. He is the author of *Rhetoric and Marxism* (1994) and *Selling the Free Market* (2001). He has two autistic boys: Nick (18) and Daniel (15).

Anthony D. Baker is an associate professor of English at Tennessee Technological University, where he directs the first-year composition program and teaches a variety of courses in writing, rhetoric, and literature. His research interests include composition pedagogy, student reflection, postmodern texts, and visual rhetoric.

Matthew K. Belmonte is an assistant professor in the Department of Human Development, Cornell University, and an affiliate of the Autism Research Centre, University of Cambridge. He holds an MFA in fiction from Sarah Lawrence College, as well as a few degrees in the sciences. Belmonte's research explores how the human mind represents perceptual experience, and how it imposes narrative order on these perceptual representations. He approaches this question within the framework of the sciences by studying the neurophysiology of attention in autism, and from the perspective of the arts by focusing on processes of narrative and symbolic representation. He is also a brother and uncle of two people with autism.

James Berger is Associate Professor of English at Hofstra University. He is the author of *After the End: Representations of Post-Apocalypse*, and editor of Helen Keller's *The Story of My Life: The Restored Edition*. He is currently writing a book on language and cognitive impairments in modern literature.

Gyasi Burks-Abbott, a 34-year-old African-American male on the autism spectrum, serves on the Board of Directors of the Asperger's Association of New England (AANE) and on the Steering Committee of the Advocates for Autism of Massachusetts. He earned his MS from the Simmons Graduate School of Library and Information Science and his BA from Macalester College, where he double-majored in English and psychology.

Kristina Chew is Assistant Professor of Classics at Saint Peter's College in Jersey City, NJ. She writes a daily weblog, Autism Vox (http://www.autismvox.com) about autism advocacy, education, books, recent scientific research, and the latest in news about autism. She is writing a book on autism, metaphor and representation and about life with her son Charlie, who has autism. She is the author of a translation of Virgil's *Georgics* (Hackett 2002).

Debra Cumberland is a professor of English at Winona State University in Winona, MN. Her essays, articles and stories have appeared in *Natural Bridge, Green Hills Literary Lantern, American Literary Realism*, and *The Journal of Pre-Raphaelite Studies*, among others.

James T. Fisher is Co-Director of the Curran Center for American Catholic Studies at Fordham where he is also Professor of Theology. He is the author of three books on the cultural history of Catholicism in the U.S. His forthcoming book *The Irish Waterfront and the Soul of the Port: New York/New Jersey 1936–1954* will be published in 2008 by Cornell University Press.

Denise Jodlowski is a doctoral candidate at Texas A&M University. Her dissertation focuses on understanding the controversial nature of autism in terms of its public, personal, and technical spheres.

Patrick McDonagh is a Montreal-based writer and part-time faculty member at Concordia University. He is a co-founder of the Spectrum Society for Community Living in Vancouver, Canada, and has written on the history of cultural representations of intellectual disability.

Bruce Mills teaches at Kalamazoo College, including a service-learning class on autism. His publications include *Cultural Reformations: Lydia Maria Child and the Literature of Reform* (1994) and *Poe, Fuller, and the Mesmeric Arts: Transition States in the American Renaissance* (2005). He has been president of his local autism society, is a board member of the Gray Center for Social Learning and Understanding, and is currently working on a collection of essays that reflect on his autistic son in the context of how we understand desire, memory, and imagination. The title essay, "An Archaeology of Yearning," has appeared in the *Georgia Review*.

Stuart Murray is Senior Lecturer in Postcolonial Literatures in the School of English at the University of Leeds in the United Kingdom, and has published widely on literature and film from New Zealand and Australia and other postcolonial contexts. He has written on contemporary fictional representations of autism in *Literature and Medicine* and is the current editor of Liverpool University Press' s *Representations: Heath, Disability, Culture* monograph series. His own study *Representing Autism: Culture, Narrative, Fascination* will appear in the series in 2008.

Majia Holmer Nadesan is Associate Professor of Communication Studies at Arizona State University's west campus. She authored *Constructing Autism: Unravelling the "Truth" and Understanding the Social* (2005) and is currently working on a new book entitled *Governmentality, Biopower, and Everyday Life*.

Mark Osteen, Professor of English and Director of Film Studies at Loyola College, Baltimore, has published widely on modern and contemporary literature and film. He is the author of *The Economy of* Ulysses: *Making Both Ends Meet* (1995) and *American Magic and Dread: Don DeLillo's Dialogue with Culture* (2000). He is also editor of *The Question of the Gift: Essays across Disciplines* (2002), and co-editor, with Martha Woodmansee, of *The New Economic Criticism* (1999). Most recently, he edited a special double issue of *Genre: Forms of Discourse and Culture* devoted to jazz and jazz writing, and has completed a memoir entitled *One of Us: A Family's Life with Autism*.

Ilona Roth is Senior Lecturer in Psychology in the Department of Biological Sciences at the Open University. She has a long-standing interest in the autism spectrum, and her contributions in this field include book chapters, conference papers and a television program. Her research on autistic spectrum poetry forms part of a wider project exploring the nature of imagination and self-awareness, and including research into awareness deficits in dementia. She is editor of *Imaginative Minds* (in press), a book based on the interdisciplinary symposium she organized for the British Academy in 2004.

Phil Schwarz is Vice-President of the Asperger's Association of New England (www.aane.org), and a board member of the Massachusetts chapter of the Autism Society of America (www.autism-society.org). He is the father of an autistic son, and an Asperger's adult himself. Professionally, he is a software developer. He earned an S.B. in mathematics at the University of Chicago, 25 years before the recent emergence (to his great delight!) of an Asperger's student organization there.

Katherine DeMaria Severson is an independent scholar and mother living in Beloit, Wisconsin.

Sheryl Stevenson, Associate Professor of English at the University of Akron, has published essays on a range of women writers, including Djuna Barnes, Stevie Smith, Muriel Spark, Barbara Kingsolver, and Sarah Waters. She has also published articles on representations of AIDS in poetry. Her current book project took shape in 2001, when she interviewed English novelist Pat Barker. The interview and part of one of her book's chapters appear in *Critical Perspectives on Pat Barker* (University of South Carolina Press, 2005).

Index

A

aesthetic modernism 101, 108–10
Applied Behavioral Analysis (ABA) 61
Armstrong, Tim 107, 108
arousal 74–75
Asperger, Hans 87, 99, 102, 103, 105–6
Asperger's syndrome 5–6, 99, 271, 278,
          286, 294; and communication
          172, 173; diagnosis, emer-
          gence of 11, 84, 88; fictional
          portrayal *see Curious Incident
          of the Dog in the Night-Time*;
          and historical figures 12, 100;
          and imagination 148, 151;
          portrayal in film 30, 32–33,
          251; research into 78; and
          self-awareness 149–50; in Sili-
          con Valley 92; support group
          256, 257, 258
Autism and Creativity (Fitzgerald) 12
autism and narrative 16–17; cogni-
          tive skills, virtue of necessity
          172–75; as defense against dis-
          order 166–68, 175–77; narra-
          tive organization 167, 168–69,
          171, 173; physiological
          causes of impairment 168–69;
          psychological consequences of
          impairment 169–71; self-con-
          scious narrative and autism
          175–77; social communication
          171–73
autism, construction of: cognitive
          psychology 88; contamination/
          pollutants 85–86; genetics
          discourse 89–91; in medical
          literature 79–84; normality
          and pathology boundaries
          86–87; psychosis/psychoanaly-
          sis 87–88; risk factors 88–89

autism conversion narratives 53, 54, 58,
          59, 61–62; counternarrative
          62; *see also Dibs: In Search of
          Self; Empty Fortress: Infantile
          Autism and the Birth of the
          Self*
Autism: Explaining the Enigma (Frith)
          121–23, 125–26, 291–92
autism, history of 102–7
autism imagery 113–15
Autism Society of America 203
autistic biography: autobiography
          25–29, 113–14, 150, 295;
          by fathers 193, 194–95; by
          mothers 184, 185–87, 188–92,
          197–99, 203; by parents
          17–22, 193, 194–95, 212–25;
          by siblings 22–25, 183,
          184–85, 187–88, 192–93
autistic brain and process of narrative
          166–77
autistic cognition 172–75
autistic creativity 12–13, 15, 148, 149
autistic identity 22, 27–28, 30, 33–34,
          110, 263
autistic idiolect 134, 142, 143
autistic imagination 13–14, 117–18,
          126–31
autistic poetry 150–51; conventional
          literary devices 153–54;
          distinct genre 157–58; early
          influences 158–59; imaginative
          language 154–55; influence of
          other poets 160; inspiration
          159–60; poets' reflections on
          their work 158–61; and self
          155–57; as self-expression and
          communication 160–61; study
          of 152–62; style 152–53;
          teaching, role of 158–59

autistic spectrum 7, 272, 277–78
autistic symptoms: communication
impairment 168, 171, 172,
173; executive dysfunction
169, 172, 174, 222; imagination impairment 117–18,
124, 126, 127, 145, 147–48;
language impairment 127,
137, 138–39, 172, 173; social
interaction impairment 168,
171–73, 271; theory of mind
in 122–23, 124, 148, 149,
171, 291–92
autobiography 25–29, 113–14, 150,
295; *see also Emergence:
Labeled Autistic* (Grandin);
Thinking in Pictures (Grandin)
awareness of self 145–46, 156, 161,
264; definition 146–47;
medico-scientific view 147,
149–50
Axline, Virginia Mae 54, 55, 56–57, 58,
60; *see also Dibs: In Search of
Self; Play Therapy: The Inner
Dynamics of Childhood*

B
Baron-Cohen, Simon 114, 122, 123,
124
Beautiful Mind, A (Howard) 254
Becker, Ernest 166
Beckett, Samuel 101
bedwetting 216–17, 219, 220–22
Beowulf 175–76
Bérubé, Michael 201–3
Bettelheim, Bruno 65–66, 76, 171; audi-
ence 67–68, 69–70; context
66–67; expert ethos 67–68;
milieu therapy 71; rhetorical
strategies 68–75; scientific
method violations 69, 70–71;
see also "Individual and
Mass Behavior in Extreme
Situations"; *Empty Fortress:
Infantile Autism and the Birth
of the Self*
biolooping 82, 83
Bissonnette, Larry 137–38
Bless the Child (Russell) 231, 232, 233,
234, 235, 238, 249
Bleuler, Eugen 102, 103
Boy Who Went Away, The (Gottlieb) 37
Breaking the Code (Wise) 264–66
Broken as Things Are (Witt) 37

C
Carson, Anne 136, 137
central coherence 121–23, 125, 130,
169
Child Called Noah, A (Greenfeld) 18,
193, 195
Cinema of Isolation, The (Norden) 30,
244
cinematic representations *see* film and
autism
clinical constructions 9–12
cognitive impairment 5–6, 169, 244–45
cognitive skills 172–75
Coleridge, Samuel Taylor 119, 120
Collins, Paul 20, 193
communication, impairment of 168,
171, 172, 173
compassion 8
concentration camps 67, 68, 70
construction of autism in 20th century:
cognitive psychology 88; con-
tamination/pollutants 85–86;
genetics discourse 89–91;
in medical literature 79–84;
normality and pathology
boundaries 86–87; psychosis/
psychoanalysis 87–88; risk
factors 88–89
conversion narratives 51–52, 54, 55,
56, 299; autism subgenre 53,
54, 58, 59, 61–62
Couser, G. Thomas 16
Cube (Natali) 241, 252; autism,
spectacularization of 235;
autistic film formula 231, 232,
233–34, 248–49; parental
absence 238
culture: as causing autism 59; postwar
58
*Curious Incident of the Dog in the
Night-Time, The* (Haddon)
39–40, 271; alterity, relativ-
ity of 283–86; Asperger's
syndrome and detective genre
278–81; Asperger's syndrome,
portrayal of 271, 272–73,
294–95; literality in language
273–74, 293–94; narra-
tive 273–76; theory of mind
281–83, 292–93

D
Daniel Isn't Talking (Leimbach) 34–35
Deacon, Terrence W. 276–78

deductive reasoning 70
developmental theory 68–69
Diagnostic and Statistical Manual of Mental Disorders (DSM-IV) 117–18, 124, 271
Dibs: In Search of Self (Axline) 53–54, 55–56, 57, 58–60, 61
disability studies 1–3, 4, 5, 7, 8, 301
disruption of narrative 168, 169, 171, 173

E
echolalia 53
egoism 14, 105, 108–9, 110–11
Eight Basic Principles 54–55, 56–57
Emergence: Labeled Autistic (Grandin) 26–28, 126, 129
Emerson, Ralph Waldo 118–19, 120
empathetic scholarship 8, 297, 300–301
empathy 8
Empty Fortress: Infantile Autism and the Birth of the Self, The (Bettelheim) 53, 59, 65, 66, 68, 69, 70–75, 76
"Epilogue, Fifteen Years After" (Park) 128–29, 205–6; *see also Siege, The* (Park)
executive dysfunction 169, 172, 174, 222
Exiting Nirvana (Park) 18, 133, 200–201, 204, 205, 206–9
"Extreme Situations" (Bettelheim) 67
Eye Contact (McGovern) 35–36

F
facilitated communication 200
false beliefs 66
Fan, Jennifer 153
fancy 119–20, 121, 122
father memoirs 193, 194–95
Feminism and Disability (Hillyer) 199
figurative language 133, 155, 293–94; *see also* metaphor; metonymy
film and autism: actors portraying autistic characters 250; autism, representations of 229–31, 236, 244, 245–46, 248; autism, spectacularization of 234–37; autistic formula 231–34; critical studies 245; family relationships 252–53; parental absence 237–39; positive identity and

self-awareness development 259–60, 266, 268; reconciling portrayals 239–42; savant skills 232–33, 235–36, 237, 249, 250
For the Love of Ann (Copeland) 185
Foucault, Michel 120–21
Fox, Nicholas 81
fractioned idiom 133–42
Frank, Arthur W. 11, 17, 22
Frith, Uta 99, 118, 121–23, 125–26, 149

G
Garland-Thomson, Rosemarie 204, 205
genetics discourse 89–91
geniuses 12–14; *see also* savant skills
George and Sam (Moore) 21–22
Giddens, Anthony 107–8
Girls of Tender Age (Smith) 23–24
Glastonbury, Marion 14, 101, 113, 150
Gould, Glenn *see 32 Short Films About Glenn Gould*
Grandin, Temple 26–27, 129–30, 173, 272; *see also Emergence: Labeled Autistic; Thinking in Pictures*
Greenfeld, Josh 18, 193, 194–95
Gross, Alan 69, 76
Growing Up Severely Autistic: They Call Me Gabriel (Rankin) 21

H
Hacking, Ian 9–10, 41, 83
Haddon, Mark 39–41, 271, 289–90, 291; *see also Curious Incident of the Dog in the Night-Time*
Happé, Francesca 125, 149
Heilbrun, Carolyn 183
high-functioning autism 84, 88, 148, 172, 173, 256
Hillyer, Barbara 199
historical figures, diagnosis if autism 259–60
Hobson, Peter 66
Hollywood and autism *see* film and autism
Hollywood, critical studies 245
Hopkins, Gerard Manley 137
House of Cards (Lessac) 248, 249, 251, 252
Hughes, Bill 4

I

Ideas of Order in the Novels of Thomas
    Pynchon (Hite) 176
identification with films 260, 261–62,
    263
identity: autistic 22, 27–28, 30, 33–34,
    110, 263; modern 107–10
idiolect 134–35, 137
idiosyncratic language 14, 105,
    109–10
imagination 117–18, 121–24, 126,
    145–46, 161; definition
    146–47; different ways of
    knowing 125–31; impairment
    in 117–18, 124, 126, 127,
    145, 147–48; medico-scientific
    view 147–49
imaginative play 117, 124, 126, 128,
    131, 147
impairment: in cognitive tasks 5–6,
    169, 244–45; in communica-
    tion 168, 171, 172, 173; in
    imagination 117–18, 124, 126,
    127, 145, 147–48; in language
    127, 137, 138–39, 172, 173;
    in social interaction 168,
    171–73, 271
indexical thinking 276, 277, 278
indifferent kinds 9, 82, 83, 100
"Individual and Mass Behavior in
    Extreme Situations" (Bettel-
    heim) 67
inductive reasoning 70
interactive kinds 9, 82, 100
Iron of Melancholy, The (King) 52

J

Jakobson, Roman 134
James, William 52
Joyce, James 109, 110, 221

K

Kanner, Leo 52–53, 74, 75, 87, 99,
    102–5, 106; description of
    autism 104–5
King, John Owen 52
Kirschenbaum, Howard 55
Klein, Melanie 60

L

Lakoff, George 139, 140, 143
Landsman, Gail 203

language: and evolutionary neurology
    276–78; impairment in 127,
    137, 138–39, 172, 173
Lawson, Wendy 153–54, 157, 158–59
Lemke, Thomas 90–91
Let Me Hear Your Voice (Maurice) 54,
    60, 61
Levenson, Michael 108
literary modernism and autism 14–15,
    101–2, 107, 113; egoism
    105, 108–9, 110–11; identity
    101–2, 110, 111–12, 113;
    language 109–10; literary case
    studies 110–13
Little Green Man (Armitage) 36
*"Little Rainman": Autism—Through
    the Eyes of a Child* (Simmons)
    201
local coherence 14–16, 122, 126, 127,
    128–29, 131
Loos, Eugene E. 134
low-functioning autism 7, 18, 172

M

Mad Travelers (Hacking) 83–84
mainstream cinema *see* film and autism
Making of Americans, The (Stein)
    109–10
Man Without Qualities (Musil) 111
Maurice, Catherine 54, 60, 61
McDonnell, Jane Taylor 188–92,
    193–94, 200, 204, 205; *see
    also News from the Border*
McGovern, Cammie 62
medical literature, constructing autism
    79–84
memoirs: autobiography 25–29,
    113–14, 150, 295; by fathers
    193, 194–95; by mothers 184,
    185–87, 188–92, 197–99,
    203; by parents 17–22, 193,
    194–95, 212–25; by siblings
    22–25, 183, 184–85, 187–88,
    192–93
mentalizing 122
Mercury Rising (Becker): autism, spec-
    tacularization of 235; autistic
    film formula 231, 232, 233,
    234, 248, 251; family relation-
    ships 238
metaphor 134, 138–39, 143; used by
    autistic poets 155
metonymy 133–34, 136, 139–40, 142

milieu therapy 71
Mind Tree, The (Mukhopadhyay)
140–41, 145
*Mindblindness: An Essay on Autism
and Theory of Mind* (Baron-
Cohen) 122
modernism and autism 14, 101–2,
107, 113; egoism 105, 108–9,
110–11; identity 101–2,
110, 111–12, 113; language
109–10; literary case studies
110–13
Molly (Duigan): autistic film formula
231, 232, 233, 234; family
relationships 238, 252; reconciling portrayal of autism
241
Morrice, Polly 290
Morson, Gary Saul 275
mother-blaming 60, 87–88, 92, 192,
193, 197; *see also* refrigerator
mother
mother memoirs 184, 185–87, 188–92,
197–99, 203; *see also Exiting
Nirvana* (Park); *News from
the Border* (McDonnell);
Siege, The (Park)
mothers: communication and advocacy
role 203–4; gendered role 199,
202, 203
motor impairment 172
Mozart and the Whale (Naess) 30,
32–33
Mrs. Dalloway (Woolf) 111–12
Mukhopadhyay, Tito Rajarshi 140–41,
145, 156–57
Musil, Robert 111

N
narrative and autism 16–17; cognitive skills, virtue of necessity
172–75; as defense against disorder 166–68, 175–77; narrative organization 167, 168–69,
171, 173; physiological
causes of impairment 168–69;
psychological consequences of
impairment 169–71; self-conscious narrative and autism
175–77; social communication
171–73
Nazi concentration camps 67, 68, 70
neurological disabilities 5, 6

neurological theory 74–75
News from the Border (McDonnell)
188–92, 200, 205
Nobody Nowhere (Williams) 27, 28
nondirective therapy 55, 56
normally autistic 299–300
Not Even Wrong (Collins) 20, 193
novels: with autistic characters 34–36;
with autistic narrators 37–41;
by parents of autistic children
34–36, 38; portrayal of autism
271, 272–73

O
onscreen representations *see* film and
autism
Orthogenic School, University of Chicago 65, 66
otherness 31, 201, 272
otherworldliness 230

P
parent-blaming 58, 60, 194, 239,
298–99; *see also* refrigerator
mother
parent/child relationship 75
parent memoirs 17–22, 193, 194–95,
212–25; *see also Child Called
Noah, A* (Greenfeld); *Exiting
Nirvana* (Park); *News from
the Border* (McDonnell); *Running with Walker* (Hughes);
Siege, The (Park)
parent support groups 203
parental self-blame 298–99
Park, Clara Claiborne 17–18, 19, 135;
see also Exiting Nirvana
(Park); *Siege, The* (Park)
Park, Jessy 133, 135–36; *see also Exiting Nirvana* (Park); *Siege, The*
(Park)
Peirce, Charles S. 276
perceptual organization 167
Perelman, Chaim 69–70, 73
Pervasive Developmental Disorder
(PDD) 84, 85, 88
Place for Noah, A (Greenfeld) 193,
194
play 117, 124, 126, 128, 131, 147
play therapy 56–57, 60
*Play Therapy: The Inner Dynamics of
Childhood* (Axline) 54, 55,
57

poetry 150–51; conventional literary devices 153–54; distinct genre 157–58; early influences 158–59; imaginative language 154–55; influence of other poets 160; inspiration 159–60; poets' reflections on their work 158–61; and self 155–57; as self-expression and communication 160–61; study of 152–62; style 152–53; teaching, role of 158–59
"Politics and the English Language" (Orwell) 293
Pollak, Richard 67, 68, 77
postwar American culture 58
primary imagination 119, 120, 121
pronoun reversal 74, 77
psychoanalysis 52, 66, 67
Punch-Drunk Love (Anderson) 248, 251

R
Rain Man (Levinson) 229, 245, 246, 250, 252; autism, portrayal of 248, 249, 294–95; autism, spectacularization of 235, 249; autistic film formula 231, 232–33, 234; parental absence 238, 239
Raine, Craig 212
recovery narrative 11, 19, 26, 29, 38, 61, 299
refrigerator mother 52, 60, 65, 66, 72, 197
Refrigerator Mothers (documentary) 203
Reis, Elizabeth 51
repetitive behavior 168, 171
resistance theory 41
restitution narrative 11, 12, 19, 22
Rhetoric of Science, The (Gross) 69
Ride Together, The (Karasik and Karasik) 24–25
Rimland, Bernard 74, 75
ritualistic behavior 167–68, 169, 170, 173, 174
Rogers, Carl R. 55, 58, 60
Romkema, Craig 154, 156
Running with Walker (Hughes) 20–21
Russell David E. 58, 60

S
Sacks, Oliver 13–14, 31, 272, 289
Sartre, Jean-Paul 110–11, 112, 113
savant skills 12–13, 148, 249, 277; in film 232–33, 235–36, 237, 250; in novels 271 *see also Curious Incident of the Dog in the Night-Time*
schizophrenia 102, 169–70
Scott, Robert L. 69
Secret of Roan Inish, The (Sayles) 266–68
self-awareness 145–46, 156, 161, 264; definition 146–47; medico-scientific view 147, 149–50
self-conscious narrative 175–77
selfhood 51, 53, 59, 61
Send in the Idiots (Nazeer) 14, 28, 29, 42
Seroussi, Karyn 61
"Short Talk on Autism" (Carson) 136
sibling memoirs 22–25, 183, 184–85, 187–88, 192–93
sibling novels 37
Siege, The (Park) 17–18, 62, 127, 185–87, 200, 202, 207; epilogue 128–29, 205–6
Silent Fall (Beresford) 31, 248, 249, 252–53
Smoke Signals (Eyre) 262–64
social autism 280–81, 284
social construction of autism 80–84, 90, 91, 101; cognitive psychology 88; contamination/pollution fears 85–86; normality and pathology boundaries 86–87; psychosis/psychoanalysis 87–88; *see also* construction of autism in 20th century
social construction of disability 1–4, 5–6, 81
Social Construction of What? (Hacking) 81–82, 100
social interaction, impairment in 168, 171–73, 271
Speed of Dark, The (Moon) 38–39
Stephen King's Rose Red (Baxley) 231, 232, 233, 234, 235, 238
stereotypes 30, 244
Stranger, The (Camus) 112–13
symbolic thinking 276–77
Szasz, Thomas 170

T

theory of mind 122–23, 124, 148, 149, 171, 291–92

Theory of Mind Mechanism (ToMM) 122, 123, 124

Thinking in Pictures (Grandin) 126, 129–30

32 Short Films About Glenn Gould 260–62

toilet-training 212–14; *see also* urination

ToM *see* theory of mind

ToMM *see* Theory of Mind Mechanism

Turing, Alan 33, 264–65; *see also Breaking The Code*

Turner, Mark 139

U

United States of Leland, The (Hoge) 29–30, 253

universal audience 69–70, 71

University of Chicago, Orthogenic School 65, 66

Unraveling the Mystery of Autism and Pervasive Developmental Disorder (Seroussi) 61

urination 214–18, 220; bedwetting 216–17, 219, 220–22; as communication 223, 224; as control 214, 215, 222–23, 225; executive dysfunction 222; therapy 218–20; toilet-training 212–14

V

vaccinations 78, 85, 86

Varieties of Religious Experience, The (James) 52

W

Waltz, Mitzi 59

Williams, Donna 27–28, 114, 154, 158–59, 161, 162

Wiltshire, Stephen 13–14, 148, 149, 159

Woolf, Virginia 107, 111–12, 197

CPSIA information can be obtained at www.ICGtesting.com
Printed in the USA
LVOW042127050712

288925LV00002B/53/P